KU-612-283

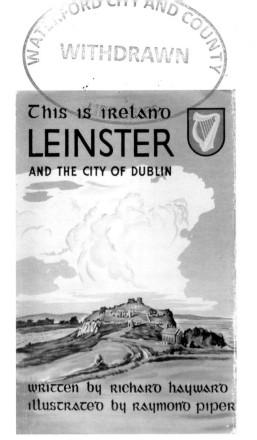

This is Ireland
LEINSTER
AND THE CITY OF DUBLIN

written by Richard Hayward
illustrated by Raymond Piper

This is Ireland
ULSTER
AND THE CITY OF BELFAST

written by Richard Hayward
illustrated by Raymond Piper

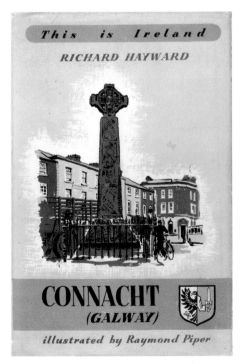

This is Ireland
RICHARD HAYWARD

CONNACHT
(GALWAY)

illustrated by Raymond Piper

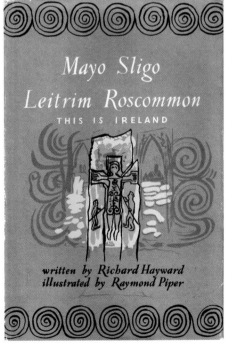

Mayo Sligo
Leitrim Roscommon
THIS IS IRELAND

written by Richard Hayward
illustrated by Raymond Piper

ROMANCING
IRELAND

Richard Hayward in his early thirties, painted by
David Bond Walker and exhibited in 1926 at
the Royal Hibernian Academy, Dublin.

ROMANCING IRELAND

RICHARD HAYWARD

1892–1964

PAUL CLEMENTS

THE LILLIPUT PRESS
DUBLIN

By the same author

Bookshops of Belfast
Irish Shores: A Journey Round the Rim of Ireland
Jan Morris: A Critical Study
The Height of Nonsense: The Ultimate Irish Road Trip
A Walk through Carrick-on-Shannon
Burren Country: Travels Through an Irish Limestone Landscape
Insight Guide Belfast

As editor

Jan Morris, Around the World in Eighty Years: A Festschrift Tribute
*Legacy: A Collection of Personal Testimonies from People Affected
    by the Troubles in Northern Ireland*
*The Blue Sky Bends Over All: A Celebration of Ten Years of the
    Immrama Travel Writing Festival*

Contributing editor

Fodor's Guide Ireland
Insight Guide Ireland

To fellow travellers through Hayward's landscape

First published 2014 by
THE LILLIPUT PRESS
62–63 Sitric Road, Arbour Hill,
Dublin 7, Ireland
www.lilliputpress.ie

10 9 8 7 6 5 4 3 2 1

ISBN 978 1 84351 624 8

The publishers and author wish to acknowledge that the
research, writing, printing and publication of this book has
been generously supported by the Esme Mitchell Trust, and:

Set in 11 pt on 15 pt Bembo by Marsha Swan
Printed in Spain by Castuera

Contents

Author's note on names

Throughout this book, the spelling of place names, mountains, lakes and other topographical features of the Irish countryside has been retained in the original way in which they were published in Richard Hayward's writing.

List of abbreviations

ARP	Air Raid Precautions
BBC	British Broadcasting Corporation (formerly Company)
BFI	British Film Institute
BGS	Belfast Gramophone Society
BNFC	Belfast Naturalists' Field Club
BNL	*Belfast News Letter*
BRTC	Belfast Repertory Theatre Company
CC	*Corrib Country*
CDB	Congested Districts Board
CEMA	Committee for the Encouragement of Music and the Arts
DH	Dorothy Hayward
DLB	*Dictionary of Literary Biography*
DNB	*Dictionary of National Biography*
ENSA	Entertainments National Service Association
GI	Government Issue
HB	Hubert Butler
IFI	Irish Film Institute
IKK	*In the Kingdom of Kerry*
ILT	Irish Literary Theatre
INJ	*Irish Naturalists' Journal*
IPU	*In Praise of Ulster*
IRA	Irish Republican Army
IRJ	*Irish Radio Journal*
ITMA	Irish Traditional Music Archive
JP	Justice of the Peace
JRSAI	*Journal of the Royal Society of Antiquaries of Ireland*
KAS	Kilkenny Archaeological Society

LCD	*Leinster and the City of Dublin*
LHL	Linen Hall Library
LOL	Loyal Orange Lodge
MCC	*Munster and the City of Cork*
MSLR	*Mayo Sligo Leitrim & Roscommon*
MW	Maurice Walsh
MWP	Maurice Walsh Papers
NAI	National Archives of Ireland
n.d.	no date (specified)
NLI	National Library of Ireland
OBE	Order of the British Empire
OPW	Office of Public Works
OS	Ordnance Survey
OUP	Oxford University Press
PEN	Poets, Playwrights, Editors, Essayists and Novelists
PRIA	*Proceedings of the Royal Irish Academy*
PRONI	Public Record Office, Northern Ireland
QUB	Queen's University Belfast
RH	Richard Hayward
RHA	Royal Hibernian Academy
RHA, BCL	Richard Hayward Archive, Belfast Central Library
RHA, UFTM	Richard Hayward Archive, Ulster Folk & Transport Museum
RIA	Royal Irish Academy
RIC	Royal Irish Constabulary
Ricky H	Ricky Hayward
RMS	Royal Mail Steamer
RSAI	Royal Society of Antiquaries of Ireland
RUA	Royal Ulster Academy
RUC	Royal Ulster Constabulary
TCD	Trinity College Dublin
TLS	*Times Literary Supplement*
UCD	University College Dublin
UFTM	Ulster Folk & Transport Museum
UIDA	Ulster Industries Development Association
UJA	*Ulster Journal of Archaeology*
UL	University of Limerick
ULTC	Ulster Literary Theatre Company
UTDA	Ulster Tourist Development Association
UTV	Ulster Television
UVF	Ulster Volunteer Force
WLYC	West Lancashire Yacht Club

Timeline

13 December produces *Hip Hip Hooradio*, first all-Ireland theatre relay transmitted from Belfast via Dublin to Cork

1929 Records first two songs with Decca, 'The Bonny Bunch of Roses' and 'The Ould Orange Flute'

Sets up Belfast Repertory Theatre Company with James Mageean; forms the Empire Players

1931 November appears in *The Land of the Stranger*, Abbey Theatre, Dublin

1932 Sings in first indigenous Irish sound film *The Voice of Ireland*

Stages, and acts with Elma, in Thomas Carnduff play, *Workers*, at Abbey Theatre, and Empire Theatre, Belfast

19 December death of mother Louisa ('Louie') Eleanor Hayward

1935 Sets up Irish International Film Agency

Releases popular feature film *The Luck of the Irish*

30 October birth of second son Richard Scott (known as Ricky)

1936 Sings and acts in two films: *The Early Bird* (with Elma Hayward) and *Irish and Proud of It* (with Dinah Sheridan)

Sails to US on Cunard liner to promote Irish films

Publishes novel *Sugarhouse Entry*

1937 Produces/acts in *Devil's Rock*; starts film production company

Sings for the first time with Delia Murphy

1938 First travel book *In Praise of Ulster* published, illustrations by J.H. Craig

Releases documentary *In the Footsteps of St Patrick*

1940 *Where the River Shannon flows* published, photographs by Louis Morrison, accompanied by travelogue *Where the Shannon Flows Down to the Sea*

1941 15 April Hayward home in Belfast damaged in Luftwaffe blitz

1942 Narrates and produces Stormont government film *Simple Silage*

1943 Publication of *The Corrib Country*, illustrated by J.H. Craig, with accompanying film

Narrates and produces Irish government film *Tomorrow's Bread*

1944 Travelogue *Kingdom of Kerry* released

1945 Appointed honorary life member of the Carrick-on-Shannon branch of the Inland Waterways Association of Ireland

1946 *In the Kingdom of Kerry* published with illustrations by Theo Gracey

Releases documentary *Back Home in Ireland*

1949 Publishes *Leinster and the City of Dublin* with illustrations by Raymond Piper (first book in *This is Ireland* series)

1950 Publishes *Ulster and the City of Belfast* with illustrations by Piper

1951 President Belfast Naturalists' Field Club, leads field trip excursions all over Ireland, sets up folklore section with Brendan Adams and starts work compiling Ulster dialect dictionary

20 February first grandson Paul Semple Hayward born

1952 *Connacht and the City of Galway* published with Piper illustrations

Publication of *Belfast through the Ages*, illustrations by Piper

His arrangement 'The Humour is on Me Now' used in *The Quiet Man*

1953 Addresses twenty-fifth International Congress of PEN, Belfast

1954 *The Story of the Irish Harp* published

Involvement in Hubert Butler's Kilkenny Debates

1955 Publishes *Mayo Sligo Leitrim & Roscommon*, illustrations by Piper

1956 His *Orange and Blue* chosen by UK music panel as one of the six outstanding recordings of the year

1957 *Border Foray* published

1958 Appears in *Titanic* film *A Night to Remember*

1959 17 March first BBC Northern Ireland TV appearance

Appointed Doctor of Literature, Lafayette College, Pennsylvania

31 October sings on opening night of Ulster Television

1960 Receives Insignia of Honorary Capataz of the San Patricio Bodega

1961 11 April Elma Hayward dies

1962 23 February remarries: Dorothy Elizabeth Gamble

1963 Elected Honorary Life Associate of British Institute of Recorded Sound

1964 12 June appointed OBE

July represents Ireland at International Congress of PEN, Norway

August *Munster and the City of Cork* published, illustrations by Piper

26 September birth of second grandson Richard Laurence

13 October killed in car crash, Ballymena, County Antrim

4 November memorial service, St Anne's Cathedral, Belfast

In the Kingdom of Kerry

The scholar in him shows us the Chi-Rho Crosses in the crumbled abbeys, the jester in him laughs at such phenomena as an unsinkable man; the zealot in him denounces the intrusion of sham villa on good landscape or the glazed tile on grey graveyard; the anchorite in him leads us up grass-grown roads and the imp and the acrobat in him takes us out on dizzy pinnacle of Skellig Michael and leaves us there with our vertigo for good company.

Extract from *The Bell* review by Bryan MacMahon
of Richard Hayward's Kerry book, 1946

Introduction

The Richard Hayward Archive is eccentric and eclectic, a haberdashery of an adrenaline-fuelled life. A vast array of topics reflect every facet of his work: travel, writing, singing, films, plays, broadcasting, lecturing, journalism and selling sweets wrapped up with a polar bear. Sifting through the detritus of his personal effects at the Ulster Folk and Transport Museum near Belfast is a pleasurable if daunting task.

When I first explored it in 2009, the archive had not been catalogued and no one had been there before me. This is because Hayward's second wife, Dorothy, was the gatekeeper of the flickering flame of his memory. For many years after his death in 1964 she guarded his estate with zeal, controlling queries from writers or researchers wishing to use or quote from his work. The sole legal beneficiary of his estate, including royalties, Dorothy had the right of veto over any use of his published, printed or recorded works and only she could approve of requests to quote from it. When she died in 2005, the museum took over ownership of the archive and copyright. In the words of the curator, Hayward was 'an intellectual magpie'. Since he never threw anything away, more than half a century's worth of correspondence and cuttings are crammed into boxes and plastic bags.

Hayward belonged to the age of letter-writing. Through his involvement with a range of organizations, he knew many people, which led to a broad sweep of friends, acquaintances and correspondents within the parallel worlds in which he worked. Hoards of letters from family and friends are crammed into padded envelopes or Jiffy bags. Others, from admirers of his books, films and songs, come with comments on his work.

In his own letters his character leaps out vividly, and although they are by no means the full picture of his personality, they provide an angled glance at his life and work.

No signposted route or index of contents guides me through the chaotic heaps of envelopes of hotel menus, guidebooks to Irish towns, cathedral, abbey and church histories, and publishers' foxed book catalogues. Chaos has its advantages; serendipity triumphs to discover 'Odds & Ends'; a brown box, labelled 'Boys' Shirts', marked 'Magic Tricks'; a bright orange crate overflows with documents and magazines. Poignantly, a long drawer holds 'Correspondence after death'.

Cardboard boxes of film stills house hundreds of black-and-white photographs reflecting character roles from his big-screen appearances. Some crumpled photographs are held together with flaking Sellotape or staples. Promotional brochures for films and records deal with the collection of royalties. Handbills for his theatrical performances turn up in unlikely places alongside loose scraps of paper, backs of small envelopes, book dust jackets and postcards, all used to make notes.

To ensure he received articles written about him, Hayward employed the services of two cuttings agencies – one in Dublin and the other in London. The press clippings include interviews with him, appraisal and commentary on his work, and reviews and profiles of his latest ventures. Unsurprisingly for a man who spent much of his life driving the Irish roads, the map collection is extensive. Two boxes contain half-inch to the mile Ordnance Survey folding sheets of every county in Ireland. Some, in pristine condition, are mounted and linen-backed; others are torn and pen-marked. Bartholomew's one-inch sheets of Ireland for Limerick and Shannon, Connemara and Sligo, and Donegal and Enniskillen are folded neatly to their concertina shape. Priced at three shillings, they are mounted on cloth with orographical colouring and roads. Hayward liked them for their detail, which included principal roads marked in red, good motoring roads in yellow, other serviceable roads, those not in general use, approved roads crossing the frontier, private roads as well as bridleways and footpaths. The Donegal and Enniskillen sheet contains pencil notes on his itinerary: 'Bundoran: 9–10.30, Enniskillen 12 lunch, Castlecoole 3.30, Tea in Armagh or Dungannon.'

The highlight of the archive for me was coming across in two cardboard boxes the battered notebooks from his Irish travels with the artist Raymond Piper, one of five distinguished illustrators of Hayward. They provide an engaging insight into his modus operandi of recording information. Twenty ruled hardback books contain closely written notes alongside disjointed thoughts and sudden ideas that came into his head, which he quickly wrote down. These fragments are the repositories of his on-the-spot experience, meeting people, attending events, studying buildings and observing what was going on around him.

Reading the notebooks produces a sharp frisson of the immediacy of the personality and his time. He worked in a methodical and systematic way, writing in black, blue and green ink, sometimes in pencil, mostly in longhand. Occasionally he sketched a rough pen drawing, perhaps of a high cross or a ring fort, as aide-memoire (even though in his literary travels he was accompanied by a professional artist). For the most part, the notebooks do not contain personal information, but focus on place with moments of protest about the weather, which do not appear in the published books. Hayward took care with Irish place names, spelling them in capital letters and noting the exact wording of inscriptions on statues and gravestones. After returning home he frequently scored vertical or horizontal lines through the pages, crossing out sentences. He then chose the important information he required to begin the process of writing a draft. Selectivity was a key aspect since he made many notes that were discarded.

The archive, and in particular his notebooks, drew me into his orbit. I wandered the landscape with him, felt the heavy showers of rain and empathized when Piper tied an umbrella to a tree for shelter to draw a sketch in the Swiss Valley in Leitrim. Their immediacy offers the full sensory experience, the complete Haywardian vibes of seeing the initial nibble notes – the raw material – made in scrawling writing, his corrections, scratching-outs, scribbles, pencil doodles, underlinings, reflections and additions. Grace notes, bracketed asides and whimsical lines all bring him touchably close. Handling them, smelling the paper and ink, and wondering why he chose certain phrases feels like slipping out of linear time into the company of the man who wrote them seventy years ago. His excitement and curiosity is tangible.

The notebooks provide a portal into his thought processes and private world. Although they are a contrast with his published books and lack the polish of the finished product, they are important in understanding how he worked. As I read through them, the scale of the accretion of information he gathered becomes apparent; they are trophies of tens of thousands of miles of energetic travel representing a remarkable record. Nothing passed his gimlet eye and everything was grist to the Hayward writing mill. From my immersion in the archive one day a week for six months it is clear there are many Richard

Haywards. Not only was he a writer, but he was also a singer, film star, stage actor, folklorist, dialect-collector, freelance journalist, broadcaster, entrepreneur and sweet salesman. I was in awe of his versatility and the sheer exhaustion of his expenditure of energy.

The highest form of travel for Hayward was the discursive quest, seeking out historical detail, bringing alive the people he met and recording the unusual. For the student of historical topography, and for a *feel* of what Ireland was like during the middle years of the twentieth century, his work is indispensable. This overdue book is part biography, part testimonial and part social history of an older simpler land. It is important to consider the impact on the cultural and literary geography of Ireland as well as Hayward's historical and contemporary relevance. My purpose in writing it is to retrieve his legacy for a twenty-first-century readership and rekindle interest in his work. As well as reflecting the absorbing life of a many-wayed man with an omnivorous appetite for living, I have tried to present a balanced evaluation of his achievements.

When I got married in 1987, as a wedding present my wife gave me a special tooled-leather edition of *In Praise of Ulster*. Since then it has been in my top ten to-grab-in-case-of-fire list. This set me off reading his books and for three decades he has been part of my marital and mental furniture. I wanted to write about him but was unable to free up time from work and other preoccupations until 2008. The trigger came with the unofficial release of the marvellously disorganized archive in 2009. With the knowledge gleaned from the triangulation of letters, press cuttings and notebooks, I set about tracking down anyone still alive who could shed light on him, only to be met in most cases with a shrug or questioning blank: Richard Who-wood? In libraries, manuscript, archive, history and heritage centres the response varied from Robert Hayworth and Rupert Howard to Roger Wayward and Ritchie Hayweed … 'was he in the Fraternity of Man, or a drummer with Little Feat?' a puzzled librarian wondered, her eyes filled with dim recollection; or, on another occasion, 'Edward Hardware – did he write detective thrillers?' I never met Richard Hayward but in some ways he has stalked me through his books and in his friendship with Raymond Piper. Now I plan to stalk him, spending time in another century, taking myself on a journey into the past.

Paul Clements
Belfast, 2014

Prelude

More than three million visitors each year tramp the streets of central Oxford, making tourism the city's biggest industry. Few cast their eyes to the ground, ignoring the cobbled medieval streets and pavements splattered with bird droppings, cigarette butts and chewing gum. But unwittingly many of these tourists are standing on circular manhole covers or rectangular pavement lights, a long-established part of the street furniture. If they looked carefully they would see pig-iron manhole covers decorated with a five-petalled raised pattern and embossed capital lettering bearing the words:

HAYWARD BROTHERS PATENT – UNION STREET BOROUGH –
LONDON – SELF-LOCKING

Hayward Brothers self-locking manhole cover outside Balliol College, Broad Street, Oxford. Hayward's forebears ran a foundry in Borough in London and the covers can still be found in ubiquitous clusters in Oxford as well as other British and Irish cities.

Some covers are barely readable. Others retain a pristine freshness, and with their circles and diamonds, chevrons and stars, trefoils and quatrefoils, are as clear as the day they were installed. In the world of eye-catching Oxford tourism, drain spotting comes firmly at the bottom of the must-see list. The humble manhole cover – for the operculist (lover of lids or covers) an aesthetic work of beautifully cast decorative symmetrical art – cannot compete with 100 amusing gargoyles of mermaids, musicians and monsters, or carved heads high up on college facades decorating entrance arches. Millions of visitors, as well as dons, undergraduates and locals have trodden these pavements ignorant of the industrial heritage underfoot. But what they have never stopped to ponder is that the company which fitted these utilitarian and durable covers, the Hayward Brothers, are the ancestors of Richard Hayward whose name too was cemented – not in the streetscape – but more glamorously in Ireland's national culture.

Hayward Brothers pavement lights are widespread in central Dublin and can be seen along College Street, Dame Street, Suffolk Street and in this photograph at South Anne Street, off Grafton Street.

His forebears ran a London foundry in Union Street, Borough. Since 1783 William and Edward Hayward had been trading as glaziers. In 1838 they bought an ironmongery business producing coal plates and later patented the addition of prisms with glazed glass that admitted light to the basement. To this day, these manhole covers and pavement lights – some with cracked glass – can be seen in parts of the capital as well as other towns and cities, including Dublin, Galway and Belfast. Nowhere are they found in such ubiquitous clusters as Oxford, a place where their presence commands so little attention. But as a tourism tag, 'The city of dreaming drains' lacks the allure of the dreaming spires. Those town drains and street gratings, like the life of Richard Hayward, have been woefully neglected. In a stark analogy with the man, they have become unnoticed, uncelebrated and invisible, trampled into history by the passing of the years.

ONE

'Soaked in Irish songs and stories'

(1892–1910)

The main street lined with open booths heavy-laden with yellow-man, hard nuts, cinnamon buds, and divers other tongue-tickling morsels. And old Mary Kirk nearby with her oranges and Larne Rock, and Ned Welch, and "Zig Zi Ah" Alec MacNichol, and ould Jimmie Morne. I don't know Jimmie's real name but he was always called Morne because he came from Magheramorne. Alec always affected a straw hat and a white waistcoat, and even as a child I used to envy his carefree life.

Richard Hayward, In Praise of Ulster, 1938

Although he took pride in his Irishness and had a great love for the country, Richard Hayward was born in Lancashire. On 24 October 1892, at 21 Forest Road, Southport, Harold Richard became the fifth of six surviving children. Within three years of his birth the family moved to Ireland where he grew up on the east coast of County Antrim. In later life he grappled with his birthplace trying to mask his English origins. His passports contain conflicting places and dates of birth. One states that he was born in Larne, County Antrim on 23 October 1893 and gives his profession as actor and singer, while a later passport in which he is described as an author, lists his place of birth as Southport and date of birth 24 October 1892.

His father, Walter Scott Hayward, the son of a London ironmonger who owned a foundry, was born on 17 April 1855 at 20 St James Walk, Clerkenwell. The company was called Hayward Brothers and was based in Union Street,

Borough. They made manhole covers that are still visible in Irish, British and foreign cities bearing the name Hayward. During the late 1860s as a teenager, Scott Hayward spent time in deep-sea voyages before beginning a yachting career in 1871 with a small five-ton single-mast sailing boat, *Rover*. When he moved from London to the north of England he continued a lifelong interest in designing and sailing yachts. His first club was the Royal Temple in London, which he joined in 1871, racing his boat in club matches. His parents moved around different locations in England; firstly to Brighton on the south coast in 1873 where he joined the local sailing club, and then north in 1877 to Manchester. There he became a member of three clubs: the prestigious Royal Mersey Yacht Club, Cheshire Yacht Club, and New Brighton Sailing Club. Cruising and racing on the Mersey, as well as involvement in coastal regattas and local matches, took up a good deal of his time.

Conflicting passport details show that Hayward tried to disguise his English place of birth: the left-hand passport states that he was born in Southport on 24 October 1892 while the one on the right incorrectly lists his place of birth a year later as Larne, County Antrim on 23 October 1893.

With his handlebar moustache, Scott Hayward comes across as a confident dashing figure, perpetually busy, mixing business with his passion for sailing. After taking an examination in 1878 he was awarded a Board of Trade certificate as Master – a distinction achieved by few amateurs – and the following year chartered a small schooner, *Resolute*, making a trip to the coast of Morocco. On his return he was soon on the move again, settling in Southport where the attraction of the sea and opportunity to pursue his sailing skills held immense appeal. In 1880 he married at Ormskirk registry office Louisa Eleanor Ivy, the daughter of a local silk merchant, John Robson Ivy. Known as Louie, she was born on 24 January 1859 at Shoreditch in Middlesex and was four years younger than her husband.

Hayward's father, Walter Scott Hayward, one of England's leading yachtsmen, photographed in 1896 with his Royal Mersey Yacht Club cap and Liver Bird badge.

Hayward's mother Louisa Ivy, known as Louie, was born in 1859
and was the daughter of a silk merchant.

The newly married couple lived in a redbrick house in an affluent area
fifteen minutes' walk east of the town centre and close to the main central
station. The advent of the railway from Manchester in the late 1840s had brought
the wealthy to Southport. Alongside them were the elegant mansions and
well-appointed residences of prominent cotton industrialists, mill owners, jam
manufacturers and a large Jewish business community. Forest Road, which ran
through a tunnel of ash trees at one end, was a mix of terrace, semi-detached and
detached houses with their own gardens. Many were built with the distinctive
Accrington brick that gave a glazed shining effect. Surrounding roads, some lit at
night with cast-iron lamps, reflected the Victorian arboreal fascination.

It was the era just before the arrival of the electric trams in Southport at the turn of the century. When baby Richard was born in 1892 horse-drawn trams and milk delivery carts plied the cobbled streets along with cyclists and the occasional landau carriage. As a baby he was taken in his pram to the Fairground or the Winter Gardens with its conservatories, promenade walkways, aquarium and roller-skating rink. He was too young to be aware of the newly installed and controversial 'Aerial Flight', which carried visitors high overhead in gondolas suspended from wires across from the fashionable Marine Lake. It was not to everyone's taste. Some residents complained vehemently that it spoilt the vista from the promenade and it was removed in 1911.

Locals cared passionately about their views. From the long seafront promenade the mountains of Cumberland and the Wyresdale hills of Lancashire stretched away to the northwest while to the southwest from the esplanade, the Welsh hills, ending in Great Orme Head were visible in the distance. Lying between the estuaries of the Ribble and Mersey rivers, Southport, facing the Irish Sea, was less brash than Blackpool, its neighbour to the north. Since the 1860s the town had developed considerably as a genteel tourist resort. Day-trippers enjoyed the mild climate and bracing flat coastal walks along the beach or over the sand dunes as well as secluded sea bathing. Sand-yachting was also a popular feature of interest to holidaymakers. They dined in the tea rooms and coffee houses lining the fashionable boulevard of Lord Street where handsome glass-topped wrought-iron verandas stretched out in front of the shops. The resort was noted for traditional family seaside entertainment such as coconut shies while sweet stalls offered toffee, chocolate, boiled and health sweets, and the must-have labelled stick of Southport rock. By 1891 the population of the borough had risen to 41,406. It had become a desirable residential town and the ideal place in which to bring up a young family.

Some ancestral Hayward details are difficult to verify. But a letter to Dorothy Hayward from one of Richard's brothers, Rex, after his death in 1964, claimed a fascinating family history, including a connection to Haywards Heath in Sussex – although this was never established:

> Richard must have told you that our father was a famous swordsman. I have a
> photograph of him with his breast covered with medals. Both he and his wife
> were crack shots. Mother could hit a three penny piece with a revolver at 20
> paces. My father used to cut an apple in half on my mother's head.[1]

Whatever the potency of the Hayward name, his forebears appear to have been colourful characters, and for the children it was to be a peripatetic existence during the early years of their lives. The exact birth date of their first child and only surviving girl, Gladys Ivy, is unrecorded but was most likely in early 1883. Her first brother, Charles Hembry, was born on 19 February 1884 at Oakford in Devon, and was followed by another boy the next year: Basil Dean, born on 18 October 1885 at Oughtrington, Lymm, in Cheshire. Just over three years later, Reginald (known as Rex) Ivor Callender was born on 21 October 1888 at Altrincham in Cheshire. Harold Richard became the second-last child when Louie gave birth again on 24 October 1892, and Casson Boyd was born on 6 January 1899. Three other children had died in childhood, including twin girls who succumbed to an epidemic disease. The surviving family comprised one daughter and five sons.

Even with a large family to support, Scott Hayward threw himself completely into the local sailing scene, emerging as the leading small yacht racer in the northwest of England. He helped form the Southport Corinthian Sailing Club, becoming the first vice-commodore, a position he held for three years. He later became captain for three years. At the start of 1899, the *Yachting World* carried a 500-word profile of him in its series 'Yachting Celebrities' along with a full plate photograph showing him wearing his Royal Mersey cap complete with its Liver Bird badge. The magazine outlined why he set up the club:

> During 1894, seeing that something must be done if Southport wished to take a position as a yachting centre, Mr Hayward decided to form a yacht club, purely for the improvement of the sport and for the education of the younger men, this being barred to a very large extent by the difficulty which attended becoming a member of the existing clubs.[2]

Apart from his involvement with this club he was instrumental in forming the West Lancashire Yacht Club (WLYC) of which he was commodore for six years. On its formation, he was also appointed commodore of the Rhyl Yacht Club in north Wales. In 1887 he bought the *Nautilus*, a four-tonner, which he raced for several seasons. Five years later, in 1892 – the year of Richard's birth – he owned a dinghy to which he gave the fun name *The Slut*. Highly successful with it in sailing competitions, he won 165 prizes and seven annual championship cups. Boating honours and prizes continued to flow during his years in the northwest. He won 100 first prizes, forty-five second prizes and twenty third prizes. At different times in his sailing career, he owned forty yachts and ten motor boats collectively winning more than 2000 prizes. But Scott Hayward was renowned as much for his work designing boats as for his sailing prowess and organizational ability in forming new clubs. He was responsible for the design of a number of open boats and small yachts as well as fishing boats and motor yachts. One of his ventures attracted publicity in 1896 when he designed the largest motor yacht to have been launched on the Mersey. In total he designed more than fifty yachts and motor launches and his designs were adopted nationally and internationally.[3]

In the midst of all his water-based exploits, the family decided in 1895 to move to Ireland, choosing firstly Omeath in County Louth. An area with a scenic backdrop of the Cooley peninsula, and the Mourne Mountains on the other side of Carlingford Lough, it seemed to offer the ideal sailing potential sought by Scott Hayward. But they stayed only a short period, relocating to Larne on the coast of County Antrim, later settling fifteen miles south in a large house at Greenisland just north of Belfast. When he moved to Ireland, Hayward maintained his nautical interests, becoming a member of the Royal Ulster Yacht Club, the Royal North of Ireland Yacht Club and Donaghadee Sailing Club. He was honorary secretary of the Ireland branch of the British Motor Boat Club, the Motor Yacht Clubs of Ireland and Scotland, and the Yacht Racing Association.

Harold Richard Hayward aged four years and nine months in his fashionable sailor boy outfit with his toy yacht. He described his childhood in Larne as being 'soaked in Irish songs and stories.'

Tour parties gather outside MacNeill's Hotel in Larne for the start of a trip along the Antrim coast in the 1890s. This scene was familiar to Hayward as a child and one he later described in his first travel book *In Praise of Ulster*.

The Ireland in which the Haywards arrived with their young children was a country going through sweeping social change. Many organizations that would alter the cultural, political and working landscape were founded in this period. Radical ideas were taking root, new movements were formed and a host of practical groups emerged to help the lot of working people in what for many was a time of poverty and serious hardship. Workers throughout the country were united under the Irish Trades Union Congress banner; tenant farmers came together in a mass movement called the United Irish League, and the Irish Co-Operative Agricultural Movement and Pioneer Total Abstinence Association were founded. The Gaelic League and the Irish Literary Theatre (later the Abbey) were also building early foundations.

Much of this did not impinge directly on the life of people in Larne in the far northeast of the country. Historically the town was best known for the events surrounding the landing of Edward Bruce (brother to the Scottish hero, Robert) when he came to Ireland on a futile mission of conquest in 1315. Larne's name means 'district of Lahar' (a legendary prince before the Christian era). Built straddling the River Inver, it was a meeting place of roads and people on the move. Of all County Antrim's towns, it was more rambunctious than most. Neighbouring places such as Ballyclare, Ballymena and Antrim were humdrum market towns, but because of its situation as a port, Larne's raffish air attracted visitors and a never-ending passing stream of travellers. Each day mail and passenger steamers linked the port to Stranraer in southwest Scotland, the short route across the North Channel, and many visitors passed through on their way to other parts of Ireland. Aside from this, steamers from the State Line, sailing around the coast between Glasgow and New York, called at Larne to embark passengers. A lively steamer trade also operated between Larne and Dublin, Derry, Glasgow, Liverpool and Ayr.

Throughout the 1890s the harbour was a scene of bustle reflecting the importance of the sea trade, bringing prosperity and employment. The Larne Shipbuilding Company was thriving while elsewhere jobs were created in engineering works and foundries as well as for smiths and millwrights. Towards the end of 1895 the British Aluminium Company opened a factory to convert locally mixed bauxite into pure alumina by chemical means giving employment to 100 men. The other main industries included flour milling, linen weaving and paper milling. But big money was being created around the new business of tourism and the train connected Larne to Belfast, helping social mobility. The place that Hayward knew was a small town of crowded streets. Writing many years later in his first travel book, he unlocked early memories to paint an evocative vignette of the time: 'Religious fanatics, ballad singers, dancers, tramps, naturals, clowns, all in a motley crowd, no doubt attracted by the custom and largesse of Larne's growing tourist traffic.'[4]

Handsome public buildings lined the streets. Six churches and three banks as well as the impressive town hall and the McGarel Building were familiar to Hayward as a child. Thatched houses were still prevalent. Three on the main street, five between the main street and circular road, and nineteen in the old town were all inhabited.[5] But the focal point for visitors was MacNeill's Hotel on the main street. Henry MacNeill set up business in 1853 with a fleet of horse-drawn cars and wagonettes for excursions into the countryside. A pioneer of tourism in Larne, MacNeill capitalized on the new railways and ferries to Scotland, selling 'package holidays'; his tour company brought in many people. Young Hayward met him when he was in his sixties and later drew an engaging pen portrait:

> The architect and deviser of Larne's bounty of swarming thousands from Lancashire and Yorkshire, dear old Henry MacNeill, old 'Knock-'em-Down' as he was known to everyone, what a character was he. I always used to

connect him in my childish way with Buffalo Bill and I was always inor-
dinately proud to be seen talking to him. Many a shilling he gave me, all
unknown to my elders, and I should blush to say that I was unmannerly
enough to accept his gifts. Human, all too human! And I'm so glad to be
able to remember that I wasn't a perfectly-behaved little prig! I can see now
that Henry MacNeill was a man far in advance of his time, a genius whose
circumstances led him to the tourist business.[6]

To accommodate the growth in trade MacNeill's Hotel expanded in 1895
while another hotel, the Olderfleet, had already added a new wing the previous
year. Larne's population was increasing rapidly and in 1892 the town boundary
had been extended. At the start of the decade, in 1891, the population stood
at 4217, while by 1901 it had risen by just over a third to 6670. A progressive place, it was the first town in the north of Ireland to have public electric
street lighting, which was installed in 1891. Larne had followed the example
of Galway where in 1889 the electricity was generated by a dynamo replacing
grinding machinery in an old water-driven flour mill – although in Larne's case
this was not a success and had to be replaced by steam-driven plant in 1892.[7]

At the turn of the century the narrow streets were filled with thirty grocers
and the same number of drapers. Butchers, bookmakers and spirit retailers were
all well represented in the business of the town. The rhythm of the agricultural
year was important in the life of Larne. During the hurly-burly of the twice-
yearly fairs on 31 July and 1 December, stalls and sellers attracted farmers and
their families from outlying villages. The streets were also thronged with crowds
attending hiring fairs that took place in May and November while a pig market
was held on the fourth Wednesday of each month and a straw market each
Thursday. The memory of those days stayed with him and in his later singing
career Hayward recorded a popular ballad, 'The Old Larne Fair'. George Baine's
bakery and confectionery shop, which also sold groceries and fancy goods,
employed twenty bread servers and bakers, and was a popular haunt. Hayward
recreates the atmosphere of the time, glancing back at a parade of some notables:

> The main street lined with open booths heavy-laden with yellow-man, hard
> nuts, cinnamon buds, and divers other tongue-tickling morsels. And old Mary
> Kirk nearby with her oranges and Larne Rock, and Ned Welch, and 'Zig Zi
> Ah' Alec MacNichol, and ould Jimmie Morne. I don't know Jimmie's real
> name but he was always called Morne because he came from Magheramorne.
> Alec always affected a straw hat and a white waistcoat, and even as a child I
> used to envy his carefree life.[8]

Lester's Café Royal Hotel, referred to as the Royal (English) Hotel, was bought by Ebenezer and Florence Drummer and later renamed Drummer's Commercial Hotel; the couple were affectionately known to locals as 'Eb and Flo'.[9] Another prominent figure in Larne that Hayward loved, and someone who brought his childhood to life, was the town bellman, Johnny Moore:

> He was a character for whom I had great respect, for I always associated him with medieval romance and for some reason with Shakespeare's *Love's Labour's Lost* which I was reading at school. I'm afraid the children of the town were not similarly impressed, for they used to torment poor Johnny with pointed remarks about his feet, which were not small. Indeed, he was always known to the irreverent as 'Acres'. But I thought he was grand and ancient and traditional and all that, and I used to love the measured beat of his bell and the sound of his voice announcing an auction, some lost property, or information about the town water being turned off at seven o'clock each night on account of the drought. This always meant the filling of baths and buckets and basins and the use of far more water than would ever have been drawn had the supply been left unchecked.[10]

There is romanticism about his recollections of Larne, a place that stirred an interest in people that would stay with him all his life. A bright child, he was alert to the sights and sounds of what was going on around him. He lived in an area rich in history and archaeological ruins, and was becoming conscious of the past and the natural world. The Antrim coast road led north to quiet valleys, to the dramatic scenery of the glens and the tourist attraction of the Giant's Causeway. When Thackeray came to the glens fifty years earlier he dubbed Glenarriff 'Little Switzerland'.

All told, it was an exhilarating place. He became familiar with hidden coves and coastal beaches. On a clear day he could see across to the Scottish coastline. But nearer home it was the thin peninsula of Islandmagee linked to Larne by a ferry – a place with a dark past where early eighteenth-century witchcraft still remained part of local folklore – that took possession of his imagination. He wandered the country lanes and flower-filled meadows of this isolated part of east Antrim and was intrigued by the 'Druid's Altar', a dolmen at Ballylumford. On one occasion when he was taken to the Gobbins cliff path – a stretch of coast on the southeast side made accessible by metal walkways and ladders, with caves and colourful basaltic cliffs – he was told the story of a religious massacre in 1642. A group of Presbyterians descended at night on Islandmagee murdering Catholic men, women and children by driving them over the edge of the Gobbins path into the sea. This was said to be a reprisal for the harsh deeds against Protestants in 1641. 'I remember how, as a child, I used to shudder when I was shown the seaweed which was, so I was gravely informed, still dyed red with the blood of these poor people.'[11]

For all their myth-making, the Haywards were church-goers, business-people and solid citizens. The family placed importance on the value of a well-rounded education as a passport to a decent job. Scott Hayward was a Unionist and a member of the Church of Ireland, attending Jordanstown parish church. The young Richard became a member of the church and was confirmed by Bishop Frederick MacNeice, father of the poet Louis.

As a child, Hayward was known as Harold, a first name that stuck until his twenties when he switched to Richard. The family lived firstly in Beach Vista beside Larne harbour, later moving round the corner to Chelmsford Place, a quiet cul-de-sac off the main coast road at Sandy Bay. Their house was a distinguished three-storey terrace in an identical row of six. Each had small round-headed windows on the top floor, a one-storey return, and enclosed gardens surrounded by hedges. Views from the bay windows stretched across the water to Larne harbour while at Sandy Bay Point stood the 90-ft-high granite Chaine Memorial replica round tower erected in 1887–88. James Chaine had expanded the port of Larne in the 1870s and local legend says that he was buried upright in the tower.

At the age of seven, Hayward developed an interest in music, not just from the singers he heard on the streets of Larne, but also in the household. As a relatively prosperous family, they employed two servants; one, a teenaged girl from Ballybay in County Monaghan, taught him his first songs. From her he learnt Irish ballads that struck a special chord, leading to a lifetime's interest in traditional songs and an abiding passion for the harp. The maid's wide repertoire included 'The Ould Leather Breeches', 'The Fair of Athy', 'Sweet Mary Acklin' and 'Wicked Murty Hynes'. Right through the day, from morning till late evening, the maid sang as she carried out her duties. Hayward later served up an account of this defining musical moment: 'Some of these ballads I learnt and still sing, but others I have completely forgotten, for it was not for many years that I acquired the prudent habit of writing down what I heard.'[12]

Partly because of this, he describes his childhood in Larne as being 'soaked in Irish songs and stories'. He does not name the maid but in the 1901 census she is listed as Lezzie Carroll, an eighteen-year-old Roman Catholic speaking Irish and English. The other servant was John Wilson, who was fifteen. A total of eleven people, ranging in age from two-year-old Basil to a fifty-two-year-old woman, Lily Leah Lucy, described as a 'visitor', were then living in Chelmsford Place. Hayward provides glimpses of his early schooldays. In the middle years of the 1890s, he attended Miss Cunningham's school on main street and later Carrickfergus Model Primary School before transferring to the grammar school in Larne. 'As if it were yesterday I can remember the voice of Miss Cunningham telling some unruly pupil that he was "the essence of disobedience".'[13]

In the summer, his parents took him on trips with his brothers to different parts of Ireland. Given his father's interest in boats it is no surprise that these were water-based holidays or coincided with yachting and sailing events. One was a boat journey along the River Erne from Cavan to Donegal, which ignited an interest in rivers and lakes. The young boy loved poring over maps of Ireland, discovering the names of mountains and lakes. He wrote later about being confused by the Upper and Lower Lakes of Lough Erne in County Fermanagh:

> The Upper Lake is about ten miles long by three and a half miles wide, and lies to the south of Enniskillen. I remember as a schoolboy wondering why this should be the Upper Lake when on the map it is visually the Lower one, and I don't think I have ever reconciled myself to this childish dilemma![14]

With its quiet waterways and serene lakes, Fermanagh was a long way from life on the Antrim coast but became a favourite family holiday destination. In separate years around the turn of the century they spent a week at a time at the annual regatta in Enniskillen, staying in the Rossclare Hotel at Castle Archdale. The regatta was a huge event and Scott Hayward persuaded some English yacht-owners to take part in it. One year, in a spirit of adventure, he brought his children from Belfast Lough to Fermanagh by crossing the north of Ireland on an idyllic, if slow and lengthy journey, through inland navigation channels. En route, as well as appreciating the history and wildlife, they camped on river banks and small islands. For a boy, the excitement of once sleeping on a barge was a thrilling experience. 'Those were the days, and I boasted about that night on a barge for many a month.'[15]

But it was a boat trip off the north Antrim coast, during which he came into contact with a celebrated name in the Irish cultural world that left the biggest impression on him. Hayward was just nine when, on a memorable journey in 1901 to Rathlin Island, he met Francis Joseph Bigger. A flamboyant historian and antiquarian, Bigger was an outspoken Ulster Protestant supporter of Irish nationalism. He was interested in reforging trade links between Rathlin and the Western Isles of Scotland, which had been extensive in the eighteenth century. The motor launch sailed on from Rathlin across the Sea of Moyle to Scotland although, to his chagrin, Hayward was not taken any farther and his adventure ended on the island itself. He was left with local people while the group went off to explore business possibilities. Longingly he looked across to the shadowy outline of the Mull of Kintyre, wishing he could have joined them. Nonetheless Rathlin, which he liked to refer to by its old name Raghery, cast a magic spell on him and he treasured the memory:

> What dreams I had during the absence of the boat, and what a place was I left in for the nourishment of them. On the return of the voyagers I heard all about their triumphal entries into little Scottish harbours, and it was much later that I came to think of Francis Joseph Bigger's immense flair for the historical background, which transmuted a small experiment in trade into a magnificent affair of merchant adventuring.[16]

Although nearly thirty years separated them, a friendship developed between the two and Bigger was to become an important influence on Hayward. His Presbyterian ancestors came from the lowlands of Scotland in the 1630s. They were part of a consortium of merchants who bought their own trading vessel, *The Good Ship Unicorn of Belfast*, one of the first trading ships ever owned by local merchants. By profession a solicitor, Bigger was also a writer, archaeologist and lover of Ireland who had many conversations with Hayward about the country and its past. He was elected a member of the Royal Irish Academy and was actively involved in the Belfast Naturalists' Field Club, serving as secretary and president. During his association with the Gaelic League he served on its executive committee, befriending Douglas Hyde, Eoin MacNeill and Roger Casement. He also revived the *Ulster Journal of Archaeology*, becoming its editor. Although Bigger was well regarded by the scholars of his day, subsequent generations of archaeologists were less enthusiastic. They felt his approach and the purple prose of his writing were more akin to those of a romantic historian rather than a serious archaeologist. In some of Hayward's writings, stylistic echoes of Bigger shine through and it is clear that he inhaled his perceptions.

The Irish landscape and coast, the play of light, the colours of the countryside and its waterways were imprinted on his mind from an early age. It was a leisurely era. The speed limit for the few cars on Ireland's roads in 1902 was twelve mph. But in between the travels that brought him into contact with a range of people, he had to fit in his academic studies. The Hayward brothers were educated at Larne Grammar School. Founded in 1888, when it opened it had just nineteen pupils though the figure rose quickly to forty-five, including nine boarders. Lack of money prevented many parents in Larne from sending their boys to the school. At the start, the fees were a guinea per term for boys under twelve for English and Mathematics, rising to £2 6s. 0d. for the whole course for boys over fourteen. The school also offered French, Latin, Greek, Euclid, algebra, drawing, natural philosophy and bookkeeping.

Set in its own grounds, Larne Grammar School prided itself not only on the quality of its education, but also on its location. Hayward boarded at the school during the early years of the twentieth century because his family had moved from Larne to live at Greenisland near Belfast.

At the time, Larne Grammar was for boys only. By the turn of the century, numbers had declined to just fourteen and some pupils did not attend with any regularity. Conditions were basic and the school lacked money to develop. Facilities for sport were poor. In Hayward's time, in the early years of the twentieth century when he was a boarder, there were up to ten teachers for forty pupils. During those Edwardian days, bullying rituals had been established to initiate new pupils. Some boys were put into a barrel and rolled down a steep slope at the side of the rifle range, making them violently sick. On other occasions boys were thrown over a thick holly hedge in the school grounds by sixth-form pupils, then thrown back by boys of the fifth form. More than forty years after leaving school, with memories still vivid, Hayward recalled his first few days and a ceremony that he had been put through to test his resilience to torture; it was not a happy experience:

> I can remember the terror of being initiated as a boarder at the Larne Grammar School. And little wonder, when that ceremony consisted of being grasped by several senior boys and of having one's head held in a place never intended for such a purpose. How could I, how could anyone, fail to remember those horrible seconds of waiting and the eventual roar and rush of waters as one of the initiators pulled a chain! And how I strutted after it was all over and agreed with everyone that it was a necessary and glorious institution.[17]

The pranks did not leave any lasting wounds and Hayward appears to have been cheerful, submitting himself to the rules and conventions of boarding school life. It opened up a whole new theatre of people and ideas to him. A diligent student and literary-minded boy, he was quick on the uptake, with a retentive memory. His reading included Shakespeare's poems and plays, which led to a love of drama. He realized the versatility of the English language and the power of expressive words in prose and poetry. This early interest in literature gave him a sense of creative possibility and he picked up on the turn of phrase, building stanzas and producing emphatic endings to pieces of writing. All this was cast into memory and proved fruitful in his later acting roles. A new headmaster, William Smyth Johnson, took over in 1901 determined to redress the school's decline and promote education in the area. He brought a new lease of life and within a year, attendance more than doubled from twenty to forty-two. But he found it an uphill battle and left after just three years. When his replacement James MacQuillan took over in Hayward's time in 1904, the school entered a new phase. MacQuillan's tenure lasted thirty-three years. An influential headmaster and teacher, his love of English literature rubbed off on Hayward. He encouraged the boys to read more Shakespeare, nurturing their talents through honest criticism. 'He was willing to have a go at teaching almost any subject, and could supervise an experiment in the lab., or conduct the school choir, or re-enact the Battle of Hastings with equal facility.'[18]

Hayward never lost affection for the school. Years later he attended annual dinners as well as prize-givings at which he donated to the library signed presentation copies of several of his books. The annual magazine, *The Old Grammarian*, shows that in 1956 and 1963 the school awarded a Richard Hayward Prize to pupils. He was also asked to judge a school writing competition.

Around 1904, when he was twelve, the family moved to live in Silverstream House in Greenisland overlooking Belfast Lough. Under the watchful eye of her father, his sister Gladys went on to become one of the few British women to gain recognition as a competitive helmswoman. She accompanied Scott on many of his trips across the Irish Sea to take part in a range of events. Initially she built up experience in a 10-ft dinghy and with her first boat *Sandpiper* won a first and two third prizes. Her father had taught her to sail in the WLYC, most likely on the Marine Lake in Southport and she crewed for him in this boat at all the club's Seabird races during 1900.[19]

Gladys Hayward, Richard's sister, being taught to sail in Belfast Lough by her father who designed motorboats and ran a marine engineering works. Gladys became one of the few British women to gain national recognition as competitive helms before 1914. Her husband was killed at the Somme in 1916.

17

SCOTT·HAYWARDS - 1906

Hayward family Edwardian studio portrait from 1906. Standing in the back row, from left to right, are Charles, Basil and Rex; seated, left to right are Richard (aged fourteen), their father Walter Scott, Gladys, mother Louise, and the youngest child Casson, aged seven.

Gladys was a member of the Royal North of Ireland Yacht Club, Liverpool Bay, Rhyl and Donaghadee Sailing Clubs. While never achieving the national renown of her father in the sailing world, she was nonetheless a respected yachtswoman. In 1907, despite its title, she merited an extensive biographical entry in *British Yachts and Yachtsmen*. In a male-dominated sport, Gladys sailed consistently to a high standard during the early years of the twentieth century, winning prizes at Southport and the Menai Straits regattas. At home she took part in the Belfast Lough and Silverstream regattas as well as competitions at Donaghadee. In 1906 she raced on the Clyde in *Curlew* winning three firsts and one second; that same year she entered the Welsh regatta and drove and steered the 12-ft motor dinghy *Pop*.[20]

Music swirled around his teenage years and his parents encouraged a love of it. In 1908 Hayward acquired his first phonograph, which worked in the same way as a turntable but with a large trumpet-like attachment instead of speakers. It was one of the latest gadgets but the only tune he had was 'Stars and Stripes' which, to the consternation of his brothers, he played non-stop for the first few days. 'It did not appeal to my elders,' he later wrote, 'as much as it did to me after its hundredth performance. They found it rather monotonous, to put it mildly.'[21] As the months went by and his musical appreciation developed, he bought other cylinders and played them in the seclusion of the hayloft above the coach house. They were his solace and delight. He later became the proud owner of one of the new Edison Amberola phonographs, which he bought from Thomas Edens Osborne, a dealer he knew from visiting his shop in Donegall Square in Belfast. He described Osborne's as a 'welter of safes, filters, bicycles, soap powders, oils and plaster statuary, all of which he sold with equal enthusiasm.'[22] Aside from music, one other curious and noisy hobby that he indulged in during his boyhood was making fireworks. In the Edwardian era this was regarded as a fashionable activity for young boys; at Halloween he took delight in putting together rockets, bangers, crackers and Roman candles.[23]

Although he enjoyed the sea air while walking near his home, Hayward does not seem to have taken part in competitive team sports. There is no evidence that he ever played the traditional grammar-school sports of soccer, rugby or hockey. Gladys, Rex, Charles and Basil were all active members of Silverstream hockey team, which their father coached during the early 1900s. Between them, the Haywards made up nearly half the team but Richard preferred more sedentary activities. It was a conventional childhood with a secure and sheltered upbringing and while music played a large part, literature was prominent too. A bookish boy, he was an avid reader of literary classics. Culturally, the period was dominated by a generation that grew up with Thackeray, Dickens and Sir Walter Scott. But notions of freedom and escape played on his mind and he devoured boys' adventure stories. His passion was stoked by *Robinson Crusoe*, which gave him a love of islands.[24] The teenage romantic showed evidence of wanderlust in his soul and dreamed of running off to a desert island. For the writer-to-be, it was a nourishing diet. His passing reference, envying Alec MacNichol's 'carefree life' is a telling remark.

Another illustrious figure he met was Percy French. In Hayward's childhood, French's 'Phil the Fluter's Ball' and 'The Mountains of Mourne' were sung everywhere – in homes and pubs, at ceilidhs and hiring fairs on the streets of Larne. Hayward wrote about him later, saying he came to know him as a youth and the personal contact with him was, 'one of the most benign influences in my artistic life.' No details of the circumstances of their meeting are recorded but Hayward wrote that, 'I know of no man who brought more wholesome entertainment and genuine laughter to his generation.'[25]

Scott Hayward continued with his sailing exploits, helping popularize marine motoring in Ireland and attending numerous regattas in the north-west of England and north Wales. During the late 1890s, despite the fact that he was now living in Ireland, he still managed to take part in a large number of widespread events. In the 1880s he had served on committees helping to arrange annual regattas and at the turn of the century was still organizing the summer Southport regatta where he held the position of Officer-of-the-Day. In 1905 he formed the Seabird, Seashell, Cariad and Gael One-Design Association, becoming its president two years later. During this period he also joined the Scottish Motor Boat Club and the Motor Boat Club of Ireland.

Although sailing was his passion, other sports and hobbies interested him. He was a famous swordsman. For three years he held the amateur singlestick championship of the British Isles and the quarterstaff championship of Lanca-shire and was for a time the English champion in trick swordsmanship. He was also an active member of the New Ross Harriers and Foxhounds Club. He had a reputation as one of the best cross-country riders to hounds and rode horses that few others could ride.[26]

Apart from sailing, Scott Hayward enjoyed hunting and was an active member of the New Ross Harriers and Foxhounds Club. He died in August 1910 on a business trip to Asia and was buried at sea aged fifty-four.

His main business interests were in marine engineering and he ran Messrs W. Hayward & Co., marine motor engineers based in the Atlantic Buildings in Waring Street, Belfast. His business thrived alongside a flour mill, linen and cotton merchants, shirt makers, solicitors and accountants. The *Belfast Street Directory* contains the following business entry for Walter Scott Hayward:

Hayward, W., & Co., Marine Motor Engineers, Paraffin, Petrol, and Suction Gas Yachts, Fishing Boats, and Cruising Launches Designed and Built; Speed Launches and Hydroplanes – 28 Waring Street. Works, Greenisland and Port-stewart. Tel. No. 879X Telegraphic Address, Auxiliary.[27]

One project that absorbed much time came about when the Congested Districts Board (CDB) of Ireland commissioned him to develop the use of motorized fishing boats along the west coast from Donegal to Galway. Set up as a government agency in 1891, the board's remit was to develop small industries in the overpopulated west as well as to assist fishermen and help modernize farming in areas with high levels of poverty. The CDB replaced squalid hovels, building slate-roofed stone cottages. They also built cut-stone piers, fishery stores, fish-curing stations and renewed harbours. In conjunction with the Land Commission, they divided large estates into strips, distributing them among tenants. In some areas the board divided up grazing and seaweed rights. Hayward's role involved working closely with fishermen in ramshackle ports and straggling villages along the coast and on small remote islands. Stormy conditions in 1905, especially on the Aran Islands, had damaged many boats and competition from foreign steam drifters was creating problems for the local industry.

Between 1906 and 1909, Hayward drove hundreds of miles by motor car along poor roads to talk to herring and mackerel fishermen in parts of Donegal, Galway and Mayo, installing motors in their boats.[28] Once he reached the area he was driven around in a 'long car' since there was no way to travel but by hired outside car. This was the method used by J.M. Synge and Jack B. Yeats who journeyed through the Congested Districts in the summer of 1905 just prior to Hayward's time.[29] Synge wrote a series of topographical essays for the *Manchester Guardian* on the harsh lives of ferrymen and fishermen, kelp-gatherers and boat builders while Yeats sketched the hardships of rural life.

Some fishermen owned basic rowboats while others had currachs or wooden sailing boats, and a small version of a hooker – a fishing smack known as a *púcán*. With his engineering skills, boating knowledge and energetic approach,

Hayward helped bring some relief to the industry. The west of Ireland through which he travelled was a completely different place from the world of polite yacht club society that he had known all his life. Although it was sixty years after the Famine, most people still subsisted on only a basic diet of potatoes, meal flour and tea. They lived in poverty to such an extent that some years earlier a parish priest on Aran, Fr Michael O'Donohue, is said to have sent a telegram to Dublin Castle stating: SEND US BOATS OR SEND US COFFINS [30]

Scott Hayward completed his work with the CDB towards the end of 1909, returning back home to his family in Greenisland. A few months later he set off on an intrepid business journey to Asia. His mission, in April 1910, was to travel to Vladivostok on the Trans-Siberian Railway to advise Russian fishermen on the use of motor boats. He planned to continue to Hong Kong where his sons, Basil and Rex, were setting up a car dealership, and then to visit San Francisco on the way home. After he had completed his business in Vladivostok, on the journey to Hong Kong, he contracted influenza. Complications developed in his health and when he arrived in Hong Kong he was admitted to the Peak Hospital. Partially recovered, he left for England with Basil on 16 July via Suez on SS *Pembrokeshire*, a Royal Mail Packet Steamer, while Rex returned home on the Trans-Siberian Railway. [31]

The family in Greenisland waited anxiously for news. Initially, they were given hope because of reports that he was recovering. But his health changed dramatically. The family received a telegram from Port Said with the tragic news that he had died from tubercular disease of the left lung on 15 August as the ship passed through the Red Sea. Basil had written to Rex from Suez stating: 'Poor dad got on so well to Colombo that I began to have hopes of getting home safe.'[32] Basil described the final days with cabin temperatures on the ship rising to ninety-three degrees and how his father was carried up on deck mentioning help from a Mr and Mrs Ellis on board.

On 16 August Scott Hayward was buried at sea at the age of fifty-four. The cause of death was stated as tuberculosis in his left lung. Yachtsmen from clubs around the northwest of England and in Ireland paid glowing tribute to his tireless contribution to yachting and the development of motor boats.[33] Under the heading, 'Death of Noted Mersey Yachtsman', the *Yachting World* reported the circumstances, describing him in an obituary as the 'prime mover' in the inception of the very successful West Lancashire Yacht Club. In the year of his death he had been a member of ten yacht clubs and of the Yacht Racing Association. The magazine said he was very well known and would be very much missed especially in motor boat circles.[34] Some months later, the magazine reported that the captain of the SS *Pembrokeshire*, Richard Hayes, had laid an evergreen wreath in the Red Sea near the spot where Hayward was buried and confirmed the details:

At 3.20 p.m., November 8, the Pembrokeshire was steamed over the position, viz., lat. 22 deg. 17 min. N and long. 37 deg. 26 min. W.; the engines were stopped, the wreath deposited in the sea, the ensign 'dipped', and the ship proceeded on her voyage.[35]

A prominent obituary in the *Belfast News Letter* noted that Hayward had done a great deal to popularize marine motoring in Ireland.[36] In his book celebrating the centenary of the WLYC, Roger Ryan summed up his contribution to the sailing world:

The successful creation and leadership of the WLYC was certainly a high point among Scott Hayward's many achievements. He was truly an individual with the ability to identify when and where to initiate changes. Of course, he had the wealth and social background needed to fit in at any yacht club in the country ... There were doubtless many wealthy 'yachtsmen' who were members of numerous clubs and did little or nothing about it. Scott Hayward stood apart from that type.[37]

Their father's death was a devastating blow. Louie was left in a plight. Her husband, although wealthy, 'may have lived to some extent above his means'.[38] She had six children, although four were well into adulthood and independent. Casson was just eleven while Richard, seventeen and now fatherless, was finding his own way in the world and had started studying naval architecture. He was also cultivating literary and artistic tastes, striking out to explore the city on his doorstep and becoming aware of the sense of life's possibilities. Belfast was a fast-developing place with plenty to feed his imagination. The culmination of his teenage years presented a golden opportunity to witness a spectacle that would remain indelibly imprinted in his mind.

TWO

Sweet poetic aspirations

(1911–1924)

On a golden day of the Autumn,
I walked where the fallen leaves
Lay soft as a carpet beneath my feet,
And tempered the ever-joyous green
With a pensive thoughtfulness

'An Autumn Day', *Poems*,
by H. Richard Hayward, 1920
Dedicated to his wife, Elma

No one who was there would ever forget that day when tens of thousands of people lined the shores of Belfast Lough in brilliant sunshine. For Hayward, 31 May 1911 was to be one of the most memorable days of his life. He had been stopped in High Street by the caretaker of the Albert Clock, Mr MacFall whom he had known from a previous visit to study the clock's mechanism. One of Belfast's most eye-catching landmarks, the clock tower was erected in 1870 to commemorate Queen Victoria's consort. MacFall invited Hayward to climb the steep steps to the top from where he enjoyed a grandstand view of the launch of RMS *Titanic*. Gingerly, the eighteen-year-old followed the caretaker and stood on a narrow ledge of cut stone high above the street. At 140ft it afforded the perfect elevated position from which to witness proceedings. Forty-seven years after the event, he wrote about that day:

I have always had a good head for heights, but I can recall even now a slight feeling of dizziness and a great sort of panic of desire to press my body tight into the unyielding masonry. There lay the great ship, fabulous creation of Ulster brains and Ulster muscles, quiet as a sleeping child in its cradle.[1]

Now apprenticed in naval architecture, Hayward was keen to see the ship being launched. In the preceding years he had followed the developments at Harland & Wolff shipyard in Queen's Island and was impressed with the size of the three Olympic-class liners being planned. After the idea of building the ships – *Olympic*, *Titanic* and *Britannic* – was conceived by the shipyard chairman, Lord Pirrie and the White Star Line chairman, Bruce Ismay in 1907, two new slipways and steel gantries were built. Over the next three years the building of the *Olympic* and *Titanic* gave employment to thousands of men. The *Olympic* was launched in October 1910, eight months before *Titanic*.

On the day of the launch a palpable cloud of excitement hung over the streets. From early morning, sightseers swarmed every vantage point, from the roofs of coal sheds to the masts of harbour shipping, in an atmosphere of gaiety. The dignitaries included J.P. Morgan, owner of the White Star Line. Tickets had been sold for a reserved enclosure at the Albert Quay. During the morning, Hayward had watched as workmen added the final touches. Several minutes after noon, a red flag was hoisted to warn the fleet of boats in the River Lagan to 'Stand Away!' The vessel was being held on slipway No. 3 by hydraulic triggers, which required the opening of a valve for release to allow the huge bulk to glide into the water. Just after midday three successive rockets were fired before the 26,000-ton hull started down the slipway. Gangs of workers scrambled clear, and with little ceremony and not even a modest bottle of champagne to break over the bow, Pirrie launched the ship to shouts of 'There she goes'. *Titanic* reached a speed of twelve knots before six anchor chains and two piles of cable drag chains, weighing almost eighty tons, brought her to a halt. The entire process took just sixty-two seconds. With his bird's-eye view, Hayward provides a vivid description:

On the stroke of twelve, with the sound and fury of a thousand steam-hammers, and as the *Titanic* started to move down the slipway I was almost hurled into the street below. Panic came back to me with redoubled force, and as I suddenly realized that eleven more devastating blows were to follow I thought I was lost indeed. But somehow the second stroke seemed less fierce than the first, and long before the last of the dozen had sounded I was so absorbed in the spectacle of the launch that I was listening, not to a noisy gong, but to a great chorus of horns and sirens and hooters that came swelling up from all over the area of the docks and quays and beyond.[2]

Within an hour the ship, which was launched as an empty shell, was moved by tugs to a deep-water wharf where work began to make her seaworthy. The engines and propelling machinery were installed while carpenters, electricians and sixty-seven other trades fitted out the passenger accommodation. Hayward summed up the significance of the event:

> Epoch-making indeed, and epoch-annihilating too, for that was the era of Edwardian complacency and leisurely comfort, the era of sharp social distinctions and smug self-sufficiency, the era in which man was deluded into the notion that nature was at last his slave; an era which died with the *Titanic* itself.[3]

Also in the crowd that day was a six-year-old boy, William MacQuitty, the son of James MacQuitty, owner and managing director of the *Belfast Telegraph*. He was to later become a merchant banker, film producer and founder of Ulster Television as well as a close friend and business associate of Hayward. He wrote about the occasion in his autobiography:

> All at once the workers on board gave a cheer in which the crowds on shore joined. The slide had begun. Every ship in the lough sounded its siren, the noise drowning the roar of the piles of restraining anchors as they were dragged along the ground. Slowly gathering speed, the *Titanic* moved smoothly down the ways, and a minute later was plunging into the water raising a huge wave.[4]

Many local reporters covered the event and eighty-five members of the press from England and Scotland were ferried across the Irish Sea from Fleetwood in Hayward's native county of Lancashire on a specially chartered steamer, the *Duke of Argyll*. Sea trials were held and ten months after the launch, on 2 April 1912, the *Titanic* left for Southampton where the first passengers embarked. Twelve days after the departure, when news of the sinking reached Belfast on 15 April, the city was numbed with disbelief. For a long time after, the disaster was barely spoken of. Hayward took away a vivid impression of the day and it remained an abiding image in his mind. Later in life he occasionally spoke of it with his family, reflecting on the colour of the moment and the excitement of the crowds;[5] in his later singing career he recorded a song called 'The sinking of the Titanic'.

In early adolescence Hayward liked spending time in Belfast, soaking up the pomp of the bustling Edwardian city. He loved its situation at the head of

the lough surrounded by hills and enjoyed wandering the redbrick streets dominated by warehouses. Belfast was a prosperous and growing industrial city. At the
turn of the twentieth century its population of 350,000 had increased fourfold
since 1850. It was the twelfth-largest city in the United Kingdom and the biggest
port in Ireland, surpassing Dublin in size. Linen mills, shipbuilding, rope-making
and tea machinery works were amongst the major employers. The imposing new
city hall, opened in 1906 on the site of the White Linen Hall, was built in the
Edwardian Imperial architectural style. Hayward later bemoaned the demolition
of the Linen Hall – 'a building of solid traditional quality.'[6] He was developing an
eye for architecture and admired the late Georgian elegance of Clifton House in
North Queen Street, built in 1771, and the city's oldest public building.

He was also becoming familiar with the pleasures of theatres and music
halls as well as the museum and art gallery. This was the era of stylish Victorian
department stores such as Robb's, the Bank Buildings, Anderson & McAuley,
and Robinson & Cleaver. S.D. Bell's in Ann Street was a grocery emporium
while Sawers in High Street supplied fish and meat to the well-to-do. Hayward
hung around Gibson's Corner in Donegall Place and Singer's Corner, both
landmarks that have long since disappeared. The quirky side of city life intrigued
him: barefoot newsboys selling the *Belfast Telegraph* with their cries of 'Telly'
echoing around the streets; old women, many with shawls, sitting on stools on
the pavement on the Queen's Bridge or in Arthur Square, their baskets full of
boiled periwinkles, which they sold in pennyworths; street traders such as Jenny
King, known as the 'Queen of Flower Sellers', who plied her wares at Gibson's
Corner where she had a pitch for more than fifty years. With her black wavy
hair and Mediterranean looks, her image was captured on canvas by the artist
William Conor who later became friendly with Hayward.

Often he wandered along Clifton Street where the trace horses of the
horse-drawn trams dragged their heavy loads uphill to Carlisle Circus, an important junction for hackney carriages and trams. He listened to the clippety-clop
mixed in with the cries of the trace boys, and the clink of the chains hooked
to the vehicles smelling of paraffin lamps, damp upholstery and horseflesh.[7] He
delighted in the city's black humour as well as the directness of its people.

One of his diversions was scouting. In his late teens he became involved
with the scout movement and was leader of the 3rd Belfast Troop. It was the
early days of the boy scouts and interest was growing. He accepted a role as
scoutmaster with a group known as 'Our Boys' Hall' in Manor Street off the
Cliftonville Road in north Belfast. Hayward showed an ability to bring together

young boys of varying backgrounds, some from tough areas of the Cliftonville and Crumlin roads. He helped knit them together, giving them an opportunity to take part in boxing and wrestling as well as providing instruction on the new-fangled internal combustion engine. They were given opportunities to stage plays on wet evenings and he organized outings, bringing them into the hills around Belfast, showing them places on their doorstep they had never been to. On one occasion, in the summer of 1911, the troop camped at Bally-walter Park in County Down. It was a trip that Hayward relished planning and that involved road, rail and sea journeys culminating, to the scouts' delight, in a motor-launch bringing them on the final leg from Donaghadee to Ballywalter. Hayward benefited from his time with the scouts. Not only did it help develop a gift for leadership and organizational skills – something that he was to be renowned for later in life – it also fuelled an ever-growing interest in drama. Equally importantly, he was a positive role model for impressionable boys.[8]

Although Francis Joseph Bigger and Percy French had been significant to him as a boy, it was not an Irish writer who was to influence him most but an English one, George Borrow. A nineteenth-century author and polymath, Borrow was born in 1803 in Norfolk of Cornish ancestry, the son of a military officer. In the 1820s he had tramped through Wales, England, Germany, France, Spain, Portugal and Russia meeting people on the road, whether nomads, tramps or farmers, and developing an affinity with Romanies. His travel book, *The Bible in Spain* (1843), made him an overnight celebrity and as well-known in his day as Thackeray or Dickens. He wrote novels and travel books, including the acclaimed *Wild Wales* (1862), a picaresque novel-cum-travel journal based on a three-month tour of Wales in the summer and autumn of 1854. The book is a quixotic mixture of road-walking and doggerel verse based on a series of comic meetings with storytellers, poets and innkeepers as well as other digressions along the way. A lover of gypsies, Borrow was a rambling man of the open road. One of his best-known books is the quasi-autobiographical *Lavengro: The Scholar, the Gypsy, the Priest*, published in 1851, which Hayward read when he was twenty. He was electrified. It was, he wrote years later in a Dublin newspaper, a book that 'glorified the countryside and the people who lived in it'.[9] Reading it was a seminal experience, providing inspiration and ultimately setting him on a path that would lead to authorship. He recalled what he most enjoyed in Borrow's work:

His curious and remote knowledge, his racy personality and great gift of seeing things from his own individual angle, his love of country people, his hatred of pomposity and above all his innate and magnificent quality of quick friendship and immediate warm contact with his fellow-creatures of all classes and creeds and races … filled me with a desire to emulate him according to my smaller lights.[10]

Borrow had shown an interest in place names, which ignited Hayward's imagination, sending him off on a philological track that 'ever since yielded treasure to me':

He tells us that his father sprang from a family with property in Tredinnock in Cornwall, a Celtic name which being interpreted means the House on the Hill or more properly the Hillock, and from that day I have never heard a place name without seeking to find out its meaning, or written a book of topography without some attempt at the elucidation of the corrupt English forms that cast such an ugly veil over the meaningful native originals that so often light up a landscape or a region with the logic of their making and the music of their sounds.[11]

Published when he was seventy, Hayward's article looked back on his lifetime of writing. He described the significant influence of Borrow, which led him to the work of R.A.S. Macalister as well as to his affection for the Irish countryside:

I don't suppose there are many mountains or hills in Ireland that I have not climbed, or many islands round our coast that I have not visited, and. it is the fact that my interest in archaeology and my curiosity about our prehistory have led my wandering feet into almost every nook and cranny of our fair land, remote regions that remain unknown to most people who are accounted sane. For the impulse that first sent me along those endearing ways I must look to Borrow and for the pabulum that nourished my continuing enthusiasm I must thank Macalister, that staunch pioneer in his field who it is sometimes the fashion to denigrate in these thin graceless days.[12]

Borrow came to Ireland at the age of twelve, accompanying his father's regiment to Clonmel and Templemore. At the military barracks he learnt to sing 'Croppies Lie Down'. He attended the Protestant Academy and was introduced to the Irish language by a fellow student called Murtagh who in a celebrated deal tutored him in return for a pack of playing cards. In Borrow's distinctive voice, Hayward found stimulation that gave him the impetus and desire to explore in a similar way. It was a book from which he imbibed a vast amount. Significantly, he had learnt the importance of contact with country people as well as the value of place names and of the Irish language.

Life in Ireland at this time was marked by a decade in which considerable political, social and economic change was about to take place. At the beginning of 1912 the country was an integral part of the United Kingdom but within a ten-year period the Irish Free State had been set up while the six northern counties remained part of the UK. It was also the start of a tragic and violent decade in European history. The ten dramatic years were to be marked by a world war, political agitation, electoral upheaval and at home the Easter Rising, the war of independence and civil war.

The third Home Rule Bill giving Ireland legislative independence was published in April 1912 and a crisis was looming. It seemed destined to pass through the Westminster Parliament despite strong opposition from Ulster Unionists and British Conservatives. On 28 September – in what became known as Ulster Day – the signing of the Ulster Solemn League and Covenant took place at Belfast City Hall, marking the Unionist protest against efforts to introduce home rule. The Unionist leader, Sir Edward Carson, was the first to sign the petition and almost half a million people followed him in registering their opposition, some even signing in their own blood. Most Catholics were indifferent to what was going on around them and continued with their everyday lives. There is no evidence that Hayward signed the Covenant; his name does not appear amongst the 400,000 held in PRONI, and as a Gladstone liberal supporter he most likely decided against signing it. Early the following year, in January 1913, the Home Rule Bill was passed by the House of Commons but rejected by the House of Lords.

Dinner-table conversation amongst the Hayward brothers produced vigorous discussion about the political controversies of the time. Hayward had disagreements with two brothers in later years and conflicting loyalties developed. By now, all nearly grown up, they closely followed the unfolding drama of events although some were becoming restless and wanted to see the world. With his lively enquiring mind, Hayward read newspapers and was keenly aware of major political developments. It was a busy household with twelve people, including two visiting relatives from Switzerland, living in it in April 1911. At the age of fifty-two and with the death of her husband the previous year, Louie assumed the position as head of the family. Gladys had already left and married. Basil, now twenty-seven and Charles, twenty-five, were both working in marine engineering while Casson was at school. The family still had a maidservant and employed a gardener.[13]

Now an adult and having left grammar school, Hayward had started his first job as a naval architect. Still living at Silverstream, he was turning over career ideas. But the family was breaking up and his brothers were soon to disperse to different parts of the world. Rex and Casson developed diametrically opposed views to his on religion and politics. In 1912 they emigrated to South Africa. Rex was twenty-four while Casson, who was half his age, converted to Catholicism in 1918, partly in an unsuccessful attempt to gain acceptance by a South American family as suitor for their daughter's hand.[14] Casson never married, although both Rex and Basil married Catholics and their children were brought up in the Catholic faith. Their brother, Richard (still known as Harold), had no plans to emigrate and liked Ireland too much to think of going to live abroad. Opportunities for work in industry were never greater with the Belfast shipyard alone employing 14,000 people in 1914. His brother Charlie, who became a naval officer in the First World War, had gone to Liverpool to work in the Cammell Laird yard at Birkenhead. Later he emigrated to Venezuela before settling down with his wife to live in Port of Spain, Trinidad.

Political divisions were becoming sharpened and resulted in a militarization of life with the formation of a citizens' militia, the Ulster Volunteer Force, to resist home rule and support the Unionist cause. They embraced every class and were commanded by a retired Indian Army officer, General Sir George Richardson. The force (or 'farce' as some called it) was a private army that eventually consisted of 100,000 men organized along military lines. In April 1914, 35,000 rifles were brought in to arm the UVF. A hundred miles south, in Dublin in the summer of 1912, John Redmond had brought the British prime minister Herbert Asquith to the city to show him the intensity of passion for home rule. And the following year, in response to the forming of the UVF, the Irish Volunteers was established in November 1913 with more than 160,000 men signing up. During the second half of 1913, the turmoil in Dublin was taking place at the same time as a strike by the Irish Transport and General Workers Union, which led to a lock-out by the employers and labour unrest.

In Larne, a place that Hayward had now left behind, Loyalists were mobilizing in serious opposition to the plans. On the nights of Friday, 24 and Saturday, 25 April 1914 they secretly smuggled in guns early in the morning, dispersing them efficiently throughout the north. Twenty-five thousand rifles and three million rounds of ammunition were brought in on a coal boat, the SS *Clyde Valley* (its cover name was the *Mountjoy*). Both the army and the RIC were informed but decided to take no action against the UVF, believing it to be a training exercise. One of those closely involved in the elaborate operation, codenamed 'Lion', was Captain John Edward Jenks: Hayward's brother-in-law. Jenks, who was known as Jack, had married his sister Gladys. They lived near the harbour in an area called Moyle. Jenks was employed by the Shamrock Shipping Company and commanded the Larne harbour section of the Volunteers, many of whom worked there. He helped lead the operation, becoming Commander 'A' Company, organizing the movement and distribution of weapons and ammunition.[15]

Jenks was the assistant to William Chaine, commander of the 2nd battalion of the Central Antrim UVF and chairman of the company that owned the harbour. Through their jobs they were able to make secret arrangements, and after the cargo was unloaded a burst of activity erupted with more than 570 cars passing through the town that night on swift distribution runs. Gladys' role, as part of Larne UVF Nursing Corps, was to support and back up the volunteers. Early on the Friday morning she told two other women, Lucy McNeill and Nora Rankin, that the landing of the guns was expected that night. Their job was to provide ham and egg sandwiches and drink. They would also supply white armbands with safety pins for the 300 men who would be on duty:

> A week of memorable happenings when the Mount Joy carrying arms was expected, very few were in the know. Jack was ready with the arrangements for her discharge – I was ready with food and drink and two helpers, we were just on secret duty and knew no more. Our signal came when the police were locked up and the telephone lines cut. An inrush of cars from all parts and in she steamed to Larne Harbour and what a hungry crew. Buckets and buckets of hot drinks all night long for car drivers and workers and Larne Harbour was 'lit up.' What a display of car lights coming and going and what organization and what rest for the police! [16]

The potential for an Irish civil war was looming but the build-up of arms by both sides was overshadowed by a much bigger event that was about to engulf Europe – the First World War. Hayward would have seen soldiers on the streets and observed regiments on the march as they prepared to head off to battle. The conflict broke out on 28 July 1914 and by 4 August Britain was at war with Germany. Many people thought it would be over quickly – perhaps by Christmas or just after – but were soon shown to be wrong. The Antrim volunteers of the UVF made up the new 36th Ulster Division and moved to Newtownards as part of the 108th Brigade. After being transferred to Seaford in Sussex, they were mobilized for war in October 1915, landing at Boulogne, and were engaged in action on the Western Front.

Hayward's wife, Elma, whom he married in 1915, was a member of the Belfast Radio Players. She was a talented actress appearing alongside her husband in stage plays and films, and supported his wide spectrum of projects.

The following summer the horrors of the muddy swamps and trenches of the Somme in July 1916 resulted in the deaths of thousands of soldiers. It also claimed the life of Hayward's brother-in-law. Jenks had joined the Royal Irish Rifles rising to the rank of temporary captain in the regiment's 12th (Service) Battalion. He died aged thirty-six on 4 July of wounds received near the village of Hamel. His division had taken over a complete section of the front line between the valley of the River Ancre and the Mailly-Maillet to Serre road, a few miles northwest of Thiepval Wood. On the first day of the battle, 1 July, 19,240 British soldiers died. Many were untrained volunteers, most still teenagers. Jenks posthumously received three medals for his war service: the Victory Medal (also called the Inter Allied Victory Medal), the 1914 Star, and the British War Medal. These three medals were sometimes irreverently referred to as Pip, Squeak and Wilfred. The names came from a popular comic strip in the *Daily Mirror* (Pip was a dog, Squeak a penguin, and Wilfred a young rabbit).

Just before the outbreak of war, a friendship had blossomed between Hayward and Wilhelmina 'Elma' Nelson, a bright and attractive north Belfast girl in her late teens. They first met while dancing at a roller-skating rink in the city and with her dazzling hazel eyes and brown hair, Hayward was drawn to her. After this they met regularly and began, as it was called in Ireland, 'coorting'. They had common interests and a shared past. She had happy memories of childhood days spent on holidays in Islandmagee and was familiar with many of the places such as the Gobbins cliff path where Hayward had spent time in his youth. Although the 'war to end all wars' was dragging on and cast a shadow over life, their courtship developed. They fell in love and in buoyant spirits decided to tie the knot. On 9 July 1915 they were married by the Rev. William Watson in a simple ceremony in Ballygilbert Presbyterian Meeting House near Crawfordsburn in north Down.

Elma was born on 3 September 1895, just a few months after the death of her father William Nelson. He had worked in the Belfast silversmiths firm, Riddels, until he retired because of ill health. In his honour she was given the female version of his name and as a girl, and through her adult life, was known as Elma. On their marriage certificate Hayward's profession is listed as 'Engineer' while nothing is listed under Elma's name. At nineteen, she was three years his junior and because of her age, a licence of marriage granting consent from her mother had to be issued as a legal requirement.

Through his brother's connections at Cammell Laird, Hayward received an offer of full-time work at Birkenhead. Like Harland & Wolff in Belfast, the company was at the forefront of shipbuilding. With Charlie's help in getting him established, he decided to take up this opportunity even though it meant leaving Ireland – at least temporarily. Given their late father's connection to the Mersey and his contacts in the area, it is not surprising they decided to go there. The newlyweds lodged in one of the most prized addresses in the city – Rodney Street in Mount Pleasant, a dignified Georgian area. According to architectural guidebooks, 'Its length, width and straightness was unprecedented in Liverpool.'[17]

Rodney Street was known as the 'Harley Street of the North' because of the large number of doctors who held surgeries and consulting rooms there or who lived on it alongside the city's professional elite. The remarkably well-preserved street was built in the early 1780s. Today many of the houses are listed buildings bearing plaques testifying to illustrious names that lived there: Nicholas Monsarrat, Liverpool's famous seafaring son, who wrote *The Cruel Sea* (1951); the biographer, historian and member of the Bloomsbury group, Lytton Strachey; the poet Arthur Hugh Clough, and Thurston Holland, the pioneer of radiology. W.E. Gladstone, elected prime minister in a minority Liberal government in the year of Hayward's birth, was born in 1809 at No. 62. Each morning

Hayward joined thousands of other workers on his daily commute, walking to Pier Head to catch a ferry for the eight-minute journey across the Mersey to Birkenhead where he disembarked at the Woodside Ferry Stage. Six ferries plied across the river in those days. Two of the Wallasey boats were pressed into service for the war, accompanying the Royal Navy at their landing at Zeebrugge in Belgium in April 1918. During Hayward's employment at the yard, Cammell Laird adapted to the needs of the British war effort and was not building or designing cruise ships. Since shipyard work was a reserved occupation Hayward was exempt from military service. His role was in ship repair and maintenance. Work was confined to battleships, armed merchant cruisers and merchant ships, destroyers and submarines, which were converted to carry mines. Cruise liners were turned into troop carriers. *City of Belfast*, a vessel built for the Barrow Steam Navigation Company's Barrow to Belfast route, was turned into HMS *City of Belfast*, operating as an armed boarding and inspection vessel. Convoys gathered in the Mersey to face submarines in the North Sea while small coastal vessels were fitted with guns.

It was a time of uncertainty and fear. As had been the case in Belfast, young men were signing up for war service. In Liverpool some of the regiments were called 'Pals' because the soldiers went to war surrounded by their friends. Nonetheless life continued as far as normality permitted in what was a flourishing port that was also the departure point for passengers on liners to the US. Hayward and his wife became acquainted with the city streets, wandering the narrow thoroughfares, admiring the buildings and feeling at home amongst the tall redbrick industrial warehouses so prevalent in the city across the Irish Sea. They were impressed with the imposing monument to Queen Victoria in Derby Square unveiled by King George V on 16 May 1911 and appreciated Liverpool's two newly erected mythical motifs – the liver birds installed in 1913 on the clock towers on the Royal Liver Building at Pier Head. Hayward would have reflected on how a badge featuring the cormorant-like bird had adorned his late father's Royal Mersey cap. Walking along Lord Street and Bold Street they discovered some of the city's elegant department stores on a par with Belfast.

Their Liverpool years are thinly documented but undoubtedly Hayward's time in the city helped widen his vision and develop networks in the artistic world in which he was increasingly interested. Occasional return trips were made to Belfast and in 1917 with the war in stalemate they said their goodbyes to Liverpool. The Ireland they returned to was a country in upheaval. Up to 200,000 Irishmen fought in the British armed forces in the First World War, an event that was to shape the twentieth century. At home the Easter Rising in 1916 saw Ireland plunged into a new period of conflict.

Three years after their marriage, their first son, Dion Nelson, was born on 20 November 1918. His arrival was just nine days after Armistice Day so it was a time of double celebration for them. But the world was changing and Hayward's life was changing too. With fatherhood came responsibilities and the tough search for work began in the aftermath of the war. His years at Cammell Laird had given him his first taste of employment and he was looking for a job that would provide stability with a regular income to support his family. He did not wish to be tied down with full-time work since he wanted to spend time nurturing his creative side and soon he found an ideal compromise. He became a freelance commissioned agent in the wholesale confectionery trade, working two days a week for two leading English firms, Fox's Glacier Mints of Leicester and Needler's Chocolate Makers of Hull. Hayward was not employed on the staff by either firm but acted as an independent representative for them, paid on a commission basis. It was the start of a long and happy association. He was to spend forty-three years working for Fox's and thirty-nine years with Needler's. When some of the artistic and cultural enterprises that he embarked on did not raise sufficient income, the bread-and-butter earnings from his confectionery job kept the family housed and fed, and helped pay for holidays. As well as a financially pragmatic safety net, the sales job gave him a sharpened sense of purpose, releasing time to explore artistic work and formulate ideas.

He started with Fox's Glacier Mints in 1922, just a year after the company placed Peppy the polar bear icon on its mint wrappers. Needler's (cable address: 'Needful Hull') was an older company founded by Fred Needler in 1886 and one of the largest employers in their area. Before the First World War their product range of 576 lines included forty types of toffees, thirty-eight different boiled sweets, fifteen labelled sticks of rocks and fourteen pralines, but by the early 1920s the English market was depressed. Profits and sales were hit as many people could no longer afford the luxury of chocolate but the company expanded into the Irish market and signed up Hayward in 1924 when they were still a well-known name. Typical of the sweets that he sold were Buttermints and Maltona Toffees, Mixed Fruit Pastilles, Chocolate Bon Bons, Niagra Nuts ('clear as crystal and an excellent aid to digestion') and the popular Buttered Brazils – nuts hand-dipped in toffee and priced at eight pence a quarter. Jars of medicated sweets ('safety first cough tablets') were also sold in the 1920s. Company advertisements claimed that they packed and sold 1,850,000 boxes of chocolates each year.[18]

'Peppy', the polar bear, first appeared on the Fox's Glacier Mints sweet bag wrapper in 1921, the year before Hayward joined the company. He spent more than forty years as a part-time commercial sales representative with the firm and was known to some as 'The Glacier Mints Man'.

Travelling in the early months of his job by train, his work for Fox's took him all over Ireland until the setting up of the newly founded Northern state. Most towns had a sweet shop, some of which also sold fancy goods and cigarettes, and he got to know many shopkeepers. His territory shrunk in December 1922 with the establishment of the Free State and the introduction of laws restricting cross-border trading. On 1 April the following year new measures included the setting up of manned customs checkpoints to raise revenues. This protected local manufacturers in the South and along with import duties, meant Hayward's confectionery sales were thereafter confined to the North. His navy ledger of customers contains a handwritten list of fifty villages, towns and cities stretching from Antrim to Warrenpoint. In his bookkeeping, as in all his activities, he was methodical and efficient. Shop owners' names are scrupulously listed in neat black pen with a code number, cross-references and invoicing details; in some cases, names have been crossed out with the word 'Bankrupt' written beside it. The Belfast entries of more than 400 run to twenty-three

37

pages, covering a diverse range of customers such as Anderson & McAuley Ltd., the fashionable department store, St George's Market, Harland & Wolff shipyard and several cinemas. Also listed were corner shops on the Ormeau and New Lodge roads along with the Sweet Centre and Candy Corner.[19] In County Tyrone, Davy Young's fine-sounding establishment, The Sweeteries, in Market Square, Omagh, was known as a local Houses of Parliament since it was the hub of everything happening in the area.

He settled in well to his new job, enjoying the congenial work and relishing the opportunity to meet new people. Alongside this, his artistic and cultural interests were burgeoning; in between his wartime work and spending leisure time with Elma, Hayward had already been dabbling in poetry with a burning desire to publish. The war years saw a flourishing of poets in England; the work of Wilfred Owen, Siegfried Sassoon and Edward Thomas was becoming well known and may have held resonance for him. With his literary intentions firmly trained on what he saw as a new calling, Hayward set about developing his writing of verse.

His first published work was a slim collection of seventeen poems, simply called *Poems*, which came out in 1917 when he was twenty-five. It was published by Morland, based in Amersham in Buckinghamshire, and was followed three years later by another hardback volume of poetry from the same press. Also called *Poems*, it included a small gold shamrock leaf embossed on the green cover. It contained thirty-eight poems, twelve of which had been included in the earlier edition. A profile portrait frontispiece of Hayward from a charcoal sketch drawn by Grace Henry, wife of the artist Paul Henry, was inserted. He is pictured wearing a bow tie and sketched with an expressionless faraway gaze in his eye for which he was to become known in portraits and photographs from this period. In another sketch, drawn in 1927 by the artist Frank McKelvey for the cover of *Ulster Life and Opinion*, he portrays the look of a dandy. The images show a sensitive serious-minded young man with a distant look. It may perhaps have been a cultured aesthete pose that he cultivated but it was one that he employed for both artists and photographers. One of the finest images stems from an outing with the Royal Society of Antiquaries of Ireland in which he is photographed with a group in a charabanc. In the picture, Hayward is the only person not looking at the photographer Albert Campbell. Even in his late twenties, he presented to his friends a youthful appearance which led, according to his son Ricky, to his being called Peter Pan, 'I think because he was slow to give up his appearance and ways – rather than unwilling to grow up.'[20]

A. RICHARD HAYWARD
FROM A CHARCOAL SKETCH
BY MRS. PAUL HENRY

For his second collection of poems, published in 1920,
Hayward chose as a frontispiece a charcoal portrait
sketched by Grace Henry, wife of the artist Paul Henry.
One poem in the collection, 'A Praise of Connemara',
is dedicated to Mr and Mrs Paul Henry.

One poem in the 1920 collection, 'A Praise of Connemara', is dedicated to Mr and Mrs Paul Henry, both of whom he knew in Belfast's artistic life after they returned around 1917 from Achill Island where they had lived since 1910. The Henrys had mounted annual exhibitions in Belfast and in 1917 held their first in Dublin where they moved to live two years later. Another poem, 'An Autumn Day', was written for Elma. His poetry gives an insight into the company he kept and circles in which he moved. Others were dedicated to Abram Rish, a playwright, W.B. Reynolds, a composer and music critic, and James A. Hogg, an uncle of the well-known photographer Alexander Hogg. Hayward embraced a range of styles, experimenting with French lyric poetry, and resulting in a mix of villanelle, sestina, rondel, rondeau and ballads. Filled with the flowery diction of youthful exuberance, his poems were expressions of love of the countryside as well as a love of life. None reflected the political turmoil in Ireland or the events of the First World War but some have a Romantic sentiment. Several dealt with music while others showed an interest in the classical world. Imagery of nature is a thread apparent in titles such as 'The Swallows in my Garden', 'The Cuckoo', 'The Cornfield', 'March Winds …', and 'The Lake'. Some were observational while others, such as 'Islandmagee' were personal, harking back to his happy engagement with the natural world in his east Antrim childhood.

> Child of the mainland! Island but in name!
> What tales of fancy thou dost hold for me:
> Witches and sprites and fairies by the sea
> Accord a magic wonder to thy fame.
> The waves that wash thy borders are the same
> That drank the blood of friend and enemy,
> When, in the boisterous past, o'er Gobbin's Brae
> Thy sons cast forth the foe as nightfall came.
> Still on thy grim, forbidding, rock-bound coast,
> The children point with fear to crimsoned stone
> And weed, as relics of that bloody fray.
> Still at the witching hour – the peasants boast
> With many a fearful glance!–a sound is blown
> Across the land, of fairies at their play.[21]

'Two men I honour and No Third' is dedicated to the memory of Thomas Carlyle, the Scottish satirical writer and philosopher whom Hayward had read. 'To a Buttercup' in the second collection was written for his friend William Newman. After Hayward's death, Newman recalled his early verse in a newspaper tribute:

Few people are aware that he started his literary career as a poet and a damn bad poet at that! He had the wit to perceive this fact for himself after a long mental struggle, and abandoned verse for the smooth and polished prose which turned out to be his natural medium and for which he has never received his due mead of praise.[22]

Whatever he may have been going through, Hayward's poems, written in his late teens and early twenties, do not suggest inner turmoil or a troubled soul. It is likely he had rewritten them and worked on them for several years. The critical reaction is not documented but they do not appear to have taken the literary world by storm, and from what Newman states they were not well regarded. Some were forced for grandiose effect, while others were pretentious and artificial, reflecting the cloying sentimentality of adolescence. Banal dialect, 'girls is quare', and antiquated flourishes crept in: 'thee', 'thou', 'o'er', 'perchance' and 'sylvan ease'. But still the poems continued to stream forth. In his thirtieth year, his third and final volume *Love in Ulster and Other Poems* was jointly published in 1922 by the Talbot Press in Dublin and Unwin in London. The forty-five poems in this reflected natural history and Irish folklore while some, such as 'The Man in the Moon', 'The Red Lane', and 'The Snail', were for children.

In a note, Hayward explained that some of the pieces appeared in the pages of *Banba* and of the American magazine *Tempo*.[23] *Banba* was a monthly Dublin journal that ran for just over two years in the early 1920s. Contributors included Brinsley MacNamara, George Shiels and Daniel Corkery. It was described in tone as 'an odd mixture of militant nationalism and chatty popular journalism (including several cowboy stories) … halfway through the run the literary content veers rapidly downmarket into low populism.'[24] Eventually he recognized that poetry was not his forte. In spite of their lack of literary virtues, he was enjoying the *réclame* of authorship. He had satisfied himself of an urge to be stirred by the muse and produced the first published work from his pen. Nearly ninety poems had been put between the hard covers of three books but his poetic ambition was declining and he wanted to try other forms of composition.

A passion for the outdoors, reflected in his poetry, was animated through membership of several organizations in the early 1920s. Hayward wanted to learn more about the layers of the countryside and joined the Belfast Naturalists' Field Club (BNFC), extending his interest in the natural world that had been fired as a child. Ireland's cultural history, as well as its natural history, had seeped into his consciousness as a boy and he was now cultivating a love of landscape in its historical context. The field club had a proud history stretching back to its formation in March 1863 and was formed as the first of a series all over the country. The Dublin Naturalists' Field Club was set up in 1886 and the Cork and Limerick clubs in 1892. Modelled on those in England, the purpose of the BNFC was to promote the practical study of natural science and archaeology. In the 1890s the club had introduced talks on folklore and ethnography. Two prominent figures in the Gaelic Revival, W.B. Yeats and Douglas Hyde, addressed the society. At a meeting in November 1893 Yeats spoke on Irish fairy lore while Hyde delivered a talk the following year on Celtic language and literature. But by the turn of the century the club's interest in folklore had declined and it was to be another fifty years before it was reawakened.

Hayward joined the club on 19 April 1921 at the age of twenty-eight. He was proposed and seconded by T.E. Osborne and Sidney Stendall. Interest had developed after the war and a big recruitment drive saw 167 people joining that same year, taking the membership up to 456. Hayward already knew Bigger, a former president and secretary, and got to know club stalwarts such as Robert Bell, R.J. Welch and Stephen Bennett who was president between 1920 and 1922. Welch, a celebrated photographer, took many images of the *Titanic* and travelled thousands of miles all over Ireland by train and jaunting car with his cameras and cumbersome gear. In the same year that Hayward joined, Welch became an honorary member and later had the distinction of having a spider – *Erigone welchii*, which he discovered – named after him.

The club's raison d'être appealed to Hayward's searching mind. During the 1920s many summer excursions were organized to various parts of Ireland including Dublin, Derry and north Donegal, Lough Erne, the Black Pig's Dyke in Scarva, Armagh, and the Giant's Causeway. Trips were also made to hilly regions such as the Mourne Mountains in south Down and Slemish Mountain near Ballymena. Hayward took part in many of these including one to Duncrue Fort at Woodburn, Carrickfergus, in August 1923 and a day trip on 31 May 1924 to Garron Point, one of the most conspicuous features on the Antrim coast. Fifty members attended the Garron Point tour conducted by Welch and A.M'I. Cleland. Amongst those attending were another photographer, Albert Campbell along with his wife and daughter and Hayward's friend, Thomas Edens Osborne, the owner of the junk shop where fifteen years earlier he had bought his first phonograph and who had proposed him for club membership. Campbell's photographs from the trip have been preserved in a club album covering the period and Hayward is pictured with the photographer's family.[25] Their coastal journey, in the area where Hayward spent his youth, took them through Ballynure and Larne. They inspected Straidkilly, known as the 'slipping village', which was built on slippery Lias clays and was sliding downhill to the sea. When they reached Garron Tower the party scattered to pursue their various interests. Hayward joined the zoologists and botanists climbing up through a steep wood searching for shells and plants including the polypody fern and a rare bedstraw. The party also examined what was claimed to be the finest eucalyptus tree in the British Isles.[26]

Another trip he relished was to the Clogher Valley in south Tyrone in

August 1927. The group travelled by train on the Great Northern Railway from Belfast to Tynan. From there they connected with the much-loved thirty-seven-mile narrow gauge Clogher Valley Railway, which he wrote about eleven years later in his first travel book. The railway chugged through the main streets of Augher, Clogher and Fivemiletown, reaching a maximum speed of twelve mph. The train's approach to Fivemiletown was often blocked by Maggie Coulter's goat, which would move only after the fireman pelted it with burning coals to clear the line.[27] Standing on the footplate, Hayward liked to follow the course of the road, which ran alongside the track for much of its length. They spent time in Clogher Cathedral, lunched at serenely beautiful Lumford's Glen near Augher and walked through a forest to climb the hill of Knockmany at 779ft. From the tour leaders Alexander Pringle and Albert Campbell he heard stories about William Carleton, the eighteenth-century novelist who was born at Prolusk near Clogher in 1794 and wrote poems about Knockmany. At the hilltop's central Ulster position, Hayward looked down on the undulating and fertile countryside of the Clogher Valley. With sweeping views west across to the mountains of Sligo and Donegal and southeast to the Mourne Mountains, it was an ideal place to grasp the shape of the countryside.

Although actively involved in attending meetings and trips, partly because of his age, Hayward did not hold any committee positions during his time as a member in the 1920s. In 1925 he was nominated to be an ordinary member of the committee but at the annual meeting was not elected. He enjoyed the friendship and making new acquaintances, as well as immersing himself in Irish history and culture, which would inform much of his writing. Many years later he wrote 'some of the happiest days of my life have been spent with the Field Club.'[28] Stimulated by the company of older men and women, and the knowledge of the conductors, his thirst for information about Ireland was steadily increasing. Now in his early thirties, Hayward was becoming well versed in local lore and enjoyed networking, furnishing his mind and indulging in what the *Irish Naturalists' Journal* called 'social intercourse.'[29]

He did not confine himself solely to BNFC trips; around this time excursions were also run from Belfast by the Royal Society of Antiquaries of Ireland. At the end of July 1924, he signed up for a trip to the Giant's Ring, a large neolithic earthwork focused on a dolmen at Ballynahatty, a few miles south of the city. A stylish photograph shows the expectant group, including Hayward, sitting in a charabanc as they prepare to head off from central Belfast.[30] Connections were made with some illustrious names and he befriended the expert

All aboard the charabanc: members of the RSAI prepare to set off from central Belfast, outside the Robinson & Cleaver building on their summer 1924 outing to the Giant's Ring south of Belfast. A hatless Hayward, seated in the centre of the vehicle, cuts a distinctive figure in faraway reverie. He is the only person in the picture not looking at the photographer Albert Campbell.

guides. On-site talks by group leaders such as the archaeologists Profs R.A.S. Macalister and H.C. Lawlor made the past come alive. Macalister, who was Professor of Celtic Archaeology at UCD, was president of the Royal Society of Antiquaries of Ireland in 1924 and later of the Royal Irish Academy (1926–1931). As well as being a gifted musician and composer, he was also a linguist. Published widely in scholarly papers and learned journals, he was the author of *Ireland in pre-Celtic times* and *The Archaeology of Ireland*. He enjoyed sprinkling his talks with humour, entertaining as well as informing his audience. Archaeology was a comparatively young science and Hayward was stirred by tales of ancient Ireland. He heard from Macalister (whose work had taken him all over the country as well as to Palestine) about medieval Irish legends. Some of the other topics that he spoke about included ogham inscriptions, ring forts, standing stones, kitchen-middens, rock scribings and historical ruins. After Macalister's death in 1950, the writer and geographer Estyn Evans highlighted his important contribution to Irish archaeology:

The antiquaries assemble for a group photograph at the Giant's Ring, the largest henge and stone circle in Ireland. Hayward is in the centre of the picture in the second row.

Small in stature, he was a stout-hearted champion of many causes, with something of the endearing pugnacity and fighting spirit of a cock-robin … Pleading always for a scientific approach to archaeological problems, he lacked scientific training, and the outstanding qualities of his work lie in his vivid imagination and his great literary gifts … A man of extravagant theories, he was quick to condemn other peoples' [sic] extravagances.[31]

An exuberant of many subjects, Macalister was a big influence on Hayward as outlined in his later travel books. In his Kerry book published in 1946, he described him as 'a never-failing mine of information, guidance and heart-warming courtesy.'[32] In *The Corrib Country* he wrote that with the 'invaluable assistance' of Professor Macalister [and others] he had pieced together a reasonable version of an inscription he found on a stone built into a plinth.[33] Hayward knew Lawlor through his work at the BBC in Belfast as he broadcast a series of talks on the archaeology of Ulster. Between 1922 and 1924, Lawlor had excavated the site of Nendrum Monastery on Strangford Lough, County Down, and was the author of *Ulster: Its Archaeology and Antiquities*.

Taking a keen interest in learning not only about archaeology but also about botany and geology, Hayward listened to both men admiringly. As they talked, he made notes and had a retentive memory for the stories he heard. He had developed a fascination for making connections between people and place, as well as the built heritage and artefacts. He remained in the field club until his membership lapsed in 1931 but rejoined with renewed vigour in the mid-1940s. The outdoor talks during the field trips were a masterclass in excellent schooling and stood him in good stead for his own tour guiding in future years. He stored up the experiences to be put to artistic use later. Tramping the countryside was an immensely pleasurable way of getting to know Ireland and helped form a rounded personality, but there was no clear sign of what kind of a writer he might become. Fortunately doors of opportunity were opening, allowing him to refocus his writing from poetry to plays, sketches and journalism.

During his early twenties he had gradually built up a network of friends in artistic circles and now set about turning his knowledge into published articles, striking out in a different direction. With a rising media profile, he began writing critical journalism for newspapers and magazines. These included book reviews and portraits of eminent writers and painters. He contributed to the *Ulster Review* that styled itself 'A Progressive Monthly of Individuality', as well as to the leading Belfast daily newspapers, the *Belfast Telegraph* and the *Northern Whig*. In October 1924 he wrote an affectionate appreciation of William Conor, who captured scenes of Belfast street life and later became a portrait painter. Conor, who had a studio in Chichester Street (and later at Wellington Place and on the Stranmillis Road) had exhibited at the Dawson Gallery and the Royal Hibernian Academy in Dublin, and in 1921 at the Royal Academy in London. That same year he painted the opening of the Northern Ireland Parliament by King George V at Belfast City Hall – a painting which hangs today in the Senate Chamber of Parliament Buildings at Stormont.

There had been a flowering of interest in painting in the first two decades of the century. Hayward had an eye for art and appreciated the work of painters, some of whom he had been schmoozing and were now his friends. Many worked in paid employment as lithographers or poster designers, both of which were jobs that Conor had done. The son of a craftsman skilled in working in fine metals, he had developed a reputation through an exhibition of war drawings. Hayward admired his work, regarding him as 'the greatest of all local painters':

He is unquestionably the established painter of the lower strata of Belfast life, so much so that it is hardly possible for one to see a group of laughing mill-girls returning from work, or a beshawled mother holding her child, without visualising a Conor drawing … We cannot give William Conor too much praise for his having accomplished the extraordinarily difficult task of presenting scenes, which to the ordinary eye are sordid or commonplace, in a new and yet perfectly truthful light. The form of magic by which a rather dingy street becomes a fit setting for a romantic piece of lovemaking, is a secret of the artist's, and seems to be akin to the thaumaturgy of the poets, which touches similarly commonplace words to music and beauty.[34]

The same month he reviewed the fourth annual exhibition of the short-lived Ulster Society of Painters at the Pollock Gallery in Belfast. Most of the society's twenty members were known to him. Fifty-five paintings were exhibited so Hayward chose only a small number to write about. He liked stoking controversy, describing the work of R.S. Rendle Wood as being 'nothing less conventional nor more original than could reasonably be asked for':

Indeed at first sight the very novelty of his vision is distasteful, but gradually one gets the hang of his work. It is all very well to ridicule every progressive move in artistic expression, but it must be borne in mind that the ugly in art has not yet been discovered … In his 'Carrickfergus Castle' Mr Rendle Wood gives us not a photograph of the harbour and castle, but a cunningly rearranged design in which the decorative features of the image are cleverly emphasised and lovingly fondled in an embrace of colour. The mass of red in the centre is rather disconcerting, but is perhaps essential to the equilibrium of the whole.[35]

He went on to discuss the work of James Hodgen, Donald McPherson, Stanley Prosser, Hunter Jeffrey, J.S. Hogg and Alfred Baker who founded the society and was its first president. In particular he singled out the work of a young painter, Theo J. Gracey, with whom he was to collaborate on a book. 'Mr Gracey's 'Mourne Mountains' is also among the very best things in the show, and it is really impossible to praise too highly this artist's command of tone and clean clear draughtsmanship.'[36]

In these early articles, Hayward had shown a depth of artistic knowledge and an ability to capture in a few words the essence of the work of painters. It is possible to discern his characteristic critical qualities of thought. He wrote that Prosser, a watercolourist whose work was also exhibited in 1924 at the Empire Exhibition at Wembley, had, in 'The Little Town', 'very perfectly realised his subject. There is an air of brooding quietness, a grey countryside stillness, about the picture which is utterly compelling, and as one looks at it, "little towns" of varied memory come flooding in upon one's mind.'

Through wide reading he became an authority on certain authors and was developing literary enthusiasms. One of these was Donn Byrne, the pseudonym of Brian Oswald Donn Byrne who was born in New York in 1889 and became an Ulsterman. Brought up in south Armagh and the Glens of Antrim, he was a prolific novelist combining Gaelic and the Anglo-Irish tradition in dramatic plots set against scenic backgrounds. One of his best known books was *Blind Raftery* published in 1924. In a profile of him in the *Northern Whig*, just before the book's release, Hayward wrote that Byrne was not well known in Ireland but deserved to be. He described his first book *Messer Marco Polo* as 'an astonishing piece of prose in form and content':

> An Eastern tale whose hero is a giant of history, it is related by a Glensman, one Malachi Campbell, in the dialect of the Glens. The effect is at once striking and harmonious, and the book was an immediate success and widely read everywhere, except in the North-East corner which inspired it.[37]

He praised two other novels, *The Wind Bloweth* and *The Foolish Matrons*.

> Donn Byrne's diction too is a most captivating blend of the American and Ulster manners of speech. It is highly probable that he does not know this himself, but I have been to some pains to study this interesting subject very closely, and cannot imagine that the mere rhythm of his prose could fail to bring intense pleasure to an Ulster ear ... Here is one who has been acclaimed by the whole of the English-speaking America and it is high time that he has a little encouragement and applause from his own countrymen.[38]

The minuscule fees he received for these articles would hardly have kept his wife and young son, but they were steps forward and helped build his portfolio of published work. Full of imaginative energy, by the early 1920s he had immersed himself in multifarious cultural events. Everything he had embarked on in recent years – the field club outings, visits to the theatre and opera as well as his poetry, art and literary criticism – had enhanced his cultural programming. The Hayward of this period was a young man in a hurry. On the verge of new excitements, his life was about to implode with a host of artistic activities, which would absorb his energies and emotions for many years to come.

THREE

'They lie who say I do not love this country!'
(1920–1937)

Nothing is so vital to the national consciousness of a people as a theatre mirroring faithfully its every desire, dream, ideal, whim, and peculiarity.

Notes about the foundation of a Belfast Repertory Theatre, Hayward

There wasn't the butt end of a Woodbine to be picked up, let alone work.

Thomas Carnduff

In the early 1920s Belfast, like many parts of Ireland, was going through a violent phase in its history. The city was rife with bigotry and sectarianism. It was a place of injustice for many Catholics and a world away from the happy-go-lucky Larne of Hayward's childhood. Under the Government of Ireland Act, the country was divided and the Northern Ireland Parliament, comprising six counties, was opened in Belfast by King George V in June 1921 while the other twenty-six counties were governed from Dublin. In the nascent state of Northern Ireland – the most disadvantaged region of the UK – a new social and political landscape was emerging. Between January 1919 and July 1921 Ireland was embroiled in a war of independence followed by a civil war. In April 1923 the republican order to 'dump arms' marked the end of a revolutionary decade. Many hoped that normality would return and their lives would settle down.

Unemployment was soaring in the big Northern linen and shipbuilding industries, but despite the poor job prospects, as well as the volatility of the times, cultural life thrived. There was a striking contrast between the politesse of social life and the violent unrest that impinged on it. The public had found distractions in new forms of entertainment such as the radio and cinema.

Hayward's interests flourished at the same time as he was settling into his confectionery jobs. In his teenage years he developed a passion for the performing arts, attending plays and musicals, especially at the Theatre Royal in Belfast. Illustrious names from the late Victorian and Edwardian eras, such as Martin Harvey and Sir Herbert Beerbohm Tree (half-brother to Sir Max Beerbohm) appeared in the city. At the Grand Opera House in Great Victoria Street, magnetic performances by Ellen Terry and Sir Henry Irving in *The Merchant of Venice*, as well as annual visits each January by Sir Frank Benson and his Shakespearean Company, brought magic to his younger days, firing his interest and love of the Bard.[1] Apart from the plays of Shakespeare and George Bernard Shaw, the shows were dominated by big musicals. Regular seasons of the D'Oyly Carte Company were held at the Opera House (also called the Palace of Varieties between 1904 and 1909) and Hayward attended the Easter pantomime, *Cinderella*.

It was a dynamic social scene. Music halls, such as the Alhambra, Hippodrome and Empire, attracted large numbers of people every night to watch local and international musicians, comedians and entertainers. Many held twice-nightly performances: the 'out-of-towners' went to the early shows at 7 pm and the 'townies' the 9 pm performance. In the polarized city of the time, at some venues, Protestants and Catholics attended on different nights. Inhaling much of this entertainment as a teenager motivated and influenced Hayward. His work with the scout movement had given him an early taste of acting and experience of life on the stage. At the end of the First World War he widened his cultural scope within the theatrical sphere. In the years that followed, not only did he write plays, but also acted in them and multi-tasked in a variety of roles that included producer, director, adviser and adjudicator. It was through theatre that he was to find a happy cultural milieu establishing lifelong bonds of friendship.

Having experimented with poetry, he tried his hand at writing a play, substituting the muse for drama and looking to see where best he could find a voice that he could develop. Crossing paths with local writers and actors, he moved easily and confidently in the theatrical world. Many of those involved in the business had been around since Victorian times and Hayward – still in his late twenties – brought a fresh enthusiastic burst of the chutzpah of youth. The call of the theatre was strong. After the war, he had made important connections in the Ulster Literary Theatre (ULT), a company he joined around 1920. Hayward's early work involved acting and he later became manager while still continuing in an acting role.

The ULT grew out of the Irish Literary Theatre (ILT), founded in 1899 by W.B. Yeats, Augusta, Lady Gregory and Edward Martyn. It was organized firstly as an Ulster branch of the ILT in 1902, but when Yeats refused permission to use its assumed title the group set up on its own, renaming itself the Ulster Literary Theatre and staging their first plays in 1904. One of the early members was Sam Waddell, an Ulster actor and dramatist who used the pen and stage name Rutherford Mayne. The most successful of his plays, *The Drone*, a rural comedy, was performed at the Abbey in April 1908 and at the Grand Opera House the following year. The new theatre company, also known as the Ulster Players (abbreviated in 1915 from the Ulster Literary Theatre to the Ulster Theatre) quickly gained support. Mayne's play was their first big success.

Hayward appearing as Holy Joe, alongside Charlotte Tedlie in Charles K. Ayre's comedy *Loaves and Fishes* at the Gaiety Theatre, Dublin in 1921.

By 1920 Hayward had finished a one-act play, *The Jew's Fiddle*, a farce written in collaboration with Abram Rish. The theme was about the jealousy of John O'Connor for his wife Mary. Hayward played the part of the Jew. Just before Christmas, on 18 December 1920, it was presented by the Players for the first time at Dublin's Gaiety Theatre. It was a turbulent time of bloodshed in the Irish capital. On 21 November, less than a month before their appearance at the Gaiety and on what became known as Bloody Sunday, the IRA shot dead fourteen British intelligence undercover agents working in Dublin. Later that day the British authorities retaliated at Croke Park, also killing fourteen people. Months of political manoeuvring during the second half of 1921 culminated on 6 December in the signing of the Anglo-Irish Treaty. Hayward did not write about these events, choosing to stay clear of the politically explosive situation. That same year, at almost thirty, he took to the stage with 'a confidence that belied his inexperience',[2] appearing as Holy Joe in Charles K. Ayre's comedy *Loaves and Fishes*, in which he also starred the following year.

Actors from the Ulster Players stroll through St Stephen's Green, Dublin in 1923. They were performing in Rutherford Mayne's *Phantoms* at the Gaiety for a week. From left to right are: Mrs Gerald Macnamara, Rose McQuilland, Walter Kennedy, Miss Woods, Gerald Macnamara, Rutherford Mayne, Richard Hayward, who was manager and actor with the Players, and J.G. Abbey.

The Players' work was not confined to Ireland. In early September 1922 the Ulster Theatre in Repertory crossed the Irish Sea to stage a week-long series of plays in Liverpool. When he was working there during the First World War, Hayward had established theatrical contacts, which enabled him to organize the week. The plays were *The Drone, Loaves and Fishes*, two by Harry Morrow who used the pen name Gerald Macnamara: *The Mist that Does be on the Bog* and *The Throwbacks, The Jew's Fiddle*, and two comedies by Lynn C. Doyle: *Turncoats* and the matchmaking *Love and Land*. The last was based on a story called 'The Widow' taken from Doyle's highly popular book *Ballygullion* with illustrations by William Conor. Their performance was greeted with enthusiasm by the papers on Merseyside. The *Liverpool Echo* said the 'acting throughout is on a very high level and gives one the impression of absolute confidence and familiarity with the life portrayed.'[3]

The following month, from 6 October, the company staged the same week-long series of seven plays at the Grand Opera House. Doyle, a bank manager whose name was Leslie Alexander Montgomery (his nom de plume Lynn C. Doyle was adapted after he spotted the words linseed oil on an invoice when he was looking for a pen name to put under his first story) was a regular theatre-goer, taking an intense interest in the production of his plays. He was pernickety about the actors adhering closely to his script and took Hayward to task for massaging a line in *Love and Land*. He played the leading part of Peter O'Hare while Elma Hayward played Mary O'Connor. Interviewed about Doyle in a later BBC radio portrait, Hayward described the playwright's reaction:

I had a line where I said 'Well indeed Miss O'Connor now, am bothered, aye am bothered … bothered' and Doyle came afterwards with a big notebook – everything that had been said in the play he had notes about – and said: 'Richard you've a bothered too many.' And I said to him but Lynn Doyle surely that's what I *felt* like at the time – I felt that that extra bothered suited and made me more bothered, and he said well I made you bothered enough and I'm the author and I don't want you to put in words that I didn't write.[4]

At this juncture, without a permanent home, the Ulster Theatre had become a touring troupe and Gaiety audiences loved their performances. Hayward was involved in many successful productions in Dublin. These included Rutherford Mayne's *Phantoms* in 1923 and the following year no fewer than three plays: Dorothea Donn Bryne's *The Land of the Stranger*, a three-act Ulster-American comedy by the widow of the Irish novelist Donn Bryne, St John Ervine's *The Ship*, and the second of Hayward's own plays *Huge Love*, a burlesque melodrama that he called a 'crude essay in novelette drama in four short acts'.[5] These three plays were also produced at the Opera House two weeks before Christmas 1924.

When the civil war ended, parts of Dublin were in ruins. While the political dramas were being fought out Hayward was more interested in the drama being brought out on the stage. V.S. Pritchett, who went on to become a novelist, essayist and travel writer, visited the city as a young journalist working for the *Christian Science Monitor* early in 1923 and painted a vivid picture of the grim street life. After attending the Abbey, watching plays and satires such as *General John Regan* and *Thompson in Tir-na-nog*, he described the atmosphere:

> The Abbey was poor, its productions were simple, for the company had only a job lot of scenery, but these actors and actresses, who came out of shops and offices and not out of drama schools, were natural actors ... The Abbey awakened Dublin. They certainly awakened me and I am grateful to them.[6]

These were the early years of partition and its cultural consequences were still unravelling. Hayward travelled regularly by train between Belfast and Dublin during his final two years with the Ulster Players. He particularly enjoyed the acclaim from the Southern audiences and the social scene, establishing important contacts and meeting actors and journalists. Even though the company tried to reinvent itself with its new name, by the late 1920s its fortunes were waning with its best days behind it. It had produced several dozen plays but was now relying on revivals of past hits. Hayward had loosened his ties with them and after a difference of opinion on the question of future policy, felt the time was ripe to go his own way. Between 1921 and 1929 he had, by any standards, built up an impressive string of acting credits, appearing in more than a score of stage plays.

Other doors were opening and his attention was partially diverted to broadcasting and singing. His thirties marked his coming of age in terms of acting. In between his public appearances, he was carrying on his confectionery job as well as working on a novel. One of the first addresses in which he and Elma lived was Hopefield House, a detached property on the Antrim Road in north Belfast. The house was divided into flats and a famous occupant was Harry Ferguson, the inventor of the tractor and known as the 'mad mechanic'. (He achieved worldwide fame when he invented a three-point linkage system that forms the basis of most tractors made today. Ferguson encouraged their son Dion to take an interest in engines and offered him an apprenticeship – an opportunity he turned down. Dion, who was educated at

Belfast Royal Academy, was a keen sportsman. He was interested in the rough and tumble of the outdoor world, later taking part in motorcycle scrambling and high diving.)[7]

Writing in *The Ulster Theatre in Ireland*, Margaret McHenry said that with 'the knowledge that his radio broadcasting of songs and plays takes much of his time at present, it is unsafe to hazard how soon Mr Hayward will be contributing more plays to the Ulster Theatre.'[8] The answer to this uncertainty came soon as Hayward carried on enthusiastically with another eight years of life in the theatre while at the same time moving on to the burgeoning film industry. Although he would have preferred a permanent home, he was undaunted by the itinerant nature of the business. He was a swift worker and got things done.

By 1929 Hayward was a distinctive presence in the theatrical world, and was confident enough to break out on his own. That year he set up the Belfast Repertory Theatre Company, joining forces with his good friend Jimmy Mageean, a dynamic thespian he had known for some time. Mageean, who was born in Boston in 1891, had worked for seven years with Benson's Shakespearean Company in the US and Canada, making his debut as Petruchio's servant Nathaniel in *The Taming of the Shrew* in 1911. He made appearances in the West End playing many parts and for a time was the company's stage manager. During the First World War he held a commission in the Royal Irish Rifles and when the war ended he returned to Ireland joining the Ulster Theatre. He had roles in Gerald Macnamara's *No Surrender* and *Who Fears to Speak* at the Opera House. Like Hayward, Mageean was gregarious and socially cheerful. The two shared a love of theatre and forged a close bond, which was important to both of them.

The new repertory company – with Hayward as director and Mageean as producer – styled themselves the Empire Players, or the Belfast Players. To a large extent they took on the mantle of sustaining Northern drama. They put on an annual season at the Empire winning success with initial productions such as *French Leave*, a light comedy by Reginald Berkeley (1929), *Love and Land* by Lynn Doyle, and in 1931 *The Land of the Stranger*. The last play, described as 'a comedy of realities', was staged at the end of November 1931 at the Abbey and was a rewritten version of the one that ran in Dublin in the early 1920s. Hayward took delight in combining the parts of an Italian gangster with that of a rustic Orangeman, garnering appreciative notices in the press. The *Irish Times* critic praised his acting, saying the play was a 'considerable improvement on the earlier version and was received with complete approval by a large audience.'[9]

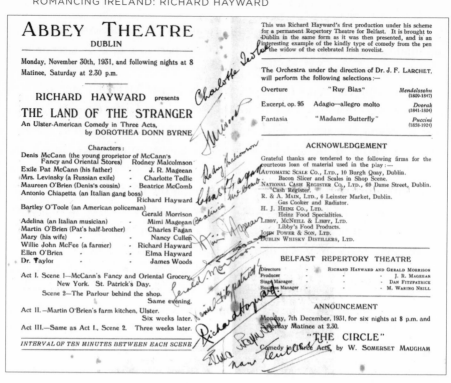

A signed programme from the Ulster-American comedy, *The Land of the Stranger*, by Dorothea Donn Byrne, staged at the Abbey Theatre by the Belfast Repertory Company in November 1931. Hayward combined two parts in the play: an Italian gangster and an Ulster Orangeman.

The company had no official connection with the Ulster Theatre although Hayward still kept links with them, bringing George Shiels' play *Cartney and Kevney*, produced by the Abbey Players, to Belfast for his Players, later turning it over to the Ulster Theatre. Like the UT the repertory company also performed the work of new and established playwrights but they did not have a theatrical home and continued to travel to Dublin for successful annual appearances. In later productions in the thirties, the programmes clearly stated that the Belfast Repertory Theatre had no connection with any other groups of Players in Ulster.

Hayward had a vision for the theatre. His ambition was to establish a Little Theatre in Belfast along the same lines as the Little Theatre of Citizen House in Bath, which was recognized by universities in England and Scotland. He believed strongly in the need to showcase the growing interest in native Ulster dramatic literature. Belfast, he felt, should have a permanent theatre to allow work to be shown alongside the best of English, American or continental playwrights. He had high hopes. For him, a local theatre was vital to the national consciousness to 'mirror faithfully its desire, dream, ideal, whim and peculiarity.' It was important too that it should be a commercial success. He firmly believed the audience was ready and that such a theatre would include a school of acting to encourage students to become involved in drama. It would, in his view, have tremendous cultural value, offering classes in acting, speech, diction, dialect, make-up, costume, lighting and other aspects of the job. Never known to think parochially, Hayward's ambitious plans pictured the theatre touring Canada and the US with a carefully selected repertoire of Ulster plays.[10] (Moves were already afoot to establish a Little Theatre in Belfast, which ran for five years. Hayward was not connected with the company, which staged plays at the Ulster Minor Hall. They enjoyed only limited success and changed their name to the Belfast Thespians Repertory Company, later renaming themselves the Little Theatre Repertory Company before closing in April 1937.)

Hayward was busy championing writers whose work he thought would appeal to locals and would be appreciated by a more urbane Dublin audience. The early plays veered towards light entertainment but he wanted to find someone with a rawer edge to his pen. Into the picture stepped Thomas Carnduff, an unemployed shipyard labourer. Born in the Protestant Sandy Row area of Belfast in 1886, Carnduff had reinvented himself as an essayist, playwright and poet, becoming an important cultural figure. His father, who came from County Down, had been a sergeant in the East India Company's Bengal Artillery, which he joined during the Indian Mutiny of 1857–58. His mother was from Newbridge in County Kildare.

Educated at the Hibernian School in Dublin's Phoenix Park, Carnduff was later a binman with Belfast Corporation. In the First World War he was a sapper in the Royal Engineers and later served in the Ulster Special Constabulary. Known as the 'Shipyard Poet', he was an acute observer of Belfast life. He had come to prominence with two collections of poems: *Songs from the Shipyards* (1924) and *Songs of an out-of-work* published by the Quota Press in 1932. And without work himself for three years he was living in the depths of poverty. Carnduff had ambitions to make his name as a poet in the style of Robert Service but was encouraged to write a play by Richard Rowley (the pseudonym of Richard Valentine Williams), a poet and president of the Northern Drama League. Within four months of their discussion he had written *Workers*, a realistic play about Belfast shipyardmen. He handed it over to Rowley who found it impossible to sign up enough dialect speakers while another group, the Rosario Players, said it was too revolutionary. The Ulster Theatre accepted the play and began rehearsals but the manager of the Opera House turned down permission to perform it, feeling it would be a threat to family values and because of its 'working-class tendencies'.[11]

The BBC in Belfast broadcast some of Carnduff's poems and this connection led to an introduction to Hayward who read the *Workers* script, saw its potential and agreed to take it on. Although it was a risk, he believed he could stage it successfully and immediately cast the players in rehearsals. The company had already staged six week-long Irish seasons in Belfast, while three separate weeks were held in Dublin. Hayward was planning a run in Dublin in autumn 1932 and arranged with the Abbey (whose actors were on a tour of the US) to split the week with three nights of Doyle's *Love and Land* followed by three nights of *Workers*. On 10, 11 and 12 October Hayward again played the part of Peter O'Hare in *Love and Land*. To help promote the company and Carnduff's play, he gave an interview before the performance to the *Irish Independent* in which he advocated the need for a Little Theatre in Belfast:

> 'The idea was', said Richard, casually plucking out by the roots a fragment of red crepe hair that was climbing into his mouth, 'that we should show the public that we could give them plays, carefully produced and that, if we had a home of our own, which is badly needed, we could justify our existence and – if you will forgive the cliché, provide a long-felt want.'[12]

The writer of the article, John Parker, added:

> I made a noise indicating loud cheers, because I was wholeheartedly with him. I know what he has done and can do. He has taken the principal parts in many plays, with the Ulster Players and in his own company (recruited from the most promising members of the Belfast amateur societies of note).[13]

Both Richard and Elma Hayward were 'outstanding' wrote the *Irish Independent* critic who went on to describe the play as having 'delightful freshness … it is intensely Irish, but essentially different from our own efforts.'[14] In its review of *Love and Land*, *The Irish Times* said that anything that is new is worth seeing for its own sake:

> However much we regret that absence of our players in America, we can welcome the Belfast Repertory Theatre Company … it would be heresy to say that the actors attain to the same standard as that of the Abbey Players, and, in any case, it would not be true. But the play is very well produced and Mr Richard Hayward is, perhaps, the best of an excellent cast.[15]

Just thirteen days short of his fortieth birthday, it was a gratifying endorse-ment for Hayward of his hard work and skill in bringing the Belfast Players to Dublin. But the acid test was to come. The cynosure of the Dublin critics and audiences quickly switched to *Workers*, which premiered to a crowded house on Thursday, 13 October. With first-hand experience of his years as a driller in the shipyard, Carnduff articulated the workers' sense of despair and hopeless-ness at being unemployed in the depressed thirties. 'There wasn't the butt end of a Woodbine to be picked up, let alone work', he later said.[16] Written in the Belfast urban idiom, the play held a mirror up to city life. Through the voices of his hard-swearing and hard-drinking characters, he brought a remarkable realism to the stage as well as sympathetic concern. Not content with directing Carnduff's play, Hayward also acted in it. He took on the role of John Waddell, a drunken shipyard worker, wife-beater and husband to Susan, played by Elma, while Jimmy Mageean was Sam Hagan, a shipyard labourer. *Workers* ran for three consecutive nights in October as well as a Saturday matinée and won an ovation from the Dublin theatre-goers. In a curtain call, Carnduff presented himself as the Worshipful Master of Sandy Row Independent Loyal Orange Lodge and addressed the audience: 'I don't know what they will say in Sandy Row when I tell them I have been standing for the 'Soldier's Song' but anyway it is a fine tune, the best I've heard, except of course for 'Dolly's Brae'.'[17] Carn-duff also said that he was the only Sandy Row man who 'took a bow on the stage of the Abbey Theatre.'[18]

The play's topicality won it praise-filled reviews in the Dublin papers. *The Irish Press* described it as 'a tremendous piece of realism.'[19] Comparisons were made by critics in *The Irish Times* and *Irish Independent* between Carnduff's realism and the work of Sean O'Casey. Although there was some criticism of the stage construction, the *Independent* review started on a high: 'Deafening cheers, a dozen curtains and imperative clamour for the author marked the end of the Belfast Repertory Theatre's production at the Abbey Theatre last night of Thomas Carnduff's three-act play 'Workers'.' The *Independent* said: 'the play has the photographic realism of Sean O'Casey without the writer's stagecraft but Mr Carnduff has distinct possibilities.' The paper said Hayward was 'distinctly good' as John Waddell and praised Elma's acting skills.[20] The *Northern Whig* called it a play with 'wit and humanity', saying: 'it is marked by natural, at times brilliant and often witty dialogue, and it displays admirable character delineation.' The *Whig* said the men in the play, including Hayward, 'were extremely good … but the two women need to speak up, as much of their conversation was lost.'[21]

RICHARD HAYWARD

presents

FOR THE FIRST TIME IN BELFAST

WORKERS

A BELFAST SHIPYARD PLAY
By
THOMAS CARNDUFF.

WITH THE IDENTICAL COMPANY THAT RECENTLY
PERFORMED THE PLAY TO CROWDED AND ENTHUSIASTIC
HOUSES AT . . .

THE ABBEY THEATRE, DUBLIN.

Preceded each Evening (except Saturday) by

TURNCOATS

AN ULSTER COMEDY IN ONE ACT
by
LYNN DOYLE.

The Company includes

RICHARD HAYWARD
J. R. MAGEEAN
RODNEY MALCOMSON
CHARLES FAGAN
R. H. MacCANDLESS
WILLIAM CREAN
DAN FITZPATRICK
ELMA HAYWARD   CHARLES E. OWENS
NANCY CULLEN
CHARLOTTE TEDLIE

Belfast Repertory Theatre

(No connection with any other group of Players in Ulster).

Director	Richard Hayward
Producer	J. R. Mageean
Stage Manager	Dan FitzPatrick
Business Manager	M. Waring Neill

One month after its Dublin success, Thomas
Carnduff's *Workers* was performed at the Empire
Theatre in Belfast. Elma Hayward's role in particular
was highlighted by the press and described by the
Irish News as 'a wonderful piece of dramatic art'.

The following month, on 22 November, *Workers* was performed at the
Empire in Belfast and two years later the theatre staged it for five nights from
23 to 27 April 1934. For its first outing the theatre suspended its twice-nightly
house to accommodate the production. The *Belfast News Letter* said the play had
set the company on course as a 'power in the land ... with Hayward unswerving
from his purpose of creating something which will be as vital a force in the
dramatic life of Northern Ireland as is the Abbey Theatre in the South.'[22] The
Irish News said that 'many of the forceful lines excited spontaneous approval ...
virtues and failings are presented with faithful feeling':

Richard Hayward and his first-rate cast gave the play every possible chance
and its success is in no small measure due to them. Mr Hayward himself played

the role of Waddell with fine fire … The role of the wife called for great powers of restrained emotion and Miss Elma Hayward had those powers. Her portrayal was a wonderful piece of dramatic art.[23]

The *Northern Whig* said 'the author has taken a slice of the home life of the shipyard workers and placed it on the stage with rare verisimilitude.' But the paper was not impressed with Richard Hayward's performance:

> Miss Elma Hayward, as Susan, and Mr Rodney Malcolmson as Jim Bowman share the acting honours. As John Waddell, Mr Richard Hayward was disappointing. He tried hard throughout to give the bullying, blustering drinking John Waddell an appearance of reality without achieving much more than a measure of success and one was left with the impression that he had been wrongly cast.[24]

Playwriting was not lucrative work for any writer in the 1930s. Carnduff was desperate to earn money to feed his wife and four sons. Hayward ran a tight ship. He drove a hard bargain with the playwrights and actors he dealt with, evident in Carnduff's unpublished autobiography:

> Hayward offered to give *Workers* a show at the first opportunity, reducing the royalties down to 5 per cent and retaining the full dramatic rights to himself. I would have taken 1 per cent had he offered it. I was at my wits' end to make a shilling or two, and I didn't care where it came from, who supplied it, or why. My whole family wanted something to eat.[25]

Carnduff also provides a vivid description of the Dublin atmosphere surrounding the play:

> Then came the announcement that *Workers* would be produced at the famous Abbey Theatre by Hayward's company on the 13th October, 1932. Next to being buried in Westminster Abbey most Irish playwrights yearned for their play to be produced in the Abbey Theatre. Sure enough it caused the sensation Hayward wished for. He believed if we could only manage an audience the play would do the rest. The weeks between were agony for me. I haunted the rehearsal rooms, and Sunday papers haunted my office.[26]

It was a proud moment for Carnduff. Hayward was pleased that he took the accolades, but for the man who made it all possible it was also perhaps his finest moment in the theatre. Writing many years later, Noel Carnduff said that his father earned £15 from *Workers* and commented, 'It threw us a life line out of the swamp.' His son noted that the one criticism of *Workers* was from a communist paper, which thought 'it was not radical enough.'[27]

EMPIRE THEATRE, BELFAST

Week commencing MONDAY the 21st of JANUARY, 1935

TWICE NIGHTLY at 6.40 and 8.50

RICHARD HAYWARD presents

FOR THE FIRST TIME ON ANY STAGE:

CASTLEREAGH

AN ULSTER PLAY OF 1798

By THOMAS CARNDUFF

(Author of "Workers," etc.)

A Play of Old Belfast in the Days of

HENRY JOY McCRACKEN

BEAUTIFULLY DRESSED IN AUTHENTIC COSTUMES OF THE PERIOD FROM ONE OF THE WORLD'S MOST CELEBRATED WARDROBES.

THE CAST INCLUDES:

RICHARD HAYWARD	ELMA HAYWARD
CHARLES FAGAN	NANCY CULLEN
R. H. McCANDLESS	MYRTLE ADAMS
HAROLD GOLDBLATT	
CHARLES E. OWENS	
RAYMOND THOMPSON	
R. FORSYTHE BOYD	
BRUCE DAWSON	

J. R. MAGEEAN, Producer.   Stage Direction: DAN FITZPATRICK.

NO INCREASE IN PRICES

Stalls 2/4. Back Stalls 1/6. Circle 1/3

All Numbered and Reserved.

BOOKING AT THE THEATRE 11 a.m. till 8-30 p.m.   TELEPHONE: BELFAST 3155

Handbill for the historical drama *Castlereagh*,
set in the summer of the 1798 Irish Uprising.
The play was Carnduff's final work for
Hayward's repertory company and enjoyed a
successful run early in 1935 at both the Empire
and Abbey theatres, drawing large crowds.

Hayward took on three more full-length Carnduff works. He and Elma again had starring roles in *Machinery*, a four-act play about Belfast factory life in a weaving mill on the Shankill Road. Performed at the Abbey early in March 1933, it was given a mixed reception by the media although playgoers received it warmly. The *Sunday Dispatch* critic described the actors as a 'company of Belfast amateurs' to which Hayward responded with an indignant rebuke saying as his 'company was run on a completely professional basis, the appellation 'amateurs' was harmful.'[28] For its part, *The Irish Times* was not impressed, saying that Elma's lovemaking 'lacked conviction' and 'although Mr Carnduff's dialogue is as lively and as natural as before, he has yet to write a really satisfactory play.'[29] The *Dublin Evening Herald* reported that: 'In something like a frenzy of appreciation the packed house roared for the author when the play came to an end.'[30] Two weeks later *Machinery* was staged at the Empire. Critics and the Belfast public were unanimous in acclaiming the play.

In early 1934 the company staged what is regarded as the most powerful of Carnduff's social observations. *Traitors*, a four-act play set in the grim inner city life of Ballymacarret in east Belfast and focused on the unemployment riots of 1932. Opening night was 22 January 1934 at the Empire. Playing the part of Tom Russell, an unemployed joiner, Hayward cast himself as lead role while Elma played Jane Watson, a factory girl and daughter of Jim Watson (Charles Fagan). The play was produced by Mageean and directed by Hayward. Noel Carnduff was cast as a Belfast newsboy, a part created for him by his father. The *Belfast Telegraph* said the play had eclipsed all Carnduff's previous achievements and praised Elma's bravura performance: 'She got through her lines in a masterful manner and thoroughly deserved the loud plaudits which greeted her clever dramatic action in the final scene.' *Traitors* first ran at the Empire, followed by a successful run at the Gaiety.

Carnduff's final work with the repertory company, *Castlereagh*, was a three-act period play set in the turbulent summer of the 1798 Uprising. The characters included Henry Joy McCracken, Thomas Russell, Jimmy Hope and the informer Belle Martin. The play dealt with Anglo-Irish aristocratic life and Lord Castlereagh's plans to hang the Rev. James Porter, a plain-speaking clergyman from Greyabbey in County Down. Castlereagh had written a letter of congratulation to the French revolutionaries but learns that it has fallen into the hands of Porter who has publicly exposed the Chief Secretary's methods of government. The play opens with them devising a scheme that will compromise Porter by inveigling him into a meeting of the United Irelanders in a Belfast tavern. Both Haywards played the lead roles of Lord and Lady Castlereagh. R.H. McCandless took on the part of Hope while a young actor, Harold Goldblatt, made his debut playing the part of Alexander Knox, Castlereagh's secretary. With Mageean again in the production hot seat, the play opened for a week-long run at the Empire on 21 January 1935, drawing large crowds and creating strong attention. Shows were twice-nightly, at 6.40 pm and 8.50 pm. The *Belfast News Letter* said it was presented in a most 'capable manner':

> Richard Hayward was excellent in the title role. The impression he conveyed was that of a man of strong conviction, determined to pursue what he conceived to be the best policy for Britain. Elma Hayward acted with distinction as Lady Castlereagh, her appeal to Castlereagh for the reprieve of Rev. James Porter of Greyabbey being imbued with real power.[31]

Years later, in his survey *The Theatre in Ulster*, Sam Hanna Bell, the novelist and BBC radio producer provided a humorous description of attending the Empire performance of *Castlereagh*, which he described as 'highly successful':

> I can recall Hayward throwing open a lattice and with a wave of his hand to the scenic backcloth crying: 'They lie who say I do not love this country!' – a declaration which we in the Gods received in silence broken by a storm of jeers, groans and orange peel.[32]

Castlereagh quickly moved to Dublin and a month later was presented for a week at the Abbey with a generally positive reception. Dramatizing history was new territory for Carnduff and different skills were required. The play went smoothly although the critics were divided about Hayward's acting. The *Irish Independent* felt that he never showed Castlereagh the man of genius. 'His Castlereagh was weak, waspish, and melodramatic, and tended to make the play seem more melodramatic than it is.'[33] While praising the cast in general saying they were 'word-perfect', *The Irish Times* declared the performance 'suffered from a lack of background to give the action of the play the political significance it ought to have.' The paper's critic complained that Castlereagh does not emerge with 'sufficient sharpness':

> Lord Castlereagh, indeed, might have been more convincing if Richard Hayward's interpretation had been more lively. His performance was free from any definite fault, but somehow he did not seem to get as much from the lines as was in them.[34]

The Irish Press on the other hand – whose critic described it as 'an exhilarating evening' – gushed about his performance: 'Richard Hayward acted the part of Castlereagh with a quiet dignity which at the same time expressed every subtlety of mood; his manner and speech were always in character and in period.' The paper said the acting deserved the highest praise with 'authentic portraits admirably interpreted,' and that it had been 'an almost perfect production'.[35] The *Dublin Evening Herald* reviewer wrote that *Workers* and *Machinery* were Carnduff's natural métier and because of this *Castlereagh* was all the more striking and worthy of praise. 'A very fine play and an excellent company,' was the critic's verdict: 'Richard Hayward had interpreted Castlereagh 'in a manner which could not but elicit great praise'. The *Herald* reviewer also said that Elma had filled her role 'admirably.'[36]

The Haywards and the company were in celebratory mood. His decision to take on the Carnduff plays had been vindicated. The company had achieved its apotheosis. Dublin audiences gave an important seal of approval. Critics had praised the clever dialogue and acting ability of the cast: 'I do not say it to flatter, but Dublin audiences are lovely to play to,' Hayward told an interviewer from the *Sunday Independent* when asked if he liked playing to them. 'They know good stuff – and whisper – bad stuff too, and they are most appreciative.'[37]

Soon there was further cause for joy; in 1935 Elma became pregnant again, the year of their twentieth wedding anniversary. Their second child was conceived around the end of February at the time of the *Castlereagh* celebration. Another boy, Richard Scott (known as Ricky) was born on 30 October, seventeen years after the birth of their first son Dion. He arrived into a busy household – just like the one his father would have known in the 1890s. Apart from the drama being acted out on the stage, there was also domestic drama to cope with. They were living at Richmond Lodge on the Cavehill Road in north Belfast when baby Ricky suffered a convulsion. Their parents were not in the house but fortunately Dion was on hand and put him immediately into cold water, which Ricky believes saved his life.[38]

Dion Hayward, aged seventeen, around the time he saved his baby brother Ricky from drowning after he suffered a convulsion. He put him into cold water, which Ricky believes saved his life. Dion once turned down a job offer from Harry Ferguson, the inventor of the three-point linkage tractor. During the Second World War he served with the North Irish Horse and was seriously injured while driving a tank in Italy in 1944.

As 1935 gave way to 1936 the company varied their theatrical diet producing some lighter work as a contrast to Carnduff's tough-edged plays. On 20 January, they staged *The Early Bird*, a four-act comedy of rural life by James Douglas, which was also turned into a film by Hayward. He took the lead role of Daniel Duff, an elderly farmer who decides to marry a widow, which Susan Duff – his niece played by Elma – is determined to foil. On the same bill, as a curtain raiser to *The Early Bird*, a short one-act sketch, *Passed Unanimously*, by N.F.Webb preceded it. This play marked the stage debut of a third member of the Hayward family: Dion, aged eighteen, played the part of David Kirk. Although he may have toyed with the idea of a career on stage, Dion did not end up following in his father's footsteps. He decided the life of an actor was too precarious, choosing instead the security of a job in the Bank of Ireland.[39]

Another playwright whose work Hayward brought to the attention of the public was Hugh Quinn, a teacher who collected street songs. Originally from Coalisland in County Tyrone, his family moved to Belfast when he was a child. He shared a similar interest to Carnduff in exploring working-class life and bringing local characters on to the stage. In October 1933 Hayward directed Quinn's play *Mrs McConaghey's Money*, a dark three-act drama portraying a Belfast working-class family. Written in broad local vernacular, the play reflected the humorous side of life during the early years of the Great Depression. It had played two years previously at the Charta Theatre in London and the Abbey under the title *Money* and was praised by the London and Dublin critics. Elma played the role of Mrs McConaghey around whom the action of the play revolves while Hayward was Mickey, her husband. Her casting provided one of the first central female roles in Northern theatre. There was warm praise again from the critics. The *Daily Express* said the audience had been left 'breathless' so realistic was the play, and described it as the most difficult work yet tackled by the repertory players. The paper's correspondent went on to lavish praise on Hayward: 'Seldom have I seen Richard Hayward in so pathetic a study. He revealed the pathos of a man mentally deficient, the butt of a nagging, mercenary wife, and the delight of the children "round the doors".'[40]

While many of the company's plays were unquestionably popular, Hayward was finding it increasingly difficult to devote the time required to theatrical activities. In his parallel worlds in the mid thirties he was distracted by film-making – something he was to be heavily involved in for four years – as well as recording songs and writing books. The financial strains were showing. Rehearsals, travelling to and organizing venues as well as shouldering the administrative side of the operation absorbed a huge amount of time. He was a practical and pragmatic man and had taken business risks. Directing two of Quinn's one-act plays, *Collecting the Rent* and *A Quiet Twelfth*, was to be his swan-song. After a run of both at the Gaiety on 6 and 7 December 1937 the company folded. To make ends meet, some of the actors were double-jobbing, moving their talents, making the switch to the big screen and the newly emerging world of cinema where the prospects and lights appeared much brighter.

The Empire, one of Belfast's leading entertainment venues, had helped Hayward by promoting him both in drama and singing. During the 1930s, the theatre, run by Gerald Morrison, staged vaudeville, burlesque, cabaret, and a range of comedy shows, classical music nights and military baton dances. Amongst the entertainers were Maureen Potter, Jimmy O'Dea and Harry O'Donovan. Other names included Canada's leading radio stars, Al and Alf Thomas, Mexano's Accordeon Band, Navarre – the 'Radio's Prince of Mimics', and the Great Levant, the Australian illusionist with a company of international variety performers. The most illustrious touring name from that era to appear at the Empire was a sixteen-year-old radio, stage and screen star called Hughie Green. On 27 April 1936 he appeared with his all-children concert party, Hughie Green and his Gang in Radio Rhythm. Green went on to present the long-running television talent show *Opportunity Knocks* and the quiz show *Double Your Money*.

For eight years Hayward had presented highly regarded work on stages in Belfast and Dublin. But the business side of the operation was not easy and he had a decision to make. He had struggled to find a professional home for his company and was forced to hire commercial theatres at exorbitant rents often unsuited to the type of entertainment he was offering. Despite this, he managed to produce original and engaging plays, some of which achieved box-office success. It was an exciting period of creativity.

The company became the driving force behind new Northern Irish theatre writing. Sam Hanna Bell's verdict was that they were 'a highly-skilled company and for about eight years filled the gap left by the declining Ulster Theatre.'[41] Hayward encouraged, nurtured and developed talent, giving a voice to playwrights who would not otherwise have had a chance of having their work showcased. 'He immediately imposed,' according to the Ulster actors' website, 'a parochially aesthetic raison d'être vigorously promoting the works of local writers who espoused ethnic themes.'[42] He also opened up many new theatrical possibilities. The remarkable work of Thomas Carnduff might never have been given an outlet without Hayward's support and he had put his own reputation on the line by staging the plays. Carnduff became a prolific writer, producing a dozen plays including radio drama, two books of poetry, and more than 150 features on Belfast for newspapers and magazines such as the *Irish News* and *The Bell*. His main focus was local drama and politics, as well as Ulster working-men poets. In the early 1950s he was appointed caretaker at Belfast's Linen Hall Library. Carnduff died in April 1956. An obituary described him as: 'a man of outstanding character, kindly and tolerant, with a gift for friendship that brought him the regard and affection of numerous men and women in Belfast and Dublin and throughout the Ulster that he loved so well.'[43]

Hayward's specialty was plays about working-class Belfast. They reflected a sense of comedy, tragedy and drama, which many theatre-goers had not previously had the opportunity to see. The characters were portrayed as living and likeable; the plays teemed with life and he brought the audience face-to-face with themselves for the first time. He took care over casting, music, lighting and costumes but it had been an uphill struggle. Frequently he compared Belfast as the poor relation to the Irish capital. Dublin had four repertory theatres: The Abbey, The Gate, The Peacock and The Torch while Belfast lacked a single one. He was aggrieved that the Irish government paid a yearly subsidy of £600 to the Abbey and sent its company on an annual tour of America in the interests of national publicity. In the North, much to his annoyance, theatres were unsubsidized, relying entirely on box-office takings, and he lamented the lack of financial support from the government, something that was the backbone of drama in Europe. 'Drama in Belfast,' Hayward noted in frustration in 1938, 'is not in a happy state ... and I confess myself at a loss to explain the present position ... I found myself up against the stone wall of finance, and to-day I seem to be farther then ever from a realisation of my plans ... I can only say that there was no lack of enthusiasm and hard work on my part and on the part of my players.'[44]

He did not sever his ties completely with theatre. A new company, the Playhouse, which in 1937 grew out of the Little Theatre repertory company, sought his help. Along with Mageean, McCandless, Gerald Morrison and David Kennedy, Hayward became a member of the Honorary Provisional Advisory Board, a committee that came up with a list of twenty-three Ulster plays for production. He said that owing to previous arrangements he was unable to act in any of them himself.[45] But the plan to showcase local plays was short-lived and the curtain quickly came down.

Few facets of Hayward's life epitomize the tireless vigour, energy and flair that he brought to the theatre from 1920 to the late 1930s. He had become the standard-bearer of Ulster popular culture, reflecting urban and rural life. His fellow actors and contemporaries admired and respected his work, and the fact that he had made sacrifices of time and money. Through his knowledge of the tricks of stagecraft and his business acumen he succeeded in his initial aims of bringing urban dramas of working-class life to a music-hall audience. Plays of distinction, new in atmosphere and humour, and which proved an unequivocal triumph had been brought to Southerners. He helped interpret Ulster drama for the rest of Ireland and, crucially, was seen by the Dublin press as contributing to 'an understanding of our Northern cousins.'[46] Hayward's departure from the theatrical scene marked a watershed in his artistic career.

FOUR

Crusaders of the ether

(1924–1950s)

We crusaders of the ether were constantly cheered and uplifted by the thought that nobody was listening.

Tyrone Guthrie, BBC Belfast producer

There were many sides to Hayward's broadcasting life and he had a remarkable variety of talents. As a freelance he spread himself around the BBC, Ulster Television and Radio Éireann. His work was heard on the Northern Ireland Home Service while his talks and music were broadcast on the General Overseas Service (later the World Service), which brought a wider reputation. The main bulk of his freelance broadcasting was with the BBC and stretched over a forty-year period from the 1920s to the early 1960s. Sometimes there were gaps in his appearing on air, partly because he was busy with so many other artistic projects including filmmaking, theatrical work, writing books and recording songs.

His voice was well known as a contributor to a range of radio music and feature talks programmes. He worked on some of the most imaginative and inventive programmes made in the Belfast studios and claimed to be the first person to broadcast Ulster dialect on the BBC. In 1924 he became involved in the new studio and offices of 2BE – the call sign allotted to the Belfast station of the then British Broadcasting Company, and based in a converted warehouse in cramped rooms in Linenhall Street in the city centre. At the formal opening on 24 October, the prime minister of Northern Ireland, Lord Craigavon, amused the audience by suggesting that 2BE stood for 'the second city of the British Empire'.[1]

The original BBC Belfast building in Linenhall Street where Hayward recorded his 1920s' radio plays and sketches with Tyrone Guthrie. A former linen warehouse, it was described as 'ugly, ill-shaped and most undignified'.

Hayward's first broadcast was with Elma and involved scenes from five Shakespeare plays. Elma was an accomplished all-round actress with mimetic talents and a flair for anecdote. They were part of a group of freelance actors known as the Station Players providing humorous sketches in the interludes between music. Along with Tyrone Guthrie, Hayward set up the Belfast Radio Players, one of the earliest radio repertory companies. Guthrie's first job at the BBC in Belfast after coming down from Oxford in 1924 was junior assistant to the head of the new station. Although just twenty-four, he quickly made his mark, going on to become a producer at the Old Vic, administrator of the Sadler's Wells Theatre, and an internationally acclaimed theatrical director.

Hayward's broadcasting in the 1920s ran parallel with his role as manager of the Ulster Players but the medium of radio drama, then in its infancy, appealed to him and he was irresistibly drawn to it. By now he was turning into a literary and social celebrity. He had started to write playlets and sketches for broadcast, acting in all of them and spreading his net wide over the repertoire of Irish drama as a whole – he wrote more than forty of these. They were broadcast by the BBC in Belfast, Glasgow, Edinburgh, London, and at the Dublin broadcasting station. Hayward scripted a series of innovative dialogues in Belfast dialect called 'Double-Sided Records', made up of two vignettes. They depicted city life in titles such as 'At the Cinema', 'In the Tram' and 'Seeing Them off at the Liverpool Boat.' The *Irish Radio Journal* praised his sketch, 'A Trip to the Isle of Man', part of which was broadcast in the open air:

> The author and producer, with his knowledge of the legitimate stage acquired from his very creditable work with the Ulster Players, has set himself the task of solving the problems of radio drama, and perhaps his greatest achievement as a producer is the skilful manner with which he weaves into his broadcast suggestive sounds which do literally take the place of scenery as it is known in the theatre.[2]

Holding centre stage, Hayward (seated centre front) at a BBC concert party in Belfast in 1925 outside the Linenhall Street studio. The cast was rehearsing one of his most popular sketches, *A Trip to the Isle of Man*. Included in the photograph are from left: Elma Hayward, Kitty Murphy, Richard Hayward, Charlotte Tedlie, Jimmy Mageean, and standing to the right in the white shirt, Tyrone Guthrie.

The Belfast station director, John Cowley, was also impressed and wrote to Guthrie in the summer of 1925, praising the work of the Radio Players. Although he did not name the performance, he referred to 'an excellent evening's entertainment':

> The songs were familiar but the 'atmosphere' that was created by the company with laughter, jests, and generally 'carry-on' made the listener feel as if he was actually taking part in a rollicking night at a country farmstead miles away from the nearest railway station.[3]

Hayward was continually experimenting with new forms and was a pioneer in creating realistic sound effects, an aspect of his broadcasting highlighted by the *Radio Times*: 'Ever since the opening of the Belfast Station, Richard Hayward has been closely associated with the dramatic and poetic side of its work. He has done much to improve the technique of Radio drama.'[4]

Listings from the *Radio Times* from 1927 provide a flavour of the different types of work Hayward was involved in with the BBC. In January he presented a J.M. Synge play, *In the Shadow of the Glen*, in which both he and Elma took on parts. The following month, two songs that he collected, 'The Ould Bog Hole' and 'Willie Reilly's Courtship' were used in a traditional programme of old Irish music, and in April he broadcast a talk called 'Ulster Folklore'. This in turn led to his branching out into fact-based speech programmes with wide parameters. His talks featured general historical Irish and antiquarian topics as well as a series 'The Story of the Alphabet', which, amongst other subjects, looked at Egyptian hieroglyphics and Cretan writing. In *Children's Corner*, a forty-five-minute radio programme, later renamed *Children's Hour*, he sang Irish folksongs. The programme began in 1924 and was initially presented by Evva Kerr and later Cicely Matthews. It was transmitted at teatime and was an immediate success. Children were encouraged to take part by singing, telling stories, reading poems or playing instruments. Hayward, who was known as 'Uncle Richard', told Ulster legends and for many was the voice of childhood. More than 3000 children in the Belfast area joined a club called the Radio League.[5] A Dublin Sunday newspaper that profiled the Belfast station described Studio No. 2 as resembling a comfortable music lounge:

> The decorations are in dark oak with panelling of Japanese design in buff and gold. Here are performed plays and chamber music, and the studio is also used for talks and what is probably one of the most popular of all transmissions – the *Children's Hour*.[6]

Despite its popularity, when Gerald Beadle became station director he stopped the chatter between the participants, quickly abolishing the labels of 'aunts' and 'uncles'. Guthrie, whose creativity had inspired Hayward, later looked back on the extremely basic set-up when the station opened. He painted an atmospheric portrait of unpleasant broadcasting conditions in Linenhall Street 'up a dark little stair – a series of poky offices, just cubby-holes, leading off a dark passage that, in its turn, led to The Studio'.[7] In those days since it was necessary to prevent any echo, the room was draped in heavy pleats of curtain with thick carpet to muffle the ceiling:

> The colour of all this was a particularly evil 'off-mustard', with a wide band about a foot from the floor of Greek key pattern in mauve and silver. The light fell from great chamber-pots suspended by muffled chains from the muffled girders in the muffled ceiling – a cold, hard, glaring light. Three minutes in this chamber of horrors would have meant asphyxiation; so there was a 'plant' which filled it – and us – with ozone. One minute of deep breathing of this ozone was, we were assured, the equivalent of a fortnight at Blackpool; the funny little smell of rotten eggs was merely proof of its invigorating, tonic, bracing excellence. You can imagine the effect upon the spirit of those who had to perform here – the smell, the gross, crass ugliness of it all, the neuralgic glare from the chamber-pots, and above all, the acoustic deadness… None the less, we crusaders of the ether were constantly cheered and uplifted by the thought that nobody was listening.[8]

But people were listening and radio's popularity was growing. The first all-Ireland theatre relay broadcast – a musical comedy – took place from the Empire Theatre in Belfast's Victoria Square on 13 December 1927. *Hip Hip Hooradio* was a revue of Hayward's transmitted from Belfast via Dublin to Cork and simultaneously broadcast through the stations in each of the cities with the Lord Mayors of Belfast, Dublin and Cork greeting each other over the airwaves. The following year Hayward recorded a series of six programmes called *What Do you know About your own Country Towns?* The broadcasts looked at the history of Northern towns or cities, covering Armagh, Omagh, Antrim, Enniskillen, Derry and Downpatrick. These detailed historical talks, with a five-page script, lasted up to thirty minutes; ten years later they formed the basis for sections of Hayward's first Ulster travel book.

With the new station only five years old and still finding its feet, many listeners were driven to write letters of complaint to the press. Correspondence on a wide range of issues encompassed the quality of drama productions, talks and music programming. Some were written anonymously and included one

Belfast News Letter correspondent annoyed about the dialects used in local plays, who signed his letter 'Pro Bono':

> Local productions by the Northern Drama League and the so-called Belfast Repertory Theatre deserve all the support we can give, provided they avoid in future the sordid outlook portrayed and the language used by writers in plays such as 'The Long Voyage Home', 'The Spook Sonata' and 'The Land of the Stranger' to name only a few. I have been distressed by the number of friends who have asked me from time to time to write to you regarding the quality of plays broadcast by the BBC, whose repeated references to the misrepresentations of Ulster folk life from the local station, are, I regret to say, more than justified … I hope someone … will do something quickly to put a stop to the absurd and ignorant dialects used.[9]

A signed copy of the programme from the Empire in Belfast of the first all-Ireland theatre relay broadcast, *Hip Hip Hooradio*, a musical comedy revue by the Belfast Radio Players. The performance was transmitted on 13 December 1927 via Dublin to Cork, simultaneously linking up the Lord Mayors in stations in each city who greeted each other over the airwaves. Hayward sang and acted in the show, which included a playlet, *The Cherry Seagull*, described as 'a study in Russian cheerfulness'.

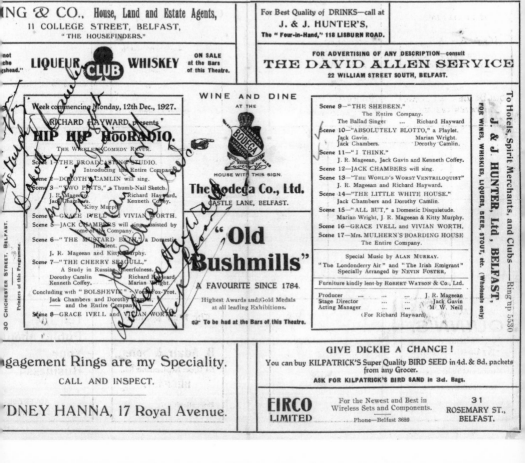

The popular Empire Theatre in Belfast's Victoria Square from where Hayward staged the first all-Ireland theatre relay revue. It was also the scene of many of his theatrical triumphs during the 1930s.

Five days later, in an unsigned reply, a lengthy defence of dialect was published in the *Belfast News Letter*. In his history of the BBC in Northern Ireland, Rex Cathcart detected Hayward's hand in the writing, saying it was 'probably' by him.[10] The letter writer said he had contributed 'many sketches of Ulster life and always with warm love for my fellow Ulstermen in my heart':

> I have tried to portray their loveable nature, their keen sense of humour, and their undoubted ability to laugh at themselves and their idiosyncrasies … A writer of playlets is accustomed to find he cannot please everybody all the time, and I shall say no more on that head. But 'Pro Bono' proceeds to speak of the 'absurd and ignorant' dialects used. It is not quite clear if he means to impute the concoction of bogus dialects to us who write the sketches. If not,

then alternatively, he must mean that the dialects are absurd and ignorant in themselves. Taking the first alternative I am prepared to stand over every dialect, word and phrase I have ever written ... 'Pro Bono' should know that the ordinary man may not come into contact with every dialect, word and phrase used in Ulster; and even I, who have a collection in dictionary form which numbers thousands, am constantly meeting new ones. The second alternative is even less justified. A dialect is not absurd. It is a natural thing in the evolution of a language. It is the backwater of the language canal, if I may use the simile. It is not ignorant, except in the sense that it is not the standard language of the country.[11]

It seems likely that the letter was Hayward's handiwork. Dialect was something that had interested him and more than twenty years later he was involved in a major project compiling a dictionary of Ulster words and phrases. To avoid any controversy he may have decided it politic to remain anonymous but uncharacteristically, the modest anonymity pay off said, 'I seek no self-advertisement, therefore I sign myself: Yours &c., X'[12]

In the early 1930s Hayward's broadcasting was restricted to a few talks and songs on *Children's Corner*, partly because of a heavy workload recording songs, making films and staging and acting in plays. But he had his radio admirers. One correspondent, writing in the *Northern Whig* with the sign off 'The Irish Emigrant', detailed a lengthy list of complaints that included a lack of Irish national music and a call for the use of more local talent. In an unnamed reference to Hayward, the writer exempted *Children's Corner* saying, 'My grateful thanks to the "Uncle" who often sings our beautiful old songs.'[13]

During the Second World War regional broadcasting in Belfast mostly closed down although Hayward continued to carry on with sporadic work on the Overseas Service. In 1941 he received a letter from Ursula Eason, the first woman to be appointed to a senior position in BBC Northern Ireland and acting Head of Programmes. The letter was written just after the Luftwaffe air raid attacks on Belfast. He was asked to give a recital of songs he had arranged and to sing and present a thirteen-minute programme. Hayward replied saying he liked the idea, submitting a script and suggesting four songs: 'Down in Glasloch', 'Among the heather', 'The Inniskilling Dragoon' and 'The Banks of the Bann'. He sent a script outlining details:

The songs are typical of the music made in the homes of the people of Ulster from time immemorial and they are, for this reason typical of all Irish folk music, but they also have a peculiar Ulster slant – subtle building of Scottish and English flavour with the tang of native Irish peat.[14]

THE BRITISH BROADCASTING CORPORATION

Head Office: Broadcasting House, London, W. 1

31 Linenhall Street, Belfast

TELEPHONE AND TELEGRAMS: BELFAST 25834

RP/UE   6th May 1941

Dear Mr. Hayward,

      Thank you for your letter of May 5th
and for your suggested script. I like it very much
indeed, but suggest that you might make it a little
simpler in expression and make the sentences rather
shorter. Short-wave broadcasting has so many "ups
and downs" that short sentences are absolutely
essential.

      I note that you would like to change
"Johnny I hardly knew ye" to "Among the heather".
Actually I have billed the other in our Overseas
publications but it will not matter making the alter-
ation at the time of the broadcast.

      I hope that apart from the falling
plaster you and yours have managed to get through the
raids safely.

Yours sincerely,

Ursula Eason

Richard Hayward, Esq.,
7 Bedford Street,
BELFAST.

Even after seventeen years in broadcasting, some practical tips were offered to
Hayward in a letter from the BBC's Ursula Eason in response to one of his scripts.

Eason responded saying she liked his script but suggested that he should
make the sentences shorter and keep it simpler in expression. 'Short-wave
broadcasting has so many 'ups and downs' that short sentences are absolutely
essential.' She added, 'I hope that apart from the falling plaster you and yours
have managed to get through the raids safely.'[15] Hayward's singing was certainly
noticed and elicited affection, even in the corporation's higher echelons. One of
the BBC's most distinguished national radio announcers, Franklin Engelmann,
wrote to him just before Christmas praising his singing. Engelmann, nicknamed
'Jingle' in the BBC, was best known for hosting such programmes as *Down Your
Way*, *Gardeners' Question Time* and *Pick of the Pops*.

First, to introduce myself – I'm a programme announcer in London on Home and Forces programmes, a dogsbody who does everything except read the news! This should establish for you that I'm mostly "hard-boiled" in respect of most items. Yet, second, I want to tell you how much I enjoyed both your presentation – you and your co-artist's singing and the choice of songs in Irish Songs on Tuesday at 2.40 yesterday. I was at home sick from canteen food-poisoning feeling pretty low but I listened throughout, thought it excellent and decided you'd like to know. Most especially I liked the Cassidy Lass and the Down through the Heather song. Full marks and thank-you.[16]

Hayward played in the BBC with Anna Meakin for a recital on *Music of Britain* in April 1941. The corporation kept a tight grip on the purse strings in those austere wartime days and it was pointed out to him that he would have to pay his accompanist at 'your own expense'.[17] Money was tight everywhere and the confectionery trade was experiencing a difficult spell since sugar was hard to come by but as usual Hayward kept himself fully occupied in other spheres. He was engaged during the war on no fewer than three separate Irish travel books. He was also working for the Entertainments National Service Association, ENSA (known comically as 'Every Night Something Awful'). Made up of dancers, musicians and comedians, it was formed in 1939 to provide entertainment for British and American troops. Many GIs were stationed in Northern Ireland and they particularly enjoyed Hayward's Irish songs and stories as well as the warmth and humour that he brought to his shows. He performed at several army bases in Belfast and County Down for which he was paid £10 a week. Hayward made it his business to build up contacts and get to know people in the armed services, which led to his leading tour groups, another string to his ever-growing list of 'performance' activities. During the war he brought a large party of US soldiers to the south Armagh border on an 'instructional tour':

They took far more interest and delight in standing with one foot in Ulster and one in Eire than in any historical or geological knowledge I was detailed to impart to them. That invisible line across the road, which separated the two parts of Ireland one from the other, made an irresistible appeal to their typical American sense of boyish fun and curiosity. Many a camera clicked to show the folks back home how their boys were able to cope with land frontiers that seemed to give the natives an awful lot of trouble.[18]

In the postwar years Hayward resumed his broadcasting with humorous conversation slots and song recitals. One of the most popular sketches was the eponymous *Richard Hayward Himself*, described as 'a drawing room conversation'.

It was aired on the Northern Ireland Home Service on *Variety Flash* in May 1946. In this ten-minute broadcast Hayward followed a short section of humorous dialogue of himself in conversation with an announcer with three songs: 'Galway Shawl', 'Nellie Bly' and 'Girls of Coleraine'. He was accompanied by Sally McGifford playing violin, Richard Adair on flute and Eddie Pearl at the piano.

By the mid 1950s he was back on a regular basis in Broadcasting House in Ormeau Avenue where he had become a familiar figure. During this period he recorded a series of short musical programmes for what had become known as the BBC Northern Ireland Home Service. For more than five years he contributed to a wide range of programmes and by this stage was a household name. The titles of some of these included *Ulster Songs and Ballads, Ulster Magazine, Sounds of Ulster, Ballads, Songs and Snatches, Ceili Band, Traditional Music* and *Ulster Edition*. In his appearances singing traditional songs, Hayward frequently played the harp. For *Sounds of Ulster* he performed 'The Cuckoo' accompanied by a talk about the tune's history.

Calling themselves the Irish Troubadours, Hayward and Anna Meakin sang together on programmes on BBC radio and Radio Éireann in the 1940s, and recorded a duet 'The Shannon Shore' with HMV.

Several programmes, including a talk on the harp, were broadcast on the Pacific Service and in *Ulster Magazine* he sang three Irish folk songs broadcast on the Overseas Service. The harp was one of the instruments with which Hayward was most associated. He played both the organ and piano and although he had an early interest in the cello as well as drumming, he decided they were not for him; instead he developed a love for Irish harp music. Initially he was taught lessons by two nuns at a convent in Lisburn, County Antrim. The sisters helped him learn the basic skills after which he continued to practice assiduously on his own until he had mastered the instrument.

In his publicity material, such as book catalogues and fliers to promote his recitals and talks as well as covers of magazines, he is pictured with a concentrated look playing the harp. The instrument became a leitmotif in his writing. The embossed image of a harp appears on the cover of his Leinster travel book. In 1957 he was caricatured playing the harp on the front cover of his *Border Foray*. On his travels around Ireland, he frequently slips in references to the harp. He was intrigued by the profusely decorated Cross of Muiredach at Monasterboice in County Louth with its series of pictorial homilies: 'On the east face, the delicious conceit of a bird, perched on the harp of a musician into whose ear it is whispering inspiration.'[19]

He had bought a historic harp dating from 1657 from a collector, R. J. Woods, in Bangor, County Down. Mostly made of sycamore, it was either English or Welsh in origin and had been in Ireland a long time prior to his acquisition. In the 1780s it was played in the streets and parks of Belfast by Paddy Murphy, an itinerant harper. Hayward felt the harp was of too great a value for a private collection and in 1947 he presented it to the National Museum of Ireland. 'The Richard Hayward Harp' contains an Irish inscription on the forepillar, which translates as 'May you never want a string while there's guts in an Englishman.'

He donated two other harps to the Ulster Folk and Transport Museum. One was Georgian and the other was his own travelling harp in a case that had accompanied him on his journeys around Ireland. His knowledge of the instrument was reflected in his twenty-four-page booklet *The Story of the Irish Harp* published in 1954 by Arthur Guinness & Son at five shillings. In the frontispiece Hayward is photographed playing his 1825 Egan Dital Harp. John Egan was the leading Irish harp maker working in Dublin from 1801 to 1841. He made more than 2000 harps during his career and was famous for his invention of the 'Royal Portable Harp'. In the introduction Hayward quotes John Good, a

Catholic priest in Oxford who opened a school in Limerick, and who wrote in 1566: 'The Irish love music mightily, especially the harp. Strung up with brass wire, and beaten with crooked nails, it is very melodious.'[20]

Traditional Irish harp playing, Hayward wrote, was confined to a few points of technique: 'The use of specially shaped long nails as plectra, the use of metal strings of varying character and thickness, a style of playing which demanded damping before the plucking of the next string, and other devices of this kind to offset the excessive vibration peculiar to the metal strings.' Special reference is made to what was known as the 'Meeting of the Harpers' in Belfast in 1792. Of the ten harpers present, six of them, including ninety-seven-year-old Dennis Hempson of Derry, were blind, and Hayward describes it as 'the last of a dying band'. He includes a section on Turlough Carolan (1670–1738), often called 'the last of the Bards' whom he says should be more accurately described as the 'last of the Harper-composers.' In a review, the *Manchester Guardian* said it was a 'charming booklet and should be a stimulus to the welcome movement to re-establish the harp.'[21]

Frequently Hayward accompanied his own singing and wrote solo instrumental items for the harp. His playing was regarded by some as a touch of showbiz. Nicholas Carolan, Director of the Irish Traditional Music Archive, describes him as 'an attention-seeking showman with an instantly recognizable voice. The harp is not a good instrument in a variety concert as it is hard to hear. It is more of a domestic instrument but is fine on record and all Hayward's recordings are of a high quality.'[22]

By the end of the 1950s Hayward's BBC appearances were monthly; he was called in to take part in programmes such as the *St Patrick's Day Shamrock Special* in March 1959, which marked his first television appearance. He sang five songs: 'The Bard of Armagh', 'The Low-Backed car', 'Little Bridgit Flynn', 'She moved through the Fair', and 'Eileen Aroon'. His small-screen career continued sporadically with occasional appearances on a variety of music and culture programmes. Sometimes he quibbled with the BBC over money. On one occasion they had wanted to pay him a fee of one and a half guineas for a reading of 'The Tale of Finn MacCool' taken from *In Praise of Ulster* and he asked for an increase. Miss D. L. Ross from the copyright department wrote to him stating that for entirely original material they paid a guinea a minute and they would not pay as much for a retold legend but, in a spirit of generosity, she added, 'My heart has melted and I am willing to increase the fee to 2 guineas.'[23]

In the 1950s broadcasting firmament Hayward rubbed shoulders with many of the best-known voices of the time including Michael Baguley, Walter Love and sports broadcasters Ronnie Rosser and Jimmy Hughes. Love, originally from Belfast, joined the BBC in London as a staff announcer. After spending a year in Edinburgh he returned to London, and later Belfast where he worked in presentation covering holiday relief before becoming a studio manager. He went on to be one of BBC Northern Ireland's longest-serving and most esteemed broadcasters. He introduced some of Hayward's live music programmes and he recalls him periodically coming into Studio One in Broadcasting House and meeting Havelock Nelson. Originally from Cork, Nelson founded the Dublin Orchestra Players and conducted the Radio Éireann Symphony and Dublin Grand Opera. In 1947 he was offered the post of resident staff accompanist and music producer at the BBC in Belfast. He later became conductor of the BBC Northern Ireland Orchestra and Belfast Grand Opera. He also founded the Studio Symphony Orchestra and Ulster Singers. On one occasion Nelson came into the studio and claimed that Hayward was playing one of his arrangements. The name of the song is not known but Nelson was clearly annoyed and Love recalls that he 'raised his eyebrows in disapproval'. Love knew Hayward by reputation from his films and acting days and occasionally was in his company in the BBC canteen for tea or a meal:

> He was quite a character in his own way and there was a bit of whimsy about him but he was very well respected in music circles. The BBC in Belfast was a happy work environment in those days with about 100 people on the staff. Some of the radio output was spasmodic with sometimes no evening programmes. Television was developing and Hayward was very interested in everything that was going on at that time.[24]

There were other eyebrow-raising moments in the corporation. Michael Baguley came across Hayward when he was recording *Ulster Magazine* for a World Service broadcast in the late 1950s. Baguley, who read the news and was one of BBC Northern Ireland's pre-eminent broadcasters, presented the programme. He remembers Hayward's business acumen, saying he was 'a very astute, talented businessman':

> A group in the corner led by Hayward, played Ulster folksongs. I was put off the music of Schubert for life because Hayward set words to the song 'The Trout' (*Die Forelle*). I remember in particular the line 'Boy, the maiden on her throne, shall be a maiden still' – a reference to Derry. Hayward was a bit

of a chameleon, as a folksinger he always seemed to be happy in whatever company he found himself but was never seen in a pub.[25]

Another BBC employee, Andrew Crockart, then a young floor manager, had joined the organization in 1954 and worked on *The McCooeys*, a popular local sitcom broadcast on radio on Saturday evening. He recalls Hayward's visits to Broadcasting House, especially one unexpected incident which epitomized his largesse:

> I was *The McCooeys* door-opener and made the noise of footsteps at the start when I began work at the age of seventeen-and-a-half. The atmosphere of the BBC was great as it was all Christian names while in other businesses it would have been mister this or mister that or surnames. Somebody said to me that Richard Hayward fancies himself and I don't think that my colleagues took him all that seriously. But subsequently I realized that in fact he did a lot of work that was very good. When he would come into the studio to play the harp, he would open his music box and out would come the Fox's Glacier Mints, which were distributed all round the studio. Everybody said 'Och thanks very much Richard'. They were pleased to see him because he was jolly and was a good performer. There were never any take twos. He was well prepared, knew what was wanted and knew what was expected of him. He sang with the harp and performed monologues, and in between times he's talking nineteen to the dozen. I think people were more reserved then so when Richard talked a lot it tended to produce the reaction, 'He's a bit of a blabbermouth' and he probably was, but underneath it all he was an intelligent man doing a lot of serious work.[26]

Hayward teamed up with the multi-talented Seán Maguire, a Belfast-born musician who lived at Dunmore Street on the Springfield Road. Maguire, whose father came from Cavan, played the piccolo, flute and tin whistle, and was classically trained. He also played guitar, piano and uilleann pipes. In 1949, at the age of fifteen, he recorded his first broadcast on BBC Overseas Radio. Maguire later made his name touring the US and Canada with the Gael-Linn Cabaret presenting an acclaimed programme of Irish music. He formed the eponymous Seán Maguire Ceili Band made up of local musicians including drummer Gerry Hobbs, an old school friend. In January 1957 Maguire and Hayward recorded *Words and music of Ireland* for Beltona, a subsidiary of Decca, and produced an LP priced at twenty-four shillings. Hayward spoke, sang and played the harp while Maguire sang and played the pipes, tin whistle and a historic Guarnerius violin from 1711. The album cover featured a painting of Donegal by Frank McKelvey. The LP, with twenty songs, was recorded in a studio in the BBC in Belfast and

Maguire invited Hobbs to come and watch. As a member of the St Gall's Boys' Choir, Hobbs had recorded songs for one of Hayward's films *In the Footsteps of St Patrick*. He recalls being invited to attend the first recording partnership between the two musicians. Apart from the technicians, he was the only other person present and remembers a consummate performance:

> To get warmed up they practiced 'The Royal Blackbird' and 'The Bonnie Bunch of Roses' and recorded all the songs in just two takes. They were well suited to each other with a good rhythm and rapport. Maguire's masterpiece was 'The mason's apron', a reel that he played on the fiddle and another old one of his 'The black woman of the glen'. After Hayward had sung 'Master MacGrath', Maguire would say 'Master Hayward, you sang that extremely well – it was wonderful.'[27]

Seán Maguire joined forces with Hayward to record *Words and music of Ireland* in the BBC in 1957. The record is a selection of verse, song and melody made into 'a little garland'. Hayward played the harp and sang while Maguire played the uilleann pipes, tin whistle, guitar and fiddle.

'Master MacGrath' was a ballad in honour of the greyhound that won the Waterloo Cup three times and was a favourite song of Hayward's. The musicianship of this once-in-a-blue-moon experience has stuck in Hobbs' memory; Hayward was 'quietly serious' when performing:

As a professional musician he concentrated intensely. He was emotionally engaged, closing his eyes while playing the harp. Maguire would come in and sing his part and then Hayward came in on his part. Hayward did not have the best singing voice in the world – it was not outstanding but it was a very strong voice and he delivered the songs confidently. He was a true gentleman and a fine musician who played the harp in a fluent, delicate and tinkling way. The recording took most of the afternoon and it was a memorable occasion for me. Watching two outstanding musicians perform so well together was one of the happiest days of my life and something I'll never forget. It was pure musical magic. I just sat there spellbound and never opened my mouth. To see how they gelled was a wonderful experience and I was privileged to have a private audience.[28]

Hayward did not offer his broadcasting services exclusively to the BBC – as a freelance he touted his talents elsewhere. The launch of a commercial television station in Belfast in 1959 in a derelict former hemstitching factory gave him the opportunity of reaching a wider audience through the new medium coming into people's homes. On 31 October 1959, the opening night of Ulster Television, Sir Laurence Olivier introduced Hayward as 'Ireland's son with the minstrel hand'. He handed over to him to present the first programme *Talks of Ulster* and Hayward sang and played one of his own songs. His TV persona was smooth and unruffled. The station's animated logo was a musical jingle based on Percy French's 'The Mountains of Mourne'. On the opening night, the first voice heard was that of the continuity announcer, James Greene, whose acting career later included credits starring in Stewart Parker's television and stage plays as well as many other film and TV performances. He recalls the excitement of the new station and meeting Hayward on the first night: 'He was part and parcel of that memorable opening night in 1959 and was a very nice man although I didn't know him very well. I would say he was quite keen on himself and he was certainly no shrinking violet.'[29]

FIVE

Master of his art

(1920s, '30s, '40s)

> He has done some excellent work; what he has accomplished is only an
> earnest of great things to come – if he "hitches his wagon to a star."
>
> F. J. Bigger review of Hayward's Ulster ballads book, *Irish News*, 1925

It was just by chance that Hayward's musical career began. When a singer failed
to arrive on 6 July 1925 at a rehearsal in Belfast of *A Trip to the Isle of Man* – a
play written by Hayward for the BBC – Tyrone Guthrie asked him to stand in
and sing 'The Ould Man of Killyburn Brae', one of the songs vital to the plot.
He liked what he heard, decided he should sing it in the actual production and
the broadcast led to Hayward's first recording contract. Until then he had never
considered being a professional singer although he had an interest in traditional Irish songs and ballads. An executive of the Columbia label was listening
in London and invited him to come to record two songs at the company's
studios in Petty France: 'The Bonnie Bunch of Roses' and the famous song of
Orangeism, 'The Ould Orange Flute'. The latter was a humorous song known
throughout Ireland, which later led Hayward into a controversial court case
over copyright. The recordings in London took place early in 1929 and marked
the start of a lengthy musical career.

   The fortuitous break helped him become a well-known singer of Irish
ballads, not just in Ireland, but in others parts of the world. As a hobby he sought
out the company, and studied the methods and style, of the old singers whom

he regarded as the direct descendants of the Irish bards or *shanachies*. As he trav-elled the roads from town to town he began collecting songs. This dovetailed with his new confectionery job, bringing him into villages and small towns. He always kept his eyes and ears open for an opportunity.

In the ensuing years, ensconced in late-night pubs or impromptu concerts, attending wakes, sitting around the turf fire in convivial kitchens at house ceilidhs or researching material for his books, he would observe performers. Listening carefully to a murmuring voice from a mountainy man in a suit, he would pay particular attention to the lyrics as well as the melody. Often, he would question them on the provenance of a particular song and immedi-ately note down the names of rare and rip-roaring ballads, mournful laments or long-forgotten fragments of songs. Some of these were based on historic battles or were rousing rebel or Orange songs; others were anti-war ballads, nostalgic street songs full of tenderness, or stories of courtship and innocent love. Much of this folk balladry reflected the sentimental humour of Irish country life at a hiring fair or market day while local characters featured men of the rambling roads. Some songs came to Ireland with returning migratory agricultural workers who sought seasonal employment in the harvest fields of Scotland. Painstaking in his efforts to preserve them, Hayward felt strongly that it was important to rescue them from obscurity and record the oral tradition for posterity. On occasions, drink might be offered to tease out another half-remembered verse, and sometimes he sang to a ready audience. Whatever the occasion, he wasted no scrap of musical experience.

Some traditional songs were hundreds of years old and he spent hours arranging them, working them up into his own style. His enthusiasm for this bloomed and within a few years he had built up a staggering collection of more than 400 titles. One, 'Among the Heather', a delicate tune set to an accompani-ment he devised, was collected in Birdstown glen in County Donegal; another, 'County Mayo Fragment', came from hearing a ballad singer in a pub in Mayo. Hayward later described it as 'a delicious little cradle song, and if it may raise a slight blush it is none the worse for that.'[1] Another song, 'County Kildare Fragment' came about in the same way. It consists of a single verse in Irish that Hayward overheard in a pub near Athy. He later sang it unaccompanied in his own English translation on his *Irish Saturday Night* record released by Decca in 1954, thirty years after his public singing debut at the BBC. On the same LP, he sings 'Nora Lee' with an orchestra and male chorus, and explains where he picked it up:

It was in the region of Dungannon, in the County Tyrone, that I first heard this song. I was only able to gather a few words of it and from these I made this present version. I well remember the old man, who sang for me, coming to a puzzled stop in the middle of the first verse, with the exasperated remark: *Dambut, there's a hole in the ballad!*[2]

As he mulled over his notes, the lyrics ran through his head and he learnt the songs in the same way as he had as a child in Larne. The idea of bringing some of them together was bubbling and he decided to assemble them in a book. This came to fruition with the publication of a collection of fifty-five songs and ballads with titles and lyrics. Many favourites such as 'Dolly's Brae', 'The Ould Leather Breeches' and 'Kitty of Coleraine', a song loved by Thackeray, are contained in his anthology *Ulster songs and ballads of the town and the country*. Published by Duckworth in September 1925, it was priced at five shillings. The opening verse of 'The Ould Bog Hole' from County Antrim gives a flavour of the humour in the collection.

> Oh, the pigs are in the mire and the cows are on the grass,
> And a man without a woman is no better than an ass,
> Oh, my mother likes the ducks, and the ducks like the drake,
> And it's sweet Judy Patterson I'd die for her sake;

The title page notes that the songs were collected and set down by H. Richard Hayward. His name is followed by the letters F.R.S.A. (Ireland), standing for Fellow of the Royal Society of Arts. In a prefatory note he wrote that he would like to also publish a companion volume to his collection where he would set down the airs of the songs and ballads he had presented in the book. He thanked his friend Francis Joseph Bigger and others for their help and noted that the ballad singer is fast disappearing. 'The coming of the kinema [*sic*] to even the smallest of our Irish towns is completing his extermination, which has already begun with the advent of national education and the cheap newspaper.'[3]

In the introduction, the dramatist, novelist and biographer St John Ervine described Hayward as a poet and antiquarian who was 'high in the councils of the Ulster Players'. He said the book 'would dispel the grotesque legend that there is neither fun nor civility in Ulster. I find a warmth and humour even in the ballads of bigotry which are irreconcilable with the character of grim and graceless people.'[4]

Like Hayward, Ervine said one of his earliest recollections was hearing a servant girl singing 'Willie Reilly and his Colleen Bawn.' He said that he 'knew of few spontaneous entertainments so heartening and pleasant as the sound of Ulstermen singing their country songs.' Ervine and Hayward had struck up a friendship. Born in east Belfast, the son of deaf-mutes, Ervine served with the Dublin Fusiliers in the First World War, losing a leg from wounds in France. Originally a Nationalist, he became an ardent Unionist after the Easter Rising, writing adulatory biographies of Edward Carson and Lord Craigavon. Ervine's groundbreaking play, *Mixed Marriage* (1915), a study of bigotry in Belfast and a poetic tragedy, was produced at the Abbey Theatre after a meeting with W.B. Yeats. (Nearly 100 years later, in February 2013, the play had a successful two-week run at Belfast's Lyric Theatre). In 1915 Ervine became manager of the Abbey but left in protest after the Easter Rising. Throughout the 1920s and thirties he wrote novels and popular comedies; one of the best known, *Boyd's Shop* (1936), was based on memories of his grandmother's Belfast shop.

Writing under the pseudonym Cloghroe, Bigger reviewed the collection for the *Irish News*. He started with the mistaken spelling of Hayward's name as Haywood in the opening sentence, although future references were correct. Bigger described Hayward as a 'popular, prominent and interesting figure in the literary and artistic life of Belfast,' and added:

> He has done some excellent work; what he has accomplished is only an earnest of great things to come – if he 'hitches his wagon to a star.' No doubt, as a relaxation from his more serious labours, Mr. Hayward turned his attention to old ballads.[5]

Bigger queried the geographical locations of some of Hayward's songs and in several instances questioned the lyrics:

> I am not a collector, nor an expert on this subject; but there are only four of Mr. Haywards's fifty-four poems that I have not seen somewhere in print before his volume came into my hands. 'A Dream of Dolly's Brae' is probably older than the extraordinary production entitled 'Dolly's Brae.' No one will dream of denying that either had its origin in Ulster but there is a doubt in the cases of several lyrics and ballads in Mr. Hayward's books. 'The Blackbird' dates from the early Eighteenth Century; the tune and the words are from the South. I find it hard to understand how an old ballad beginning 'On the road to Clonmel, at the Sign of the Bell, Pat Hegarty kept a neat cabin', is particularly associated with Cullybackey, Co. Antrim; it figured in the famous Cork 'broadsheets' a century ago. 'Lord Waterford is Dead' was resurrected by the late William Ludwig; it had just the same connection with Co. Antrim as with Sligo, Louth or Kerry. 'The Ould Bog Hole' was as well known in West Cork as in Desertmartin, fifty years ago – perhaps further back; these

wandering products of semi-illiteracy changed their shape materially as they travelled from mouth to mouth – from one remote printer's shop to another.[6]

The collection was worth making, Bigger felt, and worth securing and preserving. He kept his vitriol for Ervine's introduction.

> But why did Mr. Hayward disfigure his interesting book by printing the outlandish pages of screaming, yelping and howling contribution by Mr. St John Ervine and called an 'Introduction'? The screed does not introduce the Songs and Ballads; Mr Ervine refers casually to them in a patronizing fashion, mentioning that he had heard a servant-girl singing 'Willie Reilly and his Colleen Bawn'. William Carleton left it on record that he heard his mother singing the old mid-Ulster ballad; that must have been long over a century ago. I don't suppose anyone in Ireland – even a lyrical servant-girl in County Down – has sung, or chanted 'Willie Reilly' within the past twenty or thirty years. Many more have heard a few stanzas; but the great novelist's mention of his Tyrone mother developed into Mr. Ervine's memory of a 'servant-girl in County Down'.[7]

Another reviewer, William Dawson, also criticized Ervine's introduction. He said the reader's enjoyment of the ballad or song is considerably enhanced by a knowledge of the air or 'tune', while in quite a number of others it is handicapped by his ignorance in this regard:

> No doubt Mr. Hayward, himself a songster in every sense, can sing each and all of the ballads contained in his book. I should dearly like to hear him troll 'The Ould Man of Killyburn brae' with its whistling refrain, or 'Craighilly Fair' … even as I have heard him do 'The Ballynure Ballad' in right merry style. It is to be regretted that Mr. Hayward sought out his fellow-countryman, St John Ervine, to provide the 'Introduction.' The venom in which he steeps his pen when writing of those Irish who do not enjoy the good fortune of having been born in Ulster is noticeable in his introductory remarks to the anthology which Mr. Hayward has made 'with care and affection' and will give offence to such of his readers as permit themselves to be annoyed by manifestations of the 'Portydown' mind.[8]

Music overlapped with many aspects of Hayward's working life. He did not just perform publicly but often sang in private houses. During his Dublin trips when he was in the city for his theatrical work in the 1920s, he visited George Russell, who wrote under the pseudonym 'Æ'. A celebrated poet, painter, playwright, philosopher and mystic, Russell, who was a senior figure in the Irish literary revival and known as the 'Socrates of Dublin', was editor of the liberal weekly *The Irish Statesman*. He also wrote criticism and reviewed Hayward's book of ballads two weeks before Christmas 1925. Russell called it 'a charming anthology,' suggesting it would find many readers, not only in Ulster but in the other provinces:

> It will give Leinster, Connaught, and Munster men a very different idea of the Ulsterman and a much truer one than he will get from reading the newspapers … It is well that these ballads should be collected, for the broadcasting station, the cinema, and the gramophone are three dragons whose fiery breath is shriveling up folk-sentiment and tradition. The countryman is going to be dragged into the highways of the world and he will listen in future to what the wireless shouts from the city rather than to what the ballad singer whines at the fair.[9]

Born in Lurgan, County Armagh, Russell moved to Dublin in 1878. Frequently he held at-home soirées in Rathgar attended by writers, poets and musicians. He enjoyed chanting Yeats' poetry as well as some of his own and liked quoting from Whitman.[10] Hayward visited his house singing 'My Lagan Love', 'The Humour is On Me Now', and 'The Inniskilling Dragoon', and telling stories at Russell's behest. 'I well remember at those marvellous Thursday nights of his at Ranelagh how he used to make me sing Ulster folk songs and tell Ulster stories and how the light in his eye proclaimed his birthplace before all men.'[11] [Hayward may have mistaken the address and the night as Russell lived at 70 Rathgar Avenue and held his soirées on Sunday nights].

From the start of his musical career Hayward proved popular with audiences and his singing had a special character. The music press took an interest and he won early critical praise. *Gramophone* magazine, founded in 1923 by Compton Mackenzie and later run with his brother-in-law Christopher Stone, consistently reviewed his new records from 1929 until after his death when some were released posthumously. Hayward travelled to London to record traditional songs on 78s with the newly-established Decca Record Company. Decca were impressed and his recording career took off. He was back in London in early February 1931, this time with Elma, to record five comedy sketches in Ulster dialect with his friend, the actor Jimmy Mageean. Over three days they recorded fourteen short sketches and songs. During 1931 he revisited London in June, October and November to record further batches of songs, totalling thirty-four. Many were Irish ballads and folksongs that became a standard part of Hayward's singing repertoire on the radio and at concerts in the years ahead. They included 'The Aughalee Heroes', 'The Ballynure Ballad', 'The Maid of the Sweet Brown Knowe', 'Skibbereen', 'Dolly's Brae', 'The South Down Militia' and 'The Mutton

Burn Stream'. In spring 1931 Decca produced an Irish supplement featuring many Hayward songs. *Gramophone* described him as 'a pukka Irish folk-singer; he sings songs from goodness knows where, traditional, from their whole characters obviously genuine Irish folk-songs, innocent of 'composition' as we know it.'[12]

In a break from singing, he with other actors recorded a series of monologues in July 1934 with Decca. These included a two-part speech recording 'Hands Across the Border' with the Dublin actors and comedians Jimmy O'Dea and Harry O'Donovan. Later that year, together with Elma and Mageean, they recorded several other speech-based pieces called 'Jolly Old Pals', 'His First Boots', 'The Wee Drum', and 'The Derry Train'. The following year he recorded a further four monologues in May with O'Dea and O'Donovan, two entertainers who formed their first partnership in a revue in Dublin in 1924 and went on to have a thirty-seven-year association. During the mid thirties, O'Dea and O'Donovan were regular performers on the Belfast stage, taking part in the Christmas pantomime *Jack and the Beanstalk* at the Empire Theatre in December 1935 and an Easter comedy show, 'O'Ds on Parade', which ran for two weeks at the Empire in April 1936.

By the end of 1933, after five years with Decca, Hayward had recorded more than a hundred songs, many with orchestral accompaniment. Compton Mackenzie described his work as 'the best bit of genre singing that the gramophone has ever given us'. Along with Elma and Jimmy Mageean, he also recorded a series of comedy sketches in Ulster dialect.

A Complete List to the 31st December, 1933, of the

Records of RICHARD HAYWARD

(Traditional Ballad Singer, with Orchestral Accompaniment, except where otherwise stated.)

F 2266	THE OLD LEATHER BREECHES	arr. Hayward
	THE CASTLE OF DROMORE	arr. Hayward
F 2282	THE AUGHALEE HEROES	arr. Hayward
	THE FLOWER OF THE COUNTY DOWN	arr. Hayward
F 2283	THE SHEPHERD'S BOY	arr. Hayward
	SKIBBEREEN	arr. Hayward
F 2284	THE BALLYNURE BALLAD	arr. Herbert Hughes
	MAID OF THE SWEET BROWN KNOWE	arr. Hayward
F 2406	THE SASH MY FATHER WORE	arr. Hayward
	PROTESTANT BOYS	arr. Hayward
F 2407	THE PAPISH GOAT	arr. Hayward
	THE ORANGEMAN AND THE DIVIL	arr. Hayward
F 2408	DERRY'S WALLS	arr. Hayward
	THE BATTLE OF GARVAGH	arr. Hayward
F 2433	THE GREEN GRASSY SLOPES OF THE BOYNE	arr. Hayward
	NO SURRENDER	arr. Hayward
F 2434	DOLLY'S BRAE	arr. Hayward
	THE BLACK MAN'S DREAM	arr. Hayward
F 2435	THE HAT MY FATHER WORE	arr. Hayward
	WILLY REILLY'S COURTSHIP (with Piano Accomp.)	arr. Hayward
F 2555	THE OULD ORANGE FLUTE (with Piano Accomp.)	arr. Hayward
	THE OULD ORANGE TREE	arr. Hayward
F 2556	THE SOUTH DOWN MILITIA	words and arrgt. by Hayward
	THE RELIEF OF DERRY	
F 2602	THE MUTTON BURN STREAM	arr. Hayward
	THE BONNIE WEE WINDOW	arr. Hayward
F 2603	THE GIRLS OF COLERAINE	arrgt. words and music by Hayward
	THE BANKS OF THE BANN	arrgt. words and music by Hayward
F 2604	THE BALLAD OF MASTER McGRATH	arr. Hayward
	THE BONNY LIGHT HORSEMEN	arr. Hayward
F 2605	MRS. MAXWELL OF SANDY ROW	words and arrgt. by Hayward
	THE WEE SHOP	words and arrgt. by Hayward
F 2606	THE ORANGE LILY	arr. Hayward
	THE MURDER OF McBRIARS	arrgt. words and music by Hayward
F 2707	THE BRIGHT SILVERY LIGHT OF THE MOON	arrgt. words and music by Hayward
	THE OLD THREAD MILL	arrgt. words and music by Hayward
F 2779	UP THE HILL TO BALLYCASTLE	Morrison
	THE FLOWER OF DONEGAL	music by Morrison, words by Hayward
F 2780	THE THIRSTY COBBLER	words and arrgt. of music by Hayward
	THE LITTLE THATCHED COTTAGE	words and arrgt. of music by Hayward
F 2794	THE MAN FROM GOD KNOWS WHERE	Wilson
	(a) LOVE IN ULSTER (b) MOTHER'S SONG	Hayward
F 2572	THE YELLOW ROSE OF TEXAS (Accordion and Guitar Acc.)	words and music
	GRANNY'S OLD ARM-CHAIR (Accordion and Guitar Acc.)	arr. by Hayward
F 2899	CHAPEL FIELDS	words and arrgt. of music by Hayward
	THE BELFAST TELE BOY	words and arrgt. of music by Hayward
F 2900	RED BIDDY	arrgt. of words and music by Hayward
	NELL FLAHERTY'S DRAKE	arrgt. of words and music by Hayward
F 2901	MRS. MAXWELL'S DAUGHTER	words and music by Hayward
	THE WOMAN WITH THE RED NOSE	words and arrgt. of music by Hayward
F 2902	SWEET KITTY WELLS (with Instrumental Accomp.)	arr. Hayward
	NELLY GRAY (with Instrumental Accomp.)	arr. Hayward
F 3124	THE SPRIGS OF KILREA	arrgt. words and music by Hayward
	DAVIE BROWN'S FAREWELL	arrgt. words and music by Hayward

Records of RICHARD HAYWARD—contd.

F 3125	CARRICKMANNON LAKES	arrgt. words and music by Hayw
	THE FACTORY GIRL	arrgt. words and music by Hayw
F 3165	MAGGIE MURPHY'S HOME	arrgt. words and music by Hayw
	WON'T YOU BUY MY PRETTY FLOWERS	arrgt. words and music by Hayw
F 3281	THE ORANGE APRON TRIMMED WITH BLUE	arrgt. words and music by Hayw
	THE LADIES' ORANGE LODGES	arrgt. words and music by Hayw
F 3283	BALLINADRAE (Guitar Accomp. by Len Fillis)	Gerald Morr
	THREE LEAFED SHAMROCK FROM GLENORE (Guitar Acc. by Len Fillis)	Hayw
F 3294	A MILITARY TRAGEDY (Novelty Orch. Accomp.)	Morrison, Pagden, Hayw
	THE WATERLOO PUP (Novelty Orch. Accomp.)	Morrison, Pag
F 3354	MY BANJO ON MY KNEE (Banjo Accomp. by Len Fillis)	words and arrgt. by Hayw
	WHEN THE ROSES BLOOM AGAIN (Guitar Accomp. by Len Fillis)	words and arrgt. by Hayw
F 3374	THE INNISKILLING DRAGOON (with Harp Accomp.)	arr. Hayw
	THE FLOWER OF SWEET STRABANE (with Harp Accomp.)	arr. Hayw
F 3419	THE HAZEL DELL	arrgt. of words and music by Hayw
	THE LITTLE BROWN JUG	arrgt. of words and music by Hayw
F 3448	GIVE US A WAG OF YOUR TAIL	arrgt. of words and music by Hayw
	THE WIFE IN DERRY	Morrison, Hayw
F 3449	MOLLY DARLING	arrgt. of words and music by Hayw
	THE DRUMMER BOY OF WATERLOO	arrgt. of words and music by Hayw
F 3450	BINNORIE (with Harp Accomp.)	arr. Hayw
	THE ROYAL BLACKBIRD (with Harp Accomp.)	arr. Hayw
F 3595	THE ORANGE A.B.C.	arrgt. of words and music by Hayw
	THE ORANGE MAID OF SLIGO	arrgt. of words and music by Hayw
F 3596	THE BOYNE WATER	arrgt. of words and music by Hayw
	THE BOYS OF SANDY ROW	arrgt. of words and music by Hayw
F 3622	AMONG THE HEATHER	arrgt. of words and music by Hayw
	A SONG HEARD AT NIGHT	arrgt. of words and music by Hayw
F 3736	THE OLD MAN OF KILLYBURN BRAE	arrgt. of words and music by Hayw
	THE MUD CABIN ON THE HILL	arrgt. of words and music by Hayw
F 3775	THE SINKING OF THE TITANIC	arrgt. of words and music by Hayw
	THE SHIP THAT NEVER RETURNED	arrgt. of words and music by Hayw
F 3776	THE RAMBLING IRISHMAN	arrgt. of words and music by Hayw
	CAMPBELL MILLER'S MARE	arrgt. of words and music by Hayw
F 3778	BARNEY BACKED A WINNER	arrgt. of words and music by Hayw
	THE BURN WAS BIG WITH SPATE	arrgt. of words and music by Hayw
F 3814	NELLY BLY	arrgt. of words and music by Hayw
	MY DARK VIRGINNY BRIDE	arrgt. of words and music by Hayw

ELMA and RICHARD HAYWARD
(Comedy Sketches in Ulster Dialect)

F 2278	THE SODA BREAD	Hayw
	RICHARD HAYWARD and J. R. MAGEEAN	
	BIG BILL MUCKLE AT THE MINISTRY OF LABOUR	Camp

ELMA HAYWARD, RICHARD HAYWARD and J. R. MAGEEAN
(Comedy Sketches in Ulster Dialect)

F 2264	MRS. McWHA AT THE MINISTRY OF LABOUR	Camp
F 2287	ALL BUT	Hayw
F 3126	THE ACID TEST	Git
	ALL OVER NOTHING	Git
F 3282	MRS. McWHA AT THE COURT OF REFEREES	Rid
F 3353	UNCLE JAMES GOES TO THE TALKIES	Gib
F 3648	MRS. McWHA CLAIMS A PENSION	Rid

" *These Richard Hayward Records . . . among the most precious in the wh of my collection.*"—*Compton Mackenzie.*

The 1930s was a remarkably creative time for Hayward with his drama and film work running in tandem with his singing. Throughout the decade, his song recordings flowed thick and fast. No fewer than five songs from the film *The Luck of the Irish* that he made in 1935 were promoted by Decca in their catalogue. During this period he chalked up with the company a total of 140 songs including some remakes. In total, over more than thirty years, he collected, arranged and recorded 156 traditional Irish songs. For many of them he arranged the words and music with instrumental or orchestral accompaniment.

As well as Decca and HMV, Hayward also recorded with Fontana. The sleeve cover of *This is Ireland* features Derry's Guildhall, seen over the city walls from Shipquay Street. On this record he sang four songs and was accompanied on two by the Saint Patrick Singers: 'The Wee Shop' and the Munster folksong 'The Muskerry Sportsman'.

From the Irish Roads was one of his early long-playing records produced in 1948 with ten songs. With the grandiosely entitled Richard Hayward Orchestra, it included songs that were to become his recognized signature tune such as 'The Wee Shop', 'The Inniskilling Dragoon', and 'The Stone Outside Dan Murphy's Door' which, he said in the accompanying sleeve notes, 'in almost any *ceilidh* is a real roof-lifter!' He also reflected: 'At one time the ballad singer would have been a familiar figure, with his handful of narrow ill-printed ballad sheets but is now only seen on rare occasions.'[13] In his recording he wanted to be true, he said, to this ancient tradition of singing since he felt there was, 'much nonsense written about folksong and about Irish folksong in particular by scholars and fanatics alike who advanced the wildest and most fantastic theories.'[14] Hayward believed that the authentic folksinger always has a story to tell:

> Usually he achieves his ends by direct statement and endless repetition, means which the lovers of the sophisticated art song often finds tasteless. The trained singer also is rigidly bound by his tempered scales, but the Irish folksinger harks back to an older freedom and often seems, to the uninitiated, to be singing out of tune. I hope, in some of my songs, you will feel the same about me, for that is part of the authentic tradition. It is known to our country people as *singing rough* and here and there it slightly flattens or sharpens a note out of the tempered scale, for the purpose of colour, feeling or subtle emphasis.[15]

Hayward pointed out that the tailpiece, 'Orchestral Postlude', is based on the folksong 'Carrickmannon Lake', a melody known to Beethoven through the collection of Irish airs he edited and arranged. He wrote that it was, 'interesting to observe that the first seven notes of this melody are identical with the first seven notes of the Beethoven Violin Concerto in D Major.' With his musical life a busy round of songs and recitals, recording and revues, his work was stirring up considerable interest in the press, attracting the attention of the leading music critics. An insight into his song collecting appeared in a profile in the *Daily Express* in 1934. In an article entitled, 'Records that Pluck at Your Heartstrings', Christopher Stone – known as the first radio 'disc jockey' – threw some light on his performances:

> When he was in London last week he recorded four songs which brought his total up to 112 and every one of them is arranged by himself. He told me he has 200 more of the old ballads in his desk awaiting their turn for recording. He never misses a chance of going to an Irish 'wake,' and often singing a ballad or two himself. Then others of the mourners follow his lead, and he is unlucky if during this evening he does not hear a ballad that is new to him. He pins it down, melody and words, and takes it home like a moth to put in his desk. One of the most striking of all the Hayward series is the arrangement of 'Nelly Bly' in which a cor anglais plays a prominent part. But all of them are popular in Northern Ireland, and many of them are treasured all over the world ... Richard Hayward has the authentic style of singing them.[16]

The most celebrated of all the settings for his songs was a long way from the London studios and took place in the unlikely surroundings of a courtroom in Glasgow. In 1936 a Scottish music publisher brought a case against him in a copyright row over 'The Ould Orange Flute', one of the first songs Hayward recorded. Robert Wallace, from Glasgow, who traded under the music publishing name of James S. Kerr, took the action against rival Glasgow publishers Mozart Allan as well as Hayward, claiming it as their copyright. The case, heard in Glasgow Sheriff Court, was brought in an attempt to prevent either of the defendants printing, publishing, selling or distributing the song and requesting them to hand over all copies they owned or controlled.

Wallace told the court that he had composed the version in question in 1913 and in the courtroom he played two versions on a piano accordion. Before he began, he said that he was not in the habit of playing the instrument but he promised to do his best. When he took the witness box, Hayward said that with a traditional air no one could claim the copyright of the melody. He then sang two songs to illustrate his contention that certain tunes were not suitable to the spirit of traditional Irish songs. Apart from his own musical performance, Hayward filled the court with singers and fiddlers from Ballycastle and the Glens of Antrim as witnesses who were able to prove that their grandmothers had sung the song seventy years or more beforehand and they had learnt it from them. With his impressive line-up of musicians and strong force of argument, Hayward won the case. The papers took delight in the details. Squeezed in between stories headlined 'Tense Situation in the Punjab' and 'Fashionable Residential Quarter in Flames in Bilbao', was 'Concert in Court':

> Melody floated from Glasgow Sheriff Court yesterday. Enchanting Irish melodies were sung from the witness box, a piano, accordion and gramophone rendered pleasing airs and Sheriff Berry himself joined in and whistled in faultless time and rhythm.[17]

The shadow of legal action over copyright was something that hovered around Hayward's singing career at various times and plagued him through a variety of claims and accusations. Years after the Glasgow case, in an interview to celebrate his twenty-first anniversary as a recording artist with Decca, Hayward was quoted about the court proceedings by the music critic Moore Orr: "Twas great fun, but a little tense, for I stood to lose a lot in damages, expenses and costs if I lost. I am sure it has gone down in legal history as the most amusing copyright case on record. Thank God I hadn't to foot the bill!"[18]

That same year, 1936, the talk was of unrest in Europe again. A coup, led by General Franco, tipped Spain into civil war; Stalin was beginning his purge while Hitler's remilitarisation of the Rhineland was causing a crisis. The British prime minister Stanley Baldwin argued for restraint, ignoring calls from those who said the Nazis must be confronted. In Ireland a party of 700 Blueshirts under Eoin O'Duffy left for Spain to support Franco's nationalists. At the same time 200 republicans and socialists under Frank Ryan joined the International Brigade in support of the Republic.

An import tax was imposed on records in Ireland in 1936 because they were regarded as luxury items, so Decca and HMV opened Irish offices and set up a disc-manufacturing plant in Waterford. This led to a programme of recording Irish artists with Hayward acting as a talent scout for Decca. He was instrumental in nurturing, advising and bringing other singers to the fore. As a regular performer on the circuit of variety shows, concerts and parish hall entertainment he was in an ideal position to spot talent. Nicholas Carolan, of the Irish Traditional Music Archive, says Hayward was 'plugged into what was required':

> He knew many people and could recognize a good singing voice. If he saw someone with talent he would put the word out and organize auditions. Hayward had a strong performance gene himself, an urge to perform. He liked being in front of the microphone or camera and reaching more people than in a hall. Showboating was important for him and he indulged in a form of popular music. There is a legacy of song, pleasant to listen to and illustrative of the entertainment culture of the 1930s, forties and fifties and of what people listened to. There is a continuing core of material that is part of history and will always be of interest. He was so active that you could not do a complete description of Irish music and leave Hayward out of it as he was such a part of the scene.[19]

It was at a meeting of Irish PEN in Jurys Hotel, Dublin in 1937 that Hayward put his talent-spotting to good effect. He was first introduced to Delia Murphy, a then unknown singer from the west of Ireland. She sang that night along with him providing the evening's entertainment. With her strong accent and distinctive singing voice, she performed 'Three Lovely Lassies', a song he particularly enjoyed. The Dublin Centre of PEN had been founded in 1934. The Earl of Longford was the first president and he was succeeded by Maurice Walsh, author of 'The Quiet Man', who along with other writers from North and South founded the Belfast Centre in 1938. Hayward later became chairman of the Belfast branch. The organization's purpose, in its own words, 'was to maintain friendships between writers in every country in the interests of literature, freedom of artistic expression and international goodwill.' In Ireland it also helped bring writers together socially to discuss matters of interest and concern on an all-island basis.

Alongside the celebrated bandleader Henry Hall, Hayward is pictured discussing the latest HMV recordings shortly after the company opened their Irish manufacturing base in Waterford in 1936.

Several friends of Hayward were at the meeting. Apart from Walsh, they included the playwright and author of comic fiction, Lynn Doyle, who had recently published *The Spirit of Ireland*, a guidebook addressed to 'the better class of English tourist'. When Hayward heard Murphy he recognized her star quality and realized he had found a musical soulmate. At thirty-five, she was ten years younger than him but there were remarkable similarities in their childhoods. She was born in 1902, in Ardroe, near Claremorris in County Mayo. The family later moved to Mount Jennings House at Hollymount in Mayo. Like Hayward, who had heard many songs as a young child from the family's County Monaghan housemaid, she too heard traditional ballads as a child, picking up songs from all sorts of people, including the postman. At Mount Jennings she heard the uilleann pipes and fiddle music of Travellers.

She sat around the tinkers' campfires and listened to their songs a few hundred yards from the family home. Murphy was educated in Tuam, Dublin and at University College Galway where she learned tunes from the writer Pádraic Ó Conaire. As she wandered around the Claddagh, she heard seafaring songs from the washerwomen and fishermen who had brought them back from other Irish ports. As well as collecting songs she wrote some based on her own experience.

That night in Jurys marked the start of what was to be a fruitful four-year partnership performing on stage together and recording duets for HMV. Hayward was already established as a radio favourite. His music was fodder for many programmes and there was a strong connection between radio and records, which fed into sales. But accompanying Murphy brought a new dimension and gave him the opportunity of branching out and reaching fresh audiences. It also helped increase his brimming collection of Irish songs by tapping into the store of seafaring ones in Murphy's repertoire. Through Hayward's contacts with HMV, Murphy began recording from her catalogue of songs. The two singers travelled up and down the country, appearing on stage at concerts, festivals, ceilidhs and in ballrooms and dance halls. Enraptured audiences often travelled fifty miles to hear them. Their engagements took them everywhere, from Monaghan to Kilkenny, and sometimes they performed as part of a variety bill with such characters as Barney McCool of Coolaghy.

But Murphy and Hayward were the big attraction, and with their ability to hold an audience they were a winning combination. Although politically and religiously from opposite backgrounds, he was comfortable with her, and they had much in common on stage. Ever the showman, Hayward had met a match in Murphy, a fun-loving extrovert with warmth of personality who became one of Ireland's first celebrity women. Her chief trademarks were a rich compelling tone, directness and sincerity of expression. With his instantly recognizable baritone voice, they performed songs they both loved, creating a magnetic synergy with wide appeal.

Murphy's best-known song was 'The Spinning Wheel' written by John Francis Waller of Tipperary in the nineteenth century. Other popular tunes that were often requested at concerts and which she recorded were 'The Moonshiner', 'The Rose of Mooncoin', 'If I were a Blackbird', 'Thank you Ma'am, says Dan', 'The Peeler and the Goat', 'The Bantry Girl's Lament', 'The Jackets Green' and 'The Bright Silvery Light of the Moon', which Hayward sang in his first feature film *The Luck of the Irish*. They sang duets on Radio Éireann, giving the Irish ballad international recognition. Murphy's husband, Dr Tom Kiernan, was the station's Director of Programmes and later an Irish ambassador. He worked in the Department of External Affairs in Dublin where his diplomatic career stretched through the Vatican to Australia, Germany, Canada and the US. In 1963 he was the coordinating link between Ireland and the White House, organizing President Kennedy's visit that summer. Murphy became known as the 'Queen of Balladry' and was also referred to as the 'Queen of Connemara' after an old Irish boat song she frequently sang. Apart from Irish radio, her music was played on BBC Home Service programmes such as *Housewives' Choice* as well as on Radio Luxembourg. In 1939 she and Hayward, with piano, guitar and accordion accompaniment, recorded duets in the HMV Studios at Abbey Road, in St John's Wood, London. Three of the songs that were included in the summer and autumn HMV catalogues were 'What Will You do, Love?', 'Molly Bawn and Brian Og' and 'The Lovely Sailor Boy'. They were rapturously received everywhere they went.

It was at a meeting of the Dublin Centre of PEN in 1937 that Hayward first discovered the singing voice of Delia Murphy, known as the 'Queen of Connemara'. They enjoyed a fruitful four-year partnership performing on stage together and recording duets for HMV. Murphy went on to become Ireland's first celebrity woman singer.

But it was one of Murphy's solo performances that would remain etched in the memory. On Easter Tuesday, 15 April 1941, she travelled to Belfast to take part in *Céilidhe Mhór na Cásca* (The great ceilidh of Easter). Despite the war and the oppressiveness of the blackout, a holiday atmosphere prevailed in the city and life was as normal as possible. The Easter weather had been very warm and people were in good spirits. Theatre-goers had been enjoying the Savoy Players performing Jerome K. Jerome's *The Passing of the Third Floor Back* at the Opera House while at the Empire Theatre, a comedy revue, *April Showers*, attracted crowds. James Cagney and Ann Sheridan starred in *Torrid Zone* at the Ritz Cinema, and George Formby was at the Royal Cinema in *It's in the Air*. Hundreds made their way to a dance at the Floral Hall in north Belfast, a favourite social venue.

That evening Murphy sang to a packed Ulster Hall, just a few doors away from Hayward's office in Bedford Street in the city centre, but on this occasion he was not performing with her. She had always attracted enormous audience enthusiasm in Belfast where she had built up a loyal following. Amongst the songs she performed that night were 'Boston Burglar', 'Moonlight in Mayo', and 'If I were a Blackbird.' The relaxed crowd, who had paid two shillings and sixpence admission, sang along and danced – no one could have anticipated what was about to happen and that the city would be rocked to its foundations.

In a night of drama and horror the Luftwaffe attacked Belfast. One hundred and eighty bombers of the German air force dropped incendiaries that lit up the way for high-explosive bombs and parachute mines. Residential districts were the main targets. Parts of the west and the east were hit but the north of the city – the New Lodge, lower Shankill and Antrim Road with its narrow congested streets and back-to-back terraces – bore the brunt, mainly because this area had not been able to recruit any fire watchers. It was a devastating night, which left more than 900 dead and 100,000 homeless.

Belfast had no experience of what London had already witnessed many times and was hopelessly underprepared for the raids. The previous day, Easter Monday, people had made their way to shelters after a German plane was spotted on what had been a reconnaissance mission. A week before, on the morning of 8 April, German bombers had taken part in an attack on the docks, dropping showers of incendiary bombs, killing thirteen people and injuring eighty-one. On this occasion the city centre and most of the landmark buildings escaped largely unscathed but nearly half of all the homes in the city were damaged.

People at the concert became fearful. Most had no idea of the scale of the carnage, the panic and confusion on the streets, the extent of the exploding bombs, the raging fires with flames and smoke spiralling hundreds of feet, the wailing sirens and the drone of aircraft. Remarkably, through it all, Murphy kept cool on the Ulster Hall stage. She continued to sing, encouraging the audience to remain and keep singing along. Some did stay, but not all. As the bombs continued to rain down, people rushed home stumbling through the moon-light, amazed at the bright sky. Many were largely unaware of the seriousness of the damage wreaked on their city until they saw the blackened shells of build-ings and persistent fires. Gerry Hobbs, who was performing that night with the St Gall's Boys' Choir, recalls the events:

> It had been a very hot day and lots of people had turned out for the ceilidh. The hall was full to the rafters. The McCusker Brothers, a traditional group of nine brothers from south Armagh, had been entertaining the crowd from early on. About ten o'clock we went on stage and sang a Tom Moore song 'Silent, O Moyle, be the Roar of thy Water,' as well as 'The Lark in the Clear Air,' and 'The Croppy Boy.' After we had performed we heard some bangs and several loud booms. One of the Christian Brothers with us said to me 'Hobbs there's a bloody air raid on.' We were told to stay in the hall and not to move. Delia Murphy came on and announced that we were advised not to leave the hall. She said we will try to entertain you as best we can and to the delight of the crowd she started into a few dances including 'The Waves of Tory', 'The Walls of Limerick' and 'The Siege of Ennis.' She continued singing although people were on edge and we stayed in the hall until 2 am. We made it up the Grosvenor Road with two of the Brothers through a lot of noises and flashes and on to the Springfield Road where I was staying with my aunt and uncle. We got home safe and the next morning I was sent out to another aunt and uncle who lived at Killough in the County Down countryside. That was my home for the next three years. [20]

In his book on the Belfast blitz, Brian Barton states that Jimmy Magee, the gardener at Clonard Monastery who had been at the concert, left the hall hurriedly, 'convinced that he would be safer in the monastery's grounds … where he was amazed to find a number of priests sitting calmly in the garden.' But Barton points out, that for others, leaving the concert was a prelude to tragedy. 'Jimmy Doherty recalls that some of his colleagues in the air raid precautions services had also attended it. As they returned home, he last heard them walking up Clifton Street, still singing to keep their spirits up. They failed to notice a parachute bomb which came down and struck a church on Trinity Street. All of them died in the subsequent explosion.'[21]

Those who attended Murphy's Easter Tuesday concert treasured the elec-
trifying performance. It was a night that has gone down in the annals of Irish
music history, remaining in the memory of the people who survived. In its
report of the raids, which it called 'Murder Unlimited', the *Irish News* described
Murphy as 'A Dublin Heroine', saying her bravery during the height of the blitz
had been the subject of much discussion in Belfast. 'As bombs rained down,
many of the women present became fearful of the consequences. Miss Murphy,
however, remained perfectly cool, keeping singing continuously, asking those
present to join her.'[22]

The five-hour aerial bombardment, involving nearly 700 bombs, destroyed
the York Street spinning mill, Ewart's weaving mill, Wilton's funeral parlour and
the central telephone exchange, which meant that contact with the anti-aircraft-
operations control room was cut off. The Antrim Road, where Hayward lived,
was particularly badly affected. Entire rows of houses in Duncairn Gardens,
Atlantic Avenue, Hillman Street and Eia Street were destroyed. Hayward's
rented house, Richmond Lodge, at the junction of the Antrim and Cavehill
roads, where they had lived since the early 1930s, suffered serious shrapnel and
blast damage. The roof was pierced and all but two windows lost their glass.
Earlier in the day they enjoyed a family outing and lunch at the Slieve Donard
Hotel in Newcastle, later basking in glorious sunshine. Ricky, then just six, who
had lived in the house since birth, takes up the story:

> We had also watched *Snow White* in the cinema. There was a scene in the film
> in which a stone is dropped down a wishing well and causes an echo when it
> hits the bottom. On that night of the blitz I dreamt that I was dropping stones
> down that well, until the booming noises woke me. I got up and looked out
> through the window across the Waterworks and there were a lot of exciting
> fires. My parents quickly came in and found me standing in front of one of
> the two windows that weren't smashed by the blast. We went immediately
> under the stairs and stayed there for a while. They were quite calm about it.
> When I woke up the next morning the plaster was falling from the ceiling
> and dust was in the air. Dion had been on ARP duties which was fortunate
> for him since a piece of shrapnel that came through the roof of our house
> went through his bed and ended up in the table downstairs.[23]

Next morning Hayward cycled into the city centre to check if there was
any damage to his office in Bedford Street. Along the length of the Antrim
Road and at Carlisle Circus, he saw the devastation caused by the overnight
attacks and the 'horrific scenes of neighbouring streets destroyed and lives torn

apart.'[24] He passed knots of onlookers gathered in disbelief beside the craters, some picking their way through tons of debris. Smoke was curling from the ruins of burnt-out and smouldering buildings while broken glass littered the streets. When he arrived at his office he was relieved to find that it had escaped unscathed. The worst damage had been confined to residential areas rather than the city centre.

In the late 1930s and forties Hayward continued to record, although not so prolifically. When shellac, from which records were then made, became in short supply with the outbreak of war, his UK work with Decca came to an end. He switched to recording in Dublin where he also made regular appearances, flitting between both the Theatre Royal in Hawkins Street and the Olympia Theatre in Dame Street. The Theatre Royal, which had reopened in 1935, specialized in a unique hybrid entertainment package known as cine-variety in which a stage show and film were included for the price of one ticket. With 3850 seats it was the biggest theatre in Ireland and one of Europe's largest. It succeeded in bringing Hayward's work to the attention of a wider Southern audience; by now he was public property across the whole island.

In a Dublin cinema Hayward performed songs from *The Early Bird*, which had achieved success both as a play and film in 1936 and he was hailed as a 'Famous Irish film star'.

As part of a week-long comedy programme, his film *The Early Bird* was shown from 8 February 1937. A billboard listed him as one of three 'great top liners' and declaimed 'Irish film star in person'. *The Irish Times* said he sang some of his popular numbers and gave examples of 'pawky humour', which were thoroughly enjoyed. In the run up to St Patrick's Day in 1939, the theatre staged a week-long all-star cine-variety *Greatest All-Irish Show* with Hayward, the Irish-American vocalist, John Feeney, Maria Vianni, known as 'Dublin's Queen of Song' and Paddy Drew. This programme included what was described on the handbill as 'an exclusive presentation' of Hayward's film *In the Footsteps of St Patrick*.

The outbreak of war had restricted the availability of American films, paving the way for local amateur and professional variety artists to take the stage. For Hayward, with his songs, humorous revues and films, the theatre was an ideal outlet for his combined show. The Theatre Royal became a leading place of popular culture for Dubliners. Around the same time as he was appearing, the theatre's permanent high-kicking dance troupe, The Royalettes were amongst the attractions. It also fostered the careers of Noel Purcell, Peggy Dell and Danny Cummins, as well as two of Hayward's accomplices, Harry O'Donovan and Jimmy O'Dea.

In February 1941 Anna Meakin provided the piano accompaniment in Dublin when Hayward recorded nine duets with her for Decca; these included 'Yellow Rose of Texas', 'Nell Flaherty's Drake', 'Kathleen O'More' and 'Brian O'Linn'. Three years later, in February 1944, he was back in Dublin to record a further seven songs. From time to time he made appearances with Meakin. Under the name The Irish Troubadours they jointly devised a night of song, dance and story. In August 1940 they featured at the Theatre Royal on a week-long 'Irish Song and Story' holiday entertainment bill along with the soprano May Devitt. 'His melodious Northern brogue,' said the *Evening Herald*, which photographed the three singers at a race meeting at Baldoyle, Seapoint, 'is used to full advantage in song and in story. He is accompanied by Miss Anna Meakin, a clever pianiste.'[25] The same show, renamed 'A Spot of Irish,' ran twice-nightly for two weeks at the Olympia in spring 1941 and at the Royal Hippodrome in Belfast. Devitt later accompanied the Irish tenor Josef Locke on stage at the Victoria Palace in London.

Around this time, Hayward was actively involved in promoting the gramophone societies springing up in many places. He was president of the Belfast Gramophone Society in 1945 and held fortnightly recitals in the Union Hotel in Donegall Square South in the city centre. On 7 September 1949, after his talk, 'Bird Song in Music', he demonstrated the new Decca gramophone for use in education. He also gave programmes of recitals to the Dublin Gramophone Society. His notes show music and opera interests that he selected for the Dublin Gramophone Society on 7 December 1949.[26] His selections included 'If Music be the Food of Love' by Purcell from *Twelfth Night*, 'Elegy on the Death of Robert Emmet', Beethoven's Symphony No 8 in F Major and the Concerto Grosso in D by Handel. Gramophone circles, he believed, could be an aid to musical appreciation: 'Never try to play several very long works at one sitting; it is much better to have people wanting more than feeling they have had too much.'[27]

After the war Hayward resumed his visits to London, kick-starting his recording career again. During four separate sessions in the autumn and winter of 1947 in the new Decca studios at Broadhurst Gardens, twenty songs were recorded. They included old favourites 'Johnny I Hardly Knew you', 'Little Brigit Flynn' and 'County Mayo Fragment'. Hayward sang with a male quartet directed by Roy Robertson. By this stage in his musical career he was regarded as a consummate professional. Moore Orr was present at two of the recording sessions and described the scene:

> Roy Robertson with his small orchestra of selected soloists were in the Decca studios and the atmosphere was a perfect blend of extreme efficiency and good fellowship. I am sure Richard Hayward would be the first to agree with me that he had grand support, not only from this most knowledgeable conductor but also from the recordist, both of whom remarked to the effect that it was a pleasure to work with Richard because he is always in good form, never pretends to know all, takes advice like a novice and makes work into fun and more fun.[28]

At the other two recording sessions in 1947 Hayward was accompanied by two women. In September, Aileen MacArdle, a young woman he had known since her schooldays and whose career he had followed with interest, played the harp. She was the solo harp with the Belfast Philharmonic Orchestra and played with the BBC Irish Rhythms Orchestra. They recorded seven songs including 'My Lagan Love', 'The Galway Shawl', and 'The Gartan Mother's Lullaby'. At the other session, with the Roy Robertson Orchestra, he sang with Zuilmah Hopkins. Hayward had met Hopkins, who was born in Dublin, at a concert at Newtown School run by the Quakers in Waterford where Ricky was a pupil. He organized an audition with Decca and engaged her to sing duets with him. They recorded two of his best-known numbers, 'The Humour is on Me Now' and 'What Will You do, Love?'

Decca
MUSIC
REVIEW

JULY, 1950

Issued by
CA RECORD CO., LTD., LONDON

FRANKIE VAUGHAN
rise to fame of twenty-two-year-old Frankie
obably astonished nobody more than it did
self. Only a few weeks ago he was a
artist looking for a job : now he is touring
t a three-figure salary, and he has already
st recordings for Decca. Full details are on

ency   range recording

VERA LYNN   LEE LAWRENCE

VERA LYNN and LEE LAWRENCE (Vocal)
with BOB FARNON AND HIS ORCHESTRA
CHERRY STONES

VERA LYNN
with BOB FARNON AND HIS ORCHESTRA
YOUR HEART AND MY HEART ....◆F 9448
(Mid-June release)
with THE GEORGE MITCHELL CHOIR and BOB FARNON
AND HIS ORCHESTRA
ON THE OUTGOING TIDE
LOVE FINDS A WAY (From "My Dream is
Yours") .... F 9442

LEE LAWRENCE (Vocal)
with BRUCE CAMPBELL AND HIS ORCHESTRA
MARTA
THE WORLD IS MINE TONIGHT .... F 9438

LEO FULD (Vocal)
with BRUCE CAMPBELL AND HIS ORCHESTRA
C'EST SI BON
MY SONG GOES ROUND THE WORLD .... F 9434
with THE MITCHELL MEN and BRUCE CAMPBELL
AND HIS ORCHESTRA
THE SONG OF THE NEGEV
YOU'RE THE SWEETEST IN THE LAND ...... F 9411

HARRY ROY
AND HIS ORCHESTRA
STRUTTIN' IN THE STRAND Vocalists : EVE
LOMBARD, HARRY ROY and JOHNNY
GREEN
YOU'RE MY BABY Vocalist: HARRY ROY......◆F 9450
(Mid-June release)

◆ New issue this month

ROBERT STOLZ
AND HIS CONCERT ORCHESTRA
"DIE KINOKÖNIGIN "—Waltz (Robert Stolz)
"DIE KEUSCHE SUSANNE "—Waltz (Robert
Stolz) ....F 9447

THE TONHALLE ORCHESTRA, ZURICH
Conducted by ROBERT STOLZ
SELECTION OF POPULAR MELODIES No. 1
(Robert Stolz) ....K 2287
SELECTION OF POPULAR MELODIES No. 2
(Robert Stolz) ....K 2296

PAUL VAUGHAN
AND HIS QUARTET
from Selby's Restaurant, London
EASTERN DANCES (2 sides) ....◆F 9463

RICHARD
HAYWARD

RICHARD HAYWARD
(Traditional Ballad Singer)
with harp accompaniment by AILEEN MacARDLE
THE GARTAN MOTHER'S LULLABY
(HE CASTLE OF DROMORE ....◆C 16126

ARMANDO OREFICHE
AND HIS HAVANA CUBAN BOYS
CARINOSAMENTE—Bolero Vocalist : PEGGY
Walsh
RUMBA ARGENTINA—Guaracha mambo
Vocalist : PEGGY WALSH ....◆C 16124

LES SOEURS ETIENNE (Vocal)
with orchestra conducted by RAYMOND LEGRAND
LA MARCHINA—Samba
QUI SAIT, QUI SAIT, QUI SAIT—Bolero (Perhaps,
perhaps, perhaps) ....◆C 16121

◆ New issue this month

Decca Music Review, July 1950 showcased a young Frankie Vaughan as well as Vera Lynn and Lee Lawrence alongside Hayward who that year recorded 'The Gartan Mother's Lullaby' and 'The Castle of Dromore'.

In a lengthy profile and interview in *Disc* in 1948, Hayward gave an insight into the recordings and how he collected songs. The article was the sixth in the series featuring 'Gramophone Personalities', and was written by Discus:

Hayward [he wrote] had more strings to his Irish harp than most singers would claim. In all his many achievements he has succeeded in presenting the dignity and clean humour of Irish life in a way which must be the envy of many like-minded artists. Referring to his new records, Hayward spoke of his satisfaction with them. 'I'm pleased with their dynamics, their liveliness, the crisp diction in which I can hear not only every syllable but almost every letter, and their general characteristics.'[29]

Speaking about 'Johnny I Hardly Knew you', which he described as 'a grim eighteenth-century anti-war ballad – ferociously satirical', he provided a structural insight into the musicality he had put into the song:

Note the manner in which I have set it: continuous movement – never a break in the inevitable march on of events – four drum beats: verse: two drum beats: chorus: and so on, without variation, to the end. I'd very much like to say a lot about this setting which is my very own. Through years I have worked it up and now I think it is perfect in idea and suggestion. I have always wanted to do an unaccompanied folk-song. Well, I've done it, and this is how I got the chance. Percy French's delightful 'Little Brigit Flynn' left me an inch to go, so I filled up with 'County Mayo Fragment' without saying anything about it. The recording manager was cross at first and then said, 'Richard, that's the best thing you've ever done'. The fragment itself I took down in County Mayo late one night – in a pub – from an inebriated ballad singer who responded to my offer of a few pints of Guinness.[30]

'Discus' was clearly impressed with Hayward's style and his musical knowledge. At the end of the profile, he summed up how the performance had come across to him:

One is immediately infected with his enthusiasm, apparently inexhaustible energy, and warm-hearted good humour. He has an incomparable gift for story-telling and will hold one enthralled whilst he etches in the Irish scene and character with vivid, authentic anecdotes born of a lasting and abiding love for this country. Folk-song and the music of the Irish harp are an everlasting passion, and as a ballad singer he is a master of his art.[31]

SIX

Name in lights

(1935–1939)

Dublin is about to go mad over the little songs of Ulster, ripplingly-rhythmed and sung by the laughing voice of Richard Hayward.

Irish Press review of *The Luck of the Irish*, 1936

In the middle decades of the twentieth century, the 'pictures' were the main form of entertainment in Ireland. Most towns – even small ones – had a cherished picture house that was a social meeting place. Television was still some years away, but by 1939 about half of all households in Northern Ireland owned a radio and a visit to the cinema represented an escape from the drabness of the depressed thirties. When cinemas opened in the Edwardian era, civic leaders in some areas regarded them with suspicion. In Belfast, cinemas could not be built within a 350-ft radius of churches, and in Dublin license to show Sunday films by a Dame Street cinema was rejected to prevent the 'lower classes' mingling with church-goers. It was often said in Derry that the 'pictures' were more popular than prayers. Some cinemas started life as barns or shops and many were multi-functional, hosting dances, concerts and plays as well as films.

By 1936 there were more than a hundred permanent cinemas in Northern Ireland alone. Long queues often formed to see big names such as Bing Crosby, Bob Hope, Mae West, Hedy Lamarr and Clark Gable. In the cities, the picture houses attracted audiences in their thousands. In 1927 the Cinematograph Films Act raised the number of British films made and shown in the UK in the face of stiff competition and stipulated that films under this arrangement should be made in Britain or the 'Empire' with a British scenarist.

The 'quota quickie' system as it was known, forced companies such as Paramount to make a percentage of local films. By 1938, when a new act eradicated the 'quickies', the quota had risen to twenty percent. This increase matched the British production figures – from 131 films during 1928–29 to 228 films during 1937–38.[1] To help fill the percentage many poor-quality pictures were produced and some were shot in Ireland. The first Irish full-length 'talkie' *The Dawn*, filmed in Killarney in 1936, attracted crowds at the local cinema. Set in the era of the war of independence and the Black and Tans, it is part documentary, part romance. Some years earlier, a film industry had been established by the Kalem Company in nearby Beaufort. At the same time as this film was being made in the southwest of the country, 300 miles away in the far northeast corner of Ireland, filming of the first Ulster 'talkie' *The Luck of the Irish* was underway in Glynn, an Antrim coastal village just a few miles from Larne where Hayward grew up. A cast of more than a hundred, comprising actors, cameramen, technicians and extras, assembled in Glynn in mid September 1935 to start filming.

It was produced by the Irish International Film Agency, a company set up that same year by Hayward along with two other directors, Hugh McAleavey and Harold Goldblatt, an aspiring young actor. *The Luck of the Irish* was based on a novel by the writer, director, producer and former soldier, Lt-Colonel Victor Haddick, from Donaghadee in County Down who was educated at the Royal Belfast Academical Institution. Haddick was a colourful character who had built up considerable reputation as a linguist and spoke several European, African and Asian languages. He had a military career in the Leinster Regiment and was severely wounded in the Dardanelles campaign in the First World War. One of his claims to fame was as the inventor of the Haddick Field Kitchen, widely used by the Indian Army. A member of the first Everest expedition of 1924, he was the last man to see Mallory and Irvine alive on their tragic adventure.

The plot centres on an Irishman trying to save his ancestral home through the fortunes of Knockavoe, a racehorse. The film draws on the life of country people and the shopkeeping middle classes. Set in the fictional village of Tyr Owen in County Tyrone, the story concerns the fortunes of the O'Neills. Sir Brian O'Neill, played by Jimmy Mageean, borrows £2000 to bet on his horse, ridden by his son Derek, to win the Grand National. When Knockavoe wins the race the villagers descend on the pub, celebrating their luck in a communal sing-song led by Hayward playing the part of Sam Mulhern, the village factotum. However, the horse is subsequently disqualified and Sir Brian is faced with the loss of his home Tyr Owen Castle. Mulhern tries to help by coming up with an idea of making fake Celtic vases but his ruse is discovered. Sir Brian is rescued at the eleventh hour by the arrival of an American, Colonel Peverett, who pays 5000 guineas for the horse.

The film starred the grand old man of the Irish stage, R.H. McCandless, playing the part of Gavin Grogan, along with Kay Walsh, Niall MacGinnis, Charles Fagan, Harold Griffin and Charlotte Tedlie. Most of the cast knew each other since many had acted with Hayward's Belfast Repertory Company or the earlier Radio Players. Mageean, a life-long friend of Hayward's, had produced all the plays for the repertory company and shared the leading parts. In the Irish films made at this time, few if any of the actors had professional training but they gripped the public imagination and the fact that the films were being made locally guaranteed a ready audience.

Hayward played the part of Sam Mulhern in *The Luck of the Irish*. In this scene he leads the villagers in a communal sing-song as they celebrate a horse they backed that won the Grand National.

Jimmy Mageean, on the left, a long-standing acting friend from stage plays of the 1920s, raises a toast in *The Luck of the Irish*. The film marked a breakthrough in Hayward's career and in his transition from stage to screen.

The Luck of the Irish was Donovan Pedelty's directorial debut and he was also the scenarist. Hayward had met him in London the previous year when he had wandered into the Intrepid Fox, a bar in Wardour Street in Soho and began chatting to a complete stranger who turned out to be Pedelty. A writer and film talent scout with the Hollywood studio, Paramount, he was working on a Scottish drama and looking for an Irish story. He signed up Hayward to appear as the Earl of Cameron in *Flame in the Heather*, a historical drama set during the Jacobite Rebellion in 1745 and the first Scottish 'talkie'. Released in September 1935, it starred Gwenllian Gill, Barry Clifton and Kenneth McLaglen.

Haddick had given Hayward the script before he went to London to see if he could interest someone in its production, and by chance, Hayward had found the right man. It was a stroke of luck that demonstrated his knack of striking up conversation and engaging strangers, something at which Hayward was adept. Several years earlier, in 1932, he had worked with Haddick on the first indigenous sound picture ever made in Ireland: *The Voice of Ireland*, a photographic study of the four Irish provinces through the seasons. Hayward took on 'The Voice of Ulster' section, sang 'The Girls of Coleraine' and 'The Inniskilling Dragoon', and delivered commentary in the character of the humorous farmer and poteen maker Sam Mulhern, a homespun wit and philosopher. On its release, the *Belfast News Letter*, the paper of the Unionist community, called *The Voice of Ireland* 'an unqualified success', adding that Hayward's 'authentic Ulster dialect which he uses will surely come very warmly to the ears of those having connection to Northern Ireland.'[2] The Nationalist *Irish News* praised the songs, instrumental music and dialogue as being 'undoubtedly a treat' but suggested that the 'popular use of Derry for Londonderry, one would think, would have caught the local atmosphere better.'[3] *Kinematograph Weekly* described the recording as 'generally harsh' and said that 'when a close-up of a singer or instrumentalist is required, the performer is made-up in a way suggesting the crudest amateur theatricals.'[4] Years later Hayward acknowledged that *The Voice of Ireland* was a made on 'a shoestring budget with a vengeance ... but in spite of a poor sound track and many crudities in direction and production the picture was a success and turned out to be the veritable seedbed of Irish film production.'[5] It was the character of Mulhern that Haddick had enlarged into the star of *The Luck of the Irish*. Before the start of filming, the *Irish News* interviewed Pedelty who predicted it would be a big success:

> It has in its favour, that as there are more Irishmen living outside Ireland than live in Ireland, an Irish picture has an audience ready made for it all over the world. Our picture should appeal to them, as it combines comedy with a touch of sentiment, the blend of which Irish people are so fond.[6]

The film-makers' chief anxiety was the weather. Pedelty said if the sun did not appear they may have to go back to England and make the picture at Elstree Studios in Hertfordshire. Asked if the Northern Ireland dialect would not be difficult to make intelligible to cinema audiences, he replied, 'Not at all. After all, it's no worse than the Scottish.' The film led to much curiosity in Glynn. Extra police were called in from Larne to regulate the traffic and control the enthusiastic crowds. James Patton, who was a child at the time, later described the scene:

> There were lorries everywhere, with giant lights, and camera crews were everywhere, it was just pandemonium, but, standing in the midst of all this flutter was a very ordinary looking man who was pointed out as the star, the country folk of course were used to stars like Wallace Beery, Edmund Lowe and James Cagney and such, so there were mutterings of 'He doesn't luk lak a star' and 'What dae they need a' thae lights for, can they no see?' But things were different when the star sang 'There was an 'oul man from Killyburn Brae' and 'The Bright Silvery Light of the Moon.' Between takes, as they say in the film world, all the kids would rush to the centre of the set to the annoyance of the film people, but Hayward had a word for us all when the

time came to resume, it was, 'Now, there's the good childer' if you'll just move back a little way you'll all see more picture-taking,' not so with a fussy little man who told me in no refined way, 'Get back t'hell or that.'[7]

A friend of Hayward's from Larne, John Clifford, who wrote one-act kitchen country plays and performed them locally, appeared as an extra in the film. The two men met in 1934 when Hayward was staging *Castlereagh* at the Empire Theatre and asked Clifford to take part in a curtain raiser. From then on, Clifford recalled in his diaries, the two remained firm friends:

> I would never have gone to London had it not been that Richard invited me over to the Fox Film Studios in 1936 to complete some indoor shots. There and then I fell in love with London and went over there again in 1937 to remain for thirty years. I met Richard often when he came to London on business or to record some of his ballads at the recording studio. I never tired of listening to him singing to the accompaniment of the harp.[8]

Clifford became a civil servant in London, remaining there until his retirement. His enthusiasm for his old friend from Larne led to his naming his son Raymond Hayward Clifford in his honour. For the three-week shoot, the location headquarters for the crew was the Olderfleet Hotel at Larne harbour, round the corner from where Hayward grew up. The filming at Glynn featured the local post office while the steeplechase scene took place at Upton Castle, Templepatrick, in County Antrim; other scenes were shot at Laurel Hill Convent in Limerick and the rest completed in the Elstree Studios. Billed as 'Ulster's first feature film', the publicity material described Hayward as 'Ireland's Noël Coward', though it said that 'he himself deprecates the title'.

In London the trade presentation took place at the Carlton Theatre in Haymarket on 6 December 1935 and it premiered at the Imperial Picture House in Belfast a week later on 13 December. Guests at the screening, which was a semi-official occasion, included Lady Craigavon, the Lord Mayor of Belfast, Sir Crawford McCullagh, and G.B. Hanna, Parliamentary Secretary to the Ministry of Home Affairs. The film received public acclaim when it opened early the next year at the Belfast Picture House in Royal Avenue where it played four times a day and was extended for an extra week. Crowds waited several hours to gain admission and on the night of the final showing the queues were still as long as on the opening night. The *Belfast News Letter* said Hayward, 'adds droll wit to dry philosophy in a characterization subtly observed and cleverly portrayed.'[9] Describing it as 'a delightful comedy, so rich in Ulster humour,

Ulster songs, and Ulster scenery', the *Belfast Telegraph* praised 'a most accomplished cast of Ulster artistes headed by Hayward. It is a great success – and it deserves to be.'[10] The *Irish News* said the entertainment value of the picture lies chiefly in the acting by Hayward and his company and in the 'racy dialogue ... The outdoor shots are delightful but too much of the cribbed, cabined and confined in indoor settings ... and some of the groceries and advertisements were a trifle blatant in the shop scene.'[11]

On St Valentine's Day 1936, the Irish release of the film in Dublin was greeted with widespread critical approval. *The Irish Press* said it had made Hayward 'a soaring star'. 'Dublin is about to go mad,' the paper's critic chirruped, 'over the little songs of Ulster, ripplingly-rhythmed and sung by the laughing voice of Richard Hayward.'[12] The *Irish Independent* declared it 'an outstanding film success' while the *Dublin Evening Herald* said:

> The film was packed with deft humorous touches which the players appreciated very thoroughly. Richard Hayward is a real star, and he ambles through the picture easily, leaving a trail of laughter behind him, and some very fine songs ... The public like it, and it is the public who count.'[13]

The *Limerick Leader* felt that Hayward, Haddick and Pedelty had united to bring Irish films a big step forward. 'In honouring themselves they have honoured Ireland. This is a spectacular success, and it is so without having recourse to stage-Irish absurdity or the belittling of our country.'[14] Writing in the *Daily Express*, Alexander Boath complained about the title: 'The film is about Ulster, for Ulster, by Ulster,' he wrote, 'but its title is *The Luck of the Irish*. I wonder why.'[15] One reason was that Hayward and the producers felt there was more chance of winning audiences in Britain and the US by selling it as an 'Irish' film rather than an 'Ulster' one. In an editorial, 'Ireland on the Screen' the day after the press show, the *Irish News* said there was a need for a new film industry to be developed:

> It is not a super production, and the caustic critic will find flaws in it, but on the whole it is quite a creditable effort and proves conclusively that this part of the world can be put attractively and interestingly on the screen ... No other country possesses such an abundance of scenic value, and the old bogey of adverse climatic conditions has been overcome by the advance of cinematographic apparatus. A vast public of Irish exiles all over the world would welcome films made in the homeland as has been proved by the success of the few produced in their country.[16]

The Luck of the Irish marked a breakthrough for Hayward in his film career and in his transition from stage to screen. It was a courageous and ambitious undertaking. He aspired to realism and felt that the film showed Ireland as it really was. His philosophy was 'Irish players for Irish parts' and he thought audiences in Britain and the US would not be offended by any stage-Irish tricks or be annoyed by Irish parts portrayed by non-Irish players. He was determined to avoid the clichéd portrayal of Ireland that many films in the 1920s and early thirties presented. Films with drunken fighting Irishmen, the streetwise gombeen, the priests and fanatics, were anathema to him. Writing more than twenty years later, Hayward explained that he had been determined to make it a 'real Irish picture':

> I had seen too many synthetic Irish productions that had no more connection with Ireland than begorra has with normal Irish speech. English actors playing Irish parts and speaking in some astonishing jargon that was supposed to be connected with Clare or Killarney had long been the bane of my life, and I took a vow that the case of my picture would be free of this horrible plague.[17]

When the film crossed the Atlantic early in 1936 it was an immediate hit on Broadway. It opened on 15 January at New York's 47th Street Cinema on a night of severe snow. Hayward was quoted in the press saying, 'In a cable received in Belfast today it is stated that during the worst weather in living memory of New Yorkers *The Luck of the Irish* has attracted excellent audiences.'[18] *Variety* magazine felt the film would be popular with Irish-America:

> With a little of the proverbial Celtic good fortune and the application of a soft pedal on the fact that the case and story are both indigenous to northern Ireland, this all-Irish film should do well among the sons of Erin. Since most of the Irish comes from the southern Catholic three-quarters of the isle, and the animosity towards the upper eastern corner is well known, knowledge of the film's origin won't help.[19]

Hayward travelled to the US with Cunard White Star Line, disembarking at Boston before moving on to other parts of the country as well as Canada to help in its promotion and to market the Ulster film industry. The purpose of his visit was to find out if there was a demand for Irish pictures and he discovered huge interest. He hired a car in Quebec, visiting Montreal, Toronto and New York as well as small towns. In Boston he was received by Governor Curley, an Irishman at the State House. Elsewhere he met town mayors and in the interest of political correctness, brought letters of greeting from the Lord Mayors of both Belfast and

Dublin. Hayward schmoozed the American media, meeting the press and radio, addressing press clubs, Women's Leagues and other organizations, taking out a copy of the film and showing it in various states. On his return, in a lengthy interview with the *Irish News* he described the reaction in Toronto:

> The people rose to their feet after seeing the picture and cheered for fully five minutes, making it impossible for the next picture to be heard. There were cries from the audience of 'We want more of them, this is the real Irish stuff and no imitation.'[20]

Asked for his impressions of the Irish in America he said that he found them very happy. 'They are well off and glad to see me as a representative of the old country. They went out of their way to entertain me and make my visit as pleasant as possible.'[21] Another aspect of the film's production was the potential tourism spin-off. Hayward hoped that using local scenes would appeal to visitors and that the songs of the soil of the country would also find favour. In 1924 the Ulster Tourist Development Association (UTDA, precursor to the Northern Ireland Tourist Board) had been set up to promote the region. The organization was keen to market the area as a tourist destination by encouraging newsreel companies such as Pathé and British Movietone to visit as well as exhorting film-makers to include Northern Ireland in travelogues showing off its scenery. The UTDA had contributed £100 towards the Northern section of *The Voice of Ireland* in 1932.[22]

Hayward appeared in and narrated another tourist board film, *Irish Travelogue*, a documentary made in 1935 about different parts of Northern Ireland. It included shots of Belfast and Bangor, the Glens of Antrim and Dunluce Castle. He was featured on the honeycomb seat of the wishing chair at the Giant's Causeway and in nearby Coleraine is seen merrily walking through the streets of the town accompanied by six women. The UTDA realized the potential of the new film industry and launched a film fund. The company had supported features involving Hayward, which had also been assisted by the Ulster Industries Development Association (UIDA). In 1936 Hayward and Elma appeared in a UIDA publicity film *Star of Ulster*. The film was designed to promote Ulster-made products and showcase the Association's Star Emblem, a six-pointed badge representing the six Northern counties. As well as writing the script and music, Hayward appeared as Andy McDade, a fictional character based on a County Antrim farmer who encourages his wife Mary to buy more Ulster produce. A pamphlet, *Andy McDade*, produced in 1929 and written in

Ulster dialect, was published by the UIDA. In his survey, *Cinema and Northern Ireland*, John Hill suggests it seems likely that Hayward wrote this and another pamphlet called *Andy's Mary*, although both are uncredited.[23]

Buoyed by the success of *The Luck of the Irish,* Hayward and Pedelty moved swiftly on to their next cinematic venture and outlined ambitious plans for more films. On 14 February 1936, the date of the film's Irish release, Hayward set up his own company, Richard Hayward Film Productions Ltd., with the backing of local businesses including Bushmills Distillery. The company's registered offices were at his Bedford Street base. He described himself as 'actor and film artist'. He was chairman and the directors were Frederick Collier, Harold Goldblatt, James Montgomery, Hugh McAleavey and Samuel Wilson Boyd. Its share capital was £5000, divided into 5000 shares of £1 each. Hayward announced a programme of three films for 1936 and predicted to the media that the establishment of local studios could become a 'distinct possibility'.[24] A media-savvy Hayward courted the press, enjoying the publicity he received in return yet never forgetting the power of having them on his side. Paramount had collaborated with Crusade Films set up by Pedelty with Victor Greene. Crusade was responsible for two other Hayward films about to enter production, *The Early Bird* and *Irish and Proud of It.*

At the start of June 1936 work began on *The Early Bird* with filming lasting a week. The company then left Belfast on the Liverpool boat to start work at Elstree where the studio scenes were completed. Written by the Coleraine-born author and dramatist James Douglas, *The Early Bird* was a film version of the play staged by the repertory company at the Empire Theatre before the screening of *The Luck of the Irish.* The film was produced by Norris Davidson who had assisted the Irish–American director Robert Flaherty in making *Man of Aran.*

Set in the fictional Irish village of Ballytober, the location was again the Antrim coast with Glenarm and Carnlough chosen as the villages for filming. Hayward took on the central role of Daniel Duff, a small farmer. Humour was once more the keynote. It was described by Hayward as 'a very well-constructed comedy on robust country lines' that made use of the popular matchmaking theme. The storyline focuses on the rivalry between Duff and the local vet Charlie Simpson (Jimmy Mageean) for the hand of an attractive widow Rose Madill (Nan Cullen) and Susan (Elma Hayward) who played the part of Duff's niece. Musical interludes feature Hayward singing with footage of the scenery of the Antrim coastline. Among the songs he performed were 'The Comber

Ballad' and one of his favourites 'The Mutton Burn Stream', which became a
Hayward party piece.

The Belfast premiere was sponsored by the UIDA and held at the Picture
House on 27 November 1936. The film was also chosen to be shown at the
opening of the new luxury Broadway Cinema on the Falls Road in mid
December. Hayward attended, along with Nan Cullen, Jimmy Mageean and
Charles Fagan and said he was delighted to help the St Vincent de Paul Society
to which the proceeds were donated. After numerous requests from the audience he sang two ballads: 'The Bright Silvery Light of the Moon' and 'The
Ould man of Killyburn brae.'[25] The *Belfast Telegraph* described it as a 'merry
comedy of life and love … a feast of fun … the film will show Ulster at its best
and loveliest and will cause many a heart-throb of Ulster people in Canada and
the United States when it is shown there this winter.'[26] The paper later quoted
Owen Kelly, the President of St Vincent de Paul, saying Hayward's 'elevation
in his profession had been watched with great pleasure.' In its review, the *Irish
News* said the film was enthusiastically received:

> It is alive with a typical Ulster village humour and, made to suit a particular
> audience, will undoubtedly please that audience. The actors were handi-
> capped to a certain extent by the fact that there was very little in the nature
> of a sound plot. Making due allowance for that defect, they did all that was
> expected of them in a thoroughly convincing fashion. The comedy element
> is predominant, and it is this which will please future audiences.[27]

The paper found that the camera and lighting work were not altogether
satisfying, but that after a rather uncertain opening the film 'runs to a good
finish, rather novel in its way':

> Having seen both films made by these players, one cannot but wish that they
> would turn to some more artistically ambitious work where their undoubted
> talent could be exploited to much better advantage. Richard Hayward and
> his co-workers have certainly laid the foundation of an Ulster film industry,
> and *The Early Bird* is another step in the right direction.[28]

The Irish Press too lavished praise on *The Early Bird*:

> No one should miss seeing and hearing one of our greatest Irish actors
> Richard Hayward, happy-go-lucky singer from the green fields of Ulster.
> Here is something grandly new and fresh; humour clean as the Bann breezes
> and culture deep as Lough Neagh's blue waters. The harp of the North is
> gently strumming through his happy Ulster comedy. Those who have been

lucky enough to see (and hear) Hayward trilling 'By the Light of the Silvery Moon' in the film version of Victor Haddick's *The Luck of the Irish* will not miss him in *The Early Bird* and vouch here and now for your sustained amusement. In this genius from over the border (and he's another Ulster-Irishman that plans to abolish that deadline) we have a singer, stage-actor, film-star, novelist, poet and humorist.[29]

Hayward's second major feature film, *The Early Bird*, a comedy with a matchmaking theme, was released in 1936. It broke box-office records in parts of Ireland.

The positive publicity in the daily press gave the film impetus throughout Ireland, setting box-office records in some areas. At the Picture House in Belfast it was retained for an extra week. The distributors, the Irish International Film Agency, reported a record week in Dingle, County Kerry. Box-office records were also broken in Carlow and Galway. John Hill says it 'provides a fundamentally benign vision of community in which, whatever the courtship rivalries, all remain relatively united. However, unlike *The Luck of the Irish*, there is a much sharper sense of social division.'[30]

Despite the generous reviews for *The Early Bird*, the Irish film censor, James Montgomery, regarded it as 'crude and vulgar' and required cuts before its release in the Free State. 'The amount given to men in their shirts is disgusting

… it is no credit to Ireland to release such stuff,' was his verdict in handwritten notes on the Censor's Records.[31] Montgomery, who was the first official film censor in Ireland and held the position from 1923 to 1940, once said 'I take the Ten Commandments as my Code.'[32] Unperturbed at the censor's opinion, Hayward had already begun scouting locations for future films. In July 1936 he travelled with Pedelty and John Hanlon, distributor of Irish International Films, to explore possible locations for scenes in Wicklow. The men visited Enniskerry and Glendalough as well as Glencree, Featherbed Mountain, Roundwood, Sally Gap and the lakes in their search for suitable sites. Their quest also took them west to Galway. With two films already released during the year, 1936 was turning into a frantically busy one for Hayward, culminating in the autumn with the filming of *Irish and Proud of It*, the third movie in the trilogy. In between the filming, he continued to hold down his freelance job as a sales agent for two sweet companies while still managing to fit in time for his burgeoning writing career.

Hayward and Dinah Sheridan, a newly discovered English actress, share a tender moment in *Irish and Proud of It* (1936). Sheridan, who was just fifteen, took on the lead role while Hayward played the part of a dapper London-Irish businessman. Sheridan went on to appear in *Genevieve* (1953) and *The Railway Children* (1970).

Ballyvoraine was the fictional village of Clogher Head in County Louth used for filming the post office scene in *Irish and Proud of It*.

Irish and Proud of It was based on a story by Dorothea Donn Byrne. Clogher Head on the coast of County Louth was the chosen location and the director and producer again was Donovan Pedelty. It starred Hayward, Mageean, George Pembroke and Dinah Sheridan, a newly-discovered English actress who was just fifteen. She had already built up an impressive portfolio of work, having made her professional debut at eleven in *Where the Rainbow Ends* and in *Peter Pan* playing the role of Wendy. In 1935 she appeared in her first feature film *Give My Heart* but *Irish and Proud of It*, in which she played the part of Moira Flaherty, was her first film lead. She was born Dinah Nadyedjda Mec but selected her stage name Sheridan from the telephone directory.

Hayward plays the part of a dapper but irresponsible London-Irish businessman, Donagh O'Connor. He attends a dinner given by the Irish Flying Club where he is the guest of honour and meets an Irish-American business magnate. His rendering of a song about the Irish village of Ballyvoraine impresses the American who realizes it would be a hit on the radio. But in his

6. NAME IN LIGHTS

speech, O'Connor makes a reference to the London Irish not having 'the guts to go home' and offends a group of young aviators who kidnap him, fly him back to Ireland and leave him in a field near Ballyvoraine. He is found and released by Moira Flaherty. O'Connor's appearance in the village in evening dress causes excitement and speculation. Mike Finnegan (played by Pembroke) an ex-Chicago gangster, suspects him of being a government agent sent from Dublin to investigate his illegal activities of distilling spirits and forcing local publicans to mix it with their whiskey. Sean Deasy (Liam Gaffney) joins Finnegan's gang in the hope of making money on which to marry Moira but she resents this and they quarrel. O'Connor is captured and held in a secret cellar from which he escapes. He insists on Moira and Sean making up. Finnegan arrives but his own gang turns on him and a fight, which spreads to enthusiastic bystanders, results in him being knocked out by O'Connor.

The making of the film proved complex. After shooting the exterior scenes in Ireland, it took three weeks to find forty 'Irishmen' in London to take part in a large fight sequence. The publicity release for the film states that Pedelty could not stop a few of the men from carrying on the fighting off the set after the final take.[33] *Irish and Proud of It* was screened at the Imperial Picture House in Belfast on 4 November 1936. It was well received by a large audience. 'It breaks away,' reported the *Belfast News Letter*, 'from the familiar Hayward formula of farm kitchen courtship with a vigorous story of poteen making and an American gangster who introduces Chicago racketeering methods in a simple Irish village … But Richard Hayward's rollicking ballads are well sung … his starring role suffers by the sacrifice of comic drollery to a strong plot and livelier tempo.'[34] The *Irish News* headlined its review 'Best Hayward Film Yet' and said he revelled in an 'an out-of-the ordinary part'. 'His folk songs, without which, apparently, no Hayward film would be complete, are cleverly introduced, and heighten rather than hold up the action.' There was warm praise too for Dinah Sheridan:

> She is probably the greatest feminine find in Irish films so far. She has looks, charm, freshness, vivacity, a pleasant voice, and, what is more, great acting ability. Here is a young lady with the makings of a big star. She will go far in the world.[35]

The paper's prophecy proved correct. Sheridan went on to enjoy a glittering career in film, stage and television, frequently playing the part of a well-bred Englishwoman. Notably, she starred in two of the most popular comedies in modern screen history, *Genevieve* (1953) with John Gregson, and *The Railway*

Children in 1970. In 1983 she was named as one of Britain's five most sophisticated women by the London fashion house Butte Knit.[36] Sheridan died at
ninety-two at her home in Middlesex on 25 November 2012. *Irish and Proud of
It* received several honourable mentions in obituaries in the *Guardian* and *The
Daily Telegraph* although Hayward's name was omitted. Sheridan was described
as being 'the quintessential English rose because of her elegance and understated
beauty.'[37] Hayward described her 'as a joy to work with, painstaking, adaptable,
extremely biddable, highly talented and cheerful under all the circumstances of
stress and annoyance that are inseparable from open-air cinematography in the
unstable climate of our beloved Ireland.'[38]

But it was not all bouquets for Hayward. Brickbats were also thrown by
the press and although *Irish and Proud of It* was praised at home the film was not
well received across the Atlantic when it was eventually released in the winter
of 1938 – a startling contrast to the reception given to *The Luck of the Irish* two
years earlier. The drinking, singing and fighting side of Irish life that it reflected
was not to the liking of the American press. The *New York Times* thought it
'naïve and sentimental' and too heavily reliant on 'the staples of Irish films'.[39]
The *Irish Echo* went much further, and under a review entitled 'Not so Proud',
lambasted the film as 'a disgrace to the Irish race' demanding that a Board of
Censors selected from New York Irish societies take action against its 'defama-
tion' of the Irish character.[40] Sections of Irish-America appeared to have ganged
up on Hayward to discredit his work, but the most damning criticism appeared
in *The Gaelic American*, from which extracts were quoted by the *Irish News*:

> Irish producers seem to subscribe to the quaint theory that Irish romance
> can best be portrayed on the screen by a series of drunken brawls in which
> the glamour boys of Eire swing bottles at each other's head. They picture
> lovely Irish girls frequenting the lowest dives and drinking almost as heavily
> as the men ... to convey to American audiences the idea that Ireland is a
> land of poverty, dirts and drunks ... these motion pictures are designed either
> through intent, ignorance, or bad taste to place Ireland and Irish people in an
> unsavoury position.[41]

Although upset by the opinions, a thick-skinned Hayward told the *Irish
News* that he was not surprised by the criticisms, which were the work of 'sentimental Americans':

> The sort of person who writes those articles, and the people who read and
> believe them, picture this country as a place where long-haired bards walk
> the streets, and all the maidens are sweet and simple, with milky complexions

and rosy cheeks. That is a fantastic Ireland that does not exist. In their eyes any representation which does not conform to their imagined picture is dastardly … I have known sentimental Americans coming over here and being intensely angry at seeing a factory in Eire, or being most hurt because farmhouses had electricity or used telephones. They level an accusation against me which, apart from how it affects me personally, is untrue. I have spent my whole life in the study of Irish folklore, literature, archaeology and music, and, in order to kill the old Irishman of 'Punch', produced realistic plays.[42]

Hayward also told the paper that he had a scrapbook containing critical reviews of *Irish and Proud of It*. Quoting a section from the *Irish Catholic* review, he said if he had wanted to write something answering the charges levelled again him, this could not have been bettered. 'It offers Irish film-goers clean entertainment worthy of national self-respect and of Catholic tradition, constituting comedy without suggestiveness, drama without sinister subtlety, and action without immodesty.'[43]

The previous year Hayward had been reported as saying that 'a certain non-Irish influence and a preference for the stage Irishman, introducing drunken men and pigs' in his films had been the result of interference from the American company Paramount.[44] *Irish and Proud of It* was the final collaboration between Hayward and Crusade. A number of issues had arisen to make him consider future films. Funding was one of the main ones since it was proving difficult to get support. He had made overtures to the Dublin government about setting up a film industry but had no luck. Nonetheless he continued with his new film *Devil's Rock*, an hour-long romantic drama in which he starred alongside Geraldine Mitchell. One of the other actors was Tom Casement, a brother of Roger Casement, the Irish nationalist executed for treason and who frequently visited north Antrim. It went into production in the summer of 1937 and was to be his last major film. It featured the Lambeg Irish Folk Dance Society while St Gall's School Choir sang 'The Coolin' and 'The First Noel'. He described it as 'a personal, private enterprise' made entirely in Northern Ireland. The only actors from outside the North in it were Mitchell of the Gate Theatre in Dublin and Michael Gleeson of Limerick.

Hayward commissioned Victor Haddick to write 'a scenario with a minimum of interior work' and virtually the whole film was made 'in the open' using a new type of microphone that permitted recording of natural sound. The film was shot in Cushendun (described as Craigadown) in the Glens of Antrim. As he no longer had the services of Pedelty, Hayward decided to produce and

Filming of *Devil's Rock,* Hayward's final feature, took place at Cushendun on the Antrim coast in the summer of 1937. The film crew used a new type of microphone that permitted recording of natural sound.

direct the film himself but he later handed over the role to Germain 'Jimmy' Burger, a Belgian film director and cameraman on his previous two films and who was to film his travelogue based on his journey down the Shannon in 1939. Hayward resumes the role of Sam Mulhern from *The Luck of the Irish,* playing the part of a sheep–drover. The film's title is taken from a rock on which a young woman is stranded before being rescued by Mulhern and the villagers in a dramatic climax. At the end Mulhern walks off to the accompaniment of uilleann piper, Richard Lewis O'Mealy.

The Irish International Film Agency held the trade and press presentation on 30 November 1937 in the Picture House in Belfast and hosted lunch at the Carlton Restaurant, one of Hayward's regular haunts. He told the assembly that it was a film made entirely in Ulster as criticism of his previous films had been that Ulster was not shown enough. And he was at pains to point out that no

Queues form at the Picture House in Belfast for Hayward's final feature film *Devil's Rock*, a romantic drama in which he again assumed the role of Sam Mulhern.

recording was done in London – the music accompaniment and concert-scenes were made locally.[45] The invitation trumpeted that it was the 'first full-length feature film ever photographed and recorded entirely in Ulster and with an all-Irish cast'. It summed up the story as 'set amidst the glories of the Glens of Antrim, glowing with superb scenic shots, full of homely humour and embellished with Irish song and dance and minstrelsy.'

Homely it may have been but it was not well received by critics. 'Unsophisticated in the extreme' was the verdict of the *Belfast Telegraph*.[46] The *Daily Express* dismissed it, saying it was unlikely to achieve commercial success as 'the story was poor, the continuity slipshod and the whole atmosphere unreal.'[47] The *Monthly Film Bulletin* described it as 'halting and uncertain – there is incompleteness in all the incidents and a tiresome dragging of "local colour" ... the effect is amateurish.'[48]

After *Devil's Rock*, Hayward stepped back from a starring role in the cinematic world, concentrating on the business side of running cinemas and turning
his attention to travelogues. Cinema managers in many areas were delighted
with the success and the numbers of people attending the films. He held business interests in four cinemas in counties Down and Armagh. Along with
Harry Bailey and Norman Ellison he was a director of a company called HBE,
which towards the end of the Second World War and in the postwar period ran
cinemas in Crossmaglen, Warrenpoint, Rathfriland and Queen's in Bangor. One
surviving letter illustrates how popular the cinemas were. On 13 January 1945,
F.J. Caraher, the manager of the cinema in Crossmaglen, wrote to Hayward to
let him know about the success of a film, showing the scale of interest, especially
from across the border:

> As you will see from Return we had a tremendous house last night, 359
> patrons. The place was packed. We took a chance and let them all in, and
> lucky enough no one came along to question overcrowding. Some people
> walked miles, and apart from the financial point of view it would be hard to
> turn these people away. We had them from Carrickmacross and Castleblayney
> as well as the country districts of Counties Monaghan and Louth bordering
> Crossmaglen. One party came from Carrickmacross on a tandem bicycle,
> and several ladies cycled from Carrickmacross. There was not a hitch of any
> sort. We satisfied everybody in accommodation and programme, and the heat
> was grand. Our prestige has risen 100%, and a lot of our local "nobs" have
> informed me that they are now going to patronize us, now that we have got
> the heat. We have now reached the grand total of £107 2s od Nett.[49]

Two of the most famous of all Irish films, both made in the 1950s, had
Hayward connections. *The Quiet Man*, an Irish-American technicolor romantic
comedy-drama based on Maurice Walsh's story, was made in the summer of
1951 at Cong in County Mayo and released in 1952. It starred Maureen O'Hara,
John Wayne, Victor McLaglen and Barry Fitzgerald. Although Hayward did not
appear in it, his arrangement of 'The Humour is On Me Now' was used. The
ballad, which he had popularized, was a favourite of the director John Ford's,
and was sung with gusto shortly after the wedding scene.

Although Hayward concentrated on his writing during the 1950s, he still
made an occasional appearance on the big screen. The skills he honed in the
1930s' films did not lie fallow and he had a role in one of the biggest pictures
of the period, *A Night to Remember*, about the sinking of the *Titanic*, released
in 1958. Based on the bestseller by Walter Lord, the black and white film,

featuring Kenneth More, was scripted by the novelist Eric Ambler. The film was produced by Hayward's friend William MacQuitty and directed by Roy Ward Baker. Made at a fraction of the cost of James Cameron's multi-Oscar winning 1997 Hollywood blockbuster, it is regarded by critics as being truer to the facts and without the film-world glitz. Hayward's role was a victualling officer, collecting the tickets from those boarding the ill-fated liner. The movie was a big success around the world and helped revive interest in the shipwreck that had been largely forgotten about.

Showbusiness history records that Richard Hayward played a pioneering part in developing the Irish film industry. Although his movie reign was comparatively brief – the high tide was the mid 1930s – he was the dominant figure and his films were stamped with his unique personality. He succeeded in creating an industry, carving a place for himself in the history of Irish film-making, and laying the foundations for those who came after. He never made any secret of the fact that he was showing off his country and if it brought tourism spin off then that was some added value. The newly emerged UTDA was grateful for bringing in much-needed tourist revenue to the small state of Northern Ireland, only fifteen years old when *The Luck of the Irish* came out. Some commentators, while highlighting the fact that Hayward's films elaborated a Unionist culture, acknowledge that they were also strongly populist in character and conducted with a sharp business acumen.[50]

Producing films was a difficult and expensive business and although Hayward made them on a low budget and had the support of local businesses, the audience was ultimately not large enough to sustain a profitable film industry. Commercial pressures meant that he could not continue with the bigger films. The winding up of his Belfast Repertory Company and the end of his commercial filming adventures marked the culmination of an exciting phase of his life. By the end of the 1930s, Hayward could look back with pride on a crowded decade and point to outstanding achievements but as ever, in his life, he was looking forward. Using the power of his pen, he planned to reinvent himself; he would turn to the printed page and the world of writing, which would take him far and wide across Ireland over the next quarter century.

SEVEN

'As wonderful as Father O'Flynn'

(1936–1944)

Richard Hayward is packed with the loot of the past, and he is an accomplished writer who can shoot it to us. He is also a good mixer. For some time now we must do all our travelling by book, and this one will carry you to the real Ireland.

Where the River Shannon flows, review by James Stephens, 1940

With a mixture of poetry, plays, broadcast revues, sketches and critical journalism all now part of his writing portfolio, Hayward was determined to produce a novel. He had completed writing one in 1926 but, unable to find a publisher, put it to one side. *Sugarhouse Entry* finally came out ten years later in 1936, a frenetically busy year for him because of filmmaking. The book tells the story of a Protestant family at Gortaloughan in the County Down countryside and paints a picture of life in a farming community. It concentrates on a farmer, Robert Dunseith, a widower whose ancestors ran a refining factory in Sugarhouse Entry in Belfast. (The street was later destroyed in the Second World War.)

The characters – industrious, honest, truthful and kind – as well as the scenes are conjured out of his imagination. Hayward loves them and treats them with sympathy and his novel is fashioned in a homely style. The London publisher, Arthur Barker, who founded his firm in 1932, agreed to add it to their list. Barker had already had an early success with Robert Graves' *Claudius* and *I, Claudius*, as well as Dashiell Hammett's *The Thin Man* published in 1935.

A draft copy of sixty-nine pages of Hayward's handwritten manuscript in black ink, pencil and blue pen in Belfast Central Library contains a rough pencil sketch of the house drawn by him with notes on the main characters and details of the layout of the bedrooms and kitchen. From the start, the first sentence weaves in Hayward's interest in place names:

> Of all the farms in Ulster none had a queerer name than the farm of Robert Dunseith. Sugarhouse Entry! It was a name that did not sort with the countryside at all. It stood out from the picture, as it were, rather garish and impudent and exotic amongst its fellows with their meaningful native names. For in Ireland every place-name has within itself some kind of significance, historical or topographical or legendary. The names of Irish places are pleasant to hear and have about them the sounds of little songs.[1]

At one point, early on in the novel, Hayward outlines the complexities of the Ulster character, providing an insight into his own view. The mentality of the Ulster people, he wrote, is something utterly apart from that of any other people in the modern world:

> Self-contained, insular, and yet betimes universal, it stands four-square to the whole world and takes a kind of hard-bitten rugged joy in the standing. Ulster has known and felt deeply every variety of political thought during the fierce years of her moulding, from the downright and successful flouting of the sovereignty of England by the O'Neills in the sixteenth century, through the extreme Radicalism of the eighteenth century ... down to the fierce and unswerving loyalty to the English Crown of the present day. But a vital change must be noted with the passing of the eighteenth century, a change which is essential to an understanding of the Ulster character; for until that time Ulster politics arose from a burning nationalism, a great unbounded love of country, whereas ever since then Ulster politics have been bred on a fear and hatred of Roman Catholic intrigue. This one fact is perhaps the touchstone of the character of the Ulster people.[2]

The book was published in autumn 1936, priced seven shillings and sixpence, with a cheaper dustjacket at two shillings and sixpence. Both British and Irish critics paid a good deal of attention. Writing in the *Spectator*, Sean O'Faolain provided a ringing endorsement:

> It is one of the few Ulster novels with the authentically Northern mixture of toughness, taciturnity, and shy or homely poetry. The narrative has an old-fashioned, homely air ... Mr Hayward has a real understanding of children and he evokes the old, loving atmosphere of 'hearth and home' as only could a generation of writers who are now little more than a memory.'[3]

One of Belfast's leading book stores, Erskine Mayne, ran a prominent window display promoting Hayward's novel *Sugarhouse Entry*, the story of a farming community in County Down published in 1936. The display also featured the English travel writer H.V. Morton's new book, *In the Steps of St Paul*.

The *Irish Independent* carried a photograph of Hayward along with a generous review on its books page although it felt that he could have chosen a more felicitous title since 'it suggests a setting in 18th century Belfast whereas the book is really concerned with plain folk in a rural part of Co. Down living in our own day.' But the critic said the novel 'had a great ring of actuality in the telling and was a first novel of distinct promise. Hayward had reached a genuine pathos … it is a homely forthright narrative with no literary pretensions.'[4]

The *Belfast Telegraph* called the book 'a real success' and said it was a mystery how in the midst of his film, theatre and gramophone work, Hayward had time to write the book.[5] *The Sunday Times* described the writing as 'finely drawn, devoid of whimsy, and a piece of wholesome realism that is never sordid,'[6] while *The Daily Telegraph* said it was 'perfect in its Irish atmosphere, warmly sympathetic, and salted with the authentic idiom.'[7] In a lengthy critique, the *Derry Journal* called it 'a fine readable story.' The reviewer described Hayward as a man of extraordinarily varied talents:

> Sugarhouse Entry is one of the new modern Irish novels that I have been able to read, not merely with patience but with real pleasure and genuine admiration … Hayward has style, but it is the expression of his own personality, and it is based on the fact that he has something to say. It has, too, all the clarity and simplicity of the authors whose work has endured. He resorts to no such cheap verbal tricks as starting a sentence at the wrong end, nor does he seek to show how 'up-to-date' he is by defiling his pages with blasphemies and obscenities.[8]

The reviewer's only quibble was that the author had been hard to some of the children:

> Robert Dunseith, the widower, is such a fine type of the Ulsterman at his very best and so loveable in the beginning of the book that one rather resents his hard fate and his weakness. I am not sure that the psychology of the character is quite correct, and I am inclined to think that the Robert Dunseith of the opening characters would have fought harder for justice and been firmer than he is shown to have been in the result.[9]

The reviews were positive enough to give Hayward encouragement to continue writing but rather than produce more fiction – although he had in mind to write another novel – he decided to turn his hand to non-fiction for his next literary venture. Apart from the publicity gained in the press, bookshops helped generate interest by promoting his work. One of Belfast's leading book stores, Erskine Mayne in Donegall Square, ran a prominent window display with posters and a dozen copies of the book in its distinctive colour dust jacket of a green-shawled woman looking across the countryside to hills in the distance. The same display featured the newly published *In the Steps of St Paul*, the story of a journey through Greece, Italy, Turkey and Palestine by the English travel writer H.V. Morton. It was a title Hayward would later adapt for his documentary film about St Patrick. Towards the end of the 1920s, Morton had taken to the roads of Ireland pioneering a new genre of travel writing known as 'motoring pastoral', and drove around in a Bullnose Morris that he called Maud. Earlier in the decade, V.S. Pritchett wrote about travelling around Ireland by train and on a horse named Jemima. Around the same time Harold Speakman, author of *Here's Ireland*, was touring the country on a donkey called Grania for his book, which came out in 1925.

Hayward was aware of how these books opened up the countryside to readers, capturing their imagination, but he differed from these writers in that he lived in Ireland and steered clear of gimmicky names for his modes of trans-port. In the mid 1930s his life was a hectic round of drama and film work alongside his confectionery job, but at the same time he was assembling the disparate elements of what would become his first travel book, *In Praise of Ulster*, published in 1938 when he was forty-six. The book had been slowly bubbling in his mind for several years. He tapped into notes from speeches and talks, so unlike his later travel books, this one did not take the form of a continuous linear journey. The final writing, pulling together all the strands of material and prose polishing, was completed in late 1936. Ireland was still recovering from the trauma of the civil war and it was only fifteen years since partition. The divi-sion of the country did not concern Hayward as his journey took him through all nine counties of the historic province of Ulster, spending as much time in Cavan, Monaghan and Donegal as he did in the six counties that made up Northern Ireland. During his travels as a salesman driving around country roads in his Singer Saloon in the 1930s he became acquainted with many parts of the country and people in numerous towns and villages. He carried on sporadic work, keeping notes, and when time permitted translating them into crafted prose. (Car ownership was steadily growing. In 1932 there were 37,000 cars on the roads of the North; by 1935 the figure had risen to 41,502.)

The book was illustrated with forty-eight wash drawings by the Irish land-scape artist James Humbert 'Jimmy' Craig. Born in Belfast on the Orangemen's celebratory day, 12 July 1877, Craig was a self-taught artist who worked in his father's wholesale merchant tea business but left to attend Belfast College of Art.

He made his home in a red-roofed cottage at Tornamona overlooking Cushendun Bay, an atmospheric area offering plenty of scope, where he devoted
himself to art. His passion was landscape painting in oils. Apart from the
Antrim coast, Craig's other favourite Irish panoramas were Donegal – with a
penchant for fishing trips to Tory Island – and Connemara. A senior landscapist
and member of the Royal Hibernian Academy (RHA), he was a top-ranking
professional who had spent time painting in Switzerland, southern France and
northern Spain. He emigrated to the US where he lived only briefly and 'helped
put red-lead on the Brooklyn Bridge'.[10]

The landscape painter James Humbert Craig produced forty-eight wash drawings
for *In Praise of Ulster*, including the pork market in Monaghan town. In the wartime
reprints of the book, the illustrations from Monaghan, Cavan and Donegal –
with one exception – were dropped.

His subdued sketches in ink-and-wash or charcoal-and-wash are reproduced in the Ulster book on glossy pages and reflect quiet impressions of the
landscape. They range across mountains, coastal scenes, green roads, wheel-less
carts and buildings. Craig's deft handling and light touch are captured in the
crowd dynamic in such intimate studies as a point-to-point meeting, a regatta
on Rathlin Island, the pork market in Monaghan town and a diverse range of
cultural experiences and traditional pastimes. Since his boyhood in Bangor on

the coast of County Down, ten miles from Belfast, Craig had been sympathetic to boats and water. Máirín Allen wrote: 'He gets quiet, unexpected harmony out of a group of rowing boats adrift on the pinkish grey water beneath his window at Cushendun.'[11] Craig had been a lifelong friend of Hayward's and was approaching sixty when he took on the work. During the early 1920s, Hayward dabbled in oil-painting. Craig had mentored him for a period but he chose not to pursue it as a career. In the book's introduction he paid a tribute to the artist:

> He understands me as well as I understand him, he has entered into the spirit of the book and brought me much happiness with the sensitive and uncommon drawings with which he has embellished my pages. No one could better understand my feelings about Ulster and no one could better weave a pictorial beauty into the more sober fabric of my telling.[12]

A substantial volume of 372 pages, *In Praise of Ulster* was to be the first of many digressive quests around Ireland and established Hayward as a stylishly descriptive writer. A wide-ranging book, it is partly autobiographical containing recreations of his boyhood scenes and schooldays in Larne as well as his work in the film industry. The parameters are wide and the pages bristle with archaeology, geology and topography. 'This is not,' he explains in the introduction, 'a critical essay but rather an extremely personal account of the delight which I take in this country.' The overture deals with his love of the Ulster accent and how it drew on the Shakespearian age. 'It is one of my own larger vanities that I was the first person in the world to use the Ulster dialect on radio, on gramophone records, and in talking pictures'.[13] He outlined some of these expressive phrases still in common use:

> 'I was thinkin' long'…'I'll convoy you home'…'I'll bestow a song on you…' 'That's a dangersome kind of place'…'He'll rue his bargain' – these are good current Ulster phrases which would bring an arching eyebrow to the superior person to-day, but which Shakespeare, Bacon, Spenser or Raleigh would have accepted as the best standard English.[14]

Hayward uses the technique of reduplication, the process where words are created by partial or complete repetition: fiddle-faddle, hugger-mugger and topsy-turvy crop up in his work. Each of the nine county chapters is prefaced with a verse of a traditional song or ballad evoking that county through lyrics and music. Throughout the pages he makes numerous references to his interest in music, which he regarded as part of the fabric of the country. He constantly reiterates his love for the back roads and his 'weakness for secondary roads',

places where he spent many hours gathering stories, fact-checking information and drinking in the atmosphere. After the first chapter on Belfast, County
Antrim gets the largest slice of his discursive journey. On occasion, he slips into
purple prose, for example, describing the air on Rathlin Island as being like
'heady wine', or the sunset over Portrush viewed from Ramore Head: 'And I
hope as we stand on this bold headland the sun will be setting, for a sunset at
Portrush is something to be remembered for ever and a day. And that's no word
of a lie at all at all!' [15]

Hayward laced his work with humour and whimsy. 'Ballyshannon looks
better,' he wrote in the Donegal chapter, 'from a distance than it does on closer
inspection.' Describing the walk across the perilously narrow Carrick-a-Rede
rope suspension bridge on the north Antrim coast, he urged nervous visitors
to 'screw up their courage and get on with the job.' He had come to love high
places. On his diversions for his confectionery work calling at sweet shops, he
frequently drove or walked to a high point to look down on the panorama of
the countryside, which allowed him to capture the lie of the land. This was to
be a leitmotif in his books and something that had rubbed off from his field
club days in the 1920s. *In Praise of Ulster* includes descriptions of views from Fair
Head and Slemish in Antrim as well as Slieve Donard in the Mournes where
the 'magic mountains huddled together', the Sperrins of mid-Ulster, a 'veritable fairyland of mountain grandeur', and Errigal in Donegal. To gain height
Hayward would climb to the top of towers such as Scrabo near Newtownards
in County Down.

The book is brimful of information and lore. For example, Ballykinlar is
the 'Town of the Candlestick' because its rents provided Christ Church Cathedral in Dublin with their altar candles; in County Derry, the quartz crystals,
known as 'Dungiven Diamonds', are a geological wonder, so called because of
their great size. In the 1930s, Derry city had a population of 50,000, with more
than 6000 – mostly women – working in shirt factories. Hayward laments the
fact that the border dealt a 'severe blow' to the distributing trades of Derry since
it was the commercial capital of Donegal and 'at a swoop that large territory
was cut off by an impassable tariff wall':

> The situation of the City of Derry is one of striking beauty, lying as it does at
> a lovely curve of the splendid River Foyle. And in the old city there is much
> to think about, much to dream about, and lessons which will not be lost on
> those who have the parts to read and the grace to understand. [16]

Donegal's highest point, Errigal, where Hayward enjoyed walking along the 'giddy parapet' of the One-Man Path at the summit.

The pages are enlivened by quotations from writers, poets, churchmen and historical figures. He also invoked Irish contemporary writers. H.C. Lawlor, the church historian, was a much-quoted presence as well as his friend, the archaeologist R.A.S. Macalister. Many of these authors' books were in Hayward's own well-thumbed library. An avid reader, he knew the work of the leading historical and cultural historians of the day.

Donegal was his favourite county and he devotes forty-four pages to it. Since partition he had frequently crossed and re-crossed the border which he complained was 'an infernal nuisance' and 'dreadful bugbear'. 'It is bad enough for any of us, especially if we have been used to roaming about without let or hindrance since childhood.'[17] The book is peppered with Ulster phrases and words which appealed to many readers although several critics did not like this aspect of it. Words used include 'thole', 'spraghlin', 'dunt,' and 'wheerywheeble'. Nostalgia permeates his writing but Hayward's jargon sits uncomfortably with the general tone of the book. When reminiscing, he lapsed into the habitual phrase 'Ochanee, a nee oh, them was the days!'[18]

Priced at twenty-one shillings, the book came out in June 1938 and was an instant success. Written in a personable, easy-to-read and entertaining style, Hayward had found his true voice. In the tailpiece he said he had wanted to 'write the book for many a long year' and explained his modus operandi. 'I have endeavoured all along to write as though I were roaming about the country-side with an old friend and pointing out to him the places and things that have always interested me'.[19]

Over the summer, critical notices were published in many newspapers, magazines and journals. Gushing reviews, written by leading writers, appeared in the mainstream British and Irish newspapers. The book was acclaimed a triumph. In July 1938 it was a Book Society choice by the soldier poet, essayist and pastoralist, Edmund Blunden, author of the First World War autobiography *Undertones of War* (1928). Blunden described it as 'a capacious, generous, leisurely book' and said Hayward 'comes singing us into the country.'[20] Writing in *The Observer*, M.J. Farrell (the pseudonym of the Anglo-Irish novelist and playwright Molly Keane), declared the people of Ulster should raise a monument to Hayward. 'Nothing is left undone or unsaid in this lovely book.'[21] *The Times* reviewer said 'Despite a somewhat slapdash style, Mr. Hayward is well qualified to write in praise of Ulster ... and has wide sympathies and interests. The paper said 'he avoids taking sides, or almost succeeds in doing so, though he seems to take a certain pleasure in rubbing in the memory of the Republicanism of a century and a half ago as a foil to Derry and Enniskillen of the seventeenth century.'[22] The Belfast-born novelist, Forrest Reid, writing in the *Manchester Guardian*, praised 'much solid work, historical and archaeological', which had gone into 'this sumptuous book ... a racy colloquial style makes it pleasant to read, and wherever one dips one goes on dipping.'[23] Shane Leslie in *The Sunday Times* proclaimed that the book surpassed them all as 'it pours forth from a well-stored mind.'[24] The *Belfast Telegraph*, in an 800-word review, called it an 'uncommonly handsome book', saying Hayward had honoured his country and his neighbours:

> To his twinkling, anecdotal mind which loves the pawkiness of the countryfolk better than the eccentricities of politics, the changing scenes of Irish history need only a minimum of moral and argument ... he is as friendly and delightful a travelling companion as there is in the whole world. He knows every bend in the roads of Ulster. His affection for the country is complete; he is not, like some Irish writers of late, in love with his own thoughts ... In point of scenery and characteristics, and even plain gossip, Ulster has never been put on paper more beguilingly.[25]

Under the heading, 'Lamh Dearg Abu' ('Red Hand to Victory'), the *Irish Times* reviewer, Maurice Walsh, said it was finely written, finely illustrated and finely produced. Walsh, who wrote the dust jacket blurb that became a foreword in later editions, enthusiastically promoted his friend's books. Both Hayward and Craig, he wrote, had made a 'real living entity' of their own beloved Ulster:

> It is not dry as a guidebook is dry, or laconic or bowelless or indifferent …
> it is savoured and salty with wit and pawkiness and song, and the pleasantest
> gossip in the world … Richard Hayward thrusts a friendly arm through
> yours, and hales you off, laughing and happy, through his nine counties …
> When you are finished your 'hike' – and you are sorry it is finished – you can
> be sure that you know Ulster, and have lived in it and with it. You are sib.[26]

The *Irish Independent* chose it as its Book of the Month for July 1938 with an impressive three-column review under the heading 'An Ulsterman on Ulster' and a Craig sketch of Cave Hill in Belfast. The anonymous reviewer drew comparisons with Robert Lloyd Praeger's *The Way that I Went*, an *Independent* Book of the Month choice nine months earlier in October 1937. 'That is a high compliment to Mr. Hayward', the reviewer wrote, 'and it is meant to be':

> Only an Ulsterman of goodwill, for example, would have had the wisdom to
> put religion and politics sternly in the distant background at the outset and
> keep it there … He is a born rambler, with an eye ever alert for the hidden
> beauty-spots, and an ear ever open for the song of the bird, the babble of the
> mountain-stream, the droll story or the stave of an old ballad by the wayside.[27]

Less than two weeks later, Hayward's friend Lynn Doyle, author of plays, a travel book and the novel *Ballygullion*, wrote a 1000-word lead review for the sister paper, the *Sunday Independent*. Under the heading 'An Ulster Enthusiast', coverage was splashed across the page alongside one of Craig's drawings, 'The Green Road', Killevy to Lislea in County Armagh. Doyle said the book was another monument to Hayward's industry and highlighted an important skill – his remarkable aptitude for dealing with facts:

> He possesses an alert and receptive mind, and his power of assimilating infor-
> mation is astonishing. His reading for this book must have been prodigious.
> History, folk-lore, local gossip, legend, archaeology, geology, topography –
> he brings them out of his hat in turn. Conchology, I think, he has left out
> – though it is far more probable that I have overlooked it – but he has as
> wonderful a way with him as Father O'Flynn, and the reader will find himself
> lavishly informed and disposed to make further inquiry.[28]

Doyle also referred to 'the tributary of comment and surmise which, now and then is otiose.' His main quibble was that on occasion Hayward slipped into jargon for storytelling. He described Craig's drawings as 'pleasant, but sometimes a little boneless.' Doyle was correct in stating that he [Doyle] had overlooked a reference to conchology. In his County Derry chapter, Hayward refers to Downhill strand as 'a happy-hunting-ground for the conchologist, and well over a hundred different specimens of shell, many of rare species, have frequently been collected in the length of one day.'[29] The *Dublin Magazine*, a quarterly review of literature, science and art edited by Seumas O'Sullivan who had been involved in the Irish Literary Revival, ran a lengthy notice. It was written by Samuel B. Crooks (later Dean of St Anne's Cathedral, Belfast) who said the author's interest never wanes. Crooks points out that 'at several recent weddings in these parts one observed that among the presents displayed for admiration of the guests, pride of place was given to *In Praise of Ulster*.'[30]

The *Irish Independent* chose *In Praise of Ulster* as its Book of the Month for July 1938, drawing comparisons with Praeger's *The Way that I Went*.

The book was important in establishing Hayward's fluent writerly creden-
tials. The reviews, vital to its success, brought him to the attention of an even
wider audience. Decades later, in his 400-year survey of art in Ulster, the art
critic and poet, John Hewitt, criticized Craig's drawings. He felt he could only
express his vision in colour and 'his drawings lacked authority or conviction, as
if he did not much care for what he was being asked to do.'[31] Five months after
its first publication, it was reprinted by Arthur Barker in November to capitalize
on the Christmas market and, in a third edition, in December 1939. Maurice
Walsh added several sentences to his new foreword, saying 'it was easily the best
book on Ireland in my generation and I can go back fifty years':

> And it is no ephemeral book, for although it cannot be read other than with
> pleasure it is in the very highest sense what is known as a standard work. For
> any future writer or visitor or native wanting to know Ulster and the inner
> spirit and being of Ulster, must perforce consult this grand book.[32]

The publication of his first travel book coincided with a drive to put
Northern Ireland on the tourist map and a bid by the UTDA to attract more
visitors to such sites as the Giant's Causeway. During the war, paper was scarce.
Students had trouble getting copies of books they needed but the government
was keen to help Hayward reprint the book and saw its value in encouraging
visitors. A government information service report outlines how Stormont was
trying to counter bad press coverage:

> During November only in three British newspapers did letters appear
> attacking Ulster, namely in the Western Daily Press, the Economist and the
> News-Review, but they are significant to show how necessary it is for Ulster
> to be on the qui vive.[33]

The report goes on to state that Hayward had requested government
support for acquisition of paper supplies to enable a further edition of his book
to be published. It added, 'Our feeling is that in view of the scarcity of Ulster
books in circulation every effort should be made to secure a reprint of this one
particularly in view of its excellent propaganda nature.'[34]

Whether readers regarded his writing as propaganda or not is a moot
point. Few, if any of the critics thought he was wielding a rabble-rousing pen
or producing blatant propaganda. One of the ironies is that if the Northern
government viewed it as propaganda then it did not seem to trouble those in the
corridors of power at Stormont that three of the chapters featured counties in

the Free State. Unquestionably, Hayward was promoting Ulster as a place to visit and his book succeeded like no other. Few might now read *In Praise of Ulster*, but in its day it was one of the most popular books. After the third edition sold out, it was reprinted in the spring of 1943 in a fourth revised edition with changes, while a fifth and final revised edition, with the backing of the government, was published in September 1946. The revisions included textual, image and production changes to update such information as the fact that in south Tyrone, the Clogher Valley Railway on which Hayward had enjoyed journeys was closed by the government as a cost-saving measure on 1 January 1942. The prewar edition also included extra illustrations by Craig not found in the post-1939 editions because of the shortage of paper. The number of drawings in the later editions was reduced by sixteen to thirty-two. Curiously – apart from 'The Muckish Country' – all the illustrations for Donegal, Monaghan and Cavan were dropped.

Hayward's London publishers, Arthur Barker, were liquidated at the start of the Second World War, much of which Barker spent as a Japanese prisoner of war.[35] After the second printing, subsequent editions, with an index added, were published under the imprint of William Mullan & Son Ltd, publishers and booksellers with a shop in the centre of Belfast whose pedigree stretched back to 1880. Mullan's was noted for its old-world stylishness and catered for a wide range of subject matter. However, the company was not noted for prompt payment and Hayward, who dealt directly with them, struggled to get money for the books that he sold himself. He had an agreement with them for payment of royalties at the rate of fifteen percent on the published price. He calculated that on publication of 1000 copies Mullan's owed him £157.10s 0d. To offset rising costs in the postwar years they asked him to relent on these terms and he agreed to accept a reduction of one-third but by the end of 1949 he still had not received payment. 'I find it especially embarrassing and distasteful', he complained, 'to have to ask you several times for money which should come to me automatically without any request on my part.'[36] Hayward was also aggrieved that the company had allowed *In Praise of Ulster* to remain unobtainable for more than six months. But his main gripe was to receive a cheque for money owed to him:

> Do you wish to revert to the original agreement (which still stands) and pay me £157.10.00 on the 1sts of January, or do you wish to avail yourselves of the verbally agreed reduction???? I want to know. And if you wish to pay the reduced Royalty, it will be necessary for you to send me the requisite cheque by return ... Send me my cheque and let the hare sit!![37]

With two sons and a wife to support, Hayward had to keep the wolf firmly from his door but despite pressing financial worries such as squeezing money from publishers, his writing was flourishing. He followed up his travel writing debut with three more topographical books all published during or just after the Second World War and had his confectionery work to fall back on which guaranteed him a reasonable income. The work was congenial and introduced him to new people and new places. In 1938 chemists working for Needler's found a way of producing clear or *glacé* fruit drops, an area in which they were to have little or no competition until the mid 1960s. Consequently, the emphasis of production shifted away from chocolate (where Cadbury's, Rowntree's and Mars dominated) towards sweets. The prewar business was buoyant but the situation would change drastically within a few years when sweets (and their raw materials) were rationed between 1941 and February 1953. Thereafter demand, particularly for *glacé* fruit drops, shot up.

Considerably heartened by the critical consensus, Hayward contemplated spreading his travel writing wings beyond the boundaries of Ulster and exploring the wider island. He had had an interest in the Shannon region for some time and was working out the practicalities of a tour of the river and its hinterland. He had also spotted a gap in the book market: although the Shannon is the longest river in Ireland and Britain and one of the best known, no one had ever written about it in its entirety. His plan was to take the reader into what were then little-known and unfrequented parts of Ireland such as the Fermanagh-Leitrim border, remote islands in the midlands on which people still lived, and to the secluded shores of Lough Derg in north Tipperary. These were all ripe for exploration and the subject matter was close to his heart from his youthful days holidaying with his father on rivers and canals. A two-page synopsis running to 800 words, which has survived, was sent to prospective publishers outlining his ambitious scheme: 'The book would be conceived and written in a flowing informative manner – now grave, now gay, now reminiscent and always lit with that glow of authentic Irishry which only an Irish writer in love with his country can command.'[38]

He included a paragraph predicting the book would have wide sales in Ireland, England and the US. 'This is the kind of book that <u>always</u> sells – <u>everywhere</u>. And it should be noted that there is no up-to-date book on the Shannon; no book at all on the Shannon as a whole; and no book of this particular genre in existence.'[39] His original idea was to again use the services of Craig as illustrator and on behalf of the publishers he offered to arrange 'low terms' with him. As an alternative, he also suggested photographs, but added: 'The drawings would be more personal and add value to the book – and Craig has a very big following here, in England and in America.'[40] The early part of the summer was spent deciding on the best method of travelling and he opted for a different illustrative approach. To record the journey for posterity in stills photography and moving film, he asked two friends, Germain Burger and Louis Morrison, to accompany him. They discussed the best way of making the trip – ruling out either horses or donkeys – and came up with the idea of hiring a caravan. Hayward reckoned this would bring colour to the journey, supplying him good copy and attracting attention. In August he hired a Cheltenham caravan from the Irish Caravan Company in Belfast at a cost of £10.[41] Just as the world was sliding into war again, in the late summer of 1939, the three men set out on their Shannon adventure. Ever the dutiful housewife, Elma stayed at home, content to carry out her motherly roles and look after three-year-old Ricky. Dion had by now left Belfast Royal Academy and started work in the Bank of Ireland.

The three men crossed the border at Cavan in a 12hp car trailing their 12ft caravan. The Free State was neutral during the Second World War or 'The Emergency' as it was known, and there was an air of unreality about their trip. It was just twenty-one years since the end of the Great War, and on the eve again of momentous world events, Hayward presents a startling pastoral contrast in the preface about their departure, 'A warm sun in the sky, a genuine thrill of expectancy and joy in our hearts, and many and many a song in our mouths as we sped past the sweet fields of Ireland.' Rationing affected the country and a lack of public transport owing to fuel shortages inhibited social life. Three men in a caravan with their cameras, gear and supplies were a novelty.

The object was to gather material as they followed the banks of the Shannon from the source in the Cavan hills to the mouth on the Atlantic seaboard. The journey of 214 miles, encompassing eleven counties, would take at least three weeks. Accompanying the book, a travelogue would be filmed by Burger who was equipped with a 35mm movie camera while Morrison was to provide atmospheric black-and-white landscape photographs. The three enjoyed themselves meeting all sorts of people in towns, villages and on islands. Sometimes, locals trailed along behind them for a stretch. As in the case of his previous book, Hayward's journey had started before the journey began, by carrying out background reading and advance research. He was well read on the pre-history and history of the river as well as the legends and songs inspired by it. His gift for talking to people and using his guile drew stories from them in the same way as he had already demonstrated in his Ulster book.

When he quotes people Hayward reproduces a near verbatim transcription of their words. He does not attempt to clean up and improve on their language – they speak for themselves, the vernacular voice of ordinary people. Their journey took them through Loch Allen and on to Carrick-on-Shannon in County Leitrim. It was an Ireland of small shops; every town had its boot- and shoemakers still handcrafting their wares. Grocery shops and pubs, cheek by jowl with post offices, were the mainstays of most towns, some just set up in the front room of homes. Carrick was a place that Hayward had come to know well and he made friends with many people especially the staff at the historic Bush Hotel. Just twenty years earlier, in 1919, Michael Collins had spent a night in the hotel.

They passed through Goldsmith and Edgeworth country, and when they reached Athlone, boarded a boat to explore Loch Ree with a local man, Jimmy Rigney. On the Black Islands, Hayward met the Hanley and O'Hara families, the only inhabitants on a group of seven small islands and was photographed with them by Morrison for an image used in the book. He was intrigued by the islanders' life where letters were delivered twice a week and where cattle waded between each of the islands when they tired of the grass on one. He also delighted in the hospitality. Mrs Hanley made them a 'grand meal of good strong tea, fresh boiled eggs, and bread baked by herself, light as a feather, and fit for a king.'[42] But the return journey ended in drama when their boat ran out of petrol on their way back to their camp at Coosan. Rigney had made a miscalculation and they were more than two miles from home with night coming down:

> We fell to with a will, each of us taking our turn at rowing, but the boat was heavy, and our progress was slow. And to cap it all Loch Ree lived up to its name for caprice. Calm as a millpond all day, it now broke into ominous little waves, and the sky became suddenly dark and overcast. We had not gone far before a really stiff breeze was blowing dead against us, and I could see from Jimmy Rigney's face that he was more than a little worried. We got back to Coosan that night after about three hours' hard work in the teeth of a heft wind, and I must confess that even I, who was brought up with small boats since childhood, did not feel very comfortable once or twice when we shipped part of an especially large wave, or when our boatman, peering ahead into the darkness, thought we had gone off our course and might run aground in one of the shallows which abound in this part of the lake.[43]

Hayward photographed by Louis Morrison with the Hanley and O'Hara families during his Shannon journey. In 1939 they were the only inhabitants on the Black Islands, a group of seven small islands on Loch Ree.

Eventually they made it back safely to their camp, setting off next morning by road for the monastic settlement of Clonmacnoise. Hayward devotes twenty pages to the ecclesiastical history of the site, covering the life of Ciaran and weaving in detailed descriptions of the churches. Although they worked long hours, collecting information and meeting people, Hayward gives the impression of a leisurely journey. Most days started by bathing in the river, after which they frequently breakfasted on the remains of fish leftover from meals of the night before. Stops were made at Shannonbridge and Banagher, and at Mountshannon in east Clare, where notwithstanding their earlier escapade on Loch Ree, they boarded a dingy to reach Holy Island (Inis Cealtra) on Loch Derg. Hayward pondered the remains of churches, the round tower and other antiquities, providing a ten-page description of the site. The rest of their trip took them to Killaloe, into Limerick city and Foynes, before journey's end at Ballybunnion in Kerry. Hayward was particularly struck by Foynes from where the US Clipper flying-boats operated, and the village 'made a singular impression upon me':

> There was something un-Irish about the whole place; every other man you met spoke with an American or English accent; and everybody and everything in the village was coloured and influenced and shaped by the great circumstance and adventure of transatlantic flight …. There is a saying in Ireland, when you have stood a man a drink and he wants to do the same by you: 'Of *course* you'll have another. Sure no bird ever flew on one wing.'

Well, our drink was just being poured out, when over in a far corner I heard a native saying to a man who seemed to be an official of some kind, 'Of *course* you'll have another. Sure no Clipper ever flew on one wing.'[44]

In between the history, the book is sprinkled with humour, stories and verse. He writes that he had enjoyed the 'happy companionship' of his fellow-travellers, as well as 'the spontaneous friendliness of the splendid Shannon people, north, south, midways, and always.'[45] When the men returned to Belfast, Britain was at war and Hayward launched immediately into writing the book. By the spring, with the Nazis occupying Denmark, Norway, Belgium, France, Luxembourg and the Netherlands, he had completed 50,000 words. The book, with fifty-four photographs by Morrison, was published in early June. A folding map in black, white and blue featuring sketches of some highlights of the journey and drawn by Audrey Mayes, was inset before the index. During the warm summer of 1940 Hayward was delighted that the book was universally praised with critics seeing it offering escapism from the war. Writing the lead review, 'Three men in a caravan', in *The Irish Times*, Maurice Walsh said he hoped Hayward would treat the Shannon 'in the same friendly, genial, pawky and scholarly way as he did in his Ulster book and he had: It took a Northern man to do it.'[46] Walsh declared that the book showed the art of Richard Hayward:

He lays down his terrain for you in a masterly way: the great river at the centre of things, winding and widening with the leisureliness of greatness; the island-studded lakes with their silken skin; the twisty, almost secret roads under hawthorn hedges (and dust forbye); the small fields and the cows tail-twitching in knee-deep water ... Hayward folds you in friendly tentacles and carries you along. If he is sometimes wistful for the old things and dreams and song, he is also, at the back of it all, invincibly cheerful; and you will agree with him that the present time is not such a hell of a bad time at all within the basin of our grand river; that it is worth while to be alive and loitering, even now in these perilous days of world folly, and that the best way to forget the peril and folly and dolour is to sojourn with Richard Hayward where the River Shannon flows.[47]

It was a handsome tribute from Ireland's best-selling author and a warm endorsement of Hayward's work. Walsh's fame today rests largely on his short story 'The Quiet Man'. In the first half of the twentieth century he was acknowledged as a brilliant storyteller. His novel, *The Key Above the Door*, set in Scotland and published in 1927, sold over a quarter of a million copies. And his books were read not just in Ireland but in Britain and America. In February 1933 the

Saturday Evening Post published 'The Quiet Man' for which he received $2000. It was later included in his collection of stories *Green Rushes* in 1935. Hayward had come to know him through PEN, and Walsh had visited Belfast in 1938 and 1939 to support the local centre. At the organization's annual dinner in the Union Hotel in April 1939, the *Belfast News Letter* reported that Hayward had corrected Walsh in his speech after he said that he thought Belfast was the most friendly town in Ireland:

> Down in the deep South, of course, he said in a humorous reference to ideas held there, there was an impression that one would, in Belfast, meet a gunman round the corner. (Mr. Richard Hayward later corrected Mr. Walsh, remarking that one would have to turn at least two corners before meeting a gunman in Belfast.)[48]

Underneath Walsh's *Irish Times* review, in a section called 'What Dublin is Reading', the Shannon book was top of the non-fiction list. The *Sunday Independent* review by David Sears described it as a valuable book, ideal for anyone contemplating a holiday in Ireland. He regretted that he was not a passenger on the meandering caravan and while he praised Hayward's gift for warm friendship and understanding of Irish history, he had one quibble. 'If I have a fault to find with the book it is that he poured out this knowledge with too generous a hand. It is not that the knowledge is not interesting, but that the man himself is more interesting.'[49]

Maurice Healy in *The Tablet* wrote that Hayward 'is a good example of the way tolerance works; he has an enthusiasm for Ireland that could not be beaten by a Southerner. This is a darlin' book!'[50] In *The Sunday Times*, James Stephens, the short-story writer and author of *The Crock of Gold*, said 'Richard Hayward is packed with the loot of the past, and he is an accomplished writer who can shoot it to us. He is also a good mixer. For some time now we must do all our travelling by book, and this one will carry you to the real Ireland.'[51] The Rev. John Ryan, writing in *Studies*, an Irish quarterly review, praised it:

> Hoary with age and rich with numberless experience, the Shannon offers, in fact, material for a dozen volumes, but Mr. Hayward, with unerring judgement, collects all that is most interesting into this one. He has read and listened to storytellers on the spot, of course, (not to the radio) with industry and effect.'[52]

The book and the film, both of which came out in 1940, were distinguished by different titles. *Where the River Shannon flows* was the book's title, while the film was called *Where the Shannon Flows Down to the Sea*. Burger's black-and-white film, and the book, a marriage of text and Morrison's photographs, represent a late-1930s snapshot of the social history of rural Ireland. Because of a chronic shortage of paper during the war, the book was jointly published by George Harrap of London and Dundalgan Press of Dundalk, priced at fifteen shillings. George G. Harrap, who founded the company, loved travel books and helped nurture several travel writers including one of the big names of the day, John Joy Bell, who wrote *The Glory of Scotland* in 1932. Harrap had also published the work of Stephen Gwynn, including *Ireland in Ten Days* (1935) and *Dublin, Old and New* (1938).[53] Arthur Barker, which resumed business after the war, published a new edition of the Shannon book in 1950 while Dundalgan produced a further edition in 1989 to coincide with the 50th anniversary of the journey. The modern cover was decorated with a Bord Fáilte colour photograph featuring a fisherman. The book remains in demand by holidaymakers touring the Shannon region or boating along the waterways. A Canadian bookseller, Nick Kaszuk, who since 1999 has run Trinity Rare Books, a secondhand and antiquarian shop in Carrick-on-Shannon, is frequently asked for copies. He attributes this demand to Hayward's writing style and his popular technique combining research and people:

> *Where the River Shannon flows* is a standard local classic and Hayward's books are always sought after. I search for them on the internet and find them in Australia, America and all over the UK. His books are listed on ebay and they just seem to keep on selling. He was an informative traveller, a very good writer, and he always seems to form an attachment to the areas he visits. The way he describes places makes them come alive. People come from all over and they want to find out about the river's history and its literature. It is one of my top ten standards and anyone who appreciates topography will like it.[54]

For the twenty-minute documentary of the Shannon journey, Hayward wrote the script, directed the film and narrated the story of their trip. It was filmed by Burger with music recorded by Morrison. The film opens with a wide pan across the Fermanagh-Cavan countryside with references to Cuilcagh and Benaughlin mountains and the Shannon Pot where the journey started. It includes short sections on many of the places where they stopped. Apart from a brief shot of him at Ardnacrusha, where he explores the hydroelectric scheme, Hayward does not feature in vision. Action shots show men on the river catching trout by nets in Loch Ree. There are fleeting glimpses of Limerick showing St John's Castle, the Treaty Stone, and the statue of Sarsfield.

Walk-on parts by geese, swans, cattle and donkeys are all part of the make up.

It is a grainy black-and-white period piece of filmmaking, made up of slow-moving pans lasting between ten and fifteen seconds in each direction with tilts up and down buildings, and close up shots of church doorways at Clonmacnoise. Other shots are of Goldsmith Country and the Three Jolly Pigeons pub, as well as the rectory where Goldsmith lived. Shown at the Royal Hippodrome in Belfast, the film was screened on the same bill as *The Luck of the Irish* while Hayward also performed a twice-daily live stage and song show.

Despite directing most of his energy into research, travel and writing books, Hayward organized a multitude of other activities, spending a considerable amount of time in the South. In the autumn of 1943, for example, he toured Connaught with the comedian Harry Bailey. Their partnership, Hayward-Bailey Productions, was a double-act of jokes, patter and songs. Entitled 'Variety on Parade', their show was also held in other parts of the country, with the promotional tag, 'Shaking everybody with laughter'.

The humour of his shows provided escapism in the 1940s, a decade of profound change throughout Ireland. The war brought a surge in employment, especially in large engineering industries such as Harland & Wolff, Short Brothers and the Mackie foundry. But the Belfast blitz had an unsettling impact on Hayward's son Dion. Like many young men of the time, it affected him deeply, and immediately he became involved in the war. He wanted to volunteer as a motorbike dispatch rider but his mother talked him out of it.[55] Instead he signed up for the Home Guard and was part of the Air Raid Precautions (ARP) in north Belfast, helping with the issuing of gas masks and organizing air raid shelters. Soon afterwards he joined the North Irish Horse, driving tanks over mountain passes in North Africa and Italy as part of the British 8th Army. In a letter to Maurice Walsh in March 1943, Hayward referred to the war saying they had received five letters from Dion, now in his mid twenties:

> He seems to like Tunisia and the food in his off moments and the Algerian wine. He had Minestrone, Chicken en casserole, a sweet and bottle of Red Wine for 1/6 all of which seems to be not too expensive as things go. But I do wish it were all over and we had our boy back again.[56]

Far from being over soon, the war was dragging on and early in 1944 was at a crucial stage. British and American forces had landed at Anzio on 22 January for what was known as Operation Shingle and preparations were well advanced for the invasion of Normandy. Tragically the worst still lay ahead for Dion when he was caught up in a terrifying attack in Italy. As a sergeant, he was a driver of 'B' Squadron, *Bangor*. He was wounded several times and on one occasion, just after the fierce battle of Monte Cassino, nearly lost his life. His war journal notes reflect the horror of the incident:

> We were for many weeks embroiled in hide and seek among the foothills of the Lombardy plains, a deadly sort of business. During one advance an enemy S.P. [self-propelled] gun, hidden cunningly behind a false crest, registered a hit on the turret just above the drivers hatch. I was paralyzed down the left side by the blast and in the ensuing confusion of choking dust and fumes we were ordered to "evacuate tank and take cover."[57]

Within seconds of abandoning his tank another burst of fire wounded Dion's legs, then a piece of shrapnel penetrated his neck, entered his jaw, ripped his tongue and embedded in his upper palate. Dion was flown immediately to Barletta on the Italian Adriatic coast for urgent treatment. He was operated on by a team from the facial surgical unit and spent several weeks in hospital. It was an alarming time for his parents, unable to visit him in hospital and seemingly helpless to do anything. But Dion's resilience was strong and he quickly returned to active duty with the North Irish Horse. In January 1945 he was promoted and sent to Sandhurst Military Academy for officer training. The following month he went on a completely different mission, making an urgent visit to Belfast to get married to Dolly, his girlfriend of several years, who had waited patiently for him; their wedding took place on 6 February. Soon afterwards he returned to the continent, taking part in the Battle of the Bulge and driving a tank along the rubble of the once elegant Unter den Linden in Berlin. One of his final wartime actions was driving through the gates to help liberate Bergen-Belsen Nazi concentration camp in April 1945. After witnessing the harrowing scenes he remained in Berlin where, as a lieutenant with the Royal Armoured Corps, he was part of the occupation forces in the British zone. His son Paul says that at the beginning of 1947 when he was demobbed, he came back to Belfast a 'displaced person'.

> Like thousands of other young men of the period he tried to put the war years behind him and figure out how to move forward. He had gone off to fight when he was twenty-one and came back at twenty-seven having nearly died. It was a particularly long and protracted war for him and he had a horrific experience but he did a damn good job and was a great father.[58]

After demobilization on 31 January 1947, Dion returned to work at the Bank of Ireland's York Street branch in Belfast before moving to a branch in Drogheda, County Louth. He later left the bank and began a new job as production manager with Fox's Glacier Mints, the company his father still worked for. In the early 1960s, he emigrated to the North Island of New Zealand where he worked as production manager in the Irish Tapestry Company making candlewick bedspreads.

Father and son share a chat on O'Connell Bridge. Richard Hayward and eleven-year-old Ricky are photographed stopping off in Dublin en route to Newtown School in Waterford just after the Second World War. This picture was taken by Arthur Fields, a Ukranian Jew and well-known street photographer who snapped tens of thousands of passers by on the bridge from the 1930s to 1985.

One might wonder when Richard Hayward had time to enjoy any hobbies but he did indulge in recreational activities. In his sixteen-line entry – one of the largest – in the 1938 edition of *Who's Who in Northern Ireland*, apart from swimming and walking up and down mountains on his travels around Ireland, he lists his hobbies as playing golf, which appeared to be his main recreation. During the 1930s he played at Mahee, a nine-hole course on the Ards peninsula in County Down and at Scrabo golf course where he particularly enjoyed the country teas that were served in the Tower.[59] He also played the course at Castlerock on the Derry coast and was inspired to improve his game by the golf professional Davie Lyttle, who coached him with several lessons. 'He even taught me to reduce the lamentable number of my "air shots" and "hooks," and anyone who could do that must have been inspired.'[60]

In 1945 Ricky was sent off to Newtown School in Waterford. His father had noticed an advertisement in *The Bell* and liked the sound of it. 'He was enthused,' Ricky recollects, 'by the quality of the Irish history and language teaching as well as by the general Quaker style of all-round co-education. As relatively old parents, mum and dad were probably glad to have relief from daily care of a young boy and reckoned correctly that I would benefit from a lot more young company than they could find for me at home.'[61] Ricky prospered at Newtown, later becoming head boy. The school was founded by the Society of Friends in 1798 and his father, who described it as 'a very happy community', liked its ethos so much that he became a member of the Newtown Old Scholars' Association.[62]

Letters between Ricky's parents and the school secretary held in the Newtown School archive show a huge concern and interest for their son and their happiness about his progress. Sometimes they both made the long trip from Belfast to Waterford to leave him back for a new term or collect him. The teaching staff included Frederick Ernest Foster – father of the writer and historian Roy Foster – who taught Irish. The retired French teacher, Leslie Matson, recalls Ricky's parents coming to the school:

> Richard Hayward was liked and was an agreeable person who always paid his debts promptly. He gave occasional talks to the school and offered to show films and play music to the pupils. On one occasion though, when they were bringing Ricky back to the school, Elma was very upset. They used to go for a walk around the nearby People's Park in Waterford which she called 'The Garden of Gethsemane'.[63]

Following in the acting footsteps of his father, Ricky Hayward (extreme right) playing the role of Tony Lumpkin in Goldsmith's *She Stoops to Conquer* at Newtown School in December 1951. Also in the photograph are, from left, Anthony Rowntree (from the Irish branch of the Rowntree chocolate family), Roger Denny, Michael Stewart, Roderick Ross and Ken Sherrard.

In school holidays, Ricky recalls going around eighteen holes once a week with his father at Fortwilliam Golf Course in Belfast, not far from their Antrim Road home:

> As I was too young to play, I kept the score for him, maybe putting occasionally, and he was usually happy to keep below ninety. I enjoyed the companionship and his talk very much and my mother probably enjoyed the break, which may have been part of the deal. When I was a teenager we often played a round together usually at Scrabo or Clandeboye but occasionally at Antrim, Bangor or Donaghadee. I remember him telling me of hosting golf games with visiting entertainers, in particular the comedian Charlie Chester who loved golf. He had a lot of fun with him including such tricks as throwing the ball and sand up out of a deep bunker when their opponents couldn't see.[64]

Apart from the relaxation of his rounds of golf, his other hobbies listed in *Who's Who* are folklore, Irish music and the gramophone. His entry provides a snapshot of the scale of what he had achieved by the age of forty-six:

> Stage and screen actor, radio artist and lecturer; chairman of the Richard Hayward Film Productions Ltd, chairman of the Ulster Screen Productions

Ltd, director of the Belfast Repertory Theatre, leading character in recent Irish films, prominent in several major British pictures, descriptive study *In Praise of Ulster*, some albums and anthologies of Irish songs and ballads, collector, arranger and singer of 150 Irish songs on gramophone records.[65]

Whatever the future held, he could look back with pride on his achievements. It had been an action-packed two decades since he had taken those first tentative steps twenty years previously in the early days of his artistic career.

EIGHT

'A stubborn divil'

(1942–1946)

The walk from the row of cottages to the little lake in the mountains is a
fairly stiff climb of about two miles, along an avenue which goes twisting
about through picturesque woodlands and mountain scenery, with a little
singing river beside it dashing itself every now and again over some moss-
grown rocky ledge into every variety of cascade and miniature waterfall.

The Corrib Country, 1943

The Ireland of the 1940s was an austere place where barefoot children played
in the streets. The Catholic Church was all-powerful and even a hundred years
after the Famine poverty was rife, with mass emigration. For many who stayed
it was an unhealthy existence. Parts of the country, particularly along the west
coast, suffered badly from tuberculosis while other areas were entrenched in
the nineteenth century. But despite the decay, there was another more carefree
side to life, comprising poetry and song, a respect for knowledge of cultural
history as well as the myths and legends of an older time. This was the Ireland
that fascinated Hayward and about which he wrote. He had a ready market.
Some people were connected to small geographical areas and were becoming
more interested in their own country. They were developing a curiousness that
brought about a desire to get to know inaccessible villages or remote areas they
could not have previously visited.

Although there was an element of gloominess (electrification of farms and
rural houses did not take place until the end of 1946) there was generally a

welcome for visitors. In those pre-television days neighbours dropped in for a chat or a hand of cards. They were known as 'coorjeeking' houses, meaning 'visiting' or 'rambling'. It was a country where people worked in the fields, walked the roads and gathered at the crossroads for ceilidhs. Smoke poured from thatched whitewashed cottages all over the country, some as sparklingly fresh as though John Hinde had just snapped them for a postcard. The property boom and its accompanying bungalow blitz was still two generations away. Old-fashioned farming defined the landscape. Agriculture was the mainstay of the economy and creameries were local sources of employment. Sons took over farms as a matter of course when their fathers retired. The few cars on the rural roads were owned by priests, doctors or well-heeled businessmen.

Hayward had determined to explore this undiscovered country and was busy pressing ahead with his plans. He concentrated firstly on writing about two specific areas for his new travel books: the Corrib region, straddling Mayo and Galway, and County Kerry. By 1943, with Britain entering the fifth year of war and sweet rationing introduced, his sales were cut back and work was not so plentiful. As a freelance agent it is unlikely he received any retainer payments from either Fox's or Needler's during this time. The BBC effectively closed its Belfast operation although he continued to perform occasional song recitals from the corporation's new Art Deco Broadcasting House in Ormeau Avenue, which had opened in 1941.

Since he did not much enjoy being under-employed, he decided the best place to head for was the west of Ireland where he could continue working at an undiminished velocity. The groundwork for his Corrib book had already been laid and he chose an opulent base from which to carry out his research to make his forays into the countryside. Ashford Castle, still one of Ireland's most prestigious hotels, was his headquarters where he holed up for several weeks in the autumn of 1941 before returning the following spring. Originally built as a crenellated castle in the thirteenth century by the Anglo-Norman House of Burke, Ashford was extended and upgraded over the years. Rebuilt as a hunting lodge by the Guinness family in the 1800s, it was converted in 1939 into an exclusive hotel. Just two years before Hayward's visit, Noel Huggard bought it from Ernest Guinness and became the proprietor-manager. Huggard had trained in his parents' hotel, the Butler Arms in Waterville, County Kerry, and planned to cater mainly for sportsmen interested in angling and shooting. The hotel was self-contained with its own turbine. Set in grounds of 365 acres, on the shores of Lough Corrib, it was the ideal place for Hayward's tours.

Geographically the Corrib is an area stretching from Lough Mask through Corrib to Galway Bay. The book was a natural spin-off from the Shannon volume, keeping a water-based theme of lakes and rivers. Hayward had already made friends with many local people, ranging from priests and publicans to fishermen and hoteliers. From all of them he had developed a knack of extracting information to add to his own store of knowledge. He befriended Huggard when he stayed in the hotel in September 1941, talking to people in the surrounding area and building up his already extensive list of contacts. The two men had much in common and struck up an immediate friendship. Like Hayward, Huggard was a man of indomitable energy. As well as managing the hotel, he was also head chef, cooking all the meals and running the castle to a high standard. Because of the war, many guests stayed for long periods and the hotel enjoyed repeat business. Hayward frequently called in later years and kept friendly with Huggard.[1]

Eight months later, in April 1942, he returned to the Corrib, driving on a morning of 'golden sunshine' from Dublin where he had spent the previous day checking Ordnance Survey maps covering the region.[2] His route had taken him over the bog roads of Kildare and Westmeath, across the Shannon at Athlone, through Roscommon and north Galway into southern Mayo. 'West of the Shannon,' he writes, 'we moved into an Ireland that has changed very little in essential things in the last 2,000 years.'

Hayward loved nothing better than to start his working day with a swim and in the Corrib he had 145 islands to choose from. 'Although Corrib looks gentle and inviting,' he states, 'it can be tempestuous as the Irish Sea.'[3] In the book's opening sequence, he employs the technique of *in medias res* introducing a genial line to grab the reader's attention. 'Cock-a-doodle-doo! My eyes opened more slowly than my ears, and by the time I had started to wonder where I was my ears had been assailed again.'[4] The first island he visited was Inismicatreer, the second largest on the Corrib, where he was taken by two locals, Peter Foy and John Lydon. They discuss the fishing prospects before quickly launching into history. They bring him to Inchagoill to meet Tom Nevin, the island's only inhabitant. Gathered round the turf fire, they sit in his kitchen while he finishes breakfast. Hayward heard stories of how every month, whatever the weather, Nevin rows his small boat over to Cong to draw his pension and to shop. He asks him if he is never afraid of being drowned. 'These things are in the hands of God,' he replies, 'and sure if I'm to be taken I'll be taken and there'll be no more need for pensions or marketing or anything of the kind.'[5]

Written without chapter breakdowns, the book is in the form a long essay, ranging over history and legends. His travels take him to deserted villages, the Horse Discovery and Lady's Buttery caves, the Nymphsfield Circles, and Cong Abbey where he spends considerable time with Foy as his cicerone studying its architectural heritage. The pages are filled with lengthy passages of serious historical description and carefully distilled analysis. But Hayward realizes the benefits of introducing lighter moments and the text is permeated with humour, which 'tempers the solemnity of this dissertation'.[6] At Ashford Tweeds, a cottage industry set up by Huggard a few months previously, he describes thirty girls carding, spinning and weaving.

He draws on the work of the nineteenth-century antiquarian Sir William Wilde, author of *Loch Coirib its Shores and Islands* (1867), and follows in his footsteps, visiting a triangular patch of land known as Moytura Cunga, north of Cong, where he delves into a Bronze Age burial mound, a one-man cairn that Wilde explored. Wilde uncovered a decorated clay urn with the ashes of a cremated warrior in whose memory it was raised. The urn was later donated to the Royal Irish Academy. Hayward quotes the nineteenth-century poetry of James Clarence Mangan and William Rooney; he refers to a contemporary poet, Maurice Farley, whose poem 'The Last Stronghold' he had not been able to get out of his head for days. When he visits Knockmoy Abbey, he cites the work of the antiquarian George Petrie and the Huguenot artist Gabriel Beranger in their interpretation of the drawings in the chancel. And he shows a prickly side with a rant about the condition of the abbey, reflecting on the wider problem throughout Ireland:

> If you will but look for the cloisters at Knockmoy you will see that they have been virtually obliterated by that foul bane of all Irish monastic remains, the prescriptive right of certain families to burial in these sacred places. There is hardly an ecclesiastical ruin in Ireland not choked end to end, and from side to side, with ugly, and often outrageously vulgar modern tombstones, and I am afraid the sentiment against casting them out of a place from which any sense of public decency would always have excluded them, is too strong to be gainsaid.[7]

Hayward knew the value of stories from older people. One of his skills was to arrive in a village and ask around for the oldest person; or having done his research, he may already have identified someone to speak to. In Cong, based on information from a priest, Fr Neary, and the recollections of an old resident, David Carney, he compiled a list of craftsmen and traders from the early 1860s. The trades included wheelwright and turner, smiths, weavers, shoe-makers, nailers, fishermen and boatbuilders, millers, masons and tailors, from which Hayward painted an historical portrait of the village.

He referred to the story of Nicholas Noonan, who contested Lord Ardi-laun's right to take away an ancient privilege of the boatmen of Cong with the building of his new bridge at Ashford, whereby he denied them their long-enjoyed access to Loch Corrib. Noonan was evicted from his home in Cong, and from four other houses in the parish where he sought subsequent refuge. 'In this quiet little Western village to-day we can consider the problem through that long perspective of the years which brings clarity and sanity to our thoughts.'[8]

If there is a leitmotif in the book, then it is the inscriptions on memorial stones, churches and monuments. Everywhere he visits, he notes their wording, copying the lettering carefully in his journal. In the Old Kilmaine Demesne, when he surveys a six-sided stone structure known as the Temple of the Gods of the Neale, he becomes frustrated at the length of time it took him trying to decipher the inscription on the folly erected by Lord Kilmaine:

> It is nothing more than one of those ornamental farradiddles which noblemen of the eighteenth century seem to have considered necessary to the adorn-ment of any self-respecting demesne ... a more absurd conglomeration of unrelated objects never confronted the eyes of man. Above this farrago of nonsense is a smaller plinth into which are inset what are most likely three grotesques plundered from some ruined medieval church in the neighbour-hood ... Surmounting this amazing piece of monumental foolery is a still smaller plinth, topped with a pointed finial, and exhibiting round three of its four sides an inscription, mainly in Gothic characters ... but to which I was foolish enough to devote many maddening hours in an attempt to produce some intelligible translation or explanation.[9]

The passage is an example, not only of the parade of fanciful words in his canon, but a measure of how serious was his commitment to finding answers to historical puzzles. After his journey, to try to pin down the exact wording, he consulted R.A.S. Macalister and Brendan Adams, a philologist. He brought rubbings made for him by Peter Foy, and the two experts helped fill in missing letters. Hayward felt he had cracked most of the inscription but concluded: 'Who composed the lengthy and absurd main inscription, and what informa-tion, if any, he was trying to impart to succeeding generations, is something entirely beyond my comprehension.'[10]

Dancing at the crossroads was a feature of Irish country life in the 1940s. Humbert Craig's sketch, 'Roadside Dance', captures the atmosphere in *The Corrib Country*, Hayward's third Irish travel book published at Easter 1943.

To illustrate the book he teamed up again with 'Jimmy' Humbert Craig with whom he had enjoyed such a fruitful collaboration on the Ulster book. Their joint approach again proved successful. The watery light, landscape and lakes appealed to Craig's artistry. His thirty-eight wash drawings included the Maumturk Mountains, bogs, turf cutters, farmers and fishermen at work, as well as Cong Abbey and Cross, The Gods of the Neale, Ashford Castle and Lough Mask House where Captain Boycott lived. He also included eight sketches of Galway city to which Hayward devoted fifteen pages at the end of the book.

Publishers were feeling the economic effects of the war and it was difficult to get books commissioned. Through his Shannon book, Hayward already knew Harry Tempest who ran the long-established Dundalgan Press. Their publishing history stretched back forty years to 1903 when they produced their first book; in fact Tempest brought out Ireland's first motoring periodical, *The Irish Motor Directory and Motorists' Annual*, which ran from 1903 to 1916. In the early 1940s the company turned out attractive Irish volumes on topography, architecture, folklore, history and heritage. Their list included Harold Leask's book on Irish castles, Estyn Evans' seminal *Irish Heritage* and *At Slieve Gullion's Foot* by Michael Murphy. Hayward had read the books and knew well the high production values that had gone into them. Since the subject areas overlapped with his own interests he thought Tempest would be an appropriate publisher to approach.

By his fiftieth birthday, in October 1942, he was well advanced on the writing and ready to send off the typescript. Shortly afterwards he attended to the proofs and other details of publication. Unlike the Kerry book which was to follow, none of the correspondence between Hayward and Tempest for the Corrib book survives but it is clear that the latter had a significant input into its production. Tempest was a craftsman who had mastered the art of making books and cared passionately about those under his imprint. Taking a keen interest in the production of all Dundalgan's titles, he liked to be involved in the different stages and agree every point before the book went to press. He drew the map of Corrib Country and of Moytura Cunga, which was folded in a pocket at the back of the book. It included a sketch of the ornament on capitals at Cong Abbey drawn by Peter Foy. Tempest advised Hayward on typeface, quality of paper and on the cover image. He spoke to Craig about which drawings would print best and which areas needed strong shading before the blocks were made.[11]

Hayward's third travel book came out just after Easter 1943. The colour dust wrapper, replicated as a frontispiece, featured a Craig drawing of a mountain and lake with turf gatherers busy in the foreground. Priced at fifteen shillings, and with 164 pages, the book was set off with gold lettering on the front and spine. Despite the fact that it was the fifth year of the war and paper was scare, it was printed on high quality paper. Hayward was pleased with the polished finish. He had predicted to Tempest steady sales so the publisher printed 1500 copies – 500 more than the usual print run. Any doubts about its prospects were assuaged and his decision vindicated by the fact that it was reprinted four years later. It garnered considerable attention. In a substantial review, the *Belfast News Letter* praised Hayward's industry and thoroughness saying 'he is an amazingly versatile Ulsterman ... a portrayer of the Irish scene of the intimate kind.' The paper described him as 'a cheerful and well-informed enthusiast' and called it 'a fine bit of book-making.'[12] The *Belfast Telegraph* said the book had enhanced his reputation as an interpreter of the Irish scene:

> In the same personal and intimate vein as *In Praise of Ulster* and his Shannon book he discourses in print with free and easy abandon. He has been painstaking and industrious, and has unearthed a surprising amount of detail. He makes no tip-and-run raids on a countryside; he has time to stand and stare and then turn aside and detour to right or left at sweet will.

The paper called Craig's drawings 'an enrichment.'[13] The *Irish Independent* described it as a personal book with 'lively and well-informed writing'. The reviewer wondered though where the shanachies got the jargon of the Celtic twilight and concluded with a caveat, 'Not by all the "gods of the Neale" in the "Corrib Country"! Full marks for everything else, nothing for the mist that do be on the bogs.'[14] *The Irish Press* said both Hayward and Craig had an eye for everything, 'the purple mountains, shimmering lakes, ruined abbeys and Georgian houses; and Richard, being a born story-teller, has a good story to tell about them all.'[15] The *Times Literary Supplement* described it as pleasant, declaring, 'Hayward takes his subject seriously, and has been at pains to study and research.'[16] The *Dublin Magazine* said the book was a 'rippling stream of easy-flowing gossip and persons and places and things … and you could have no better shanachy to tell the stories than Richard Hayward,' and went on to say 'No lover of Ireland should be without it.'[17] The following summer, a generous and lengthy consideration in *Studies* helped give sales renewed impetus. The reviewer, named only as S. Ó C., described Hayward as the ideal guide:

> Clear and vivid in description, intimate and friendly in talking with you, and without a trace of that condescension, be it ever so kindly and well meant, that one meets occasionally in other books on Ireland. As he talks about the shores of the Corrib you might almost imagine that you were walking by his side, stopping here and there, turning down an unpromising lane which you might otherwise not have noticed to lead you to an old house, gable-end of a church or the mouth of an underground river. And there you would listen to him reconstruct the past so vividly that it would seem to live still. Mr. Hayward has the happy knack of picking out the dramatic incident, the illu-minating detail and the humorous incongruity, so that every page sparkles.[18]

However, the reviewer had 'one crow to pluck with him'. He felt Hayward had concentrated too much – about three-quarters of the book – on the area around Cong, at the expense of the west side of the lough:

> It seemed to me that the author drew mainly on books for this section of his journey. When he comes across an interesting story in them he tells it in his own racy style. But there is none of that pleasant chatting with the local inhabitants and fishermen that gives its charm to the earlier part of the book.[19]

He praised Craig's drawings. '*The Corrib Country* is not merely a Baedeker. It is the record of the impressions which that countryside made on the mind and eye of a sympathetic and imaginative artist.' The *Bell* reviewer said 'while the mere tripper will find the book altogether too leisurely for his requirements

... it should certainly serve to attract the more serious-minded tourist and holiday-maker ... and will go far to interpret for him the district with which it deals.' The reviewer, described as S. Mac P., added that the book was 'set in a framework of description and conveyed largely by way of conversation, with facts as to fishing facilities and golf unobtrusively insinuated, and the whole flavoured with mild and, it must be confessed, sometimes sentimental, sociological speculation.'[20] The book was reprinted four years later, in 1947, and again in 1954.

Once more, Hayward called on the services of Maurice Walsh to supply the foreword. Walsh declared it was Hayward's best book: 'It is an affectionate book, a gay book, a thoughtful book, a knowledgeable book; in short it is what a touring, rambling book should be to capture a reader and hold him from first to last.'[21] Walsh also reviewed the book for *The Irish Times*, saying 'no one knew his Ireland more surely than Hayward, or can write about it in a more masterly manner.[22] Apart from the critical reception, the book was given an endorsement by one of Hayward's business associates. Donovan Pedelty, his film friend with whom he was still in regular contact, wrote to him:

> It is a grand book for dipping into, but if I pick it up for ten minutes I find when I look at the clock again I've been blarneyed out of an hour ... But a lot of people like me will be grateful to you for Sir Candy's boy and Cathal of the Wine Red Hand, the Captains Webb and Boycott, and the rest of that engaging company. When it comes to webs, your work has much the same spell-binding quality as a coloured movie – with honeyed verse to it. I'm not surprised the book is a success. More power to it.[23]

The Hayward publicity machine was given another shot in the arm during a break in the filming of *The Quiet Man* in 1951 when an elegant Maureen O'Hara was photographed relaxing in a chair with a copy of *The Corrib Country*, an enduring image of the star. In 1963, twenty years after the original year of publication Hayward wrote to Tempest about producing a third edition since it was out of print. Tempest replied, 'It will not pay us to reprint at the former price and royalty. The sales are very slow if regular. We cannot invest £250 in it and wait for three or four years to get it back even if we increase the price to twenty shillings – it is not a royalty earning proposition now either.'[24] In 1968, four years after the deaths of both men, Dundalgan Press produced a third edition of *The Corrib Country* and a fourth came out in 1993 to commemorate its fiftieth anniversary. It remains the most recent reprint of any Hayward book.

On a break from her role as Mary Kate Danaher in *The Quiet Man*, Maureen O'Hara dips into *The Corrib Country*.

If he was busy with his travels around Ireland, Hayward was also busy back in Belfast. Since Richmond Lodge was damaged and uninhabitable after the blitz on 14 April 1941, the Haywards were forced to move out. For the next two years their existence was peripatetic and they lived in no fewer than five different locations. Initially they went to a small holiday chalet near Ballygally on the Antrim coast where they spent several months in late spring of that year. Ricky recalls it was a beautiful location carpeted with primroses and high above the sea. One of his earliest memories was being bathed in a tin bath in front of the fire.[25] Their next move was across Belfast Lough to Killaire House, 'a small mansion' on the loughshore at Carnalea near Crawfordsburn in County Down. With its own boathouse and lobster pots, it was an idyllic setting overlooking the lough. They shared this house with Louis Morrison and his family. Morrison had been the photographer on the Shannon book and was to accompany Hayward in producing future travel documentaries. He was also a director of Screen Productions, a company Hayward had set up some years earlier to make documentary and advertising films, and carry out publicity consultancy work.

As a counterpoint to his travelling, research and the solitary discipline of writing, Hayward threw parties and joined organizations. On one occasion he entertained more than twenty members of the Belfast PEN club at a summer gathering in August 1941 at Carnalea. From one of their family trips away they returned to discover that the armed services had requisitioned their house at Carnalea and piled all their possessions into one room. As a stopgap they moved into the nearby Crawfordsburn Inn, Ireland's oldest inn, run by Paddy Falloon, and a place with a curious history that appealed to Hayward. They remained there for a cosy three months before their next move brought them a few miles along the north Down coast to Bangor. They lodged beside the post office near the seafront at Ballyholme, noted for its sandy arc and swimming; from there they went into a rented bungalow at Baylands in Bangor.

For Ricky, then seven, being shunted around a variety of accommodation with different worlds to explore was a magical experience. But it was an unsettling upheaval for his mother as she tried to run a house and establish a routine; by the final move she was exhausted. Life in the war years was a series of departures. Added to the worry of Dion's absence on active service, and the loss of easy access to her sisters and friends in Belfast, her husband was away for a considerable length of time researching and working on his Corrib book and other projects. Although Elma had now grown accustomed to his absences and sometimes long separations, there were times when she was annoyed. On the surface at least there seemed to be few marital tensions or resentment of his trips, but moments of friction were inevitable. Ricky recalls one occasion when his father's failure to show up exasperated his mother:

> It was during a period when we lived in a bungalow at Baylands near the seafront in Bangor. I was seven and remember walking with her at Bally-holme when my father failed to turn up as promised. She said 'he's the L-I-M-I-T', but that was a rare and not repeated expression of her feelings.[26]

Avril Cotton-Taylor, whose parents were friendly with the Haywards in Bangor, remembers parties in Ballyholme. Her father was the managing director of the Owen O'Cork Mill in east Belfast and knew Hayward through his connection with the Hippodrome Theatre:

> It was a hectic social scene in Bangor in those wartime days. Richard and Elma came to parties in my parents' house on the Ballyholme Road. My mother, who played the piano, had a beautiful voice and could reach high notes. She sang songs from the major musicals of the time. Richard would

accompany her singing Irish songs. She had some of his records and loved to sing with him. I was sent to bed with my sister but we used to hang over the banister listening to them into the early hours of the morning. He was a very sociable man who was great fun and enjoyed a drink. As a child I used to play with Richard junior at the seafront. The water was very clean in those days, we would often swim in the bay and we had some great times.[27]

Towards the end of 1943 their nomadic house-hunting days finally came to an end. They moved back to their preferred part of Belfast, renting a commodious house called Clonsilla, at 352 Antrim Road in the north of the city close to two of Elma's sisters. This was to become the family home for the next twenty years, bringing stability to their lives. It was a three-storey Victorian red brick house in a row of five facing on to the main road. The front door opened into a porch with a vestibule door. The spacious rooms were set off with cornices, picture rails, and ceiling roses, while an elegant newel post with mahogany handrail led upstairs. There was ample living area for the furnishings they had accumulated. During the winter months Elma shifted the furniture around and sorted out the kitchen. Hayward filled the house with books and paintings. Downstairs the drawing room and dining room housed his radiogram, piano and harp. Upstairs his extensive library was displayed on shelves and in mahogany bookcases along with filing cabinets and a writing desk. A chest on the landing held much of his large record collection. Elma's happiness was restored; they had a house that she could turn into à home where they were able to entertain friends and relations. Each Christmas morning they held drinks parties attended by many in the artistic and literary world. A much-treasured family story revolves around one such Christmas when William Conor, who had cycled to their house, had too much to drink. 'When he tried to mount his bike on departure,' Ricky recalls, 'he went too far over the saddle and fell off on the wrong side. He appeared to be uninjured and took it in good part. As well as being a great artist, he seemed a very nice man.'[28]

Hayward was content in his new home – not that he was planning on spending a huge amount of time looking into the coals of the fire. It was a short distance into his office in the city centre and gave him a base from where he could launch his next projects. The house provided the essential components most necessary to his happiness: the company of Elma, a quiet study for writing, a gramophone and harp for musical distraction, and a library of reference books close to hand. At last he was able to organize his large library in proper bookcases. An avid bibliophile, he had assembled a large collection of books reflecting his interests in Irish cultural history, music, drama, film, biography and fiction. His shelves contained the works of R.A.S. Macalister and H.C. Lawlor, two archaeologists he had met through the BNFC. Literature on folk-lore and dialect sat next to books on Irish topography including the works of the Donegal writer, Harry Percival Swan and Estyn Evans. Some of his personal collection is retained at the Folk Museum and gives an insight into Hayward's reading habits. Drama and volumes of poetry by Yeats and MacNeice, plays by friends such as St John Ervine, Rutherford Mayne, Hugh Quinn, and Doro-thea Donn Byrne and song books by Alfred Perceval Graves were all part of his reading. Other shelves housed fiction and short stories, including the work of Maurice Walsh, Anthony Burgess, Forrest Reid, Lennox Robinson, Patrick Mahony and Percival Needler, the managing director of his chocolate company employers. Well-known books by the film director John Paddy Carstairs as well as biographies of Virginia Woolf, the Marquis de Sade and J.M. Synge filled the shelves. Reference books included *Brewer's Dictionary of Phrase and Fable*, and *A Dictionary of Derivations*.

Hayward used the first-floor library for his writing. Dion's girlfriend, Dolly (later his wife), carried out proofreading on the Corrib book, marking up the manuscript with annotations. For some of the later books, Ricky helped check the galley proofs. He has fond memories of growing up in a comfortable, if somewhat chilly house:

> My father used to sit at his desk in the study and type with two fingers. Our house had no central heating but we had gas and electric fires and he used a footmuff to protect his feet from draughts. He typed quite quickly and worked hard but always made time to talk and was a very good father to me. At night he read me poetry and stories. He sang songs such as 'My Lagan Love', 'The Inniskilling Dragoon', 'Johnny I Hardly Knew you', 'By the Margin of the Ocean' and 'The Lark in the Clear Air' which made a particular impression on me. He also sang some of the lighter Orange songs such as 'The Ould Orange Flute', 'Dolly's Brae', 'Derry's Walls' and 'The Sash'. Poems that he read to me were by James Stephens, Joseph Campbell and the Nationalist poet Alice Milligan, who was born in Omagh, while others were by Yeats or the Romantics. He also read all the Arthur Ransome stories, Lewis Carroll, Beatrix Potter, Robert Louis Stevenson's main child-friendly works, and many of Patricia Lynch's books, including *The Turf-cutter's Donkey* with its wonderful evocations of the countryside. He knew her quite well and liked her children's writing. On one occasion – most likely in Dublin and when he was much younger – he also met Yeats who didn't take a blind bit of notice of him or as my father phrased it appeared not to register his existence.[29]

Flush with confidence following the Corrib book's success and with Elma now cheerfully ensconced in her new well-ordered home, he was already laying plans for his next writing project. As the war showed no signs of ending, his sights were set on another part of the west, much farther south. This was to involve a lengthy exploration of Kerry, one of Ireland's largest counties. Barely had the ink dried on his Corrib book than he began immersing himself in the county's history, studying how the past shaped the present. In his new home, he puzzled over Ordnance Survey maps, working out routes and places to visit as well as building up a network of reliable local contacts. For this book he planned to travel with a new artist but on this occasion was not saying goodbye to his family. Elma and Ricky came along for part of the trip, accompanying the roaming writer and his artist. With its rich heritage, Kerry offered Hayward much scope to write about everything from history, legend and folktales to archaeology and architecture. The Ring of Kerry, the Dingle peninsula and the Skelligs were ripe for study and it would prove difficult in deciding which areas to choose.

In those days the Kerry landscape was largely unsullied by the proliferation of one-off rural houses that blight the area today. Apart from the cultural history of the county, its natural beauty with quiet lakes, valleys and Ireland's highest mountains was ideal territory for him. Having studied the contour lines on maps, he worked out the best approaches and had his sights set not only on Brandon and Mangerton, but also the country's biggest peak, Carrantuohill in the MacGillicuddy's Reeks. All this was quintessential Haywardland and it is not hard to understand why he was smitten by Kerry and keen to write about it.

He envisaged a book with sketches along similar lines to his Corrib one, albeit a much larger volume. Humbert Craig had died on 12 June 1944 at Cushendun, and Hayward asked Theo Gracey, a landscape painter and illustrator whom he knew, to fill the breach. Dundalgan Press agreed to take on the book. Tempest felt photographs should accompany the text but Hayward knew well the value of an artistic flourish to sit alongside his words and was adamant that a professional illustrator should be employed. In the summer of 1944 – just a few weeks after the D-Day allies launched their invasion of Europe – they took themselves to the far southwest of the country, spending five weeks gathering material.

The warm summer weather was appealing and the friendliness of the people helped their mood. It was just twenty-two years since the civil war, which had been fought more bitterly in Kerry than anywhere else. Memories were still fresh of the Free State troops landing at Fenit pier in August 1922 to surprise the anti-Treaty republicans. In Dublin Éamon de Valera had just been re-elected Taoiseach in the twelfth Dáil. Hayward does not dwell on immediate history or contemporary political issues – his focus is on prehistory, landscape and topography. The two men quartered the countryside, inspecting forts, churches and abbeys, scrutinizing antiquities such as stone alignments or the Loher Cross. They climbed mountains, sailed to islands, rode on a jarvey through the Gap of Dunloe, and spent time in August at Puck Fair in Killorglin. Hayward loved the fair's atmosphere, writing up lengthy descriptions of it. Set piece events and the quirkiness of the ceremony attended by thousands provided lively copy. The first official mention of the fair in a written document was in 1613 when a local landlord received a charter from King James I giving him permission to charge tolls, a practice that continued into the 1950s. But the most popular story is that when Oliver Cromwell and his soldiers were storming Killorglin, a goat ran down from the mountains to warn residents of his imminent approach. This story is dismissed by Hayward as being 'rather silly'. He interpreted Puck as a pagan deity capable of bringing luck and success to marriage and binding together people in a unity of gathering assembled to worship him. He saw it as 'virtually a pagan fertility festival of folk-memory … preserving an antique, celebration undoubtedly associated with the goat-footed Pan.'[30]

During his 1944 visit he made a film about Kerry; on his return the following summer, he again revisited Killorglin and included a sketch of the goat being raised on to the platform in the busy square. Nine-year-old Ricky was also with him. Hayward describes what he saw as the connection between Puck Fair and the solar festival of Lugh, the sun god of the Tuatha de Danann. From their base, Hayward organized a room on the first floor of O'Shea's cinema, giving them a grandstand view of the proceedings. With his jackdaw eye, he scanned the panorama of the square and street down to the bridge, gathering precise, jewelled detail as well as making notes. He paints a graphic description of the scene:

> The tall wooden scaffold-like construction rising in front of my window, flagged and be-ribboned for the reception of His Majesty King Puck when the great moment arrived; the concourse of showmen and their stalls crowding the small square to bursting point; the movement of frightened herds with their loud cries and bellows; the streets and pavements in many places ankle-deep in cow dung; the rather savage feeling of sound and colour and raw humanity. It was all very primitive and lively and pagan-seeming and it was all intensively exciting.[31]

The fairs of Ireland, he wrote, had appealed to the poets of the country from remote times. He came down from his own high position to walk the streets and in the best travel writerly tradition, brought the reader from the panoramic to the particular:

> For wherever I went was colour and movement and animation, and no poet worth his salt could fail to be infected with the immense energy of it all … And then over the bridge, along the road to right and left, were the caravans of the gypsies and the distinct and smaller portable habitations of the tinkers. A great riot of nomadic colour this, with swarms of children playing under the cara-vans, or about the openings of the lower tilts, and the buxom brightly-shawled women busy taking silver in exchange for news of dark-avised strangers whom they saw in the upturned palms of laughing country boys and girls.[32]

He describes how Conn Riordan of Headfort, known round the Irish fairs as 'Conn the Laces', was plying a variety of three-card tricks and how his son, referred to in the book under his Irish name, begged to be allowed to try his skill. 'I shouted down to Laces and evidently Risteard Og and he got on well together, for the young rascal soon came back with a beaming face and a pocket jingling with coppers.'[33] Hayward enjoyed the pageantry of it all, recording vividly the moment when Puck was elevated:

> Even the cattle were stilled and the raucous women at their stalls, and through the very air seemed to creep a deep sense of tradition, of the realization that now was the moment when the ritual of unnumbered centuries was to live again. It was ten seconds of extraordinary tension, and it was broken by the quavering note of a single distant violin, absurdly irrelevant and unspeakably fragile in the thin line of its stringy tone.[34]

At the end of the Puck section, he slips in one of his idiosyncratic words: 'one of our party … told me that he saw many stout farmers lying asleep on the pavements, doubtless having dropped in their tracks in the midst of a high wassail which only sleep brought to an end.'[35] Their boat trip to the Skelligs brought rich pickings. The twenty-page section includes five of Gracey's sketches, and the journey gave Hayward the chance to indulge in some adjectival prose:

> And now we were well and truly free of the land and riding high, wide and handsome over those grand rollers which were tall as a house and green as jade. The air was sharp and invigorating and heady as vintage wine, and a great exhilaration came upon us as the prospect changed in slow majestic rhythm from deep-enclosed valleys of ocean water, which shut out every-thing but their own iridescent immensity, to the savage grandeur of the rock-bound storm-besculptured coast. This was indeed the very majesty of Kerry.[36]

The natural world played a part in Hayward's travel writing and in his detailed study *In the Kingdom of Kerry*, published in 1946. He described the gannets at the Skelligs, sketched by Theo Gracey, as 'soaring and gliding and standing still ... the bird fell like a streamlined bomb.'

Hayward looked forward to tackling some of the county's highest mountains. When it came to Carrantuohill, he left Elma and Ricky behind despite protestations from his son:

> No one of my own party cared for climbing except Risteard Og, and this particular expedition was a bit beyond his years, although I did not succeed in convincing him of the fact ... we took leave of the rebellious Risteard Og and his expostulating mother, who had accompanied us thus far in the car, and set off on our long climb.[37]

Hayward set off with two guides, Tomas O'Sullivan, a local man, and James Stewart from Limerick. The hardest part of the trek to Ireland's highest point at 3314ft was negotiating the Devil's Ladder:

The Devil's Ladder is the devil itself. Six hundred feet high, and as vertical as makes no difference, it looks like the old course of a waterfall, and composed of scree and loose boulders, it is treacherous to hand, foot and ankle, as well as to the heads of those who follow the more forward climber. For my part I hugged the sides for safety, and many a sizeable boulder came clattering down beside me that I would rather have seen there than felt somewhere else. The whole upward length of the Ladder is just one solid piece of hard work, sore on the hands and on the leg and thigh muscles, but it holds nothing to daunt any actively-inclined person and I soon became convinced that Risteard Og would have taken it in his stride.[38]

He took up with him four stones: one for himself, one each for Ricky and Elma, and one for Dion, 'making more perilous ascents in Italy' – a reference to his exploits in the Second World War, which by the summer of 1945 was finally drawing to an end.

Gracey's sketch shows a group of climbers descending Mount Brandon in Kerry. Nine-year-old Ricky leads the way with his father and two guides.

Ricky did get a chance to climb Brandon, although the weather was poor. One of Gracey's sketches shows the party descending the mountain and Ricky with his walking stick out in front. With his lively eye for absurdity, Hayward was always on the lookout for unusual stories or traditional songs. He had a productive visit to Blennerville, noted for its windmills, and at one time the centre of the Munster grain trade. It was also the place from where, in the nineteenth century, ships such as *Jeanie Johnston* loaded up with emigrants to America. He picked up a rhyming chant about Paddy Spatters' bell, rung to summon emigrants to the ship:

> Let all who are goin' on the Americay line
> Be down to the windmill in ten minutes time,
> Some people laughin' and some people cryin'
> For that is the way to the end of ty-im:
> Ding-dong bell! [39]

Ricky recalls his father bemoaning the quality of many of the hotels that he stayed in during his travels around 1940s' Ireland. 'He often told me,' he said, 'that he shared his bed with fleas.'[40] One of Hayward's friends in Kerry, Dick Hilliard, was a Killarney businessman and bibliophile. He owned two stores in the town selling drapery, footwear and furniture, and a shoe factory in High Street. Hayward had made contact with him in advance of his trip and Hilliard invited him to browse his private collection of books for research in their house on the Muckross Road, a mile outside Killarney. An insight into how Hayward worked on location and the extent to which he relied on other texts is given by Hilliard's son, Richard, then a fifteen-year-old schoolboy:

My father owned an extensive library of 3000 books, many about County Kerry and travel books such Thackeray's *Irish Sketch Book*, and Arthur Young's *A Tour in Ireland*. He specialized in Irish history, church history, world history and reference books as well as anthropology. The library in Killarney in those days was rudimentary as things were pretty lean during the war and ours was a tremendous resource. My father did not have many friends but was quite happy to entertain Hayward for the week of his daily visits as generally he did not let people into his library unless he was with them. Hayward arrived each morning, had access to everything and my father left him to it and went to work. He spent time copying large amounts of detail from various books, going through them carefully. After his Kerry book was published, my father often said that he wrote it in his library. Hayward did not stay overnight with us as he was in a local hotel but my mother made him lunch and cooked him dinner each night. We lived mostly on roast beef or lamb chops and, as we had a big orchard, there was stewed apple and rice pudding. She also made pea soup and beef broth which he enjoyed. It was the end of the war but food rationing did not affect us apart from sugar, tea and butter. Hayward was polite and mannerly but hardly noticed me at all and I never talked to him. He was too busy pumping my father for historical facts and leading him on, quizzing him to get information. They discussed history and troubled times of the past. Our ancestors came from Yorkshire to Killarney to put down the 1641 rebellion and our family history interested him.[41]

On return to Belfast with a fresh crop of experiences after an arduous summer tour, Hayward immediately launched into writing up a draft. The main business during autumn and winter was the preparation of the type-script. A measure of his unremitting dedication is clear from a letter he sent to Harry Tempest, which throws light on his working pattern. He disclosed that the previous day he had written 6000 words and by November 1945 was halfway through the book with 60,000.[42] For several months the two men exchanged a flurry of letters in what turned into heated correspondence, debating the content and coverage of specific topics. Although similar in back-ground and temperament, they had strong differences of opinion. Like many writers, Hayward had moments of frustration and despair at his desk, rewriting and revising, harmonizing the text, arguing over stylistic points as well as the issue of selectivity. His happy-go-lucky front concealed a stubborn streak. Disa-greements continued to simmer, erupting into bilious letters. The immediate postwar period was a busy year for Tempest. He was publishing seven books in what was the first year of peace. Hayward worked flat-out on the manuscript. He appeared to write the book at a gallop. New projects were building up and he was wrestling with competing demands on his time. Nonetheless he was sedulous in his approach.

Tempest read an initial draft of the text and requested thirty changes. He asked Hayward to 'tone down your manner of writing and not to rake up old animosities.' He felt that some of his prose was too purple, advising him to 'avoid journalistic phrases':

> I don't like 'terrific huddle of mountains' or 'mountain-fringed eyeful of beauty' ... I repeat do not inflame old wounds – some of the phraseology is more suited to a political speech than to a pleasant book on a beautiful country. I do not mind objective history but I do not want to publish anything which tends to keep people divided instead of bringing them together again.[43]

Harry Tempest, owner of Dundalgan Press, and publisher of four of Hayward's books. He asked Hayward to: 'tone down your manner of writing ... and avoid journalistic phrases'. Hayward's *Where the River Shannon flows* is in the middle row of the top shelf.

Tempest had exacting standards. He suggested that to help with accuracy, the architectural historian and archaeologist Harold Leask be consulted to check facts about important buildings. In 1923 Leask had been appointed the first Inspector of National Monuments in the Free State and his book on Irish castles remains the standard architectural work on the subject. Another expert used by Hayward was R.A.S. Macalister, whose monographs are referred to in his text. He also requested that Maurice Walsh and a Tralee priest, Rev. Dean Reidy, known as the Dean of Kerry, should check it for accuracy. Tempest queried the priest's title with Hayward, saying he could not 'imagine how there was a "Dean of Kerry" for there is neither diocese nor cathedral of that name.'[44]

Since Walsh was a Kerry man, Hayward had asked him to write a foreword. He was ideally placed to do this, he believed, having already contributed to the Ulster, Shannon and Corrib books. In a preliminary page dedication to Walsh, Hayward dubbed him 'the father and mother of this book.' Tempest, however, was uneasy about using Walsh to write the foreword, and outlined his reservations about the hype contained in it:

It is a very nice and very enthusiastic personal letter of appreciation to you. I am not so happy about it as a foreword to the book. If as publisher I used this continued very high praise as part of a "blurb" it would be in keeping, for a publisher is supposed to cry his wares and his authors as if they were extra magnificent – though, even then, I believe in restraint and sober statement of fact. Also the public are rather suspicious of one author writing praise for another author, or reviewing another author's book. It is beginning to look like log-rolling or back scratching to them.[45]

Tempest also said that Dean Reidy had written back and he sent on the suggested changes:

They are just what is wanted – expert local knowledge and learning. We want to avoid anything incorrect, to counter wrong popular notions and to start no new pseudo-traditions based on our book … Even taking all these notes of corrections or changes into account, they are few compared to the mass of good material you have composed.[46]

Tempest moved next to the subject of Gracey's illustrations. The total he has asked to produce was 173, which Tempest felt was too many and would increase the amount of paper needed. 'You cannot expect an artist to turn out such a number quickly if they are to be well done and not commercial pot-boilers.'[47] Hayward had many enervating demands on his time. Preliminary plans were underway for two new films, one of which he hoped to make that year. He had just finished the first treatment of the script and was awaiting instructions from London about the second one. The other was a documentary on American soldiers serving in the North during the Second World War. He had also started on what he said was a long second novel. In the event it was never published but he appended two exclamation points to a wry little joke, 'But the rest of the day's my own!!'[48] In his three-page reply, an enraged Hayward dealt firstly with the question of using Walsh, before moving on to difficulties he was experiencing with Gracey delivering the drawings on time and the problem over the correct title for Dean Reidy. The Walsh question aroused in him a degree of passion:

Please be reasonable. Maurice is a best-seller and there is nothing that I can do to bring him advantage; back-scratching pre-supposes mutual benefit; but here all the benefit is one-sided. I have only just left Maurice, and what he said to me in conversation eclipses everything in that letter. He is firmly of the opinion that my book is the best thing of its kind done in Ireland for fifty years – and he should know – or anyway be entitled to his opinion … As to the <u>form</u> of Maurice's contribution, this was his own idea. I am uncertain whether you want a foreword from him at all. From what you say, his opinion, as a fellow-writer, is worthless. Please make yourself clear on this point. If you want a regular foreword, send me back the letter and I'll ask Maurice to oblige. If you want neither foreword nor letter, say so.[49]

He went on to fulminate with a torrent of scorn about a further anxiety – Gracey and the fact that Tempest had showered praise on him, while he was experiencing problems in getting him to complete the drawings on time:

You did the worst possible thing in telling this man that he was doing well. I warned you about his type, and asked you to sail into him. The result of your talk is that he has done <u>nothing</u> since he saw you, and when I took him to task today he told me that you were delighted and assured him that there was no hurry. That is his <u>type</u>, and he must be dealt with accordingly. I think you should write him a letter at once, saying that April 30th is a deadline and that drawings after that date will be useless to you – that you will then proceed to publish with what you have. Take my advice and write this letter <u>at once</u>. I will then call and do the rest. One sentence in your present letter enrages me beyond endurance. You say: "I have never seen a list of what you proposed to have drawn … etc.", whereas I went to the trouble of typing just such a list for Gracey to take with him for your interview. I confronted Gracey with your statement this morning, and he said that not only did you see the list but went through it with him. <u>Please!!</u> I am a busy and methodical man, and this sort of thing is <u>too</u> much.[50]

He then turned his attention to the wrangle over Dean Reidy's title:

His name was written down for me by one of his closest friends – John Caball, M.A., the local schoolmaster. Naturally I never suspected that a man in his position would give me an incorrect title, especially in connection with a close friend who is also his P.P. The Dean's remark that he is never known by the title is breath-taking – for during my two months in Kerry I never heard him addressed other than as The Dean of Kerry. Nor do I follow your reasoning; there is a Cathedral in Killarney, and a Bishop of Kerry – so why not a Dean of Kerry … But please do understand that I accept no blame for the wrong title and address … The tone of your letter rather suggests that I am careless in such matters.[51]

On a roll, a fractious Hayward moved on to moan about the vexed subject of revision, which he found irksome:

I have already told you that the very idea of going over my own work is abhorrent to me. I dealt with your personal suggestions, rejecting some, accepting others ... This is <u>MY</u> book, and since I have written other successful books in the same genre, I must be allowed to stand or fall by what I say myself in my own way.[52]

Hayward had shown that his fuse was short, but his most pressing problems were the exigencies of his films, songs, and other writing as well as his confectionery job, now about to pick up with the imminent ending of war:

I shall be up to the neck in work for twelve months – two films and a long novel – and I had definitely got this Kerry book off my plate in expectation of all my present commitments. To go through all that again, page by page, will be a formidable task, but I shall be able to do it – with dint and drudgery. I loathe the very idea of going over it again, but I accept my responsibility.[53]

He included a final note about the thorny issue of his illustrator:

And deal with Gracey – by all means deal with him – write him that letter and send me a copy of it. We must get something definite there. If you don't face up to this you'll find Gracey still promising to work hard after his next Christmas rush is over. I know this man so well – a good artist but an impossible 'putter offer'.[53] ... My time for the next few months will be shockingly divided between home, London and Dublin, so you can surely appreciate my plight. I never dreamt for a moment of the Kerry book as other than completed.'[54]

In his matter-of-fact businesslike reply, Tempest kept his cool, adopting a no-nonsense approach. 'I will leave to you the responsibility of dealing with the help and suggestions you have received. I am not prepared to discuss them further. If you believe Maurice Walsh's foreword makes it a better book or helps its sale, I say nothing more.'[55] Three days later Hayward replied hastily with an apologetic calm in his letter of 6 April:

I am sorry to observe a note of acrimony in your letter. I didn't want that to happen ... I am indeed very grateful to you, and our other friends, for the care they have lavished on reading my stuff, and I can assure you that every reasonable suggestion will be adopted by me. I want this book to be the best thing I have ever done. Believe me ... Please forgive if I have been awkward. It was not intentional ... I loathe people who don't keep their bargain. With me a date is a date.[56]

Tempest posted the manuscript back avoiding any controversy but Hayward would not allow matters to rest. He persisted, writing back a week later, asking for guidance: 'I can, as you say, make my own decision, but I would be grateful to you for your opinion. A more restrained formal foreword – how would that do? What I really want to get at is this – why did you suddenly take such a violent dislike to the idea?'[57] Hayward also dealt with some specifics of the Kerry book and continuing problems over the timescale of the completion of Gracey's drawings:

I left Brandon out because it has been done so often. I did not list them [the drawings] separately because Gracey asked to be given a free hand. I will remind him, but I hate going near him nowadays. He puts me into a bad temper, and that does no good to anybody. The yew at Muckross – I ask you? With so much deleted, why revive that hoary old fellow? It has been pictured ad nauseum, and so has the Friary itself. If we get half the "essential" list I'll be surprised – never mind these definitely unessential details. I'm really tired of Gracey and his continued promises and failures to keep them. He hasn't done a thing since he saw you!![58]

Towards the end of April, tempers cooled. On 24 April Hayward again wrote to Tempest. He pointed out changes he had made to the typescript as he wanted to avoid any blemishes and admitted his stubbornness:

If I have left too many 'terrifics' and things like that, we can prune them further in the proof reading; and perhaps you'll make a list now and say what I have omitted to tone down. I think I've done most of the things you asked me to do. On this, I ask your further advice. Please. I shall now look forward to hearing from you that you are completely satisfied with the book as it stands today. Revision, to me, is a hateful job, but I feel that my book is greatly improved by what I have done – and I now thank you, sincerely, for your valuable persistence. I'm a stubborn divil, and don't really deserve a publisher like you.[59]

They still continued to disagree over content and when Tempest read a second draft of the book he requested more changes. An exasperated Hayward reluctantly agreed to his suggestions. 'It will be an awful job. I detest working over a thing twice and the MS will look ghastly when it reaches you finally … this is a very important book and I am with you in a desire to remove all blemishes.'[60] Hayward wanted to include a twenty-page section in the opening chapter on four Kerry poets. A monument by the sculptor Seamus Murphy had recently been erected in Killarney to the poets and he felt this was justification. Tempest said it was far too much. He had written to the Dean of Kerry who replied: 'Twenty pages on four poets? Decidedly excessive – see Fr. Dinneen's pamphlet. Three or four pages would be a big allowance.'[61] In the end Hayward did cut back and the published book contained fourteen pages on the poets. By the spring of 1945 the copy-editing was finished but there was still much work to be done on the illustrations. Gracey had completed seventy-one drawings and told Tempest that Hayward wanted another one hundred. Hayward was in despair with the delay. Gracey's output slowed and then stopped. The help of a mutual unnamed friend was enlisted and drawing was resumed.[62] The deliberation over the text, consultations with experts and delays in sketches meant that it was not ready in time for the 1945 Christmas market. Hayward was angry. Tempest too was disappointed since he had planned a highly attractive book with extra wide margins to accommodate the small sketches and full-page drawings he had been promised. Matters were smoothed over, Hayward went through the proofs and agreement was reached on final changes.

The book was eventually published in spring 1946. *In the Kingdom of Kerry* is nearly twice as long as his Corrib book. Like *The Corrib Country* Hayward's Kerry book does not have chapter breakdowns but takes the form of a continuous essay with the text broken up by sketches. The finished book contains 109 pen-and-ink drawings, twenty-six of them full page, and fourteen marginal ones. Gracey's sketches fall into three categories: diagrammatic, land- or seascapes, and whimsical. A stylish folding map, drawn by Tempest, is included in a pocket at the back while the front endpapers are decorated with a map of the Killarney district. The wraparound jacket features a colour sketch of Loch Currane in green, black and yellow. At 350 pages the Kerry book was on a par with the scale of the Ulster volume.

The critical opinion was warm and the book sold well. The *Irish Independent* said Hayward 'combines a typically Northern thoroughness and tenacity with a puckish sense of fun. And it will readily be admitted that historical or archaeological reflection, with which this book is filled, is easier fare when it is seasoned with so liberal a dash of humour.'[63] An incisive review by the Kerry writer Bryan MacMahon in *The Bell* caught the essence of what Hayward had set out to achieve. Opening the book in 'a spirit of scepticism', MacMahon soon changed his mind and in a short perceptive portrait of the author summed up the many sides to the man and his writing:

> The scholar in him shows us the Chi-Rho Crosses in the crumbled abbeys, the jester in him laughs at such phenomena as an unsinkable man; the zealot in him denounces the intrusion of sham villa on good landscape or the glazed tile on grey graveyard; the anchorite in him leads us up grass-grown roads and the imp and the acrobat in him takes us out on dizzy pinnacle of Skellig Michael and leaves us there with our vertigo for good company.[64]

Irish Bookman reproduced on its cover Gracey's sketch of Puck Fair with crowds in Killorglin square watching the raised goat. In his review, Conal Casey said Hayward 'misses nothing, nothing out of the present, nothing out of the past':

> He chats about all things, often – granted – with the ersatz snappiness of the voice that goes with a documentary film, often the irresistible zest of the good salesman, most frequently with evidence of careful observation and a deep feeling that can approach poetry … On a few details pedants may quarrel, for Richard Hayward knows enough about archaeology to dare to write down judgments and opinions. But wise men, like myself, will admit that he has written the best guidebook ever written about Kerry, the most readable, and thanks to Theo J. Gracey, possibly the most effectively illustrated.[65]

(Fifty years later the art critic Theo Snoddy wrote that Gracey's Puck Fair sketch with the crowded scene 'is quite untypical of his work'.)[66] Writing in the *Illustrated London News*, W. R. Calvert described the book as compelling and praised Gracey's drawings. 'It is a guide to a comparatively unknown country – so far as the average Englishman is concerned – which is both appealing and informative.'[67] The *Manchester Guardian* said it was 'well mapped and carefully documented.'[68]

In 1950 Hayward wrote to the RSAI correcting a note written by Fran-çoise Henry about the Loher Cross. She had claimed that no mention or photograph of the Cross had ever been published. Hayward pointed out he described it fully in his book on Kerry as well as 'the fine slap on Church Island, Loch Currane, of which a carefully detailed drawing appears in my book. I consider this last-named drawing to be of importance, because the rapid weather of this great slab will soon render it indecipherable. As it was, we spent tedious hours bringing out the details.'[69]

A local man who featured in the book, Daniel O'Sullivan, of Caherdaniel, Killarney, wrote to Hayward: 'You made me so vain in your references to me in your Kingdom of Kerry that I have sent copies to America and three to England to friends.'[70] The book continued to sell in good quantities. Seven years after the first edition was published, the owner of the Kerry Book Shop in Tralee, Michael Glazier, wrote to Hayward asking if he would contribute an article of 2000 words to the *Kerry Annual*. He mentioned the Kerry book in the letter saying, 'The Kingdom of Kerry is the eternal bestseller; it sells on and on and on …'[71] Such success in sales terms was an acknowledgment from the book trade of his hard work and of the time, money and energy spent working on what turned out to be an enormous project. The battles that he had with

Tempest, the wrangles with Gracey, the torture over rewriting, must in the long run have seemed worthwhile. The book was reprinted in 1953, 1976, and again in 1987 with a new colour cover.

A further measure of the regard in which Hayward was held in the Irish book industry is revealed through a biographical leaflet printed in 1947 by Eason booksellers. Between 1946 and 1953, the company produced monthly bulletins, which included a series of eighty-two profiles of Irish authors. Hayward was chosen as number thirty in the series. The 1500-word article was a retrospective consideration ranging across singing, film and drama work as well as his books. He was described as being 'like most versatile artists ... a difficult man to pin down with a label':

> As a writer, Richard Hayward, is becoming increasingly popular and impor-
> tant ... Once, when he was asked what he considered to be his most impor-
> tant work, he said: "The work I am doing now," and that is as good an index
> to his strength and weaknesses as we are likely to find ... Archaeology, which
> runs like a thread of gold through his writing, is another of Richard's towering
> enthusiasms, and there is hardly an ancient site in Ireland which has not been
> probed by his roving and experienced eye. Adjudicating at Irish feisanna is
> something else in which our many-talented subject delights, and most of the
> performers who have come before him for judgment have paid tribute to the
> constructive helpfulness and fair-mindedness of his closely-reasoned deci-
> sions, based as they are on a wide and practical experience in the theatre, on
> the screen and radio and on the concert platform.[72]

As the unnamed writer of this profile highlighted, his adjudication at feis events was something that had absorbed considerable amounts of his time. Despite the wartime austerity and its accompanying problems such as a shortage of petrol as well as food and paper rationing, crossing the border and dealing with authorities and bureaucracy, Hayward produced three substantial discursive travel books between autumn 1939 and 1946 that stood the test of time and were all reprinted. Cumulatively they are a formidable achievement, and along with his Ulster book and novel constitute a total of five volumes in a ten-year period. Given the hardships of the times and the economic difficulties of publishing books during the war, on top of his punishing schedule, it is little wonder that they were written and produced at all. Moves were afoot to have his work better known across the Atlantic. He was entertaining the hope of being published in the US and about to mark a new stage in his writing career.

Hayward's exclusion, by and large, of religion, politics and any bitterness, which colours much of Irish popular history, contributed to the wide general appeal of his writing. A man in harmony with the *genius loci*, his literary star was in the ascendancy and he was ready to tackle the remaining parts of Ireland that had yet to come under his gimlet-eyed scrutiny. He had found his true voice and a unique style – one that admittedly had a certain *longuer* but in hindsight seems in keeping with the times. He was puffed up too about Bryan MacMahon's endorsement that echoed in his ear: 'He has an ability to show he could be scholarly, indignant, jocular, didactic or informal.'[73]

NINE

Ulster versus Ireland:
A 'sugar-coating' battle
(1939–1946)

> The making of films is a highly-specialized craft in which the four men of Four
> Ways Productions have skilled themselves in the hard school of experience.
> Hayward letter to Northern Ireland Government

Hayward had very much enjoyed the film making experience and the fame that
came with it but financially it was impossible to sustain long term. He wanted
to combine his Irish travel writing with documentary films so that they would
feed off each other thus maximizing publicity. In 1939 he was forty-seven. He
had ambitions to write discursive travel books about the different regions of
Ireland and had already swept into this work. The first of these, *In Praise of Ulster*,
came out in 1938 and although it was not accompanied by a film, his next three
books were. By this stage he had also published four volumes of verse and a
novel, and written and produced more than forty BBC radio plays and sketches.

He did not completely give up dabbling in films and continued over the
next ten years to produce short fact-based travelogues and two government
information films although these were a long way from the bucolic comedies
that had made him a household name in the mid 1930s.

In the meantime, the first of his 'shorts', *In the Footsteps of St Patrick*, was
shown to the trade in Dublin in March 1939 and four months later at the Classic
Cinema in Belfast. The twenty-five-minute film made by Screen Productions

reflected again his enthusiasm for the countryside. Locations included Slemish Mountain, Strangford Lough, Antrim, Armagh, Downpatrick Cathedral, Slane in Meath and the Rock of Cashel. The cameraman was Louis Morrison who had been a stills photographer on *Devil's Rock*. Filming took place during the summer and in the winter of 1938 as snow scenes feature in a sequence at Antrim round tower. One of the highlights is a scene involving hundreds of people taking part in the blessings by Cardinal MacRory on 12 June 1938 and the unveiling of a new memorial to St Patrick at the top of Slieve Patrick Mountain at Saul in County Down. Hayward, who narrated the commentary, secured exclusive rights to the filming of this scene, which in the days before television news has the look of a Pathé newsreel. The *Belfast News Letter* said it captured 'the spirit of our exquisitely simple countryside and was likely to do much to strengthen the consciousness of Ulster.'[1] In *The Irish Press* Liam MacGabhann lauded it as the best of all the previous Irish travel films by a long way. 'Richard Hayward, poet, songster, actor, producer, novelist, is a man out of Orange Ulster, And God bless this more than Irish Ulster, say I, for showing us how things are done'.[2]

Gerard Turley from Belfast was part of the celebrated boys' choir from St Gall's Monastery School, which sang 'St Patrick's Breast Plate' in English and 'The Dear Little Shamrock' and 'Hail Glorious St Patrick' in Irish. They were acknowledged, he recalls, as the top boys' choir in Belfast and were much in demand, appearing in concerts in many towns.

> During the making of Hayward's film on St Patrick in 1938, I was taken to the Classic Cinema in Castle Lane on a Sunday afternoon to make a recording for background music for the film. When it was all over we went to the Continental Café for a treat at the corner of Chapel Lane and Castle Street. Then a few weeks later we were taken to the Falls Road and dressed up as choir boys. We formed a choir and were filmed as if we were at Saul. We sang 'Hail Glorious St Patrick' in Irish but what we sung didn't matter as long as we looked as though we were singing, it all turned out very well and I was fortunate to get from a friend a sound track of the film which I treasure very much.[3]

As part of Hayward's ambitious double-purpose journey down the Shannon he made a film to sit alongside the book. *Where the Shannon Flows Down to the Sea* was shown at the Royal Hippodrome in Belfast in 1940. It was screened on the same bill as *The Luck of the Irish* while Hayward also performed a twice-daily live stage and song show. This successful joint approach – a book accompanied by a film – continued with a travelogue on the Corrib in 1942, followed the next year by the book *The Corrib Country*. The film *Kingdom of Kerry* was shown at the Savoy and Theatre Royal in 1944 and was followed two years later by *In the Kingdom of Kerry*. *The Irish Press* reviewer said *Kingdom of Kerry* is definitely not Hayward's best film and complained it was a 'rush job, jumping from hotel to hotel irrespective of weather' and the film-makers had left out many of Kerry's best known landmarks: 'Where was Staigue Fort, for instance? Derrynane Abbey? Ballycarbery Castle? Wynn's Castle?':

> Perhaps makers of travelogues have a licence to dwell on the abnormal, but he has stressed the weird. Your final summing up on the south western part of the country is that its population is mainly composed of tinkers who have never heard of hygiene, and, for the rest, composed of sporadic anglers and their gillies … But his final scenes, with much stress on the silly ceremonies at Puck Fair and an elaborate insistence on showing us the face of a puck goat, butting in ridiculously every moment as if it were the national emblem of Kerry, and his fanatic urge to pick out the most outlandish characters that grace that pagan Mardi Gras, made the whole film top-heavy in favour of the absurd. Mr. Hayward and Mr. Pedelty seem to have let their cameras lead them in this unworthy successor to their former films, and cameras, though they rarely tell lies, have not developed the science of selectivity.[4]

Other plans were stirring with Hayward. He was determined to try to tap into some financial support from the government since he was aware they were keen to promote the North and develop the potential of documentary films about it. At the end of February 1940, six months into the war, he met Sir Wilson Hungerford, a Unionist MP and leading member of the party in Belfast, to lobby support for making a propaganda film about Northern Ireland. Hungerford, who was secretary of the Ulster Unionist Council and later Parliamentary Secretary to the Ministry of Commerce and Ministry of Home Affairs, was supportive of the plan.

During their meeting, Hayward outlined his proposal for a film that would place Northern Ireland in a historic context for the wider world. He emphasized that he felt it should be made not just as part of the war effort but for more permanent value. In a follow-up three-page letter to Hungerford, Hayward stated:

> To people in England or more distant lands Ireland means the land of those desperadoes who place bombs in their cinemas and other places where their people gather for business or entertainment. Through such a vehicle we could tell – directly and vividly the story of the birth of this country, our industrial

history and worth ... in the present fight against the vile things for which Hitler, and his merry band of murderers, stands.'[5]

He outlined his skills, knowledge and experience as well as his contacts in the industry which he felt left him well placed to make the film, adding – with typical rhapsodical exuberance – a personal note:

> My whole life-work has been bent to an effort to make Ulster better known and better understood and appreciated. This I can say without lack of modesty or fear of contradiction. For me Ulster has always been the thing of greatest importance in everything I have done or tried to do ... I am entirely at the service of the Government at any time, and am ready and willing to answer any questions which may be put to me, or to give any information in my power.[6]

Hungerford wrote immediately to the prime minister, Lord Craigavon, about Hayward's plan. But a letter of reply to him from a government official, L.G.P. Freer, held out little hope of any support.

> While the Prime Minister fully agrees that Mr. Hayward's proposal has many merits he feels that such a project could only be put into effect if the necessary funds were provided by the Government. He thinks, however, that in the present circumstances it would be quite out of the question for the Government to consider putting up the substantial sum of money which would be required for this purpose.[7]

Despite the rejection, Hayward's reputation and his contacts led to his being asked to make an informational film, *Simple Silage*, for the Stormont government. Owing to the cost and shortage of imported food, the Ministry of Agriculture was involved in promoting young grass fermented in a pit and known as silage. The proposal had first been floated to the government by William MacQuitty who suggested making the film. He contacted Hayward who was immediately enthusiastic. They brought in Louis Morrison to take responsibility for camera and sound work. MacQuitty agreed to supply the farm and finance with any profits to be equally divided amongst all three. Crucially, he also agreed to bear any loss. Morrison set up his 100ft clockwork Eymo movie camera that he loaded from 1000ft cans of professional film and they set to work. The cameraman, Germain Burger, who was living in London, agreed to look after the rushes and send them back to them to monitor their progress. MacQuitty later wrote, 'The results were beautiful and made the making of silage look truly simple.'[8]

Taking on the role of narrator Hayward recycled the much-loved

189

character Sam Mulhern from his 1930s' films, this time as a farmer who is converted to the benefits of silage, although this material was omitted from the final version of the film. Not surprisingly music played a part and instrumental versions of local songs were used on the soundtrack. Most of the film was shot silent with commentary by Hayward. MacQuitty also hired a Vinten camera from London Studios with the running speed shown on a tachometer. When the tachometer on Morrison's sound gear and the Vinten both showed twenty-four frames a second, they shot Hayward in conversation with farmers. The largely instructional film featured a sequence with research staff in the Ministry of Agriculture laboratories engaged in evaluating the quality and feeding value of silage. It also demonstrated various ways for preparing silage and alerting farmers to the help available from the government. But it was not all a smooth technical process. MacQuitty later wrote of the hitches they encountered in editing and how they were able to cut away from the worst lapses to produce a polished product:

> Despite lining up the tracks exactly on their clapper-board marks, Richard's lips continually went in and out of synchronization … opticals, fades, mixes and dissolves smoothed my path; Irish music bought by the yard blended with the round tower and the shamrocks of the title.[9]

A full house attended the premiere at the Classic Cinema on 4 February 1942. The invitation list included the Minister of Agriculture, Lord Glentoran and other members of the cabinet, as well as MPs and the executive committee of the Ulster Farmers' Union. The *Belfast Telegraph* praised the film while the *Northern Whig* called it 'interesting' and quoted Hayward's closing words as conveying a message that summed up the subject. 'Every farmer must make silage this year.' The surprise is that the film received any coverage at all because the media was preoccupied with reporting war news. For example, the *Whig*'s 5 am 'War special' edition – which also carried the blackout times alongside its front page masthead – was dominated by the aerial onslaught on Singapore from waves of Japanese dive-bombers and the fierce fighting on the Kalinin Front.[10]

The *Belfast Telegraph* and *Belfast News Letter* though made space for letters about the film. The letters are thought to be written by Hayward because of their tone and sentiment and because they speak of the need for more locally-made documentary films.[11] The one written to the *Belfast News Letter*, signed 'Ulster First,' was printed above the short report of the film's release:

It puts Ulster on the map, or more appropriately, the screen. The photography and technique is excellent ... it is purely local and Ulster should be proud of a first-class job done by Ulster producers in our own province. There are numerous other subjects which could be dealt with in a similar fashion: so here's looking forward to many more films of the calibre of 'Simple Silage' and to the firm establishment of a documentary film production in Ulster.[12]

The *Belfast Telegraph* letter, signed 'Agricola,' praised the excellence of the film.[13] *Simple Silage* cost £805 11s 7d to make. It involved considerable financial risk for MacQuitty with no one in the government mentioning payment. To resolve the matter he boarded a blacked-out steamer from Belfast to Liverpool and a blacked-out train to London to meet Jack Beddington, head of the Film Division of the Ministry of Information. Beddington congratulated him on the film, encouraged him to make more, but the issue of payment was unresolved:

> 'What about the money?' I asked.
> 'Do as you did with *Simple Silage*.'
> 'But that was my money and I still haven't been paid.'
> 'I'll write to your Minister,' Beddington said. 'It's a good film.'
> They were still looking perplexed as we shook hands.[14]

MacQuitty spent time in Dublin, accompanied on occasion by Hayward, crossing paths with a wide range of the city's cultural and artistic celebrities, and where he found 'little evidence of war or rationing':

> We ate huge steaks at the Dolphin and gourmet meals at Jamet's [*sic*] We drank in the Palace bar with the clever cartoonist Harry Kernoff; with Micheál Mac Liammóir and Hilton Edwards of the Gate Theatre; with Morris [*sic*] Walsh ... and drank Red Hackle whiskey. Through Victor Waddington, the art dealer, I also met the architect, Michael Scott, the sculptress, Hilary Heron, and the painter, Jack Yeats ... Talk was stimulating and drink flowed gracefully. I had entered a world of saints and scholars, of Synge, Joyce, Michael Collins and de Valera, in which the war was never mentioned.[15]

Hayward too was spending considerable time in the South. The following year he took up an offer to make an Irish government film *Tomorrow's Bread* about the need to secure enough grain to feed people. Filmed mostly in County Kilkenny, it began by depicting scenes on Irish farms, in villages, towns, and empty docks during the years when most wheat was imported into Ireland. It emphasized the beginning of the drive of wheat tillage by showing the torpedoing of a grain ship and focusing attention on the necessity for exploiting Irish wheat resources. Sequences showed the growth of wheat, and the processes of threshing, milling and bread making. It was made by the Irish National Film Unit of the Department of Agriculture in collaboration with the 'grow more wheat' campaign. Michael Scott was the art director and Roger Greene, a solicitor and businessman, was director. Its first public screening, at the Grafton Picture House in Dublin on 15 November 1943, was attended by the Taoiseach, Éamon de Valera, the Minister for Agriculture, Dr Ryan, members of the Dáil and Seanad and the Diplomatic Corps. Also present were county agricultural instructors, farmers and teachers. It was shown twice – once with a commentary in Irish by Séumas Mac Ugo, an official translator on the Oireachtas staff, followed by Hayward's English commentary. He told the audience that the film was being distributed 'free in Eire' by General Film Distributors Ltd. Apart from help from the Irish government Hayward was assisted in making it by the Irish High Commissioner in London and the British Board of Trade.

Next morning *The Irish Press* covered the film preview as a front-page news story with a photograph of Hayward and the Taoiseach in close discussion along with Seán MacEntee, the minister for local government. MacEntee, who was born in Belfast, took part in the Easter Rising for which he was sentenced to death, although this was later commuted. He was one of a small number of Northerners in the first Dáil and opposed the Treaty because he felt it cemented partition. The paper reported that the Taoiseach and Dr Ryan congratulated Hayward on the film. He said eight copies were ready for distribution in Dublin and would be shown at cinemas in the capital in early December.[16]

A month later, in its review, the *Irish Press* critic wrote that he hoped no one gets the wrong impression from the commentator's suggestion that 'we can have white bread again when we have sown sufficient wheat.' He said although the remark is understandable, 'Mr. Hayward could not, of course, have visualized that white bread would be brought about by the use of barley with wheat, due to abuses of the whole wheat extraction method.' But the critic went on to praise the production. 'From the filming point of view the Film Unit has done excellently. Mr. Scott's art direction was very pleasing and easy on the eye as was Mr. Hayward's accent on the ear.'[17] The *Press* also felt that the film was proof of the sustainability of the Irish scene to the film camera. The *Dublin Evening Herald* said it was well produced and, apart from its propaganda value in the wheat campaign, the film made excellent cinema entertainment.[18] However, the *Irish Times* critic was not so impressed:

Amidst the Second World War headlines, Hayward was photographed on the front page of *The Irish Press* with the Taoiseach, Éamon de Valera at the launch of *Tomorrow's Bread* in Dublin in November 1943. Hayward narrated the commentary for the Irish government film about the need to secure enough grain to feed people. Also in the picture is Seán MacEntee, the minister for local government who was born in Belfast.

If we are going to make the impression on our people that is possible through the film, and if we are going to send out documentaries to other countries, we shall have to do very much better than has been done in this film. It gives an impression of having been rushed, of a scenario written in a hurry and shot in a hurry. There are too many shots of ripe fields of wheat and of harvesting operations, too little of the ploughing, the harrowing, the growth of the crop, the watching of the weather and all the other things which would lead up to the climax of the harvest … The makers of the film must either have been filling up for lack of better material, or else they lost sight of the purpose of the film, viz., to persuade our farmers to grow more wheat.[19]

After the war the close links between Northern Ireland and the US featured in a thirty-five minute Hayward film, *Back Home in Ireland*. A travel documentary made in early spring 1946, it told the story of American troops stationed in the North during the war. It was produced by Hayward and members of Four Ways Productions, and distributed by Paramount. Donovan Pedelty returned to work with him on the production as director. Morrison looked after the photography and sound, while Harry Bailey was involved in presentation ideas. The US Expeditionary Force arrived on 26 January 1942, eight weeks after the US had declared war on Germany and Japan following the attack on Pearl Harbor. The American troops – the first contingent of the US Army to land in Europe during the war – entered through Belfast and Derry. The total force eventually exceeded 120,000 spread out across different areas. They were part of Operation Bolero, the build-up of soldiers prior to the invasion of Europe, so-called because like the dance, the operation unfolded slowly. The newsreel-style film was described as an experience in screen journalism reflecting the links between the two countries and the romantic assignations that took place. Most of the GIs were glamorous, young and single; after the war, 1800 local women sailed to the States to marry them.

Hayward narrated the film jointly with a fictional American sergeant. In a burst of self-promotion, his *In Praise of Ulster* is shown in the window of a Belfast bookshop from which he emerges leading the American on a tour of locations with US connections. One village that featured was Boneybefore, on the shores of Belfast Lough near Carrickfergus in County Antrim, where the parents of Andrew Jackson, seventh President of the US, lived before emigrating. Other locations included Broughshane in mid Antrim, the home of the ancestors of Sam Houston, the first President of the Republic of Texas, and Strabane in County Tyrone, which had been the home of the grandparents of President Woodrow Wilson. Towards the end memorable shots include the GIs taking over Ravenhill rugby ground in Belfast for a baseball game.

The film includes photography of the countryside visited by American soldiers and footage of them arriving in Ireland mixed with traditional music. Irish songs and dances are performed by Ellie Mulligan and the Johnston School of Dancing and the Belfast Empire Orchestra. In one sequence Hayward plays the harp while Irish figure dancing is staged around him. General Eisenhower is filmed receiving the freedom of Belfast while the prime minister of Northern Ireland, Sir Basil Brooke, is seen arriving at the Belfast Red Cross Club to make a farewell speech to the US troops.

On 14 March 1946 the trade show was held in the Paramount Theatre in London. Three weeks later Sir Basil and Lady Brooke as well as members of the cabinet and the American Consul, Quincy F. Roberts, watched a morning premiere at the Imperial Picture House in Belfast. Afterwards Brooke congratulated the filmmakers. He said the documentary combined history with the present and would allow the parents of the 'American boys' who served in Northern Ireland to see something of the countryside and learn about the hospitality they received before going to the Front.

The *Belfast News Letter*, *Belfast Telegraph* and *Northern Whig* gave the film a warm reception but the praise was more measured in film industry magazines. *Kinematograph* described it as, 'Well-meaning but protracted and uneven … the scenes are good history-book and documentary, but the quest for feature quota footage is responsible for a tedious "where we came in" ending. Fancy trimmings very nearly defeat its high and worthy purpose.'[20] *To-day's Cinema* called it an informative survey of historical link-up between sons of Northern Ireland and America. It said the film had, 'Straightforward direction-editing, whimsically sung Irish song or two, charming scenic backgrounds at times and pleasing popular novelty.'[21] Hayward struggled to interest film distributors in taking it on. The Joint Managing Director of General Film Distributors, S.F. Ditcham wrote to him saying the film possessed 'very little commercial value … is a rather too common type of documentary.'[22] Paramount acquired the British and Irish rights but for a sum less than Hayward had anticipated. F.E. Hutchinson of Paramount wrote to Hayward pointing out, 'It would hardly see daylight except for the fact that it ranks … as exhibitor quota.'[23]

Behind the razzle-dazzle of the film's release and press coverage there had been a lengthy exchange of letters and views within the government and between Hayward and civil servants over certain aspects of the film, notably the title. The Stormont government had asked for it to be changed to *Back Home in Ulster* but Hayward had deliberately chosen Ireland in the title to appeal to American distributors. Despite several requests, both he and Pedelty refused to bow to pressure to change it. The row is revealed in Public Record Office cabinet letters between the Ulster Office in London and government officials working in the press and publicity office at Stormont. A letter from F.M. Adams at Stormont to E.P. Northwood in London set out clearly the government's position:

> From the Ulster point of view the very title of the film 'Back Home in Ireland' is not wholly acceptable. It would be far preferable if the word "Ulster" could be brought into the title. As you are aware the use of the word "Ireland" is

calculated to assist in obliterating the distinction between belligerent Ulster and neutral Eire. The psychological effect of the reiterated use of the word 'Ireland' is bound to tell in favour of the Nationalists and Republicans.[24]

In 1937, Eire had been adopted by the Irish government as the name for the Southern state. Further memos and letters show that the Stormont government kept up pressure on the producers to change the title but Hayward and Pedelty stood their ground. An internal note quoted Pedelty saying 'Ireland' had a much wider appeal and as it was a commercial proposition he was looking for a good reception for it and as wide a circulation as possible. Hayward had wanted to include shots of the prime minister in the film and the letter also suggested that his participation in it should be made conditional on the omission of the word Ireland from the title and the substitution of Ulster.[25] Hayward wrote to Robert Gransden of the Cabinet Secretariat, outlining his views:

> Some of the features that may have pleased you least – the dancing, for instance – was essential sugar-coating for the non Irish markets and it is just those features which will ensure large audiences for the vital message I had to tell. I am little enamoured of that sort of thing myself, but through the years I have come to know what non Irish audiences demand of Ireland. If, as a working artist, I have any qualities of value to the Government I place these qualities at your service.[26]

Given his passionate love for music and song and later participation as a dancer in some of Ireland's best-known festivals, Hayward's reference to being 'little enamoured' about it is curious. In the event the film had extremely limited distribution and Hayward and his colleagues were unable to recoup its costs. A request had also been made by Hayward to the government for help in distributing the film in the US. Gransden replied that he thought that there would be very little difficulty in handling it 'through the usual commercial channels but that it is a matter in which it would be very inappropriate for the government as such to take any part.'[27] Hayward responded saying that despite Gransden's opinion 'the distribution of British pictures in America is one of heart-breaking difficulty.'[28]

Hayward was undeterred by the lack of official support. The experience prompted him to suggest the setting up of a government-sponsored film unit in the North, which would properly fund the making of his documentaries. Inspired by the prime minister's generous comments on his production, he suggested a series of six films covering each of the counties reflecting history, scenery, industry, agriculture, sport, education and special crafts. (This was an echo of his proposal six years previously in which he had suggested making a general film about the history of Northern Ireland.) Together with his letter of 9 April Hayward submitted a one-page proposal entitled 'A few observations on the idea of an Ulster Film Unit'. The crux of his argument emphasized that, 'Bluntly – Ulster films should be made by Ulster people with the necessary skills.'[29] If the government was willing to produce a film about the six counties, sponsor the series, and finance the 'bare costs' then he predicted that it would in twelve months return all the outlay. 'Sponsorship would of necessity give the government sub-editorial powers over my material and finance would give the Government absolute powers over my budgeting.'[30] A month later, Gransden replied with disappointing news that they were reluctant to grant him a monopoly of government-funding production:

> The matter had received the careful and sympathetic consideration of the Government and they regret that they do not find it possible to grant your organization the official status suggested nor can they agree to confer exclusive rights for the production of Government films on any particular unit.[31]

Gransden though did not spell out in his letter the other reasons for the government's refusal, which are contained in the minutes of the eighteenth meeting of the Cabinet Publicity Committee held at Stormont Castle on 6 May 1946 and attended by Brooke and two other government ministers. The harsh reality was that the government did not appear to be persuaded of the quality of his work. The minutes state that Brooke, despite his public praise of the film at its Belfast premiere the previous month, felt that it 'did not strike him as a very promising example of the type of work which Mr. Hayward's organization might be expected to turn out.'[32] The committee decided that it was better to work with the newly established Central Office of Information. In a note, presented to the cabinet committee responding to Hayward's proposal for the establishment of an Ulster Film Unit, a senior press officer stated that the Central Office of Information 'were acknowledged by the cinema trade and by the public to be of the highest quality in every respect …'[33] The *coup de grâce* was a final point of disdain from the press officer, 'If this view of the matter be accepted it is hardly necessary to comment on the details of Mr. Hayward's proposal.'[34]

It was a surprising volte-face by the prime minister. On top of this, adding more insult to inflicted wounds, Hayward was bitterly aggrieved when he read in the papers that an English company was engaged to make films for the government similar to those he had in mind. 'It is not my desire,' a disillusioned Hayward wrote in another letter

> To encroach upon your plans in any way, but if it is a fact that I can produce films of at least equal quality, and at lower cost, than any London company, I think the argument is unassailable that this work should be in my hands. No non Ulster person could possibly pretend to deal with this country with my close knowledge and authority, and so far as technical ability and distribution power are concerned I have already demonstrated my ramifications. All the major Companies are glad to buy and distribute my product, and that fact alone disposes of all taints of the order of 'a prophet is not without honour, save in his own country.'[35]

Some inkling of how he felt is glimpsed in a final plea:

> I am a citizen of Northern Ireland, bringing up my family here and paying rates and taxes here; I have enthusiasm for Northern Ireland, as is evidenced in all my work in literature, the theatre, the screen, and the lecture platform. Surely these things speak for themselves … There can be no doubt that films must loom large in future publicity for Ulster, and it is my contention that a Unit maintained on the lines indicated in my plan would be of far greater benefit to this country than any occasional employment of London interests. Patriotism, economy and common-sense alike bear me out.[36]

The government decision rankled with him. It was a major disappointment and may well have led to his deciding there and then to forgo the film world once and for all and concentrate on the printed word, but he nursed his grievance and moved on.

TEN

'We used to row like hell at times – as good friends do'

(1947–1949)

The green roads of Ireland, populous with happy families before the Famine killed them or drove them to America, wind over the hills and through the valleys, and if it is the real Ireland you seek they are worth a thousand tourist-haunted highways for all their fine coat of tar macadam.

Leinster and the City of Dublin, 1949

In the postwar years Northern Ireland was struggling. Clothes, soap, butter, cheese, sugar, bacon, meat and tea were rationed and other food was in short supply. Tuberculosis was still rampant in many parts of Ireland and urgent measures were needed to deal with the problem. Education, health and social services were being reformed; in the North, the birth of the welfare state led to dramatic changes. The National Health Service, free to everyone, replaced the existing and inadequate Poor Law workhouse system. During the second half of the 1940s, the whole of Ireland boasted some of the emptiest and quietest roads in Europe. Few people owned cars but towards the end of the decade the country was gradually beginning to open up with thousands of families seeing the landscape for the first time. Tourism, stunted by shortages of petrol, was in its infancy. The tourist board was working hard to promote Northern Ireland in Britain, and the Republic was anxious to attract overseas visitors. Reading offered the vicarious pleasures of travel.

For several years Hayward had been mulling over a long-cherished idea of a detailed study of the country involving a sustained circuit of the four provinces. Using each as a framework for a continuous journey, he would explore all thirty-two counties, delving into little-known places and along the way turn up anecdotes from the past. Experience had shown him that to popularize his books he must produce something more than a fact-filled litany of the topography, history and antiquities of the country. He needed an additional element to help sales; this would be done by including drawings. To illustrate what turned out to be five books in a series called *This is Ireland*, he secured the services of Raymond Piper, an up-and-coming young Belfast artist.

The interweaving of the visual and verbal had already been a feature of his travel books and he was aware of the importance of attractive drawings to enrich their appearance. It was vital that he work with a trustworthy artist who could do justice to his writing and deliver high-quality sketches to a deadline. Hayward first met Piper in the spring of 1947 at a meeting of the Belfast Naturalists' Field Club. Through his connections with the club the young artist had made three separate portrait drawings of the illustrious field-naturalist Robert Lloyd Praeger, a polymathic figure and former president of the Royal Irish Academy. (One of Piper's sketches was later published as a frontispiece to the second edition of Praeger's *Natural History of Ireland*.)

A Londoner by birth, Piper had lived in Belfast since the age of six when his family moved to the city in January 1930. He was passionate about painting and although he attended an evening class at Belfast College of Art, he was largely self-taught. His father's decision, however, to send him to work in the Harland & Wolff shipyard, led to a job as a marine engineer where he spent six years. He left the shipyard in 1948, teaching for a short period before becoming a full-time artist. A tall and effervescent man, he never lost his English accent even though he lived most of his adult life in Belfast. By his own admission he had a wicked sense of humour and enjoyed teasing, poking fun and mimicking others. He was to play a significant part in Hayward's life and despite his affable manner it was the start of a sixteen-year collaboration that was not without stormy moments.

Even as he was promoting his newly published Kerry book, Hayward was making a bid to interest an American publisher in a one-volume travel book to be called *This is Ireland* covering each county. After the war he initiated correspondence with the New York publishers, Devin-Adair, to try to tease out an agreement from them to accept his proposal. The president of the company,

Devin Garrity, saw the postwar potential for such a book and was extremely keen on the idea. Hayward knew that illustrations would play an important part in a publisher's decision to take it on and immediately Piper set to work producing a selection of fourteen images, which he forwarded to New York as samples. Garrity said the illustrations were 'good' and promised to publish the book in the summer of 1948 with a hundred drawings. He suggested the manuscript should be a maximum of 100,000 words. Hayward signed a contract and received an advance on royalties of $150.[1] But he was planning a bigger volume than Garrity had in mind. He had turned round the information from *In Praise of Ulster*, updated the details and sent part of it for his consideration. He wrote to Garrity saying 'it will be impossible to make the book shorter than 200,000 words. But to try to deal with the whole of Ireland in 100,000 words is out of the question':

> You have said all along that you want this book to be important – to be capable of remaining <u>the</u> standard book on Ireland for at least fifty years. Would you please write to me by air mail just as quickly as you can? I am now <u>preparing</u> Dublin and the Province of Leinster, and I don't want to do any actual <u>writing</u> until I have your considered opinion about this Ulster section. If you agree with me that this is the sort of stuff we want, solid, informative, dignified yet light, then I shall go ahead. But I don't want to write any more of the book until I have your comments on this present section.[2]

Transatlantic exchanges involving haggling over the length of the book, its style, tone and content went on for months. By the autumn of 1947, Garrity had read the first sixty-five pages of the Ulster section but was unimpressed. He felt it was too long, too wordy, too historical and the content not right for an American readership:

> It is particularly annoying when you set out to inform Americans about their own history. Americans do not wish to be told about their own history and they particularly do not wish to be misinformed … when you tell us it was Ulstermen practically exclusively who settled here prior to the Revolution, you are definitely wrong. For every pre-Revolution town in the U.S. called Derry there are three called Clare. For every boatload of immigrants that set out for these shores in the 18th century from Northern Ireland there were two or three that cleared from Cork. The pre-Revolutionary Irish in America from the South decidedly outnumbered those from the North … While on the subject of America, we refer to the recent war as World War II, not as the Hitler war. We got in the war when Japan attacked us. The fact that Ireland remained neutral during the war would require an objective attitude in discussing the matter in a guide book.[3]

A general criticism from Garrity was that readers would gain the impression from Hayward's writing that the countryside around Belfast was 'utterly devoid of living people':

> We are told about the dead and their monuments and a great deal about who <u>was</u> who. Are there no living writers in that part of the country? No poets or artists, no interesting farmers? The whole work would be greatly improved if a little more who's-who-among-the-living were introduced … One of the best features of the section on Ulster is the geological detail. The natural history, however, is poor. We are not told anything about the trees, gardens, birds. The anecdotes and jokes are good. Dialect should be avoided at other times and wherever possible in the anecdotes … On page 23 and elsewhere, you refer to St. Mary's as being "the first Roman Catholic church in Belfast." Do you mean since the Reformation? And since this book will be bought largely by Catholics you should be reminded that Catholics like to be called Catholics over here, not Roman Catholics. They are touchy about it.[4]

Less than two weeks later, an incensed Hayward dispatched a 2500-word typewritten response to Garrity's criticisms breaking down all the matters raised. He began his five-page letter by saying it 'is the most baffling and unsatisfactory thing of its kind I have ever received':

> I don't know whether you are telling me to take my book to hell out of your way, or whether you are asking me to rewrite it, to recast it, or to burn it at the stake. My artist is left even more in the air, for he doesn't get a single <u>word</u> to bite on, and after several months of hard work he doesn't know whether you approve of his stuff or not. The worst aspect of this is the loss of time. Two months to tell me about 65 pages of my work, and you know it was agreed between us that I would not continue further until you had passed judgment on these first pages. This results in a complete stoppage of my work, for I cannot start on a novel I have already planned until I get this book of yours off my chest. I simply cannot tackle two jobs at once. I'm not that sort of writer.[5]

Hayward also said he had submitted Garrity's letter to what he called 'the greatest authority on the Irish in America' and fumed, 'I am utterly shocked by your attitude to my purely factual writing':

> I sent an abstract of your letter to my friend – easily the greatest authority on this subject alive today, and a man of wide sympathy devoid of all sectarian bias. A scholar to his finger-tips. And do you know what he said? "The facts set out in your MS. are unanswerably true. But nothing you will say will convince your Irish-American friend, for he does not wish to be convinced." I am afraid I must concur … In parts your letter can only be taken as rude in

the extreme. I was suspicious of the fact that you take a purely sectarian view of this whole matter, and I know that in <u>my</u> writings nothing of that sort ever rears its head. <u>Because I am NOT sectarian.</u> I am not out to prove a case for either Protestants or Roman Catholics. I am concerned with <u>facts</u>. In all my books – you have two of them, I think – you will find this factual texture strongly emphasised. That is why my books sell as well in Dublin and Cork and Limerick as they do in Belfast.[6]

Hayward asked for clarity from the publishers and for definite decisions about the future of the book, saying he wanted a 'clean-cut instruction' from them. He added that he had supplied the material that had been agreed between the two:

> In writing about Ulster I think I can claim to know a little more about my subject than you do, and I could never consent to bend my views to suit your particular ideas. I do not think you would ask me to do that. I am not a hack writer. What I have written about Ulster is what I feel about it, and what I think a visitor should know about it. When I come to our other three beloved Provinces I think you will find that I will deal with them no less handsomely.[7]

Garrity replied at the end of November enclosing a reader's report which although criticizing the book for too much historical background, turned out to be generally favourable. The reader – who was unnamed – felt there were superfluous sections and 'to describe every town along the main highways would seem too much of a good thing':

> We go for 6500 words on Belfast. Now no one, including apparently, Mr. Hayward, has ever mistaken Belfast for a tourist's paradise. It is a hard-bitten, un-beautiful industrial city with little to recommend it to the tourist with limited time at his disposal ... See it he ought – but merely <u>en passant</u>. Dublin, by contrast, is almost impossible to tear one's self away from ... It is full of endless charm and discovery. I strongly advise that this whole section be pared down – and given in brisker fashion.[8]

On the plus side, the report found Hayward's style 'readable and friendly ... He writes authoritatively and fluently. I particularly like the little side-remarks and local expressions, characteristics, jokes, etc ... they give 'color' and personalized atmosphere.' The reader concluded by disagreeing with Garrity on one point:

> As to your suggesting more geological, ornithological, horticultural material – I'd go easy on too much of that. For the average tourist a little of that sort of thing goes a long way – and too much of it will merely defeat our aim of trying to cut the book down to size ... I think Mr. H. has the makings of a

lively book – if only he will bear in mind that this is a book to literally be read as the reader runs. Inevitably a certain amount of scholarship (in which Mr. H. abounds, I can see) must be sacrificed in the interest of producing a practical, lively, easily carried guide-book.[9]

Hayward had again asked Garrity about Piper's sketches and was astonished to find that he had had a change of heart. 'Frankly,' Garrity declared, 'I don't think much of them':

> They are well executed of course, beautifully done in fact, but they are completely photographic and I think we can safely say today that if a camera can do the job better it should be given the assignment. In further criticism: there is no imagination evident in the figures. The harp player, the ballad singer and the prehistoric "ancients" are stereotyped, to say the least. The work is that of a finished and accomplished draftsman rather than of an illustrator.[10]

Garrity's damning of Piper's work with faint praise was a devastating blow. It was a turnaround from his original opinion on the sketches, which he had liked. It now looked as though the whole project was in jeopardy as far as an American publisher was concerned. Hayward replied to Garrity two weeks before Christmas 1947, beginning, 'Your letter of the 28th of November maddens me.' What especially annoyed Hayward was that Garrity ignored all the points that he had raised in his lengthy reply to his initial criticism. He felt Garrity's letter 'was a complete reversal of almost everything you have said,' and contained 'contradictions and inconsistency'. Hayward did not hide his discontent. He sent a questionnaire 'to be returned with plain answers' asking whether he should proceed with the book, seeking clarification on Piper's sketches and on using an Irish font as well as other stylistic aspects of the book. His patience was starting to wear thin:

> I accept your reader's report as a very helpful indication of what you <u>now</u> require … I must have some fixity of plan … To safeguard my time and temper, would you please fill in and return the enclosed Questionnaire? Please – and by return? It is essential to my work that I know exactly where I am. We have talked and written and argued and changed far too much. I want to write a book – not to run a debating society by mail … I simply cannot go ahead until I know your mind – and know that it will not be changed.[11]

Early in 1948 the response from Garrity was in the negative. He chose to ignore Hayward's questionnaire, pointing out that the cost of making books had doubled in the past eight months owing to an inflationary spiral. The state of publishing in the US was such that they would have to postpone any possibility of taking it on for at least two years and even then there would be doubt about its future. The company was sending books abroad for printing and had contracts pending for more than twenty-five:

> I don't see how it is going to be possible for us to get together considering the difficulties that exist. A book of this kind needs a great deal of thrashing out with the publisher over a table, and possibly with aid of a drop or two (on the publisher of course). We are already far too involved in a debate across a 3000 mile distance and I am afraid it might continue to the detriment of all concerned ... I think in all fairness you are entitled to retain the advance we sent you as part compensation for your work, and if you plan to complete the book anyhow we shall be glad to do all we can to aid you in finding a publisher or sponsor if you wish it.[12]

Hayward's opening line of reply in early February summed up his incredulous mood. 'To say that your letter of the 20th of January came to me as a bombshell is to put it mildly.' He followed up by launching a blistering attack on the company:

> Your present decision is quite unethical and certainly most unfair to me and to my artist. Quite a lot of publicity has been circulated here, in the press and over the radio about this book ... On this basis alone my reputation would suffer very great damage if the book were turned down. I am sure you accept this fact. And to suggest that my small advance would in any way compensate me for the vast amount of work already done, or even go <u>part</u> of the way towards paying Piper for his labours is not tenable ... Even if you let me down – which I <u>cannot</u> believe – I would feel morally bound to pay Piper for his work. That is no more than would be expected of any decent man. And on the lowest possible assessment I would not consider Piper entitled to any less than 500 dollars for the work done to date.[13]

Hayward reminded Garrity that they had a contractual undertaking. He even offered to rewrite the Ulster section, reducing its length, suggesting an overall total of 120,000 words. In the past few months, he pointed out, he had already travelled several hundred miles gathering the latest material and local colour. His self-belief in the project was as strong as ever:

> I am really boiling to get this book done ... send me back the Ulster MSS. at once and I will boil that stuff down ... I shall now have to adopt a much more lively and less leisurely style ... From now onwards I would like our correspondence to be shorter and <u>much more prompt</u>! I am really the most

friendly soul in the world, and I shudder to think that a decided note of acrimony was creeping into our letters. I can only suggest that one cause of it was your astonishing facility for taking six months to answer my letters. Can we put that bad habit behind us? It is rather wearing on the nerves, you know ... I know that this book is going to be a huge success and that it will be one of the best paying propositions on your list. Were I not well assured of this I would not persist – I would not write to you as I am writing. But I had precisely the same thing with Barker's over "In Praise of Ulster." ... Barker's talked about the cost of publishing – the length of my book – the great cost of illustration in collotype – etc., etc., – but I went on in my faith, and the result was triumphant: a Book Society Choice, a best-seller, and a book that is still selling as freely now as it did in 1938.[14]

Despite Hayward's offer to rewrite, Garrity stuck by his decision saying other books were being 'indefinitely postponed ... American publishing has hit rock bottom in a new depression.'[15] Spitting ink, Hayward wrote a final letter in early May stating that he wished to say little more:

You know how things stand by your letter of the 2nd of February. And you are content to repudiate your own contract, entered into honourably between us, because business is not to your liking. Content also to leave me to pay Mr. Piper out of my own pocket. Obviously there is nothing I can do but show you that I am fully aware of your astonishing methods. Just that, and express my bitter disappointment ... I am happy to say that I have never before been the victim of such execrable dealing.[16]

Disillusioned at the shabby way he had been treated by a publisher who had reneged on his word, he set about seeing if he could stir up interest in publishers in Ireland or Britain. All was not lost. Arthur Barker already had a relationship with him, having published his prewar books *Sugarhouse Entry* and *In Praise of Ulster*, and had restarted their business after the war. Hayward asked Piper to send twelve of his best drawings to Barker and they were delighted with his work. He signed him up and Piper resigned his job as an engineer. Barker agreed to take on the series. The company wanted to help develop his writing career and saw the sales possibilities, both at home and farther afield. The terms of Hayward's contracts show he was paid an advance of £100 for the first four books. Less than four months after the rejection by Devin-Adair, Hayward signed a contract for the Leinster book, the first in the series. He was paid £50 on signing and £50 on the date of publication. Piper was paid an inclusive fee of sixty guineas. Royalties were ten per cent on the published price of the first 2500 copies, fifteen per cent thereafter.[17]

The money was hardly munificent but Hayward had other income streams from his work, his confectionery sales as well as royalties from his earlier books and records. The two men lost no time in launching into the research for the first book. Maps were studied, routes worked out, contacts established in advance and in September 1948 they prepared to head off. They were fervently hoping for better weather than the previous winter when a big freeze paralyzed the country. Snowdrifts and five separate blizzards led to forty-two consecutive days of sub-zero temperatures. Transport had been brought to a halt, telephone lines were down and electricity power lines knocked out. Their luck was in, the autumnal weather was in their favour and they drove south on a lengthy journey away from home. Hayward had to apply for permission from the Taoiseach's office for special petrol supplies, which he was granted. Their route, covering several thousand miles and lasting three months, would take them through all twelve Leinster counties, the largest number of any of the provinces.

The book was called *Leinster and the City of Dublin* and he chose the capital as his starting point, describing himself as 'a devoted lover'. After an eight-page historical portrait he asks the reader to keep in mind the shape of the old city for perspective as this 'to-day will give depth and colour to all you see'.[18] His walking tour encompasses landmark buildings such as Trinity College, the two cathedrals, the GPO, the Four Courts, Tyrone House in Marlborough Street, the Guinness Brewery, and the Royal Hospital at Kilmainham, 'now the headquarters of the Civic Guard – Eire's smart, efficient and most courteous police force'.[19] The alleyways and courtyards off Dame Street fascinated him and he describes one of his haunts, the Dolphin, as 'a pleasant hotel and a famous old eating-house where the atmosphere remains charmingly reminiscent of a more gracious and leisured age'. Jammet's, an opulent French restaurant in Nassau Street, was another of his favourites. Opened in 1901, its main restaurant of dark wood, gilt and marble attracted the Irish literati as well as artists, musicians and actors.

Hayward had built up a substantial body of architectural knowledge and cultivated an interest in buildings through his travels. He was well versed in the lingua franca of vernacular architecture and wrote authoritatively about the built heritage, a consuming passion. With Piper by his side, he wandered around the Liberties and the Coombe where the high-gabled buildings and Huguenot houses of the weavers impressed him. He was not shy about expressing a candid opinion on something that he did not like. 'I hurried you past the statue of Tom Moore, near Trinity,' he wrote, 'because it is a poor and unworthy thing'.[20] The new loop-line railway bridge is 'a tasteless a piece of vandalism as could well be imagined'. He laments the destruction during the civil war of the Record Office in the Four Courts, which destroyed 'priceless and irreplaceable documents that the heart of the scholar well-nigh breaks at the very thought, and even the most loutish man must feel regret … it was the greatest single disaster of this insane orgy of destruction and violence'.[21]

The look of the streets dismayed him. Many areas were derelict with a sense of decay, and O'Connell Street, he found, had lost its character. 'Order has gone from it, taste has been smothered under a blanket of chromium vulgarity, and building is as haphazard as could be.' If this was not enough, he was indignant at the state of Henrietta Street: 'The whole district, which a century-and-a-half ago was the last word in aristocratic elegance and magnificence, is now an unbelievable sink of squalor and hard grinding poverty, and the impact of it will come upon you with terrible force as you walk through the streets.'[22] He liked pointing out inaccuracies. The harp adorning the Parnell Monument at the top of O'Connell Street was 'a musical monstrosity … [it] suffers from a sad defect, more poignant to me, who am myself a harpist, than to most, in that the two lowest strings are attached to the front pillar and nexus, instead of to the sound board.'[23] In St Stephen's Green he examined the bust of Countess Markievicz, 'a quixotic gallant citizen-soldier,' and noted that the Irish inscription, which he translated into English, was incorrect. Instead of reading:

> A brave valiant woman who fought in battle for
> Ireland, at Easter in the year of the Lord, 1916

It reads:

> A brave valiant woman who fought in a cat for
> Ireland about cheese in the year of the Lord, 1916 [24]

The formula Hayward used in his books was to explain the significant historic facts, setting the scene for the reader. After providing an account of the historical pedigree of the place buttressed by eclectic scholarship, he would then plunge in, walking the streets. His exploration of Dublin presents a typical approach that he applied to the other books in the series. Once he and Piper arrived in town their modus operandi involved exploring it, seeing how the streets fitted together and keeping an eye out for a characterful bar. Invariably, a local historian, an enthusiastic antiquarian, a gregarious parish priest or Church of Ireland rector would be tracked down to accompany them pointing out idiosyncratic details, which provided lively copy.

A favourite haunt of Hayward's was the Brazen Head, a bar near the Dublin quays, which Raymond Piper captured in one of his pencil sketches for *Leinster and the City of Dublin*, the first book in the five-volume regional series *This is Ireland*. The inn, which appears on some of the oldest maps of Dublin, was the meeting place of the United Irishmen.

The Casino at Marino in Dublin that Hayward included in his Leinster book on the advice of the architectural historian Harold Leask who said it should be seen by any serious visitor.

Hayward struck up conversation with all sorts of people, sometimes inter-posing a bystander. He made copious on-the-spot notes about everything they came across. Piper kept his gimlet eye peeled for the best angles for drawing. Sketchpad in hand, he then zoomed in on something that caught his attention, perhaps a time-worn historic monument such as a round tower, a seventeenth-century church or a narrow alleyway, capturing the small incidents of life that spooled around him slowly like a film but with no loss of background. When Hayward was striking up a rapport with someone, Piper would sketch their outline, which would be reproduced as a half-tone pencil drawing.

Dublin city and county took up the lion's share of the book, absorbing eighty-four of the 256 pages. Having done justice to the city and its surround-ings, they set out for the southeast of the country. Through theatre and film-making as well as adjudicating at drama festivals Hayward had become familiar with parts of south Leinster. In the mid 1930s he reconnoitred film locations, visiting Enniskerry, Glencree, Featherbed Mountain, Roundwood and Sally Gap. By early October their route, in a prewar Singer 12, took them south to Wicklow and Wexford. The permanencies of the landscape, and in particular mountains, are an integral part of his writing. At the Royal Hotel in Glen-daloch, Hayward met a man known only as Andy 'The Boots', with whom he had previously climbed Lugnaquilla. He recounts how he once made a nine-hour trek to the top via the Upper Lake, Conavalla and the slopes of Table Mountain. When he returned to the hotel the staff told him that he was an hour and a quarter over the record for the route to the top, which was held by a Mr Wright from Cornwall. A few nights later they booked into the Marine Hotel in Arklow where bed and breakfast was nine shillings and sixpence, and evening tea four shillings.[25]

In Wexford and Kilkenny he repeats the pattern that he used for Dublin by firstly looking at the history and a day was spent relying on the local knowl-edge of Dr Hadden of the Old Wexford Society. Sometimes research proved fruitless; Hayward was interested in the old Forth and Bargy dialect but could not find any information on it. Another aspect of his writing reflects his grasp of the natural world, especially birdlife with numerous asides. He was particu-larly struck by the swans at Carnsore Point, 'necks outstretched and their many wings making a clamour in the air', but he found the region 'dreary' although the views across the Saltee Islands and Hook Head redeemed it. At Fethard he was shocked how local youths had turned an old wall into a ball-alley, a 'measure of the low state of public taste'.

They headed inland to Kilkenny, 'a county of many graces', stopping on the way to the city at Jerpoint Abbey where Hayward delved into the building's architectural heritage. At Inistioge he felt the Nore Valley 'is where Leinster appears in its most richly opulent mood'. Twenty-six years on, he looks back on the burning of Woodstock House, destroyed in the civil war: 'I know of no better place in Ireland where one may stand and reflect on the folly and stupidity of those fanatics who thought that in burning down the big houses of Ireland, and driving the great families out of them, they were doing benefit to their country.'[26]

They stayed at the eighteenth-century Club House Hotel in Kilkenny, one of Ireland's oldest inns. The tobacconist, Mr Bourke, a member of the Kilkenny Archaeological Society – the oldest society of its kind in Ireland – led them on a walking tour of the city through slips and back alleys. They also spent an evening in the company of the writer Hubert Butler who was one of the society's joint honorary secretaries. Hayward made a plea for the restoration of Rothe House, the oldest merchant house in Ireland and one of the city's finest buildings dating from 1604, which was in a badly decaying state; he later became a supporter of the campaign to preserve it. In Kilkenny he purposefully avoided the landmark buildings since he felt they had been well documented in guidebooks and monographs, concentrating instead on lesser-known ones. He did though refer to St Canice's Cathedral which he described as 'one of the most beautiful churches in Ireland, pure and austere and comely as the breezes that caress the mountain tops, and the manner of its keeping has not one jarring note to detract from its full enjoyment'.[27]

In neighbouring Carlow, on the other hand, the Catholic cathedral was 'rather florid' for his taste but he was impressed with the Brownstone dolmen, the largest in Europe, weighing over a hundred tons. From Carlow they drove across to Leix and Offaly making their base in Mountmellick, the main Quaker town in Ireland. Mostly they stayed in hotels or accepted hospitality where it was offered. In this case, their hosts Samuel and Winnifred Pim put them up for a week at Anngrove, a large country house built around 1698 by the Beale family, influential Quakers from Suffolk. The Pim family connection with the house stretched back 250 years. Hayward entertained them with his Irish harp and described how they sat round the turf fire singing and telling stories. Samuel and Winnifred's son, Alan, was just nine when Hayward and Piper visited Anngrove in 1948. His sister, Elizabeth, had attended Newtown School and was in the same form as Ricky. He has fond memories of their visit to his parents' house:

They were out all day touring the countryside and I recall at night that Hayward played the harp. He had a fistful of songs, but the only one I remember him singing in our house is 'Six miles from Bangor to Donaghadee.' I have happy memories of their visit. They were very hospitable and a great pair and it was a pleasure to have them staying. My parents enjoyed their company very much and were extremely fond of them. The highlight of the visit for me though, and the main thing I remember, is that Raymond Piper drew a sketch of myself and my parents.[28]

From their comfortable base at Anngrove they toured the local towns with side trips to Portarlington, Timahoe, Portlaoise, Emo Park and the castle at Dunamase. In neighbouring Offaly their attention focused on the High Cross of Durrow and the monastic site of Clonmacnoise to which he devoted six pages. Blunt in his views on Clonmacnoise, he considered it 'a place monstrously over-crowded, mostly with tombs of the utmost vulgarity, where even ice-cream-shop effects, carried out with pieces of crudely coloured glass, are not considered out of place, and it is high time the people of Ireland revolted against this horrible desecration of their most sacred places.'[29] For his journey along the Shannon in 1939 Hayward had already spent time at Clonmacnoise and the main towns so the accounts of Shannonbridge, Banagher and Birr are perfunctory.

Many places on their itinerary were bedevilled by decline. The population was decreasing and some towns had an impoverished look. The majority consisted of one straggling main street and a number of subsidiary roads that had developed from lanes. Some retained a flavour of their old personality and local characters thrived. Any towns worth their salt had a general merchants or corner shop that was often the focal point. Family-owned shops or department stores had been owned for several generations and many larger towns boasted a haberdasher, saddler, draper and milliner, victualler, hardware store, tobacconist and cobbler. Aside from Woolworth's, there were no chain stores and apart from a church or chapel, every self-respecting village could boast up to a dozen or more pubs. Some were in one room while others with grocery stores at the front sold everything from Flahavan's porridge and Clonmacnoise rhubarb to a bottle of beer or a pinch of snuff.

Much of rural Ireland was an untidy place with pot-holed lanes, sagging farm gates, unfenced fields, ugly waysides, badly cared-for stone walls, and living conditions that, in some places, were at best slum-like. Hayward found a neglect of the built heritage with a 'complete disregard for old monuments'. From the Shannon they drove northeast through Kildare, Westmeath, Longford and

Meath, ending their long journey on the east coast at Louth. Sites that attracted their attention and gave Piper sketch opportunities included the River Boyne, Newgrange, Bective Abbey, Mellifont, and Monasterboice, 'a place of extraordinary interest' about which Macalister had written a book two years earlier. In the midlands, the Hill of Uisneach, Tara, the Hill of Ward, Slieve na Callighe, even a tree-clad hillock called Trumpet Hill at Ballymascanlon in Louth – an eminence on which, he tells readers, 'Cuchulainn stood alone guarding Ulster' – were all on the map of Haywardland. Standing on the Hill of Slane he wrote: 'If great long thoughts do not come flooding upon you in this sacred and most historic place, your mood must be far different from mine every time I stand there.'[30]

Carlow Castle and the River Barrow sketched by Piper for Hayward's Leinster book published in 1949.

Piper's sketch of the Shannon at Athlone with the castle and the Church of Saint Peter and Saint Paul, which Hayward felt 'lent a kind of alien charm to a very humdrum place'.

Hayward adopted the well-known 'monarch-of-all-I-survey' approach beloved of travellers in the Imperial Age. If there was no hill nearby, he would climb – as he did in the case of Monasterboice – to the top of the round tower. This vantage point afforded him one of his favourite views of north Leinster, stretching from the Wicklow Mountains to Carlingford Mountain and beyond to the Mountains of Mourne. As the standard of living improved, cars were starting to appear although on many days they had the roads largely to themselves. Hayward loved the minor roads. In the Republic the main roads were classified as 'T' for Trunk and 'L' for Link, while the minor roads were unclassified. They drove along dusty untarred country roads that were little more than dirt tracks referred to by guidebooks as 'roadeens'. The narrowness of the roads discouraged what *Muirhead's Ireland* in 1949 termed 'speed merchants'. As they were driving towards Loch Ennell in Westmeath, Hayward referred to 'the spreading plume of white dust behind us that hid the entire countryside from our eyes for mile after mile.'[31]

Through an easy style in reporting what he saw, he delved into people's lives, captured their language and recreated lost worlds. When he quotes people he does not attempt to improve their language; they speak for themselves, the voice of the ordinary people going about their day-to-day lives. Oral history, important as a record of the period, is reflected in the different voices that emerge. The book is enhanced by lively historical phrases and handed-down sayings. Examples include: 'Well, I'll go to Ballyhack', 'That bangs Banagher and Banagher bangs the band', 'The pardon of Maynooth', and 'Beef to the heels like a Mullingar heifer!' Elsewhere, an arresting metaphor, a quotation or lines of a song, were grist to his writing mill. Hayward had learnt to listen as a writer instead of merely 'hearing'.

He was an exponent of the early Irish genre known as *dinnseanchas*, which refers to the lore of place and encompasses the allure of topography. *The Oxford Companion to Irish Literature* defines it as a body of knowledge in which 'the land of Ireland is perceived as being completely translated into story; each place [having] a history which is continuously retold'.[32] In Hayward's case, for every place name, he lists both the Irish and English 'usually corrupt' equivalent. Throughout the Leinster journey he often ponders these names and the stories behind them. The etymology of a townland, village or town was vitally important to him as he felt it shed light on its history. 'There is a comeliness and significance about our Irish place-names that is too often smothered beneath the uncouth forms which the anglicisers of the seventeenth and eighteenth centuries put upon them with so heavy a hand … and in their original forms these names have about them the pleasant sweet sound of a song.'[33] One aspect of his travels that Hayward disliked was hotel food. Apart from an excellent meal in the restaurant of the Adelphi Cinema in Dundalk, he had eaten many inferior dinners and complains about the poor quality:

> Our average country hotel is an unattractive place, pre-Victorian in its amenities, and with a menu usually made up of dishwater soup, grey roast beef, colourless cabbage, badly boiled potatoes and unimaginative pudding … They are a bad advertisement for our country and an affront to ourselves and our guests.[34]

Towards the end of 1948, he returned to Belfast to enjoy the comforts of home-prepared food. Elma liked to cook traditional Sunday lunches and one of his favourite dishes was stuffed pork fillet followed by syrup tarts. With customary diligence, he worked steadily throughout the winter. Hayward turned again to the authoritative services of Harold Leask to check facts. Once he had completed the first draft at the end of 1948, and losing no time, he immediately sent it to him for his consideration. Just after the turn of the year, in a two-page letter of reply, Leask listed twenty separate points, answering specific queries, correcting factual errors, clarifying aspects of the built heritage, and suggesting places for inclusion, with such comments as:

> The bombardment of the G.P.O. was by a few bombs from trench mortars which set it on fire. The walls were not damaged by shell fire … I do not think that the church at Killiney is early Celtic. It is a queer jumble, mainly late medieval … Surely the Casino at Marino, as the finest thing of its class in these islands, should be seen by any serious visitor. It deserves passing mention in any case.[35]

After some fine-tuning, Hayward delivered the typescript to the publishers in early 1949. Piper added the finishing touches to his sketches and *Leinster and the City of Dublin* was published in the summer priced at fifteen shillings, becoming a Book Society recommendation. Arthur Barker had taken care to produce an appealing hardback with attractive endpapers carrying a quirky Leinster map with some whimsical notes beside the place names, alongside a geological map of Ireland. One omission was an index – the others in the series are meticulously indexed. In the foreword, Maurice Walsh wrote: 'His word-pictures of the marvellous colours of our countryside, ever-changing and fickle as any lovely woman, succeed where a painter must inevitably fail.'[36] In the preface Hayward formally acknowledged Leask's help for will-ingly undertaking 'the arduous task of reading my manuscript, and from his wide and expert knowledge, of setting me right where I had sometimes gone astray in matters of technical nicety, or even of fact.'[37] Later in the year, when he received his copy of the book, Leask wrote to Hayward saying it flowed well and was 'most attractively written'. He praised Piper's drawings, 'as nice a pencil technique as I have ever seen', adding 'You are naughty, you know, in giving me such a glowing testimonial in your own hand in so prominent a place.'[38]

The book appealed to a wide readership, especially those for whom car ownership represented freedom and status. The Dublin papers heaped praise on it with little fault-finding. *The Irish Times* said Hayward had 'succeeded in giving the reader an eminently readable description of Ireland's first province, mixing historical, antiquarian and geological information in a manner which informs but does not obtrude'. But the paper's reviewer could not understand why the author, 'who exhibits a deep knowledge and sensitivity to the feelings of his southern countrymen', refers to the Border as the 'Eire-Ulster' boundary. The paper said Piper's sketches 'possess a freshness which promises well for the future of the artist'.[39] The *Irish Independent* reviewer in the popular 'Books and Bookmen' Saturday page said 'he has woven into a pleasant narrative a congenial blend of history, topography and geology … it is a racy and competent book … and no easy task to compress everything into a single volume'.[40] One dispar-aging voice was *The Irish Press* review written by the paper's literary editor, M.J. MacManus, who said Hayward was an Irishman first and an Ulsterman second. The book 'was bright, breezy and informative', but he curtly dismissed the quality of the writing: 'His publishers claim that it is 'a lovely piece of writing.' I wouldn't say that … there is nothing glittering about it and there are few imaginative touches. It is just straight-forward, functional prose that serves its purpose effectively.'[41]

Irish Geography described it as a 'welcome addition to the literature on Leinster'[42] while the *Dublin Magazine* enthused that the book was 'written gaily and lucidly by one who has an eye for pleasing countryside and architectural decoration'. The reviewer felt it was not easy within one volume to cover so wide a territory, yet there were very few notable omissions:

> Care has been taken with nomenclature, which is given bilingually, and there
> are some helpful features not usually to be found in this class of work. The
> author's speed of travel allows time only for the briefest descriptions, which is

admirable for Modern Man in a hurry. It is an entertaining book, exploratory and directive, and careful revision in parts would enhance its validity.[43]

The *Times Literary Supplement* called Hayward 'an unrepentant romantic' and said, 'unfortunately he has not avoided the temptation to give every little town near his route its marks for good or ill and to point out each monument and prospect'. However, it added, 'Mr. Hayward's best asset is a real sense of the poetry of history, through which he peoples ruined castles and abbeys with the life of former times'.[44] Writing in *The Bookman*, Compton Mackenzie said Hayward had avoided all the pitfalls and added something of genuine value to the Irish scene: 'I wish one or two of our Scottish topographers would take a lesson from him'.[45] In an adulatory notice, Sir Shane Leslie, who reviewed it for *Truth*, described it as the best Irish guide since that of Sir William Wilde. Hayward was, he wrote, 'steeped in the language and the balladry, ready to take colloquial jaunts on foot like George Borrow'.[46] It was a perceptive judgment since Borrow, a nineteenth-century English author, had been an important influence in Hayward's early life. Leslie also praised Piper's illustrations as 'exquisite, minute, and accurate, and with the soft, dreamy character of silver-points drawn by fairy folk.'

Hayward paid tribute to Piper's work in the preface: 'I was fortunate in my choice of a young artist, who was gifted to set down with his sensitive pencil those very impressions which I wish my readers to share with me.' His artistry and sound draughtsmanship were evident in the sixty-five evocative sketches and colour cover of Dunamase castle. On the face of it, the two seemed publicly to get on well on their first collaboration and the slickly produced book was a happy partnership of text and drawings, a mood encapsulated in the book's final sentence: 'It was a fittingly melodious and friendly end to a journey that had been compact of melody and friendship every mile of its lovely way.'[47]

But behind the equable façade of humour and banter all was not well. Piper could be charming but at other times insufferable with a supercilious approach to people, while Hayward could be testy. The two had quarrelled furiously on occasion, which clouded the trip for Hayward who complained that Piper had been rude to him and given him headaches. He sent a moaning letter to Arthur Barker who replied:

> He is a very foolish young man not to appreciate the kindness you have done him. But I can set your mind at rest in advance by saying that I leave the matter of future illustration in your hands. The books are yours – you

are the author. And I leave it entirely to you to employ any other artist you wish on the Munster and Connacht volumes. But we shall have to insist on Piper completing the Ulster volume, for that is a contract on which he has accepted an advance of money, and we should take legal steps to compel him to honour his undertaking. You have all my sympathy. I can well understand how you feel when a job of work in which you took such joy, should be turned to unpleasantness by a very unaccountable young man. My own opinion is that you should get rid of Piper forthwith. He is obviously unreliable, and you should not saddle yourself with an artist who gives you such headaches, and who behaves to you in such a very rude and uncouth manner … Engage any artist you feel would be competent. Get pleasure out of this work instead of misery.[48]

Long afterwards, in an interview reflecting on their time on the road, Piper recalled some of their rows, acknowledging that not everything went smoothly in the rituals of being together for a considerably long time:

We always talked straight turkey. I was very prickly at times and sometimes quite wicked. I'm inclined to be bloody-minded and critical on occasions and some people felt I was quite hard on him. We used to row like hell at times – as good friends do.[49]

ELEVEN

'Talkative traveller'

(1950–1955)

All around us, as we travelled on, the brooding mountains cast their spell, and the far-flung stretches of ocean and tawny strands gleamed with a potent magic in the fading light of a cloudless day.

Mayo Sligo Leitrim & Roscommon, 1955

Never one to bear grudges, Hayward put the difficulties behind him, anxious to get on with *Ulster and the City of Belfast*, the second book in the Ireland series, which came hard on the heels of his Leinster volume. By the spring of 1949 he already had two-thirds of the manuscript written. And with his usual forward planning, was working out a summer and autumn trip with Piper to gather material for the next two books, both based on the west.

For his new Ulster book, Hayward had a template with *In Praise of Ulster*, which required revising and updating. It was twelve years since its publication and while his new one included stories from his previous book, it also contained fresh material. Hayward's deep love of Ireland was rubbing off on his companion. The artist had found his métier. Hayward began to interest Piper not only in the cultural history and archaeology of Ireland, but also the stories and legends. More than anything else, it was the natural history that most grabbed his artistic friend. The colour cover of the Ulster book, drawn by Piper, featured the County Antrim coastline and showed that he had well and truly caught the spirit of the place.

Hayward liked the sweeping landscape views from Knockmany Chambered Cairn near Augher, County Tyrone drawn by Piper for *Ulster and the City of Belfast*. He first visited the cairn on an excursion with the Belfast Naturalists' Field Club in 1927.

As with his earlier Ulster book, this one again considers all nine counties, starting in Belfast where Hayward had by then been living for more than thirty years. The city had suffered badly in the blitz and the face of the streets had changed considerably in the intervening twelve years. Near the start Hayward describes himself as 'a confirmed wanderer and extreme individualist'.[1] A lover of rugged country and wild mountain landscape, Hayward was particularly drawn to Donegal and awarded it his 'prize' as the greatest and most rewarding county in Ireland for those who 'take their pleasures afoot'. The county is afforded the longest chapter, twice the space devoted to Belfast.

Hayward had friends and acquaintances in every county and Donegal was no exception. Mathew O'Mahony from Glenties was a friend through the local drama circuit. He was the author of *Play Guide for Irish amateurs* published in 1946 (and in 1960 *A Guide to Anglo-Irish Plays*). On a tour of the county he had called with him but O'Mahony was not at home and he met his wife Eileen. Hayward wrote to him in the spring of 1949 asking for advice on what plays he would suggest should be staged in Limerick in March 1950 when he was adjudicating at the *Feis Luminghle*. He had proposed *The Drone, Love and Land, The Lost Leader, The Glorious Uncertainty* and *The Far-off Hills* but wanted his opinions, adding 'Please write quickly.' He also told O'Mahony that he had been trying 'rather forlornly' to hire a caravan 'to do' Connacht and part of Munster in the summer. He had planned to replicate his Shannon journey of ten years earlier, travelling by the same method but was forced to abort the idea saying 'I can't get next or near a bloody caravan.' Looking ahead to his plans, Hayward told O'Mahony 'I'll be up to my neck for a full year.' His letter ended, 'Give Eileen my love, and tell her I hope you'll be away <u>next</u> time I call. Husbands are a nuisance, and I won't have my own wife with me <u>either</u>.' In a handwritten PS, he added, 'God Bless – may we meet soon – that's a nice wee house you have and a nice wee chatelaine!'[2]

A quick turnaround of information resulted in the Ulster book coming out just a year after Leinster. It was published on 26 May 1950 by Arthur Barker, priced at fifteen shillings. By now Hayward's style had been firmly established and readers continued to look forward to each new book. The *Belfast Telegraph* said:

> Very largely this is Ulster by a writer with a predilection for its old-time Irish setting … while the book is a general guide, it is distinctly not the stereo-typed guide-book or a glorified transport timetable from which to learn when the last bus leaves for Glengormley or Stranmillis (Hayward is more at home in recalling the derivation of such names). Similarly there is a complete absence of staggering statistics of industrial output, especially in relation to shipbuilding in the city which was discounted in a single line.

The newspaper thought that his reference to Queen Elizabeth as 'the red-headed harridan of England' was an expression that would have been better omitted.[3] The *Northern Whig* succinctly summed it up: 'It is in the nature of a personally conducted tour, with Mr. Hayward leading, expounding, narrating, displaying, occasionally even singing, and doing it all very well.'[4] 'A genial collo-quially written book', was the opinion of the *Dublin Magazine*, which 'vividly traces the physiognomy of the province … a happy polish has been applied to town, country and people alike.'[5] Writing in *Studies*, Aodh de Blácam, felt that Hayward had produced 'a satisfactory, if not very brilliant, guidebook and refer-ence work. He is to be commended on his care to give the original Gaelic (with some inevitable slips) of the place-names of all nine counties; indirect testimony of the absolute Irishness of every corner of the separated land.'[6]

In a controversial review, the *Times Literary Supplement* said Hayward 'skated over bigotry in Ulster.' (In those days the *TLS* reviews were unsigned. The anonymity policy was abandoned in 1974, and at the turn of the twenty-first century the paper publicly made available the names of the reviewers of all books. The Ulster reviewer was revealed as Randal McDonnell, thirteenth

Earl of Antrim.) McDonnell complained of carelessness in the writing, citing several examples, 'Architecturally the City Hall is nothing to write home about,' and 'The annual contribution to the Imperial Government … is in the neighbourhood of several million pounds … Mr. Hayward skates over the bigotry of Ulster. It is a fact. It belongs to the majority of Ulster people. But no, Ulster must be made soft and romantic. Ireland to Mr. Hayward is the only source of romance.'[7]

By the summer of 1949 the two men were back on the road working not only on a book about Galway city and county, but also a separate volume planned on the other four counties: Mayo, Sligo, Leitrim and Roscommon. Hayward had decided there was sufficient material to split Connacht into two. Heavy July showers poured down and Hayward records with exhilaration Piper's improvisation with his sketchbook in County Leitrim: 'Downpour of rain at Swiss Valley, but Raymond got heroic sketch with umbrella tied to tree (6/7/49).'[8] It is fascinating to see how Hayward worked this up in the published book:

> Water streamed down his neck, and down ours as well, and running in streams from his finger-tips spread all over his sketching block, but his determination equalled his language in vehemence, and his reward was ultimate triumph.[9]

The following week, in Carrick-on-Shannon, their visit coincided with the funeral of Ireland's first president, Douglas Hyde, a fact noted by Hayward in his journal of the trip but not referred to in the book:

> 14/7/49: CORA DROMA RUISC: Carrick on Shannon
>
> Sketch of Carrick street, then to Rockingham, where Lady Stafford King-Horsman received us. Lovely room and two drawing-rooms, demesne beautifully kept. Beech drive a mile long, - views of lake superb island close in front. Lunch in Royal Hotel, Boyle, Sketch. Poor Douglas Hyde – watched his funeral pass. On to Drumshanbo through Carrick to Arigna … Farewell to Carrick in usual friendly style.[10]

The book contains many period sketches evocative of small-town Ireland of the early 1950s, especially the one on Carrick where three local men sit chatting on a windowsill. Carrick was a familiar place to Hayward, having featured prominently in his Shannon book. It was a staging post en route to the west or southwest of the country and he often stayed at the Bush Hotel. Tom Maher's grandmother ran the hotel during the time of Hayward's visits when it had eighteen rooms and twelve staff. Maher managed it until 1988 when he sold it and opened a B&B from his house Hollywell:

> My grandmother liked the fact that Hayward was writing about things in the area and that he was helping to preserve the history and culture of Carrick. She was conscious that Leitrim was a poor area and that through his books he was promoting the place in a way that had not been done before. He helped put it on the map. I remember seeing him coming and going from the hotel to Dunne's bar and walking around the streets. My grandmother told me that he was very musical and she had a good collection of records including some of his which she enjoyed. Hayward always had a meal in the hotel and he generally stayed a few days, finding out information and meeting friends. Carrick was a sleepy place so when he came with Raymond Piper, the word quickly went out on the Bush telegraph as we used to say, from the Bush Hotel.[11]

By now the Hayward-Piper collaboration was well established. After their summer tour they returned home, heading off again in Hayward's trusty Singer 12 as two carefree spirits on 22 September. His notebooks show the gap between his narratorial voice and personal opinions and gripes:

Thursday 22/9/1949

Set out again on our Connacht journey – Raymond Piper and myself. Left Belfast at 9.30 am. Lunched Enniskillen – the Imperial. Crossed border at Belleek and had first drink in Bundoran, for the luck of the trip. Heavy rain all the way, but beyond Bundoran the skies cleared, the Sligo hills took on a shining glory.[12]

The two men spent the autumn covering 8000 miles and driving all over Connacht. Galway city and county was explored as well as other parts of the province. At times it was hard going. The single-track western roads were rutted and dusty especially in dry weather, although notebook entries moan about the rain. For his second Connacht book, published after the Galway volume, Mayo was the launching point of the trip. His journey begins in Cong, familiar to him from his Corrib stay, where he embarks on a boat trip with Piper on Lough Mask before moving on to Achill Island. They based themselves at the Amethyst Hotel in Keel where he had a cosy room 'filled with the endearing nostalgic fragrance of turf smoke, the loveliest odour in all the world.' Achill was a poor place with few jobs. Many islanders went to work picking potatoes in Scotland or in the building trade in England returning in the summer for a few weeks to help cut hay and turf. Electricity had still not reached the island (it came around

1953). Homes were lit by paraffin lamps and candles while heat and energy for cooking came from turf fires and ranges. He shows his fondness for invoking other visitors who included the publisher Edward Newman from London and Mr and Mrs S.C. Hall on their journey in 1853 and in whose footsteps he was following nearly a hundred years later.

Although he enjoyed walking on Achill Hayward was appalled at the 'vicious devastation' that he found at the deserted village on Slievemore Mountain. He felt that the people of the island 'seem to have had small regard for their monuments of antiquity, a regard which is not greatly developed in the Irish people as a whole, and many of the Achill megaliths have been ruthlessly taken apart for the provision of materials to build houses, sheep-shelters and walls.'[13] There was little that he was not interested in. Quays fascinated him, ancient customs intrigued him, old graveyards were favourite haunts, lost names in history and stories such as those involving Fighting Fitzpatrick and Grace O'Malley all fed his curiosity. Frequently he stopped at roadside shrines and holy wells although he was unimpressed with what he found at Knock:

> The ugly assemblage of untidy wooden stalls and shacks, loud with advertisements and tawdry trimmings, the raucous loud-speakers, and the long lines of chromium-plated taps from which holy water is dispensed in a kind of production line, seem to me to be far removed from any seemly spirit of Christian devotion.[14]

On 3 October, Piper by his side, he climbed 'the dreamy unforgettable cone' of Croagh Patrick, saying it used to be known as Mount Aigli. But they did not linger long at the summit as they were pestered by 'a plague of Shield Bugs, which had obviously taken to the air in vast squadrons for our especial annoyance.' His notebooks record small detail: 'Croagh Patrick. We took under 2 hours to climb and 1 to descend: 1½ usual but too damned fast for me. Returned to Westport in rain for sketch of Reek (3/10/49).'[15]

Hayward had a quaint way with words and liked dropping in some surprising ones. After descending Croagh Patrick to Campbell's pub he discovered his 'really stout *veldtschoen*' were so badly cut and worn that he had to sit in the nearest cobbler's whilst new soles and heels were stitched and battered into place. On the way to Sligo he diverted to tour the back roads around Loch Talt and wrote of his love for them: 'For the *green roads* of Ireland ever tug at my heart, and I never tire of exploring their withdrawn beauty nor of seeking out their hidden or forgotten history.'[16]

The monastic settlement on the island of Inishmurray, County Sligo, which Hayward and Piper visited in 1952 with a local historian Robert Kirwan.

Sligo was a place of particular affection. But it was not so much the town that captivated him as the nearby island of Inishmurray and its antiquities. He devoted thirteen pages along with four pages of sketches to it. John Gallagher brought them across to the island in a small boat along with a local historian Robert Kirwan. Its recent history was fresh in the minds of locals because of the government evacuation scheme the previous year. Something about the spirit of the place touched Hayward. He was enchanted by the medieval wooden statues of saints and in particular by the face of Saint Molaise in the Oratory:

> It is a remarkable face, not easily forgotten once it has been seen, austere, other-worldly and ascetic in the highest degree. Great dreaming eyes look over high cheek-bones which surmount characteristic hollows, and if the visage suffers a little from wanton disfigurement which the statue underwent at the hands of some accursed Captain Morgan, the whole psychology of a hermit saint sill shines forth from it with compelling power ...[17]

Apart from the effigies, the deserted schoolhouse, where the teacher's chalk and blackboard stood on a stand with the last lesson written on it, had an unsettling impact on him:

There was an uncanny feeling of arrested animation about the whole place, not at all the feeling of a school that has been closed but rather that of one which might suddenly spring into life and activity without warning or reason … It was a matter of minutes before I was able to shake myself free of this unquiet mood, and when at last I turned to speak to Raymond and found that he had already departed, a terrible sense of loneliness descended upon me and made me call him loudly by name. No sound was ever more joyful to my ears than his answering call, and when he rejoined me he confessed that the feeling which I described had been shared by him in such compelling measure that he had been forced to seek the solace of the open air.[18]

He was particularly struck by the 'astonishing aerobatics' of golden plovers at a lake in County Roscommon, producing a lyrical eighty-word sentence:

Thousands of these birds passed over us from time to time, like a great swiftly-moving cloud, and then suddenly, at the issue of some command hidden from our senses, the cloud would split into two or three, and separate squadrons would pass into the hazy distance of the twilight, wheel suddenly, and simultaneously, at some other mysterious signal, reunite into one vast shimmering company, and pass over our heads again with a great sigh of whirring wings.[19]

After completing his Connacht journey, he returned home loaded down with material for two books that became *Connacht and the City of Galway*, published in 1952, and three years later the cumbersome and unimaginatively entitled *Mayo Sligo Leitrim & Roscommon* (*MSLR*). As soon as he arrived back in Belfast he wrote to Harold Leask, telling him he had just returned from the end of a three-month 8000-mile trip. 'I'm overwhelmed with notes', he declared, 'which is all to the good.' Hayward prepared a list of ten questions for Leask and described himself to him: 'I'm your watchdog and "on the spot" reporter!' The queries dealt with buildings as well as some suggestions about their care. One example is from Gort in County Galway:

Kilmacduagh. What is the degree of "leaningness" of the Round Tower? And why the lean at all? Some guide books say "seventeen feet from the perpendicular," which as, Euclid said, is absurd. And what is the curious structure to the NE of the "Bishop's House"??? I should like to know.

Clare Island murals. Being ruined by damp, I think if the belfry (?) were slated it would cure this.[20]

Leask replied two days later saying Hayward's idea for Clare Island was worth trying; in relation to the lean of Kilmacduagh he wrote, '17' is rot, of course, but the lean is considerable. I do not remember the annexe to Bishop's House.'[21] At the same time as this exchange of correspondence, Hayward sought advice from Leask about the possibility of his being elected to the Royal Irish Academy. He believed that with six books now behind him and several more in the offing, he would be a suitable candidate for membership of Ireland's most celebrated body that could trace its history back to 1785. Leask, then secretary of the Academy's committee for Polite Literature and Antiquities, had been a member since 1930. He replied by stating the Academy was dominated by scientists who are hard to convince of the merits of candidates:

> The attitude of most members of Council, when names come up for recom-
> mendation to the general body is to question a man's published work. If this
> is scientific, original research of any kind, in any bulk, he is sure of votes.
> Now practically all such work is unpaid, save for love, at worst for kudos.
> Your excellent works, being your liveliehood, [sic] are regarded, I regret to say,
> as savouring of journalism and as such, to the scientific mind in particular,
> anathema. I do not regard this as fair but can understand the minds which
> think that way.[22]

Although sympathetic to his desire to become a member, Leask concluded by advising Hayward 'not to come forward just now, at any rate, I do not think the chances good.' Leask's letter underlines how the Irish academic intelligentsia viewed Hayward, with reference to his work 'savouring of journalism', meaning that it was not held in high regard by the academicians. Hayward took it on the chin and did not pursue future election. There is no record of his ever having been elected to the RIA although he was a member of another long-established Dublin-based institution, the Royal Society of Antiquaries of Ireland whose pedigree, while not so long as the Academy's, stretched back to 1849.

While he was applying himself to his Connacht manuscripts, he was simul-taneously juggling with the Ulster book. He took time to briefly bask in the success of the first volume in the series, writing triumphantly in November to Mathew O'Mahony:

> My Leinster book has been a wow – Book Society recommendation and
> grand English and Irish reviews. Have you seen any – such as the Irish Tatler
> for September? I'm checking proofs of my new Ulster volume, companion to
> Leinster, which I was writing when I saw that charming wife of yours; and
> that book will be out in May. I'm only back from the Wesht – 8,000 miles I did
> in the yoke – and I start writing Connacht in ten days. I have to go to London
> next week to deliver two lectures on the Ulster dialect. I was in Dublin on
> Friday doing a lecture for Trinity College Music Club. I'm not idle.[23]

227

Although the critical praise for his Leinster book was largely positive, problems were arising over his delivery of the two Connacht books and if, for financial reasons, Arthur Barker was going to continue with the series after the Galway book. He was embroiled in wrangles with the publishers over finalizing the manuscript for the first of the them. Arthur Barker's health was poor and he handed over the running of the firm to one of his directors, Herbert 'Bertie' van Thal. An author and editor, he had run a short-lived publishing firm, Home and van Thal, but at Barker's he kept the general character of the company in his role in charge.[24] He was closely involved in the editing and preparation of Hayward's book and asked for the ending to be changed to read: 'Thus far we have travelled through the City and County of Galway, and I am of good hope that I have guided the steps of my readers to the more notable places in that tract of country.' He added 'I have left out the adjective "immense" since I feel that after all you are not dealing with the steppes of Russia.'[25] Van Thal had sent him back twelve sketches with the instruction, 'These need not come back to us since under no circumstances can they be incorporated in CONNACHT.'[26]

Hayward had been uneasy about the galleys and pictures being sent to Piper when they should have been sent to him. He was further aggrieved when the publishers declared they were cutting the book to 138 pages and reducing the number of sketches from sixty to fifty-one. He felt that in comparison with the companion volumes on Leinster and Ulster, the book would look 'very small and mean'. In the event they reached a compromise and the final book contained fifty-six sketches with 192 pages. *Connacht and the City of Galway* was published in March 1952 in a print run of 2000 copies. But there was a further blunder on the part of the publishers. Hayward was infuriated when he saw the finished copy. His name was mistakenly omitted from the title page owing to a printing error. Arthur Barker was a scrupulously caring professional imprint and it was an embarrassing oversight. Van Thal put his hands up offering 'sincere apologies' over the mistake. In a letter, dated St Patrick's Day 1952, he said that he would see what he could do with future reprints. 'I must confess that you have a very legitimate grouse about your name not appearing on the title page. This is a deplorable mistake on our part.'[27] In his personal copy of the book, Hayward signed his name with a copperplate hand on the white space where it should have been printed, adding in capital letters: AUTHOR'S NAME OMITTED FROM THIS TITLE PAGE.

In the chorus of notices there were some lukewarm and positively vituperative voices amongst the critics. In a snarl of disdain in the *New Statesman and Nation*, Louis MacNeice reviewed it along with a clutch of other Irish books including Maurice Craig's *Dublin*. He said it was packed with fascinating fact but he felt Hayward was 'unduly addicted to superlatives and to words like "lovely" and "veritable" and allows the landscape to wax in splendour on two pages running ... and he tends to admire too many things too much.'[28] MacNeice's comments were mild in comparison with the judgement of the *TLS*. The paper highlighted a passage, 'The sweetest little waterfall cascades melodiously down a rocky defile,' which it said gives the book the wrong kind of antiquity. On this occasion the anonymous *TLS* reviewer was later revealed as being the Mayo-born poet Richard Murphy. He wrote that Hayward is old-fashioned and 'seemed unaware that to see the country in the present it is necessary to look with contemporary eyes':

> We might be anywhere in the past 50 years propelled along by ridiculous passages about the panoramic beauties of coast or hilltop, with lumps in our throats as we amble in the ruined pleasure-grounds of Coole, to the sound of a voice that is often a poor pastiche of Amanda Ross [*sic*]. He is sound on the quality of various hotels, monuments no tourist should miss, mountains thought out to climb ... But he does not really come to grips with his subject. He does not give a proper account of the views of those who have – Synge on the Aran Islands, Yeats of Coole. Like the illustrations, the impression is slight ... he gives us in the end more ideas about the mind of a sentimental tourist than about the country he visited ... this landscape is only seen by Mr. Hayward as placid and fixed. Instead of being alive, it is insipid. Where is the animation? We are only shown Mr. Hayward's. His book would have been better had he studied the economic and social background of the country. People want information, not emotion, from a guide-book ... Many people no doubt will share the author's enthusiasm when they visit the country, but most, one hopes, will share it in silence.[29]

The Irish papers were kinder. The *Northern Whig*'s critic Alex Riddell remarked:

> The kindly guide with a good deal of knowledge – he has certainly worked to gather its great bulk – which he transmits with a hint of the manner of the good papa of the 'Swiss Family Robinson' leading his children through that marvellous island.[30]

In his review for *Irish Book Lover*, Kevin Faller, a Galwegian, said the book was 'tastefully produced' and 'remarkable for the pencil sketches of Raymond Piper, and anyone familiar with the grey, burred landscapes which predominate in the western province, can anticipate the charm and authentic atmosphere that a talented pencil spreads throughout such a work.' He added: 'I doubt if another will ever replace it.'[31] Hayward requested of the publishers that as many review copies as possible should be sent out, specifically mentioning Compton Mackenzie, which prompted a reassuringly humorous van Thal reply:

> The advance copy was sent to Compton Mackenzie, but there has been no reply from him. Reviewers never do reply to letters! And very few authors do – except on such dire occasions as when, for instance, their names have been left out of their title pages![32]

One of Ireland's leading bookshops, Kenny's of Galway had already chalked up respectable sales of his Corrib book and took on the first Connacht book. Des Kenny remembers his mother Maureen, who ran the business in Shop Street, talking about Hayward's visits:

> During the 1940s and fifties he used to come in and look around the books and talk to my mother for quite a long time. He would have been seeking information, asking questions about Galway and checking on sources. I remember her telling me years later that after they had chatted, he would walk down to the Wolfe Tone Bridge and look over the Corrib. Frequently she spoke about him and said he used to stare into the river for hours and she often wondered what he was thinking about. She never understood why he did that although he may have been taking notes and deliberating on his writing. We bought a job lot of *Corrib Country* and still have some. His books sold very well in the shop and his writing which was anecdotal and historical was popular. I would describe his work as a cross between a journalist and a serious writer. It was after Hayward's death, as well as the deaths of Brendan Behan, Kate O'Brien and Austin Clarke, that we decided in the late 1960s to start the picture gallery of authors as we realized that we did not have anything to remember them by.[33]

A somewhat less romantic portrait of the banks of the Corrib is painted by Henry Comerford, a retired solicitor. Hayward was a regular at the Galway Oyster Festival held in September. One year, accompanied by Piper, he was guest of honour at the ceremony:

> My late father, William J.V. Comerford, who was a solicitor, was a founder member of the Oyster Festival and when he was attending it Hayward used to call at our house at the Spanish Arch. Piper was sometimes with him and one afternoon there was a lull between the morning and evening sessions for the purpose of talking, singing and drinking whiskey. I saw Piper vomiting into

the flood having overindulged in oysters and Guinness during the morning debauch. Hayward was a wonderful character, my father liked his colour, and I loved his ebullience and his singing.[34]

Although the response from bookshops appeared to be positive, it was an extremely tough market for publishers. Questions were being raised by van Thal about the final two volumes in the series and whether they would be able to publish them since the books were a loss-making proposition. With Leinster, Ulster and the first volume of Connacht now available, two more were pending: one covering Mayo, Sligo, Leitrim and Roscommon, and the other on Munster. The issue was raised in van Thal's letter of 24 October 1951 – Hayward's fifty-ninth birthday:

> If we do not make a fair success of CONNACHT we shall not be able to continue and though you will no doubt be able to get your further volumes published elsewhere, I still believe it is most annoying to be told of forth-coming volumes which we, as the publishers, feel may never forthcome. I am personally not in the least pessimistic about this matter; I am being merely practical since we have already made a loss on the first three volumes. Although we have heard from you repeatedly that in the future we shall regain our money it is a slow process and hundreds of pounds are involved.[35]

Lynch's Castle in Galway which, Hayward wrote in his Connacht book, is the one single example of what the city must have looked like before the 'Curse of Cromwell' fell on it.

Hayward had learnt to deal with anxiety over sales figures from publishers and disparaging comments from the critics. Although sensitive to what the reviewers wrote, he had an unshakeable conviction in the work he was doing but the harsh realities of the postwar marketplace did not match his optimism.

By early summer 1952 Ricky had completed his education at Newtown School. Because science was not taught to a high level, he attended for a year Campbell College, a grammar school in east Belfast. Many years earlier Samuel Beckett, who had taught French at the school, had been involved in rows with the headmaster. At one meeting the head reminded Beckett that his pupils were 'the cream of Ulster', producing a memorable rejoinder, 'Yes, rich and thick'. It was noted though for its excellent physics and chemistry teaching, which stood Ricky in good stead when he went to Queen's University. He earned a senior student-ship from his first year results, which took some financial strain off his father, and graduated in 1958. In a letter to the scholar and poet Liam S. Gógan clarifying a point of history, Hayward wrote with pride about his son's academic achievement:

> By the way, my younger son, Richard Scott Hayward, has been awarded a First Class honours BSc in Chemistry at Queen's University Belfast. He was one of only three to achieve this distinction. I am very bucked about it. Clever boy: full of brains: takes after his ma![36]

The early fifties were dominated for Hayward by the huge *This is Ireland* enterprise but he took time to enjoy his first grandson Paul, born to Dion and Dolly on 20 February 1951. One event with which he was closely involved was the British Association meeting in Belfast in 1952. The retired director of the Folk Museum, George Thompson, was the local secretary of the anthropology section and Hayward helped him put together events:

> He was master of ceremonies and organized a ceilidh in the lecture room of the museum in Stranmillis. Hayward took charge of it and it was a great evening. Many illustrious names from the cultural world, including the English painter Stanley Spenser, were present. A group of folk dancers performed a French square dance *Dos-a-dos* which means 'Back-to-back'. It involved dancers passing right shoulders, moving to the right, passing the back of the other dancer at which stage the partners faced away from each other before moving backwards passing the left shoulders and returning to the starting position. Hayward directed them by calling out the movements in advance. They followed his directions closely and he did it all supremely well.[37]

According to Thompson, they had a mischievous soubriquet for Hayward:

We called him 'the Glacier Mints man' to cut him down to size a little. It was a bit of fun. He was an eminently likeable man but ambitious beyond belief and very confident. Ambition was oozing out of his pores. He could be quite ruthless – in the nicest possible way – or perhaps opportunistic would be a better description of him. I would describe it as hubris. My wife and I were involved with the Old Grammarians in Larne organizing the annual dinner in the 1950s each year in the King's Arms Hotel. Hayward, who was always willing to sing or play at the drop of a hat, often attended the dinners and liked making his presence felt. One year he brought his harp and mentioned to a few people that it was in the car park but no one asked him to play. It reminded me of the old song 'He brought his harp to the party but nobody asked him to play.' He was always ready to seize the opportunity and was annoyed that night that he wasn't asked to perform. But on the whole he could be very charming, working you round to his way of thinking and I rather liked him.[38]

In the spring of 1953 he took part in a recital of Ulster ballads during a trip to Denmark. The programme was presented by the Director of Drama and Song of the Danish State Radio. In between his travel writing, he took on many roles and involved himself in a host of activities that appeared to keep him working day and night. More than a hundred separate events are listed in his personal diary for 1951. One month's run – covering October – demonstrates a flavour of his crowded schedule:

Ballet Rambert, Casse Noissette; BNFC Conversazione; Opening meeting of YUA, speak on Ulster countryside; Annual meeting Astronomical Society, Kerry film shown; Arts Theatre; Lecture for QUB; Women's Inst; City Hall, Lady Mountbatten; Belfast Orchestra; Mariners Club lunch; saw television for first time in Belfast at Maurice Solomon's House; BNFC Fungus Foray; Slieve Donard for lunch; Inst. Manag. Assoc. for N.I., Tech, Dialect; Dental 2.20; QUB lecture, Celtic Art; BA Meeting Lord Mayor's Parlour; Astronomical QUB; Arts Theatre, The Gentle Gunman; Lunch Rostrevor; Pres. Address, BNFC; BGS; First Meeting QUB Film Society; PEN Committee; BNFC Comm, Film Show; BA Sub-committee QUB; We gave Ricky his first watch = 16; QUB International Rel. Soc.; Larne Gr. School, principal guest & present prizes; Opening meeting QUB Guild.[39]

In 1953, at the same time as the conquest of Everest was celebrated, more than 400 leading writers from around the world were arriving in Ireland for the twenty-fifth International Congress of PEN from 8 to 13 June. Based in Dublin, the week-long congress was the largest ever organized with thirty-six centres from twenty-seven countries descending on the capital. Side trips from Dublin included a bus tour to County Wicklow, a visit to Maynooth College and an excursion to the Lakes of Killarney. A special train was chartered to take the group for a day trip to Belfast on 11 June. It was the largest international gathering ever assembled in the city. The packed itinerary included a reception at Stormont, lunch in the city hall, a literary event at Queen's University and a state dinner hosted by the government. Hayward, who was then the Belfast chairman, was appointed a congress executive committee member.

Closely involved in organizing events, he made a speech. He sat at the top table, alongside illustrious names from the world of literature including the Hungarian writer Arthur Koestler, the Scottish novelist Neil Gunn, the poet and literary critic, Edwin Muir, the English writers Storm Jameson and C.V. Wedgwood, and the French novelist André Chamson who wrote in Provençal as well as French. Irish representatives included Maurice Walsh, Austin Clarke and the Derry-born writer Joyce Cary.[40] The congress theme was 'The Litera-ture of Peoples whose Language Restricts Wide Recognition' – a subject close to Hayward's heart. The programme included talks on Catalan, Hungarian, Estonian and Japanese literature, writing in Welsh and translation problems. Micheál Mac Liammóir spoke about writing in an obscure language. Hayward's speech on Ulster dialect – much to his consternation restricted to ten minutes – focused on how, when the Scottish planters came to Ulster, the language of Ulster was Irish.

Although he mostly had given up writing poetry he returned to the genre again in the 1950s submitting a poem to *Rann*, an Ulster quarterly edited by Barbara Hunter and Roy McFadden. 'The Stranger', a poem of four verses, was published in June 1953. The magazine attracted a mix of names including John Hewitt, Padraic Colum, Robert Greacen and Kingsley Amis. But Hayward's poem was not well received in some quarters. In a letter to Hewitt, the sub-editor on *The Bell*, Geoffrey Taylor, who had favourably reviewed Hayward's Leinster book, questioned why the poem was used in *Rann*:

> I've been meaning to write and say how impressed both Mary and I were with Roy McFadden. A strange, twisted and most attractive creature. On the other hand what an utter mess the last number of Rann is. Who are Daphne Fullwood and Oliver Edwards? And supposing them the right to live, why should they be given the privilege of print? And why, equally print Richard Hayward and May Morton? No standards.[41]

The controversial *Kavanagh's Weekly*, produced by Patrick and Peter Kavanagh, satirized his work as part of a wider piece on an Irish PEN anthology *Concord of Harps* published by Talbot Press. The collection included a three-verse

Hayward poem, 'Song'. The magazine reproduced the first three lines and part of line four:

> As I walked out from Carrowdore
> The song was in my mouth,
> And the whitethorn tree was flinging
> Its blossoms …

The reviewer added, 'whatever side rhymes with 'mouth' of course.' (The line finishes: 'Its blossoms to the south.') With the exception of *Old Moore's Almanac*, he said, 'it is the funniest book I have read for years.'[42]

The controversial *Kavanagh's Weekly* was produced by Patrick and Peter Kavanagh in the 1950s and satirized an Irish PEN poetry anthology published by Talbot Press which included a Hayward poem, 'Song'. The magazine reproduced the first three lines and part of line four. Kavanagh said that with the exception of *Old Moore's Almanac*, 'it is the funniest book I have read for years'.

On occasion Hayward acted as guide bringing local groups around Belfast on tours of historic parts of the city. He always brought them to Kelly's Cellars, a time-burnished pub then owned by Jimmy Tohill, and one of the city's oldest bars. In the early 1950s the owner started a visitors' book signed by scores of sporting personalities, actors, artists, and writers including Hayward, Conor and MacNeice. Tohill's son, J. J., helped out by serving customers; as a twenty-two-year-old he recalls Hayward bringing in a group and shaking hands with him:

> He was a great raconteur and could speak on any subject. In fact he sounded much the same as he came across in his books which I admire very much. On his tours he would bring in a group of ten and deliver a well researched fifteen-minute talk. I noticed when he was speaking a silence fell over the bar – the regular patrons were entranced by what he had to say. Often he would finish his tour by showing the group St Mary's chapel beside the bar which was funded by Presbyterians. My father thought that Hayward went where the money was since he was chummy with a lot of people and he said he would have hunted with hounds. He was two-faced because he was an Orangeman one day and a Hibernian the next day. But generally nobody had a bad word to say about him. He produced some wonderful books that in my view have never been equalled. He was a goer and put a lot into the country.[43]

The confectionery trade was still a constant in his life but after the Second World War it was in the doldrums and he experienced severe difficulties in getting chocolate supplies. One man who remembers him, Wilson Graham, later worked for Needler's as a sales representative. His father ran a sweet shop on the Castlereagh Road in the east of the city. As a boy he recollects Hayward calling in on his regular rounds:

> He liked chatting with my mother and father behind the counter while they booked their orders with him. But in the early 1950s when rationing was still in place he complained bitterly about supplies. His allocation was four ounces per person which equalled only two bars of chocolate. One of the most popular lines was the Richmond Selection of assorted toffees and chocolates in a jar which were high quality. Needler's had a great reputation for their sweets – their pastilles and glazed fruit drops were bestsellers. Milk chocolate was popular too, particularly in Northern Ireland, where people ate more sweets per head of the population than anywhere else in the UK. But Hayward could not get enough to spread around all his customers in the wholesale trade and the situation annoyed him very much.[44]

The uncertainty surrounding the fourth *This is Ireland* volume was resolved, after some financial agonizing, when Arthur Barker agreed to take it on, including it in the company's 1955 spring catalogue. The publishers were cautious about how many copies to produce and it was the lowest print run of any of his books, making it today the most elusive of all titles in the series. Since there were surplus sketches from the Connacht book, Arthur Barker insisted on using these, refusing to pay Piper for them a second time as they claimed they were paid for under the terms of the original agreement. Most of the research had already been done as part of their earlier journey for the Connacht book but they made a trip to Sligo in 1952 for additional sketches and material. Hayward had bought a new car, a Ford Consul four-door saloon, which first came off the production line in 1950.

The former world heavyweight boxing champion, Gene Tunney with his American friends sketched by Piper at Yeats' grave, Drumcliffe, County Sligo in 1952. Hayward is standing on the left of the drawing.

MSLR was published on 24 June 1955. In the preliminary pages an unlikely dedication is made to his American friends and in particular to one illustrious name from the boxing world:

To my good friend
GENE TUNNEY
Stalwart and worthy son of America and of Mayo,
and to his friends and mine
Allan P. Kirby, Joseph P. Routh and William M. Chadbourne
(because we all made this Western journey merrily together)

He referred in the book to Bohola, the birthplace of Gene Tunney's mother. A former heavyweight boxing champion of the world, Tunney struck up a friendship with Hayward on a trip to the US some years earlier. Tunney's father emigrated from Kiltimagh in Mayo to the US when he was nineteen and was a stevedore on the Hudson River. They lived in Greenwich Village where he grew up with three brothers and four sisters. Hayward maintained contact with him and on his Irish trips he looked him up. Tunney, a bibliophile with a library of 20,000 books and a liking for Shakespeare, had a long friendship with George Bernard Shaw.[45] When he and two friends toured in the west of Ireland for a week with Hayward he was still in his pugilistic glory. They stopped at many of the region's main tourist sites including Drumcliffe graveyard where Piper sketched the four men (known collectively as 'The Four Horsemen') standing at the grave of W.B. Yeats. In the summer of 1952 Tunney turned up in Belfast and along with Hayward drove up to the Glens of Antrim. He was well known in the area, especially from the filming of *Devil's Rock* in 1937. The date was Sunday, 24 August and Tunney was on a quest to find the house of Archie Murphy, a local farmer who once worked on the New York docks with Tunney and his father. They asked around and called at McBride's in Cushendun, one of Ireland's smallest bars. The pub was closed since the law did not then permit Sunday drinking. Hayward banged on the front door and the owner, Mary McBride, allowed them in. To keep within the law she could not take payment for alcohol but she pulled the blinds and poured them free drinks. Eleven-year-old Randal McDonnell, a nephew of Mary McBride (and sixteenth cousin of his namesake who reviewed Hayward's Ulster travel book for the *TLS* in 1950) remembers they drove a huge American car. It was thought to have belonged to John Ford who had been completing the filming of *The Quiet Man*. He recalled his aunt's reaction:

She had to treat Tunney and Hayward as her guests, so as to be lawful. I think they were embarrassed at getting a free drink, which was not their intention … Hayward was well acquainted with the glens, and acted as a guide for Tunney. Before they left McBride's they signed their names on a wall inside the pub. The signatures were preserved for years.[46]

The two surprise visitors left and shortly afterwards tracked down Murphy who was living with his aunt outside Cushendun. Denis O'Hara, the author of a book on Tunney, wrote that during the filming of *Devil's Rock*, a local farmer was employed to take part in a scene involving a sheepdog rounding up flock and was later nicknamed 'Hayward'.[47] A few days after the glens trip, when Tunney went to Belfast, the visit made both the front and back pages with news and sports coverage in the daily papers. A reception was arranged for him at the city hall where he dined with Hayward and the Lord Mayor. The *Northern Whig* carried a photograph showing Tunney signing the visitors' book along with his wife.[48]

Tunney was a regular visitor to Ireland and three years later he met Hayward in Dublin. That visit ended with a meandering cross-country road trip to Shannon Airport. In those days Hayward was friendly with Dr Thomas Carty and his wife Kate, a consultant ophthalmologist at the Charitable Infirmary in Jervis Street. Kate's sister, Mollie Quinn, a retail pharmacist, ran a shop in Lower Baggot Street near Doheny and Nesbitt's pub. Dr Carty's son, Austin, now a retired radiologist in Liverpool, recalls some of the details of that time:

My aunt Mollie held court at her shop for many of the cosmopolitan coterie of refugees in the general Pembroke flatland after the Second World War. Through the Dublin Arts Club in Fitzwilliam Street where she had a flat, she had come to know Richard Hayward. She spent her leisure socially with my parents and Richard who visited us often for lunch. I recall him being eager to put me through my conversational paces in Irish. I was doing the intercert at school and was taught Irish by a Kerryman. But I remember especially the glorious "skite" when the Tunney party, which included Mollie and Richard, undertook an odyssey from Dublin to Shannon Airport for his departure for the US. They hired a chauffeur-driven Chrysler seven-seater limo, more associated with use as a funeral car, from Murray's on Baggot Street Bridge and took Tunney on what was a fun trip, stopping at several bars en route. Mollie was infatuated with Richard. She had been with Elma and him on a trip to Spain in 1954 as he needed a translator. She was quite an extrovert and was always excited by Richard. He dominated a gathering which some would find off-putting, although for Mollie he was never boring but always full of interest and wonderful conversation.[49]

Mollie Quinn, who ran a pharmacist's in Lower Baggot Street, was friendly with Hayward in the cultural milieu of Dublin in the 1950s. According to her nephew, she was 'infatuated' with him, and thought he was 'always full of interest and wonderful conversation'.

Hayward's second Connacht book *MSLR* – the fourth in the sequence – came out in the early summer of 1955 complete with the Tunney sketch. It received generally enthusiastic reviews. Some critics praised it, adding qualifying quibbles, while others found it less than overwhelming. The *TLS* said Hayward was a 'Talkative Traveller – the words tumbled out of him: the scenery waxes in majesty until it reaches a climax of grandeur.'[50] The *Western Mail* in Cardiff was irritated by the fact that Hayward presupposes an acquaintance with all his earlier works when he writes: 'The origin and functions of these Round Towers, so typical of Ireland, I have already explained at page 178 of my Leinster volume.' The reviewer felt the book should be self-contained:

> His enthusiasm can carry him away. For example, in the absence of artifacts or other indication, it is difficult for the rest of us to accept that the shell middens at Ballysadare Bay must have been left by early man. A more pleasing feature is Mr. Hayward's interest in pre-history. 'Tis himself is the darlin' man for a megalith.[51]

TWELVE

Friendly invasion from the North

(1952–1955)

He belonged to nobody but he belonged to everybody – everybody claimed
him as a friend and he was very popular.

Peter Cavan, secretary Belfast Naturalists' Field Club

Dressed in immaculate Irish cream tweeds with turned-up trousers, shiny
brogues and hat, the dapper figure of Richard Hayward could have stepped
straight out of central casting. Black-and-white photographs show a sanguine
and self-confident man with a spring in his step. Centre stage, he cuts a distinctive style preparing to set off with his trademark cheerful spirit leading a jolly
party on one of many field trips throughout Ireland. Frequently he is accompanied by groups of redoubtable women dressed for all weathers with handbags,
umbrellas and walking sticks at the ready – known to one of his detractors as
'Hayward's pussies'.

Storyteller, lecturer, tour guide, historian and cultural all-rounder, Hayward
conducted excursions to many parts of the country through the Belfast Naturalists' Field Club. He led large groups of up to fifty, hungry for information
about the history and heritage of remote parts of Ireland that were opening
up to them. Photographs taken on departure portray a joie de vivre about the
weekend prospects in the company of a man who radiated joviality and had
an ability to charm a remarkably wide range of people. Many were familiar
with his films as well as his singing and broadcasting, and it was a journey of
discovery around an Ireland that few of them knew much about.

Hayward delivered lectures, illustrated talks, presented papers and handed out prizes for the best field work in the junior section at the annual conversazione. A regular attender at meetings, he served on the club's general committee from 1946 to 1949 during the presidency of the Queen's University geographer and writer Estyn Evans, a major figure in promoting the study of Ulster folklife. He knew Evans through his books, particularly *Mourne Country*, which had been published by Dundalgan Press in 1943. Evans's son, Prof Alun Evans, recalls his parents discussing Hayward 'with a tone of friendly disdain'.[1]

Hayward was elected president on 10 April 1951, serving for 1951–52. Other positions he held included vice-president, chairman of the junior division, secretary of the geological section and, above all, conductor of numerous excursions to many parts of Ireland. In the annals of the field club's history, he is best remembered for these trips. They ranged from one-day local summer or autumn outings to five-day spring weekends. Over a seventeen-year period he led more than thirty excursions. The Easter locations were a long way from home, involving lengthy journeys to the far west, southwest, or southeast of the country. Cork, Kerry, Limerick, the Burren, the Corrib, Achill Island, Carlow, Kilkenny, Waterford and Wexford were all on Hayward's itinerary. There was hardly a square mile of Ireland that he had not visited; the country never failed to ignite his enthusiasm and he delighted in sharing it. Early Christian and Romanesque churches, medieval ruins, abbeys, priories and friaries, Norman castles, monasteries, round towers, and holy wells were amongst the sites visited. Folklore and historical arcana were all part of the mix. He identified closely with the natural world, and had a sound working knowledge and wide vocabulary of wildflowers and birdlife. He was entertaining and informative with a breadth of knowledge from decades of reading scholarly literature.

Detailed instructions running to several pages were provided to those participating. On the Burren trip in 1956, for example, they included advice on bringing strong shoes, rubber footwear and oilskins as well as thermos flasks. Unlike today's OPW-run sites with their interpretation panels and wardens, few of the historic places had any signage to them. Hayward relied on the help of trusted historians or members of local field clubs who knew their patch. Several outings were held in conjunction with the archaeological societies of Thomond for the Limerick trip and with the Kilkenny Archaeological Society (KAS) for a visit to Leinster. They sent advance plans and produced an outline itinerary to help him and he handed over to them for detailed local knowledge.

In his presidential year Hayward, in the centre, leads a large group of members of the BNFC on their 1952 excursion to Kilkenny. *The Irish Times* described the weekend as 'an invasion from the North', while the *Old Kilkenny Review* said it was 'another outstanding event of the year ... and the 'Belfast members were most genuinely enthusiastic about their reception'.

A veritable roll-call of mid-twentieth-century writer-friends was enlisted. The Donegal topographical writer and historian Harry Percival Swan helped with a September trip to the Inishowen peninsula in 1948 when the party was invited to afternoon tea in Buncrana. Hayward's trustworthy fact-checker Harold Leask was signed up for the Boyne Valley trip at the end of August 1951 while Liam Gógan, who had written the introduction to Hayward's book on the Irish harp, led another trip to the same area in 1958; in Limerick, the antiquarian, Alma Fitt, a banker from a Quaker family of grocers and auctioneers, was on hand to help with arrangements during an Easter excursion in 1951, while his publisher, Harry Tempest of Dundalk, joined them for the tour of that region on 15 May 1954.

The destination chosen for the Easter 1952 trip was Kilkenny, a city Hayward had come to know and love. A large party of forty-eight signed up for the tour – described as being of 'general topographical interest'. Hayward invested a vast amount of time, effort and energy in organizing the trips and the Kilkenny excursion in particular – his first to the Irish southeast – was one in which he was determined to excel, especially in his presidential year. The essayist and linguist Hubert Butler, who in 1944 had revived the long-dormant KAS, had met Hayward when the latter was researching his Leinster book in 1948. He agreed to help sort out local practicalities. Butler lived at Maidenhall, the family's Georgian mansion near Bennettsbridge, five miles south of Kilkenny. As the society's secretary he was ideally placed to be an on-the-ground factotum. He had another connection to Hayward's past as he was married to Susan Margaret, known as Peggy, the sister of Tyrone Guthrie.

The KAS was a well-known Victorian institution with the Prince Consort as patron and the Marquis of Ormonde as president. It was an influential group in Irish historical studies. Butler had a deep attachment to the countryside, and by his own admission was an 'amateur archaeologist'.[2] In an essay about his life beside the River Nore, Butler wrote 'I have always believed that local history is more important than national history … Where life is fully and consciously lived in our own neighbourhood, we are cushioned a little from the impact of great far-off events which should be of only marginal concern to us.[3] The lengths to which Hayward went to ensure everything ran with precision for their Kilkenny excursion are clear from letters. In October 1951, six months before the weekend, he wrote to Butler with a plan:

> Wherever we go we ask the local club or society to arrange our itinerary and provide guides and it has long been my desire that we would one day descend upon you. I outline bare details: number of party 35. Arrive late on Good Friday, leave for Belfast lunchtime Easter Tuesday … PS: Could we also do the meeting of the three Sister Rivers. We want a bit of scenery as well. I do hope you can arrange things.[4]

On Hayward's behalf, Butler wrote to local business people, including Walter Smithwick of the brewery, organizing access to buildings and arranging guides. At the year's end, on 29 December, Smithwick replied: 'It is only a pleasure to us and quite apart from that if this is the Richard Hayward who wrote that delightful book on Kerry I will be honoured to meet him. I recommended his book to several people in London and also put it into the circulation here in the local Book Club'.[5] With the turn of the year and time pressing, Hayward got down to brass tacks, writing to Butler with a renewed sense of urgency:

> I want to book the hotels – Imperial and Club House – definitely for a party of 35 and I want to do it now. Easter is a busy time and plans must be made final within two weeks at the latest. As well as that, I am Chairman of the British Association Excursions Committee and after the end of this month

I'll be swamped with work in connection with looking after 3,000 of the blighters. So the need is all the more pressing for me to get this thing fixed and sealed. I'm sure you'll understand and agree.[6]

On leap year's day he again wrote to Butler on headed Ulster Transport Authority notepaper from the City Hotel in Derry:

I'm over-subscribed by five and I don't want to turn 'em down. I have the hotels fixed but not the transport. So look. Can you fix at once a local hack man to meet the train in Dublin, bring five to Kilkenny, take them round the bus trips and take them back to Dublin? If you can, I'm saved. I'm sure there are plenty of such men, and I can pay up to £10. I could even squeeze a couple of pounds more, not to be stuck. But £10 should do it, according to our scales here … This is very very urgent, because I must tell my five. If five too many, four would do. I can jamb [sic] one extra in the bus. So will you please see what can be done and WIRE me at once. Keep a note of the wire cost, and of any other costs you have in this show – postages, telephone etc. I'll refund all to you when we meet. Don't forget this … Anyway do wire me … This thing is a terrific success. Regards to "herself."![7]

Butler telegrammed three days later saying 'Will risk promising car twelve pounds for four, if too little … private gifts probably available.'[8] Hayward responded the next day in a follow-up postcard:

Thank you for your telegram, and I've fixed for the extra four. But I would like to make it five, as I said. There are lots of big cars in Eire, and I'm sure there is one in your ancient city that would hold five at a pinch. We could make it £14 which should be ample for the whole itinerary. So will you engage local hackneyman in commercial altercations (!) and send me another wire at once?? Please. With five fixed I'll feel fine and dandy about it all.[9]

Hayward was determined not to lose the business of a single customer. After much to-ing and fro-ing, everything was in place with the final tally rising to forty-eight. Less than two weeks later, he again wrote to Butler and enjoined him to hustle for press coverage:

I am very keen that we should get all the local publicity we can for this meeting and I hope you will key up the local press to a pitch of fever!!! A lot could come from this meeting and you and I want it to. So hammer away at the press. What about the Dublin papers???? They might very well bite at such an allIreland gathering. That's what we want to stress – allIreland – no border in science and culture. The papers will buy that.[10]

Hayward's persistence paid off with national press exposure. The day before the gathering, 'An Irishman's Diary' in *The Irish Times* carried a piece saying that Kilkenny, 'for the second time in a generation, is to have an invasion from the North at the Easter weekend':

> This year's visitors will be led by Richard Hayward, whose book on Leinster has a very pleasant illustration of the famous Kilkenny Tholsel, by Raymond Piper … The Kilkenny Archaeological Society, whose recent exhibition was a huge success, are catering for all tastes among their guests. Apart from the better-known archaeological and architectural interests of the region, the visitors will be taken to the Dunmore caves, the Hollypark coal mine, and St. Francis' Brewery – what better judge of a good beer, after all, than a good naturalist?[11]

Along with three visitors from the Archaeological Society of the Isle of Man, as well as members of other Irish field clubs, the party also visited Graiguenamanagh, Jerpoint Abbey, Thomastown, Kilfane, Swift's Heath and Bennettsbridge. So much was packed in that often there was not enough time at each stop. In the city, they inspected the relics in the Black Abbey but the scheduled fifteen-minute visit turned into two hours after which, the *Kilkenny People* reported, the group 'left reluctantly'.

As he saw it – three decades after partition – Hayward was doing his bit for cross-border relations. He produced a letter of fraternal greeting from the Lord Mayor of Belfast to the Mayor of Kilkenny; in a speech at the city hall he said he had come to know the city's history and its old buildings because he had been there 'a hundred times'. After dinner the informal evening ended with music and song. 'Nobody talked about partition or politics nor did anyone studiously ignore them,' according to the *Kilkenny People*. 'There was no need. For it is quite obvious that politicians have not yet succeeded in erecting any barriers that friendship and scholarship can easily cross over.'[12] During the speeches, Ramsey Moore of the Isle of Man Society and Governor of the Manx Museum, said they were grateful to Hayward for 'lifting them above the realm of politics and into the realm of affection.'[13] Two weeks later, the Irish government picked up on the group's Easter visit. In its weekly newsletter, interspersed between stories about the diplomatic corps in Dublin, tourism figures, trade returns, and the expansion of peat briquette production, the Department of External Affairs, reported on the outing.

> Kilkenny, famous city of Ireland's south, received at Easter a friendly invasion from the north. The Belfast Field Club, which visited Limerick last year,

chose Kilkenny for their annual outing. The leader of the expedition, Mr. Richard Hayward, the well known Ulster singer and writer, whose gramophone records and travel books are well known had already visited Kilkenny when writing his book on Leinster.[14]

Despite the intensity of the numerous postal communications involved in organizing the weekend, not everything went according to plan. The Butlers nearly missed one event, believing it was scheduled for the next day; 'In fact', according to one account, 'the proceedings proved decidedly unregimented, a combination of charm, intellect, and organizational chaos.'[15] A humorous description of the weekend appeared fifty-five years later when the Dublin writer Christopher Fitz-Simon quoted in his memoir a story from Butler's wife about what would happen on the Sunday morning:

> 'They'll have to be given time to go to church,' said Peggy, her knowledge of Ulster ways to the fore. 'Protestants in the North always go to church so as not to be seen as ungodly by their Romanist neighbours, unlike Protestants here.' Hubert felt that some of them might well be Romanists – these naturalists were known to be of ecumenical disposition.[16]

There was general agreement that it all had been a tremendous success. Butler was extremely pleased with the visit and wrote afterwards, 'I think everybody who attended the outings was aware that something very important was happening.'[17] Since reviving the KAS seven years earlier, he had organized many events including a centenary celebration of the old society in Kilkenny Castle as well as a successful Kilkenny Exhibition with the cooperation of the National Museum. 'But I think I was proudest of having organized a week's visit from the principal archaeological society in Northern Ireland; for cultural fraternizations between North and South are as rare as they are valuable.'[18] In its editorial in 1953, the *Old Kilkenny Review* – the annual journal of the KAS – the field club visit was described as 'another outstanding event of the year.'

> A large number came, the weather was excellent, the programme was well organised and much appreciated. A very full programme covered most aspects of town and country, a large number of our members reading papers and acting as guides. The Belfast members were most genuinely enthusiastic about their reception here.[19]

It had all been good knockabout fun, but later in 1952, Butler was at the centre of a controversial storm, which led to his leaving the KAS. During a lecture at the end of October at the Foreign Affairs Association in Dublin, a

furious row erupted about the persecution of the Roman Catholic Church by
the Yugoslav Communist regime. When he spoke, Butler reminded the audience about the forced conversion to Catholicism and the eventual massacre of
thousands of Orthodox Serbs by the Croatian regime that collaborated with the
Nazis. The Papal Nuncio, who was in the hall, regarded Butler's comments as an
insult, and walked out. The press launched a campaign against Butler who was
ostracized. So strong was the feeling that he was forced to resign as secretary
of the KAS since only a small number of people were prepared to defend him.
Kilkenny County Council also expelled him from one of its subcommittees.
When Hayward heard of the row he wrote immediately in solidarity. It was a
sympathetic yet characteristically blunt letter:

> You know very well that we <u>all</u> feel sorry about this rotten thing, but whether
> the BNFC will wish to do anything I cannot say. I'll try to <u>make</u> them, but
> they are an old conservative body and the Committee naturally decides about
> such things ... I do hope it all blows over. Your leaving the KAS would be an
> irreparable loss to them. They would never get anyone like you. Can't they
> <u>see </u>that this is all childish? But you know what RC countries are – or you
> <u>should</u>. And knowing that, why the hell did you shoot out your neck????
> Freedom of speech, my eye, as you know damn well. The RCs only believe
> in that when it is <u>their</u> brand of speech. My God haven't they got their own
> brand of truth???? With a special beJayzes <u>Catholic</u> Truth Society to vend it!
> Why not just TRUTH? But you know the answer to that one. I have always
> sheered off religion and politics for this very reason that has hit you. In a RC
> country you must either say nothing or be rent in pieces. Good luck to you,
> with regards to Peggy and yourself.[20]

Butler maintained his intellectual independence and after the furore died
down he started the Kilkenny Debates in an attempt to encourage discussion on a range of subjects. Organized by the Kilkenny Debating Society, a
subcommittee of the Kilkenny Arts Society, the first topic in spring 1954 was
the controversial subject of partition. He asked Hayward to come up with
the names of two Unionist leaders to speak to the motion, 'That Ulster's best
interests lie with the United Kingdom'. There had been considerable advance
coverage about the event in the press. Protests were held in Belfast about the
Unionists' participation in what was the first ever cross-border public debate.
It was also raised in the Northern Ireland Senate. The speakers from the South
were Seán MacBride, former minister of external affairs, and barrister Eoin 'the
Pope' O'Mahony, vice-chairman of the Anti-Partition Association. From the
North, supporting the motion, the main speakers were Col. W.W.B. Topping,

the Unionist Party chief whip, and the secretary of the Unionist Council William Douglas. Hayward was invited to speak along with Mary O'Malley, a Nationalist member of Belfast Corporation.

More than 200 people attended the event at the City Technical School on 23 April, St George's Day. Anticipating trouble, members of the Special Branch and the Civic Guard turned out in force but the three-hour debate ended peacefully although frank views were expressed.[21]

Chaired by Prof Myles Dillon, an Irish scholar at the Institute for Advanced Studies, the subjects debated ranged across religious, political, economic and cultural matters including the Irish language; no vote was taken. Hayward was to be a principal speaker but appeared anxious not to take sides. In the event he concluded the contributions from the platform with a general call for mutual respect.[22]

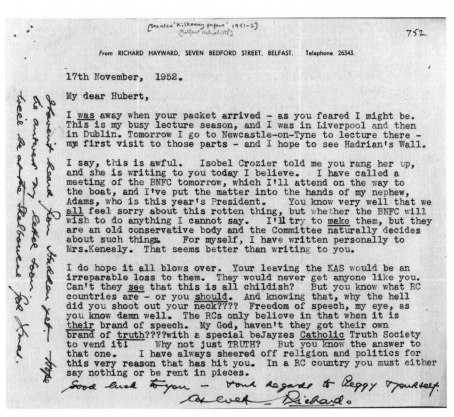

Hayward wrote to the essayist Hubert Butler in November 1952 offering support for his plight following a controversy over outspoken comments Butler made about the persecution of the Roman Catholic Church by the Yugoslav Communist regime. Hayward asked him: 'why the hell did you shoot out your neck????'

Under the headline 'Even the cats were quiet in Kilkenny', the *Belfast Tele-graph* gave the story front-page prominence covering in detail the main arguments presented by both sides. Its political correspondent reported: 'Richard Hayward said a few serious words before singing a song about a petticoat on a clothes line in Irish and English.'[23] The paper concluded: 'If nothing else, the meeting at least allowed either side to see as, one speaker put it, that "they are not all ogres north of the Boyne, nor all gunmen south of it".'[24]

Clearly Hayward did not want to upset the political applecart. Two weeks earlier he had brought a large group to the Corrib for the annual field club's Easter excursion. They stayed at Ashford Castle, touring the region for four days; it was in his interests to encourage North–South friendship. In an essay two years later, Butler reflected on the events:

> My opponents hoped that my liquidation would be decorous and quickly forgotten, but my friends and myself were little inclined to oblige them, and for a time our small society enjoyed in the metropolitan press a blaze of publicity which its archaeological activities had never won for it.[25]

The Easter excursions quickly became a permanent fixture in the field club calendar. In 1953, on a visit to the Old Wexford Society, which marked the ninetieth anniversary of the club's founding, the party was given a civic reception. Later they were entertained, according to the itinerary, 'by a selection of Irish songs mainly by Thomas Moore rendered by Miss Codd's Mixed Choir, including Miss Nellie Walsh.' This excursion attracted a record crowd of fifty-eight members each of whom paid £10 16s 0d but Hayward did not garner as much publicity as he had done for the Kilkenny trip. Amongst locations visited were New Ross, Dunbrody Abbey, Ballyhack, Fethard, Ballyteige Castle, Kilmore Quay and Hook Head where Dr George Hadden, a geologist and president of the Old Wexford Society pointed out to the party specimens of corals and crinoids in the sandstone and conglomerates.[26]

One of those present on the trip, Prof Richard Clarke, a retired Belfast anaesthetist, first met Hayward at Inver in south Donegal on a family holiday during the Second World War. He was persuaded by him to join the club and started attending meetings, some of which were held in a hotel in Linenhall Street in Belfast. Clarke kept in touch with Hayward and as a young postwar medical student developed an interest in local history. Sixty years later he looked back on some of the fun of the trip:

About seventy per cent or more were elderly ladies although there were some younger folk and it was a full bus load. Hayward was a dynamic figure and there was so much good about him. He enjoyed chatting to the ladies and buttering them up. Many were widows who wanted company and to be appreciated and although it's easy to sound patronizing, he had the ability to talk to them and make them feel important. But he also talked very civilly to younger people too. One evening in White's Hotel we had a ceilidh and danced the 'Waves of Tory' – the locals taught us how to do it. Hayward of course was master of ceremonies. He was in the prime of his life and pushed himself since he was doing what he enjoyed; he chatted to everybody freely and that was the secret of his success.[27]

Miss Codd, John Clancy and the Wexford Male Voice Choir took part in the evening entertainment while Nellie Walsh sang 'The Three Flowers', which Hayward said was an unconscious compliment to him because along with Norman Reddin, he had written the music to the song. Clarke enjoyed the experience so much he signed up for another club excursion the following year, Easter 1954, this time to the west of Ireland. The destination was Mayo and Galway, specifically the Corrib region, eleven years after Hayward's book on the area had been published:

We had a boat journey across a very choppy Lough Corrib when the water came pouring in and we all got completely soaked. I remember one elderly man stripping off down to his underclothes and drying himself in front of the fire in a small pub outside Galway, so it was all very informal and no one seemed to worry. Hayward was slick and very good at putting across the subject. He could talk about things as if he really knew them and gave the impression that he knew a lot. But he bluffed a bit – though that is perhaps unfair – as he was so good at talking, and what he didn't know, he made up. He had absorbed all the information about the outdoors to carry him through and did not make a fool of himself. For example, he could identify easily the main flowers of the Burren; names such as *Dryas octopetala* and *Geranium sanguineum* still stick in my head.[28]

On occasions Hayward brought the groups to luxurious surroundings. For the Corrib trip he booked a party of thirty-six to stay in the opulence of the Ashford Castle Hotel in Cong, County Mayo. He had written about the hotel in *The Corrib Country* when he stayed there, making friends with the owner Noel Huggard. Word of the jollity of the weekends quickly spread and for many Hayward's leadership was the unique selling point. Peter Cavan joined the club in 1956 when he was twenty and got to know Hayward well. He was appointed secretary and sat on the committee with Hayward, attending winter lectures and signing up for excursions. He cherishes the memory of brilliantly warm weather on a trip to the Shannon region at Easter 1962 when they stayed in Cruises Hotel in Limerick:

> Hayward's outings sometimes were booked out – you had to get in early if you wanted to go and the women often fought for a seat near him on the bus. He was charismatic with a great personality and a supreme entertainer. People were always asking questions and Hayward had no shortage of answers. He was an enthralling speaker because he drew on a vast fund of knowledge. There was minor climbing over ruins while he expounded on everything. Nobody would probe too deeply as they didn't want a lot of detail to confuse them and if he didn't know the answer he approximated something. There wasn't really any scientific depth to it – it was rather superficial but it gave people who wouldn't ordinarily have gone to these places, an idea of what parts of the country were like. Hayward was constantly on the go – a sparse man and tall, but very agile and active. My main memory is an army of ladies of a certain age. They were devoted to him, and he to them. They were regulars and it didn't matter to them where the location was, if Richard Hayward was conducting it, they were going on it. *He* was the attraction.[29]

Members of the BNFC line up for the camera as they prepare to set off from Belfast on the Enterprise train to Dublin en route to the Burren in County Clare on their 1956 Easter weekend excursion. Hayward's wife Elma is standing behind him while behind her, to the right of the pillar, is Raymond Piper.

Hayward had a capacity for memorization, rarely referring to notes during the talks on field club tours. Effortlessly he reeled off dates of events and plucked out other information without hesitation. He deciphered the landscape and brought the past to life with a phlegmatic and relaxed approach. This was outlined to Liam Gógan in advance of a club trip to the Boyne Valley at the end of May 1958. Gógan had agreed to share the conducting with Hayward and had compiled detailed notes on the antiquities of the area, which he sent to him. Hayward replied saying, 'I shall prime myself with all the dope. I never read to my people. I just take a few headings and then talk. We can share the thing evenly, as you wish. If you want to take Tara and Slane, or anything else, just say so and I'll leave you to it. Or we can both do a stint on everything. We know each other well enough to weave in pleasantly.'[30]

Elma and Ricky went on some excursions, including one to the Burren in 1956 with Raymond Piper. Elma was frequently accompanied by her sister, Edith Adams. Cavan recalls that they were always together:

They were very keen supporters and followers sitting together on the bus and chatting happily as Richard walked up and down talking to everybody. Elma was a quiet woman but she couldn't upstage Richard. He belonged to nobody but he belonged to everybody – everybody claimed him as a friend and he was very popular. The field club in those days was divided between those who were serious in their research about butterflies and botanical specimens while Richard on the other hand was more or less in favour of having a nice time which didn't go down too well with the more serious people. The scientific side did not like the cult of personality which they accused him of. They perceived that he was a bit of a social butterfly. But that was the wrong impression because he had a deep knowledge and love of all things. Perhaps the speed with which he communicated belied the fact that he really thought deeply. He wasn't standoffish or reserved but convivial and brought people along with him on a tide of enthusiasm.[31]

But not everything in the field club garden was rosy and not everyone enthused about Hayward. Membership was divided into two distinct camps: scientific and non-scientific. According to Cavan, Hayward's popularity annoyed some members and in particular Patricia Kertland, curator of the Herbarium at Queen's University since 1937, a field botanist and lecturer in the botany department:

He was regarded by Kertland as a bit frivolous. She was formidable and did not like women on the trips, dismissing them as flibbertigibbets and referring to them as 'Hayward's pussies'. If she didn't like you, she was forthright in her opinions and she certainly didn't like Hayward at all and made no secret of it. As a professional scientist, she thought he was in the club through sheer forceful personality. She disregarded his researches as well as his books and writings. 'That Hayward!' she would proclaim in disgust. She didn't suffer fools gladly; in fact she didn't suffer them at all. She took against him as being a lightweight. He was not fulfilling her expectation of what a member of the club should be. And because he had such a large and loyal following of ladies who hung on his every word and followed him everywhere, this annoyed her even more.[32]

The botanist Patricia Kertland, sketched by Raymond Piper, was dismissive of Hayward. She referred to the women who went on his field club excursions as 'Hayward's pussies.'

BNFC, SLIGO.   EASTER 1961

Hayward leads a field club group to Sligo from Belfast City Hall over the
Easter 1961 weekend.

During 1962, in the run up to the club's centenary the following year, there
was a possibility that Hayward would be president again. But Cavan recalls that
Kertland's hostility to him was growing and she argued that he should not be
president in the centenary year since he would 'just make a joke of it. The practice was that the previous year's president nominated his or her successor so she
engineered things to be president in 1962 and nominated James Loughridge,
the surgeon, as her successor in the centenary year. Hayward was hurt and very
cross'.[33] Notwithstanding the filibustering and blatant antagonism, his renewed
membership of the field club was a fond link with the past. In the 1920s he knew
many of the illustrious names from that time including Bigger, Robert Bell, R.J.
Welch and S.A. Bennett. In a review of Praeger's biographical work, *Some Irish
Naturalists*, he reflected on his memories of them: 'There is nothing I love more
than a man who is not afraid to declare his deep affection for such people, as well

as for the grand old club itself, which Dr. Praeger handsomely describes as 'my second university'.[34] In the preface to his 1950 Ulster travel book, he doffed his hat to the club members with whom he said he had 'spent so many rewarding hours in the fair fields of our beloved country. Archaeologists, botanists, zoologists and geologists, I thank them all for their happy comradeship.'[35]

It was during Hayward's tenure as BNFC president that he embarked on an ambitious project to compile a dictionary of dialect words. As far back as the 1890s, some members had wanted to initiate folklore studies in the club, but by 1900 the project had collapsed. At its annual meeting attended by seventy-five members on 10 April 1951 in the Old Museum, Hayward proudly took the presidential chair, 'passed by acclamation', as the minutes record.[36] The committee had already agreed on the formation of a new folklore and dialect section but a dissenting voice claimed that folklore was a branch of archaeology, that the committee had no power to split a section, and that 'ordinary members of the committee were being swamped by the increasing number of sectional secretaries.'[37] From his new seat of power, Hayward said the committee had already sanctioned the formation of the section. After a short discussion, he ruled the objection out of order, saying that it was resolved that folklore and dialect was not a branch of archaeology.[38] He undertook his year in office with diligence and had a brisk businesslike approach at meetings. Peter Cavan says if Hayward had a contribution to make he was concise: 'He knew what he wanted to say and if he wanted to persuade people he would have made the point succinctly but always with humour. He was an engaging, larger-than-life man, with an inventive mind, and always had a smile on his face.'[39]

Hayward and his nephew, Brendan Adams, were the driving force behind the section and both were involved with it until their deaths. Adams, who succeeded Hayward as club president, had a fascination for dialect and wrote papers for the *Proceedings of the Royal Irish Academy*, *Ulster Folklife* and *Bulletin of the Ulster Place-Name Society*. In December 1947 his twenty-four-page paper, 'An introduction to the study of Ulster Dialects,' presented to the Royal Irish Academy in Dublin, acknowledges his uncle's interest and encouragement of his work.[40] Adams, who originally worked as a buyer in the flax industry, was a gifted philologist. He had read the proofs of Hayward's Kerry book in 1945 and helped him with queries in his writing. The son of Edith Adams, Elma's older sister, he had been brought up in Belgium, spoke fluent Flemish and French and had acquired a working knowledge of Irish and German. He also had an acquaintance with Chinese, Berber and Coptic.[41]

With the rising influence in the 1950s of television as well as newspapers, radio and the cinema, Hayward believed that dialect was in danger of being slowly watered down and lost to future generations. A long-term interest was his love of colloquialisms. An acknowledged expert on dialectology in Ireland, he had respect for local sayings that had been handed down. Hastily scribbled lists, loose scraps of paper and notecards with oddball bits of arcane information reflecting his interest in dialect are stuffed into buff-coloured envelopes in his archive at the Folk Museum. Linguistic curiosities, words, phrases, quotations, sayings, proverbs, rhymes and a gallimaufry of random notes fall out of the envelopes: spoonbake, cleft palate, deaf colonel, Kircubbin barber, clockin' hen, gawk, and a Walt Whitman quote: 'Come lovely and soothing death undulate round the world'.[42]

He drew up a plan of campaign for what was called the Ulster Dialect Survey and work began on a dictionary with the provisional title *The History and Humour of the Ulster Dialect*. Hayward had been inspired by a gift of a Manx Dialect Dictionary when he had conducted an excursion with the field club to the Isle of Man in 1950 and he realized the potential for a similar Ulster one. When complete, he hoped the published volume would stretch to 12,000 words. Within a short time of the new section's formation sixty members had enrolled. At a meeting on 8 May 1951 to discuss policy, Hayward and Adams were elected editors of the dictionary and were in charge of the fieldwork. Eight chief collectors were appointed with twelve serving on the editorial board. The collectors were each allocated an area to look after. It was planned that the dictionary would contain two glossaries, one botanical and one zoological, which would give the common, scientific and dialect names. It would also include the pronunciation of the words and their meaning illustrated by use in phrases.

From early summer a team of people was engaged in the survey sending out 900 questionnaires, collecting words and phrases, writing up material from printed glossaries and keeping index cards. Those involved went about the task assiduously and were aware of the importance of what they were recording. The club received support from the Ministry of Education, which circulated country schools requesting teachers to reply to the questionnaires. They linked up with a linguistic survey of Scotland being carried out by the University of Edinburgh and agreed to place the collected material on to slips at the disposal of the university. Questionnaires were also sent out to retired civil servants, lighthouse keepers, fishermen and fishery inspectors, rate collectors, provincial newspaper editors and local community organizations such as history societies, Women's Institutes and Young Farmers' Clubs.

The questionnaire asked the informants for common vernacular phrases or words. Considerable interest in the press was stirred up by the research. Examples of words used to help gain coverage included 'oxter coggin' ('knockin' about') and 'sevendible' ('trustworthy'). Hayward was reported in one newspaper as saying he felt it would probe the conscience of members of the field club who had 'on various occasions spoken a little vaguely in the same vein … The time for vagueness,' he told the *Northern Whig*, 'was past.'[43] In one of his 1950s' travel books Hayward gives an insight into the 'onerous task', explaining that he and Adams plotted usage-lines for words on a series of maps. He cites one example for the varying names they collected in daily common use along the line of the Irish border for the insect – the earwig.

> Starting from Newry the dialect words for earwig are strung out along the Border like this: at Omeath, *guillioneel*; at Newtownhamilton, *earywig*; at Smithborough, *forky-tail*; at Wattlebridge, *earywig*; at Florencecourt, *dheelog*; at Garrison, *dheeal*; near Pettigo, *gailog*; at Aghyaran, *dyeeloag*; at Clady, *geelick*; at Strabane, *gullygaleen*; at Greenan, *geelug*; and finally at Derry, *gallyglean*.[44]

Looking back on the project, the curator of the Ulster Dialect Archive at the Folk Museum, Anne Smyth, acknowledged that the survey was a very good piece of work:

> At that time there was a significant flowering of dialectology and the presence in the field of very proficient academics. The study of dialect was then very fashionable and Hayward and Adams collaborated with some of the leading linguistic lights of the time. They used the all-Ireland 1950s Munster Simms maps which were popular at garages and which included remote townlands that in some cases were not on the Ordnance Survey maps. When the survey started Adams was hugely interested and was like a dog down a rabbit hole if he discovered something he hadn't seen before. A lot of people were very interested in dialect. For example, farmers coming in at night from a hard day's work in the fields, collected words and wrote out in longhand linguistic items of interest. Many people were involved out of the sheer love of it.[45]

The research was fruitful, bringing in replies with stories of humour and many long-forgotten words. All nine counties of Ulster, as well as limited coverage of counties Louth and Leitrim, were encompassed in the survey. The aim of the dictionary was to ensure that the historic form of the English language would not be lost. Mostly, the collectors were concerned with the English dialects of Ulster but they also were interested in the original Gaelic dialects of the area. A twenty-page handwritten booklet sets out much of what Hayward had already done. As an example from this he listed place names and divided the page into columns to give the local names of such phrases as Left-handed, Door-catch, Pigsty, Youngest of Brood, Call to Pigs and Yellow-hammer.[46] By the start of 1956 more than 8000 words had been collected and work continued through the fifties with the dialect section having eighty fully paid up members by 1959. The section organized lectures in the Old Museum where guests would address the members on various related topics. Some were better attended than others. In his annual report of 1959–60 to the BNFC from the section, the secretary Brendan Adams noted that 'the first dialect lecture on November 17th was unfortunately affected by fog and half-a-dozen members sat round the fire with Mr. J. Braidwood as he read his second paper on Shake-speare and Anglo-Irish speech dealing this year with vocabulary and syntax.'[47]

Hayward gave talks to the section on a range of topics, widening the param-eters to include subjects such as windmills of the Netherlands, Irish folksongs, country recipes and Spanish folk music. Eventually it became clear that owing to the length of time involved and financial constraints it would not be possible to publish a dictionary. The committee got bogged down recording every single variant and became overwhelmed with information. The matter was discussed at a BNFC committee meeting in 1959 when Adams reported that 'very special-ized work' was needed and he did not have the necessary room for storage. He suggested that all the material should be housed in the Folk Museum and be available for inspection, completion and extension.[48]

Negotiations began with the newly opened Ulster Folk and Transport Museum in County Down, which agreed to the suggestion of housing it and the collection of words eventually formed part of the dialect archive. In 1960 Adams became its honorary archivist. The results of the research were brought together in papers that made up the museum's first publication in 1964.[49] As well as Hayward and Adams, other luminaries who moved in linguistic circles became involved. They included John Braidwood, the linguist Robert Gregg, and Estyn Evans, as well as George Paterson, curator of Armagh County Museum.

The results ultimately helped provide the basis for the *Concise Ulster Dictionary* published by Oxford University Press in 1996. The book editors acknowledge that the origins of the archive go back to 1951 when Hayward and Adams began their survey.[50] Surviving material is held at the museum's Ulster Dialect Archive. Anne Smyth, who was an assistant editor on the OUP book, said there was huge interest during the 1950s in trying to preserve dialect speech and some of the phrases would most likely have been lost to posterity if the survey had not taken place:

> While their work was important it was not groundbreaking and was eventu-
> ally subsumed into a greater whole. It sounds pejorative but Hayward had
> a feeling that there was nothing you couldn't learn if you were interested
> enough and he soaked it all up. It's an attitude you don't get much today and
> it was authentic. There was no plastic heritage with him – it really was the
> genuine article. When all is said and done dialect is the speech of the ordinary
> people in the homes, fields and farms which they kept alive and Hayward's
> involvement with the survey gave an extra push to what was going on.[51]

Smyth never met Hayward but colleagues of hers knew him and he was described as an 'absolute gentleman. He had an integrated whole persona with many elements and there was no sectarian divide with him. He mixed, worked and communicated with people from all traditions, and had a holistic approach – that to me is his greatest legacy.'[52] After Hayward's death, Adams thought it unlikely that the BNFC would have launched the Ulster dialect dictionary had it not been for 'his persistence and enthusiasm in popularising the project':

> It was Dr Hayward's boast regarding English and his regret regarding other
> languages – both of which I have often heard him express since long before
> the dialect survey began – that he could never master grammarian rules or
> learn a language by systematic methods and he did not in fact possess the
> technical knowledge in comparative linguistics which would have enabled
> him to edit a dictionary of the scope which his enthusiasm for the project
> called for. In compensation he possessed a remarkable ability to reproduce
> accurately the nuances of a variety of local dialects, which was of great value
> in enabling him to put the local countryman at his ease and to elicit spon-
> taneously information that a different kind of approach might not have
> produced. To my knowledge the one language he did try to learn systemati-
> cally was Irish and, if he did not succeed in speaking it beyond the extent of a
> few phrases, he rendered valuable service by inculcating a more sensible view
> of its contribution to the Ulster cultural heritage than was held by many in
> Northern Ireland in the early years of his literary career.[53]

Adams went on to say that he had checked with the Edinburgh linguistic survey and found that Hayward's share in this part of the fieldwork amounted to finding seventy-eight out of 241 informants, 'a high proportion when we recall that eight field-workers were engaged on this part of the project.'[54]

Linked to his love of dialect, Hayward had committed to memory hundreds of hours of folk tales and a vast repertoire of traditional ballads. His voice carried the authority and authenticity of a centuries-old tradition of story-telling. Frequently he ended his talks with a song but one of the mainstays was his irrepressible sense of humour, an important part of the Hayward armoury. He possessed a sharp wit and sprinkled talks with quips and amusing anec-dotes, some apocryphal, but always enjoyed by his audiences. He poked fun at sectarianism. Many stories were recycled to different audiences in Ireland and Britain. One of the best known concerned an English visitor who was watching the annual Orange Order's Twelfth of July procession. He turned to a local man beside him in cap and scarf and asked 'Is this some special occasion?' 'It's the Twelfth,' says he, 'Didn't ye know?' 'Oh, yes, I know the date,' answered the Englishman, 'What, I wanted to know, was the occasion.' 'Ach!' growled the man, 'Away home and read your Bible.'

He also liked to tell the story of a caddy at Clandeboye Golf Club in County Down who recognized him from his film appearances. 'I saw ye on the pictures last night. Do you know, you're as like yourself as two peas?' Another one that raised the roof referred to the personal advertisements in the newspaper. 'Young farmer (32) Protestant wishes to meet young woman farmer who owns tractor. View to matrimony. Reply Box 793 sending photograph of tractor.'

Ulster humour in particular was something he had written widely about. Hayward gave many talks on dialect and humour to Rotary Clubs and members of the Round Table. He felt that the genesis of Ulster humour was satire. In a speech to the Rotary Club of Armagh in 1953 he said, 'We make fun of our weak-nesses, our bigotry, our Sabbatarianism, our tightfistedness.'[55] His talks took him to England where he addressed Ulster Associations in Liverpool and Sheffield. In February 1952 he gave a lecture on dialect to the Association in Birmingham. He was having lunch in a restaurant when a waiter leaned over and whispered in his ear: 'Man it's gran' to hear that voice o' yours.' The waiter was originally from Portadown and Hayward invited him along to that night's lecture.[56]

THIRTEEN

Many-wayed man with an 'eye for the main chance'

(1955–1959)

The Border is especially tortuous in these parts and a glance at the map will show you how Fermanagh and Tyrone, of Northern Ireland, and Cavan and Monaghan, of the Republic, continually intertwine and twist and turn in a regular Chinese puzzle of cartographical complexity.

Border Foray, 1957

It was nearly six o'clock on a warm summer's evening when Hayward approached a quiet part of the Irish border and knocked at the door of the customs hut to have his triptyque scrutinized and stamped. 'But a farmer near the end of his labour in an adjoining field saw what I was at and called out to me: "You needn't knock there, mister. Sure there's no Border at this time of the day: the man's away for his tay".'[1]

This story is recounted in the opening pages of *Border Foray*, a 200-mile 'leisurely examination' of the border featuring its folklore, legend and history, as well as reflecting the political turbulence of the time. The triptyque was an official passport document for Hayward's Morris Minor that was valid for twelve months and allowed him to cross the jurisdiction. But in those days, even with the IRA's border campaign from 1956 to 1962 – codenamed 'Operation Harvest' by its participants – there seemed to be a relaxed approach to border formalities. There were some horrific incidents though; in one of the worst, in

November 1957, five people died when an IRA bomb was being moved across the border from County Louth.

A book on the border had been germinating for a considerable time. Hayward had squirrelled away material from a variety of sources and worked on it intermittently. His notebooks, he writes, were full of stories taken down during many years of enquiry along the whole line of the Black Pig's Dyke. Some are dated from people he met in May 1953 and many go back further than that. Much of the border was well known to him since he had crossed and re-crossed it hundreds of times on his travels. It was, however, a subject neglected by writers and he wanted to combine its history with a present-day look at what it meant to those living along it.

The IRA targeted property such as police barracks and timber customs examination huts, many of which were destroyed in repeated attacks. The campaign made little impact on the broader population and ended in 1962. The most newsworthy incident was the raid on Brookeborough barracks in County Fermanagh on New Year's Day 1957. Two IRA men, Feargal O'Hanlon and Seán South, were killed and several others wounded. Hayward's research coincided with this campaign and he makes several references to attacks 'still unhappily in progress as I write.'[2] He refers to this and other incidents along the Fermanagh border, saying that in 1957, 'the Northern Ireland authorities have been compelled to blast a number of road traps against the irresponsible raids of armed terrorists.'[3]

Hayward was aware of the tricky balancing act involved in writing a book on the border and states explicitly: 'This is not a political book and I am no politician. I am a lover and observer of my country and I shall seek to set down facts objectively as I see them. Especially in Ireland this is a task of stupendous difficulty, and I know full well that in the course of my writing I shall annoy now one side and now the other.'[4] He also had the nous to realize that inclusion of specific incidents and news events would date the book and that other, more serious attacks, could well happen. In several sections he promulgates an increasingly hardline Unionist attitude, which nonetheless did not prevent him from describing the border as a 'confounded nuisance'.[5]

The funeral of O'Hanlon in St Macartan's Cathedral, Monaghan on 3 January was attended by 20,000 people. Two hundred miles away in Limerick, upwards of 50,000 mourners turned out for South's funeral on 4 January, lining the route from St Michael's Church to Mount St Lawrence Cemetery where he was buried in the republican plot. Against this violent backdrop, two days later, on the morning of 6 January 1957, Hayward started out on his journey from Omeath – the first place he came to in Ireland with his parents as a baby in 1895. His plan was to follow the line of the border through farmsteads, townlands and villages, in the well-rehearsed pattern, drawing out stories from people. The counties he touched on were Louth, Down, Armagh, Tyrone, Monaghan, Cavan, Fermanagh, Donegal and Derry. On this trip he was not accompanied by an artist but travelled instead with a local historian from the museum in Armagh, George Paterson, who worked with him collecting words as part of the dialect survey.

The early part of the book is taken up with history and legends and is followed by lengthy accounts of Newry and south Armagh. He devotes twenty-five pages to Newry and is indignant about what he describes as the 'architectural dereliction' and 'the all-pervading sense of neglect and dilapidation ... sad beyond words.'[6] There was, he complained, an 'ingrained disregard' on the part of Irish people for all their buildings of quality and interest, domestic and ecclesiastical alike:

> In England or Scotland, or on the continent of Europe, a town of the architectural quality once enjoyed by Newry would be cherished and cared for like a beloved child, but Ireland has always been devoid of public taste and civic pride.[7]

Hayward likened the border to the equator, an imaginary line but formally based on tradition and ancient territorial law. Smuggling was big business and provided him with colourful copy. He confessed to feeling 'dizzy trying to sort out the complexities of the terrain ... everything was in favour of the smuggler.' In south Armagh, the *contrabandisti* operated 'an efficient system of light signals and bush-telegraph communications' dodging the Customs Prevention Officers or the curiously named Customs Waterguards (known as 'the Water Rats'.)[8] He made the most of the contradictions thrown up by partition, especially in the region of Flurry Bridge where the border 'zig-zags madly across the road, through a barn or a house, along the middle of the road, or through the field of a small farm':

> You may see, and probably will see, a woman standing in the Republic and feeding her hens which are clucking greedily in Northern Ireland. The grain she dispenses may have been grown by her good man in a field which is half in one country and half in the other, or it may have been bought in a shop in that part of Ireland where it happened at the time to be cheapest.[9]

At one point Hayward describes himself as one of those few 'quare fellas … who keep alive the memory of artists and dreamers green and fresh through the blight of the passing years.'[10] Into this category fall John Mitchel in Newry, Rose Kavanagh in Tyrone, and especially William Carleton, long a part of his literary past. He spends time at Carleton's cottage near Augher in south Tyrone where he meets Anketell Richardson of Kilrudden House. He had read Carleton's work and regarded him as one of the great Irish writers. In his honour, he climbs Knockmany Hill for views of 'this history-soaked territory' that Carleton knew on boyhood excursions to the hilltop.

Although he notes that the old ways of rural life are mostly gone, he still ferrets out stories from farmers and countrymen. Leitmotifs in the book include his interest in dialect; in Ulster, he says, people speak an old-fashioned historical English 'pressed into an Irish mould'. His field club background was useful in identifying many different types of wild flowers. References to plant lore are slipped in as grace notes. These range from cowslip in Rostrevor to houseleek, bog myrtle and bog cotton in the Slieve Beagh hills of north Monaghan, water bistort (known as monk's blood), as well as a curious Fermanagh plant called 'Dahoe of Ardagh', said to have symbolical connection with St Patrick. Other themes, familiar to his readers, surface throughout the pages: his interest in antiquities, sweeping across pillar stones, crannogs, souterrains, ring forts, dolmens and high crosses. As ever, a sprinkling of traditional songs and poems appear, including one of his favourites from the anonymously written 'Man of the Roads':

> It wasn't the lads from Shercock
> Nor the boys from Ballybay,
> But the dealin' men from Crossmaglen
> Put whiskey in me tay.

Hayward is quick to point out that the rest of the ballad makes it clear that it was 'not hospitality that was afoot on this particular occasion but an attempt on the part of some dealers to bamboozle a poor fellow into selling his beasts at a low price.'[11] *Border Foray* is written in the style of a continuous car journey during which he fills his notebooks with the human, historic and topographical side of life. But in what turned out to be his most political book of all, Hayward introduces strong opinions. Towards the end, when he reaches the Fermanagh-Cavan border, he refers to Newtownbutler and Brookeborough, launching into a previously unseen side, and bitter criticism about the political situation:

I know my people well enough to realize that the use of force to persuade them to do anything they don't want to do has as much chance of success as the project of storing snowballs in hell! There is probably no more doggedly determined man alive on this planet to-day than your typical Ulsterman, and if the Border is to be removed, or even slightly amended, it is not by force that it will be done. That is as certain as that the morrow's sun will rise in the east ... Root-and-branch the Ulster way of life is determinedly anti-authoritarian whilst the Republic is based upon a system of government completely subservient to the dictates of an authoritarian Roman Catholic hierarchy.[12]

On a political role, Hayward pointed out that no one could deny the right of both peoples, North and South, to be governed as they think best. 'And the people of Ulster recognize that principle when they ask for the peaceful acceptance of differences that are real and vital and deep-seated as the mighty foundations of our majestic mountains.' While acknowledging that the ways of life may be 'poles apart', he felt that 'surely we can still be friends and good Irishmen all, respecting each other, helping each other, and coming together in amity in matters of common interest.' He reflects on the civil war, concluding his opinions by drawing parallels with the new outbreak of violence along the border:

This madness of 1922 is now descending upon us once again in a hateful recrudescence, and the current destroyers, in the guise of armed and irresponsible 'liberators,' are set upon another campaign of violence and destruction ... An acceptance by the Republic, in friendship and goodwill, of the accomplished fact of Northern Ireland's legal and constitutional entity, and a cessation from tiresome and futile ravings against a partition that is based on law and common sense, would without doubt result in great and lasting benefits to Ireland as a whole.[13]

The blame for the current situation, he felt, lay squarely at the feet of 'factious politicians' who were preventing the country 'pull along together in a spirit of comradeship, understanding and mutual respect.'[14] He pointed out the humour always breaking through and recounted the story of a party of smugglers who were challenged in the darkness by a special constable, and shouted 'Don't shoot, constable: we're only smuggling.'[15]

His travels ended on 28 March, three months after setting out. When he returned home, he knuckled down with his usual application to work on the manuscript, completing it by the end of May. *Border Foray* was published by Arthur Barker in September 1957 in the same uniform style as his regional books in the series *This is Ireland*. It was his last major Ulster book and the reviews were largely positive. While the *Times Literary Supplement* felt that his geological references were 'quite technical', it said the book was lightly administered. 'His criticism never goes deep but his opinions are sound.'[16] No sketches accompany the text but he employed Piper's services to provide a resplendent cover artwork, a mishmash of amusing images featuring a collection of caricatures of the mythological characters of Irish history. It includes an arresting image of St Patrick playing the harp, his face a caricature of Hayward's, alongside the Three Collas, the Black Pig, the 'Wilde Irishman', his list of words for earwig, and even scantily-clad dancing girls. Two decades later, in his 400-year survey, *Art in Ulster, 1557–1957*, the poet John Hewitt criticized the cover, saying that Piper's hand 'faltered'. 'It became a scramble of little not very original humorous groups, a marked failure of imagination. He could have drawn a black pig rotting in the ground, but not the Black Pig of legend. Still, a man should be grateful for his gifts.'[17]

Against this, the cover was chosen many years later by a British book collectors' magazine as one of the best-designed jackets of books from the twentieth century.[18] *Border Foray* was Hayward's seventh and final book published by Arthur Barker. Two years later the company was taken over by Weidenfeld & Nicolson. He was now in need of a new publisher for the final Munster volume to complete the Irish series and still had the daunting task of gathering the material.

Even towards the end of the century, the border book was still the subject of discussion by academic commentators, some of whom believe it was brought out to help deflect attention from the IRA campaign. Dr James Loughlin asserts that Hayward's books were 'travelogue-cum-propaganda'. He claims that *Border Foray* was designed to appear at a moment of political crisis to serve Unionist interests:

> It made a pro-Unionist argument in a text denying political purpose, and, among other things, focused on the distinctive character of 'Ulster'. Hayward posed and answered the question, 'is there any real difference between the folk of Ulster and the folk of the rest of Ireland?'[19]

Loughlin felt that Hayward's attempt to explain away the deep community divisions that the Ulster plantation gave rise to was 'wishful thinking', adding, 'Ridiculous as it may seem now, Hayward's views on Ulster's identity were attractive to many Unionists at a time when their membership of the United Kingdom appeared to be unassailable.'[20]

There are no doubts about Hayward's Unionist colourings shining through. He was a member of the party and had now, somewhat late in life, taken a decision to join one organization whose ranks he had up until then shied away from – the Orange Order. In April 1957 he was proposed and seconded into Belfast Eldon Lodge No. 7 by John Henderson and Peter Mayes. Traditionally the members of this 'elite' lodge were made up of politicians or military men as well as those from the business and professional classes. Aside from the political and religious aspects, it was a social networking club. Eldon's history stretched back to 13 July 1829 when it started life in Higginson's Hotel in Donegall Street. Founded in honour of the Protestant Defender, Lord Chancellor Eldon, its motto *Sit Sine Labe Decus* translates as 'Let glory be without stain'. Hayward threw himself into the Order's activities, attending meetings, dinners and other functions. In the late 1950s the annual dinners were held in Thompson's Restaurant in Belfast or at Unionist headquarters in Glengall Street, invariably starting with speeches, including 'The Orange Toast':

> To the glorious, pious and immortal memory of the great and good King William III who saved us from Rogues and Roguery, Knaves and Knavery, Popes and Popery, from Mass money and wooden shoes, and whoever denies this Toast may he be slammed, crammed and jammed into the muzzle of the great gun of Athlone, and the gun fired into the Pope's belly and the Devil into Hell, and the door locked, and the key in an Orangeman's pocket: and may we never lack a brisk Protestant Boy to kick the arse of a Papist, and here's a part for the Bishop of Cork.[21]

At one meeting, Hayward was asked to read a paper he had been collecting for decades on the history of Orange ballads. His name was suggested as chair of a committee preparing a history of Eldon and he was appointed to the newly formed Lodge of Research that was tasked with bringing together historical information on the Orange Order. Hayward had never been a member of the Order, but at sixty-five he acquired his Orange sash. His membership possibly came about through friendship with the Rev. Michael Dewar of Banbridge whom he had known for some years and had published widely on the organization. Whatever the motivating factor, he joined the ranks of respectable Orangeism; his 'brothers' in Eldon included influential acquaintances such as the Lord Mayor of Belfast, Sir Robin Kinahan, the Dean of Belfast, Rev. C.I. Peacock, who was chaplain, and Brian Faulkner, a future prime minister of Northern Ireland. Members of Parliament, the judiciary, retired colonels, wine merchants, linen manufacturers, shop owners and college lecturers were all part of the lodge's make up.[22] The secretary of Eldon in those days, Angus McConnell, recalls Hayward's participation at meetings:

> We had a big membership in Eldon and it was made up of middle class people of some standing in society. Hayward was well known to everyone and he was pleasant. He brought colour and laughter but also took a keen role in all the varied activities. After our meetings we would gather around for an informal chat and open the drinks cupboard. It was an inner circle in which politics was discussed. Hayward was part of that and was closely involved with the Lodge of Research.[23]

Clearly there were tangential benefits, in the form of writing and singing work, from being an Orangeman. With his extensive network of associates and ability to consort easily with many people, Hayward saw an opportunity to further develop his range of contacts in the commercial world. Having friends in high places was good for business. He was actively involved in encouraging new members and helped sign up his son Dion in October 1959. (His membership though was short-lived since he emigrated to New Zealand the following year.) Dion's son, Paul Hayward, remembers watching his grandfather taking part in the Twelfth of July parade in Belfast in 1958 – although his enduring memory of him is seeing him prepare to play the harp, an instrument not normally associated with Orangemen:

> We watched him on the dais in front of the Robinson & Cleaver building with his bowler hat, chain and sash on the Twelfth. He seemed to be one of the 'top brass', reviewing the troops so to speak, as the parade passed. My own reaction was one of bemusement as I did not know anything about it and was not cognizant of what it all meant. As a young boy I used to visit their house on the Antrim Road on Sunday afternoons. My grandfather was always impeccably dressed in a linen jacket while my grandmother kept in the background. I can clearly remember him filing his fingernails. He would sit on a chair with his knees together, his tongue would come out as he concentrated on the filing, and he was fastidious about this job. Then he would pick up the small harp, start plucking the strings and play and sing for us. I was aware that he filled a room with his personality. My father, as the elder son, found it difficult to be in the shadow of someone who was an extrovert while he was more introverted. It was clear to me, even as a young kid, that Richard was aware of his position. He was multi-talented, he was aware of those talents and happy with them and he wanted recognition. I think he was bordering on egomania which was all part of his creative drive.[24]

Hayward's joining of the Order coincided with a renewed interest in recording Orange songs, something with which he had achieved considerable success during his Decca career in the 1930s and forties. His work in those days had been praised by Compton Mackenzie in a review of 'The Ould Orange Flute' as far back as 1927: 'Every word is audible, the manner is perfect ... and I consider this the best bit of genre singing the gramophone has given us.'²⁵ The popularity of these songs was not confined to Ireland. His fame had spread across to Scotland and England. The recordings of his Orange songs in the 1950s and early sixties were highly regarded by the leading music critics of the time. In 1956 his *Orange and Blue* record was chosen by a British panel as one of the six outstanding recordings of the year. The commendation came from the *Gramophone* critic, W.A. Chislett: 'How perfectly our very old friend, Richard Hayward, sings these songs. I must include this glorious record in my choice of the Six Best Recordings of 1956.'²⁶ On this recording he was supported by a five-man choir, 'The Loyal Brethren', and a fife and drum band. Hayward delighted in telling audiences that he was the only Protestant member of it. The following January he recorded a second series of songs on *Orange and Blue No. 2* that included 'Dolly's Brae', 'Derry's Walls', 'The Green Grassy Slopes of the Boyne' and 'Black Man's Dream'. His recordings are now part of the music collection at the Folk Museum. Anne Smyth, a member of the museum staff, was brought up in Glasgow in the 1950s, where her family played Hayward songs in their house:

> My granny propped me up in the pram and sang me some of Hayward's well known ballads such as 'The Orange A.B.C.' and 'The Ould Orange Flute'. I still have his early recordings. He was not possessed of a wonderful voice but his diction was clear and people identified with him. They learnt the songs off his records and liked the fact that he was interested in old ballads and especially loved the homespun side of it. Essentially these are folk ballads – one of the touchstones for them is that there are many variants. The ones I heard did not have any offensive overtones, but would have been of the Unionist tradition commemorating battles of times past. People say 'The Sash My Father Wore' is a sectarian song but it is actually a drinking song that was written in Scotland.²⁷

Smyth hopes this will be carried on to the next generation:

> I have tried very hard in my lifetime to persuade people to pass Hayward's songs on to their children. If you don't have your children singing them then it won't take long before they don't exist any more. My old song books that Hayward produced are falling to bits and will not survive another generation.²⁸

Towards the end of 1959 Fontana produced *The Orange Sash: Richard Hayward with the Loyal Sons of William*, a fanciful name for four members of the Ormiston choir that backed him on some songs. The cover of the LP featured his Eldon lodge collarette and an illustration of a section of an engraving by John Hall from a painting by Benjamin West. The image shows King William on his white charger, one still used to this day by Orange mural artists decorating gable walls of loyalist parts of Belfast. The album was a mix of some of his best-known songs alongside less familiar ones such as 'The Ladies' Orange Lodges', 'The Murder of McBriar' and 'The Orange Apron Trimmed with Blue'. In a considered review in *Gramophone*, Chislett, familiar with his singing for more than thirty years, said, 'The voice is perhaps a shade darker and a trifle less agile, but it is still as steady as a rock and the words are crystal clear as always. His artistry has ripened with the years.'[29] The *Belfast Telegraph* review of the LP said 'Hayward disproves the theory that the rebels have all the good songs.'[30] Hayward's 1935 version of 'The Sash My Father Wore', regarded as the anthemic song of Orangeism and adapted from 'The Hat My Father Wore', is believed to be the first recording of it with an original air. The melody is thought to come from 'The Irish Molly O', an Irish or Scottish song about a soldier who meets a woman and wants to marry her but is thwarted by her father.[31]

Hayward regarded Orange ballads as folksongs because they were part of the folk balladry of Northern Ireland and because their authors and composers are for the most part unknown. For him the main business of a ballad was to tell a story with a clear and straightforward narrative from the days when newspapers were uncommon or non-existent or when the majority of country people would have been unable to read them.[32] He often said that the stories of the Orange ballads that he sang were plain and straightforward but to someone without Ulster connections they may be 'strange and enigmatical'. Some of his songs such as 'The Papish Goat' were what he called 'mischievously humorous' and belong to a rather unusual and uncommon body of Orange ballads inspired by bucolic comedy. 'The Ould Orange Flute' is regarded as one of his classics. He sang it and the other songs in the traditional manner of their 'birth and being' and felt to sing them any other way would be unacceptable and unforgivable.[33]

For all his singing, speechifying, involvement in public affairs and gallivanting abroad, Hayward's creativity continued unabated. His wide hinterland kept his Orange activities in perspective. He worked unremittingly throughout the 1950s, his enthusiasm for writing never flagging. Woven in between his diverse activities were several more books, separate from those for *This is Ireland*.

He was a regular contributor to the *Sunday Independent* and turned these into a collected anthology, *Belfast through the Ages*, published in 1952 by Dundalgan Press. The book reflects his knowledge of shipbuilding and linen history, and famous characters from the past. Piper's sketches of the buildings, markets, streets and surrounding hills provide the opening illustrations to each chapter. Hayward refused to gild the ugly:

> College Square was never a square other than in name, and the whole gracious plan was blown to smithereens by the much later erection of the tasteless pile of the Municipal College of Technology. A more outrageous piece of philistinism than this raising of an incongruous building, ugly in itself, to the half-destruction of the lovely prospect of a gracious late Georgian building, it would be impossible to conceive, and perhaps more than anything else this piece of wanton perversity may stand as a symbol of that cultural unawareness which began to bedevil Belfast early in the nineteenth century, and which only now is beginning to be seen as the evil thing it is.[34]

He travelled widely in Europe and his peregrinations took him to the US on three occasions. In May 1955 he went to New York where his host was Gene Tunney and two other American friends, Allan P. Kirby and Joseph P. Routh, who had been on the 1952 Sligo tour. He was guest of honour of the New York Ulster Association at their annual celebrations and banquet and stayed at the Waldorf Astoria Hotel. The following year he was back in New York for a month. He called on Irish clubs and societies, giving speeches on the Irish harp and Ulster dialect. He tried to blow off the image Americans had of Ireland as clowns, drinkers and playboys, interested only in pubs and horses:

> It is not the truth of our greatest storyteller, William Carleton, these people want, with its picture of the Irish as the realistic, often cruel, often avaricious and always strongly individual people they are, but rather the fiction of Charles Lever and his life, where the Irish countryman is shown as a buffoon tumbling and grimacing for the amusement of his hard-drinking, hard-riding landlord, and him not a thought in his head but the fun and the games, and maybe the odd ball of malt.[35]

In early summer 1959 Hayward went on a flying clipper ship operated by Pan American Airways from Shannon to the US for what was to be one of his proudest achievements. Before departure on 11 May, friends from Dublin joined those from Limerick to organize a dinner in his honour at Shannon Airport Restaurant. The menu card is autographed by Hayward, plus his Dublin friends

Catherine Quinn, Mollie Quinn, Dr T.J. Carty, and Alma Fitt from Limerick. On 5 June, in a ceremony at Lafayette College in Easton, Pennsylvania, an honorary degree was conferred on him. Many emigrants from the north of Ireland and Scotland settled in the area around Easton in the eighteenth century. Two of the college founders, Thomas McKeen and Thomas Rogers, were born in Ulster in the 1780s. The citation stated that the doctorate was awarded for 'distinguished services to Irish literature' and in recognition of his contribution to the development and spread of Irish literature. It recognized his 'love of Ireland and Irish lore' and that he 'had convened the joy in beauty and the love of the country to many.' The president of the college's board, Dr Lloyd Felmly, presented Hayward for the conferring by saying he was a man of diverse talents:

> He is one of Ireland's most recognised and best loved authorities in the fields of thought and creation which he has made his own. Mr. Hayward is known throughout the British Commonwealth, and indeed throughout the world, for his active and prolific career as a scholar, author, poet, playwright and musician.[36]

A proud moment: Hayward receives an honorary degree from Lafayette College in Pennsylvania in 1959.

Another member of the board, Dr Ronald Bergethon who carried out the conferring, said he 'portrayed the real through the imaginary':

> Challenged by the new medium of radio drama you then explored, as play-wright and player, its limitations and its possibilities. A lover of Ireland and Irish lore, you gave words to your affections for your people and your country in your books and made the talking pictures proclaim your pride. You became historian and commentator of the music and the language of Ireland on the lecture platform and as singer and harpist recorded for posterity the poignant beauty of the Irish folk song and ballad. In you the zest of appreciation has given the Irish muse the minstrel voice and hand that could link the misty realm of Irish legend to the electronic magic of the twentieth century, and convey to the many your joy in beauty and your love of Ireland. Hence, by virtue of Pennsylvania, and by Lafayette College, I confer upon you the Honorary Degree of Doctor of Literature and all the rights and privileges of that degree: in witness whereof I cause you to be invested with the hood of the degree and give you this diploma. And I certify that naught said here can be attributed in any way to that stone in your homeland at Blarney Castle.[37]

It was an acknowledgment of a lifetime's endeavour in the cultural world for which Hayward had never properly been credited at home. He used the occasion to make a long speech to the assembled audience, which was reported in the local paper in Pennsylvania. Hayward said he was the first Ulsterman, and Irishman, to be honoured by Lafayette. He referred to the Ulster link to the college founders and to the fact that 'there is almost a complete lack of knowledge of the tremendous part played by Ulster people in the founding of the United States.' He mentioned specifically the 'world-shaking event' of the printing of the Declaration of Independence by John Dunlap from Stra-bane.[38] His arrival in Pennsylvania was heralded in the newspapers. Under the headline, 'Ireland of Shillelaghs and Shamrocks is Myth, Visiting Poet Declares', Hayward gave a controversial interview to the *Easton Express*. The paper said the Ireland that Hayward knows is a land rich in heritage that he has explored with great intensity. 'The Irish', he said, 'are practical people and much like America in this respect':

> Those in the Irish Free State, however, tend to be more imaginative and superstitious than those in Northern Ireland ... these tend to slow down their productive capacities. They dwell on the fantasies of their imagination rather than on the realities of life that to them press in on their dreams. These persons do better when out of Ireland where somehow their imaginations become the basis for great creativity. The people of the Free State are highly

nationalistic. They continue to be disturbed by the fact that Northern Ireland is separate from the Free State and loyal to England. They are the Irish who clamour the loudest at St. Patrick's Day parades and talk the most of shamrocks and the shillelaghs. The people of Northern Ireland, on the contrary, are internationally minded and are much more practical and successful within their own state.[39]

Hayward's comments show how his views about the North-South divide had hardened in line with his border book two years earlier. His interview with the paper was not picked up by the Irish press and went unnoticed outside the immediate area. Hayward had brought with him a letter of reference from Viscount Brookeborough of Colebrooke, prime minister of Northern Ireland, addressed to Mr R.H. Trench Thompson, president of the Ulster-Irish Society of New York. It was dated 6 May 1959:

> Mr Hayward's visit to the Ulster-Irish Society provides me with a welcome opportunity to send greetings from Northern Ireland. He is a man of many parts – author, traveller, broadcaster and humorist. He is a shrewd observer and chronicler of the folklore and history of Northern Ireland and has done much to record the traditions and customs of the area. I am happy that Mr. Hayward should be the bearer of this message and know that you will find him a lively and entertaining personality.[40]

On his 1955 visit to the US Hayward had brought in his pocket a letter of introduction from the Lord Mayor of Dublin, Alfie Byrne, who described him as 'one of Ireland's leading writers and lecturers on Irish affairs. He is splendid company and has made thousands of friends in Ireland of all groups and parties and I think he has made more friends for Ireland outside our shores than any other man in the country.'[41]

During the 1950s his many European holiday escapes *en famille* took him to the Netherlands, France and Andorra, Spain, Gibraltar, Portugal, Italy, Germany, Austria, Lichtenstein, Luxembourg, Belgium and Denmark as well as parts of England and Scotland. In July 1951 they spent two weeks in the Scottish highlands and on 20 July climbed Ben Nevis. Hayward's diary records that Ricky took three hours and ten minutes to reach the summit while he took three hours and forty minutes; they descended in two hours. As part of their preparation, they had climbed Slieve Donard in the Mourne Mountains a week earlier. Ricky's first visit to England was to the Hornby toy factory near Liverpool where he delighted in looking around the train sets, Dinky cars and Meccano. One memorable experience, he recalls, was flying across with their car on an air-ferry aeroplane from Newtownards in County Down to Scotland where they drove up to Loch Lomond; on another occasion they took an air-ferry to France from Dungeness in Kent:

> On the holiday to southern Spain and Gibraltar in 1954 my father hired a car and we toured Andalusia. The car was a Hillman with too small a radiator, which was constantly boiling in the heat. We learned to stop only for water, wherever possible, at the top of a hill so we could push-start it. We went to Torremolinos which was then utterly unspoiled and enjoyed a horse-ride in the Coto Donana. My father liked sightseeing and leading us around. He enjoyed museums, art galleries, churches and the great architectural set pieces such as Versailles and Chartres Cathedral. One place that stands out and which we had a great laugh about was the town of Middle-fart in central Denmark.[42]

Another side was emerging too – a passionate interest in viniculture and in particular Spanish wines and sherry. In 1958 he travelled to southwest Spain with Ricky, Raymond Piper and several other friends. That year the vintage was dedicated to Ireland and marked the start of an association with sherry and the Garvey sherry firm, which had Irish roots.

Much of what occupied Hayward in the 1950s was journalism. A thread that had run through his early life was his freelance writing, which began in the 1920s as contributor to the *Ulster Review* and *Northern Whig*, writing book reviews and profiles of artists. During the 1930s and forties, largely due to pressure of work on his books as well as films and singing, he had little spare time to write for newspapers or magazines. But in the 1950s he entered a renewed and vigorous period of work for them. The article on his honorary doctorate for *Ulster Illustrated* was one of twenty that he wrote for the magazine during a three-year period in the late 1950s. The glossy thirty-two-page monthly began in 1953, providing an outlet for lengthy features, and he became a roving contributor. The magazine carried a range of articles on social life, the theatre, art and music reviews, fashion, motoring, nature and sport.

With a sports car, he toured the back roads of Fermanagh while topics such as the Christmas Rhymers, Lambeg pottery and a visit to Pinewood Studios in Buckinghamshire to write a feature on his filmmaking days, provided engaging stories. He wrote up interviews with Lord Brookeborough in Fermanagh, and with Sir Norman Stronge at Tynan Abbey, a mansion in County Armagh. Many years later, on 21 January 1981, Stronge, aged eighty-six, along with his son James, were murdered by the IRA at their home.

On the road in west Fermanagh: this photograph of Hayward in a sports car was taken on the Derrygonnelly to Garrison road when he was gathering material for a travel feature for *Ulster Illustrated*.

Hayward also contributed to many of Ireland's leading daily and Sunday newspapers, magazines and cultural periodicals, writing specific articles on travel or other subjects, either on commission or on spec. He was always happy to satisfy demand or express an opinion. Some helped promote his books while others became a short series for features editors. In the summer of 1950 he contributed a weekly series to the *Sunday Independent* on the west of Ireland. Called 'Roving the West', it ran to a total of ten features. His territory covered Galway, Mayo, Sligo and Leitrim, mirroring the area written about in his two books on Connacht.

He followed this up with another series for the *Sunday Independent*, which became *Belfast through the Ages*. This was the golden era in Irish newspaper sales. In 1952 the *Sunday Independent* had become an established weekly title bought by a staggering 400,000 readers while the daily title sold more than 200,000 copies. This readership and potential audience offered far-reaching publicity for his books. Hayward was a marketable commodity and well aware of the many ways of tapping into increased sales. He wrote a series of articles for the *Belfast Telegraph* under the title Causerie with his byline. These covered diverse topics, ranging from fairies and wine to the historic Friar's Bush graveyard in Belfast and the disappearance of Lambeg drums from Orange Order parades. He loved the quirky side of human nature. One example is his piece on the Tyrone artist Ponsonby Staples that Hayward wrote to coincide with an exhibition of his work at the Belfast Museum and Art Gallery in April 1958. Staples, who lived at Lissan House in Cookstown, indulged in the practice of nelipotting:

> The thing I remember best about Ponsonby Staples, the man, was his passion for walking barefoot for at least fifteen minutes each day, a habit which is listed in 'Who Was Who' as one of his favourite recreations. I once questioned him about this curious activity, for he was a man willing to discuss anything and not to take offence at what might seem to some people impudent inquisitiveness. He told me that in his opinion many of the ills of modern living arose from man's foolish practice of complete insulation from the earth's magnetism by the encasing of his feet in leather. 'And it's much worse my boy,' he said, 'since rubber soles came into fashion. Rubber: complete occlusion of the life force! Absolute suicide!'[43]

Hayward's work was as much sought after by editors in Dublin as in the North and he earned the admiration of many. In the summer of 1962, the *Evening Press* features editor Seán McCann asked him to contribute to a series of six articles, 'My Home Town', to run in the autumn:

> Since taking over as features editor I have been trying – so far successfully – to bring Ireland's top writers into the paper. I wonder if you can help me carry on with this campaign ... The main idea is to get the writer's eye view of the community. This can embrace hopes, memories, history as you will, Length to be a maximum of 1,500 words, payment ten guineas.[44]

Hayward joined the exalted company of Kate O'Brien (Limerick), Frank O'Connor (Cork), Walter Macken (Galway), Brian Friel (Derry), and Donagh MacDonagh (Wexford) and his piece on Belfast was published at the end of the year. He also wrote features on the Shannon region and Tipperary for the well-regarded *Ireland of the Welcomes*. The magazine had a large overseas readership, appealing especially to Americans, and a generous budget – always an attraction for a freelance writer.

Hayward with friends from the literary and artistic world pictured at a function in Dublin in the late 1950s. The painter, Cecil Salkeld, is on the left. Compton Mackenzie, co-founder of *Gramophone* magazine which reviewed many of Hayward's records, and the Irish novelist, Maurice Walsh, are standing to his left. Walsh was a champion of Hayward's work and wrote the foreword to four of his travel books.

Richard Hayward might be described as a man who could do anything and who sometimes tried to do everything: poetry, criticism, travel writing, fiction, journalism, theatre, acting, filmmaking, singing, lecturing, tour–guiding and collecting dialect words but they remain only a part of his multifarious oeuvre. During the 1950s his creative energy was channelled into many other spheres. The affairs of local government claimed his attention and he became a member of the libraries committee of Belfast Corporation. He took on civic responsibilities, including a position as Justice of the Peace. Around the same time he served on a Ministry of Home Affairs Stormont Committee looking into the treatment of gypsies in Northern Ireland, which recommended toleration and the provision of sites. On one occasion, the RUC in Derry called on his expertise asking him to help set up a display featuring a typical poteen still, a task that according to Ricky, he enjoyed very much. He was a member of the editorial board of the *Irish Astronomical Journal* to which he jointly contributed a historical paper.[45]

Although in his mid-sixties, the notion of retirement or even semi-retirement had not crossed his mind. If anything, his energy expanded with age, his interests were continually widening, and as ever he was in demand as a speaker. In the 1950s plans were being laid to open a Folk Museum near Belfast. Among those involved were Estyn Evans, George Thompson, Brendan Adams, George Paterson, W.A. Seaby (the director of the Ulster Museum) and his predecessor J.A.S. Stendall. Hayward served on the Association Committee for the new museum, a subject that greatly interested him. As far back as 1947 he had written a lengthy letter to the *Ulster Journal of Archaeology* about practical archaeology, specifically preserving artefacts. In 1946, when promoting his Kerry book, he attended the Killarney Agricultural Show. He discovered a stand displaying fifty objects of antiquity ranging from flint arrowheads and bronze pins to fragments of Ogham stones and bronze cauldrons. It had been organized by the Kerry Archaeological Survey and Hayward was impressed that someone was on hand from the Kerry Field Club to explain to farmers the significance of the objects and the specific fields they came from. The farmers, he wrote, listened attentively to the fact that they should take care of such objects and that they should remain untouched until a member of the club arrives:

> I feel strongly that something similar to the Kerry effort should be attempted here. No one knows better than I do the immense damage that has been done by uninstructed excavators to many of our ancient monuments for, tramping the Ulster countryside every week as I am, either alone or with the Field Club, I could not fail to be confronted with many sad examples of unwitting violence done to our ancient heritage.[46]

Hayward offered to help organize a similar event at the Royal Ulster Agricultural Society spring show and asked for names of people willing to form a committee to pursue the matter. He was a keen supporter of the idea of the new Folk Museum but according to retired director, George Thompson, was annoyed about not having an official role:

> He contributed quite a bit to the promotion of the idea for a Folk Museum but he was seriously aggrieved that he wasn't appointed a trustee as he felt he should have been. The problem was that his pushiness got up people's noses and they developed a bit of a suspicion about that. He was remarkable for getting in everywhere and loved the publicity. He could be very charming, working you round to his way of thinking, and you have to remember he was self-made, carving a niche for himself without any foundation.[47]

The Prime Minister of Northern Ireland, Lord
Brookeborough, stokes the model engine *Donegal* as
Hayward looks on at the official opening of the City of
Belfast Transport Museum at Witham Street in June 1962.
The Lord Mayor of Belfast, Alderman Martin Wallace is
behind Brookeborough. One of Hayward's public roles
included serving as a member of the museum committee.

Hayward attended the official opening of the Transport Museum at
Witham Street in east Belfast on 15 June 1962. But it was to be another two
years before the Folk Museum opened its doors. In the meantime he continued
his lectures on folklore and dialect with his harp by his side. Thompson Steele
recalls Hayward playing the instrument at a meeting of the Stranmillis Field
Studies Society:

> I remember having to introduce him, which was a daunting task. I think
> he must have had a frog in his throat and when he had finished singing and
> playing I asked him if he would like some Orangeaid to drink, which he
> took from me gratefully. He seemed to me to be an old man but there was
> nevertheless a freshness about him and he was lively. Hayward was very full of
> himself. Richard was only interested in Richard but he was always prepared
> to come and talk to people no matter who they were.[48]

Hayward was a member of Belfast's venerable Linen Hall Library and user of their well-stocked shelves. Founded in 1788, its radical past appealed to him along with the pervasive sense of history. Apart from his own published books on the shelves, scattered today amongst the library's eclectic collection of memorabilia is an incongruous Hayward item. A cheque bearing his signature, made payable to the library five days before Christmas 1955 and drawn on the Provincial Bank of Ireland for the annual subscription of four guineas, is framed and hangs on the wall of the Librarian's office. The cheque, which has a Dickensian appearance, was framed by the then Librarian Jimmy Vitty. The reason for this is not known. Various questions arise but few answers suggest themselves. Was it framed for reasons of posterity? Did the library have trouble getting Hayward to pay? Could the library's insouciance have led to it going astray or mistakenly being forgotten about? The current Librarian, John Killen, suggests the cheque 'may have been framed as a bit of fun; maybe Hayward was late in paying his annual subscription to the Library and Jimmy ribbed his friend about it – we may never know the real reason for it.'[49]

All his life he was a joiner and socialite. But one informal club to which Hayward did not belong was a gathering of the mid-twentieth-century notabilities of Belfast's literary and artistic circle that met regularly on the top floor of Campbell's Coffee House. The café was a popular venue opposite the flower sellers at the city hall. From the 1930s, with William Conor, Lynn Doyle and Richard Rowley as the founders, it became their haunt for several decades. Amongst the roll call of those who assembled over the years to discuss the latest books and plays were Sam Hanna Bell, Joe Tomelty, Jimmy Kelly, Denis Ireland, Patrick Riddle, John Boyd and Jimmy Boyce. Sitting alongside them were the painters Humbert Craig, Padraic Woods and Rowel Friers. There was a certain amount of teasing and gossip as well as drollery and light-hearted badinage. But those who turned up regarded it as more than just a place of hot air and cold coffee; they saw it as offering vigorous and fiery conversation as well as somewhere to exchange ideas and find inspiration from kindred spirits.[50]

When passing through Belfast on occasional visits, Louis MacNeice, Denis Johnston, Robert Lynd, Micheál Mac Liammóir and Eoin O'Mahony all dropped in on the Campbell's circle. Hayward was never part of this coterie. Although he knew most of them individually, and his Bedford Street office was a mere five minutes' walk away, he did not involve himself with the coffee-drinking chatterati. Given his workload, it is perhaps no surprise that he did not loiter in cafés like the salaried BBC men or newspaper staff journalists. The actress Roma Tomelty, daughter of the actor and playwright Joe Tomelty who created and appeared in the BBC radio programme *The McCooeys*, recalls that her father felt that Hayward's self-assuredness rubbed people up the wrong way:

> My father would never have considered him as part of the Campbell's coffee set. They thought of themselves as the crème de la crème, and the movers and shakers, whether working in the BBC or involved in writing and journalism, in the theatre or other art forms. He was never complimentary about Hayward and would say his name in a very dismissive way. He thought that he was a man who latched on to things and made them his own. He felt that if Hayward heard about something new happening he would immediately say 'I'll do that now'. He was jumping around so many different things and didn't concentrate on one thing, which annoyed my father. Some people would also have said that he was pushy and always had an eye for the main chance.[51]

Although he did not mingle in the Campbell's coffee-drinkers society's clubbiness, he frequented the Linenhall Dining Rooms. According to local bakery historian James Campbell, he had a weakness for a treat on the menu:

> Hayward liked the Linenhall Dining Rooms where the staff made home baked pancakes, which he was very fond of. My father was chairman of the company that ran the Carlton Restaurant in Donegall Place and Hayward was a regular there too. I used to go in as a boy and sometimes he sang. It was a respectable and genteel meeting place for the middle classes where ladies with their hats went for afternoon tea and enjoyed listening to musicians. In 1941, during the war, I was evacuated to the Royal School in Dungannon and Hayward used to ask me about it. I would tell him what it was like and this would provoke a catchphrase in response: 'Come in Dungannon, I know your knock.' He was a lovely soft-spoken man. He did not have the hard Belfast accent but had a gentle lilting voice, which was reflected in his singing.[52]

Not everyone enthused about Hayward's music. The Librarian of the National Museums of Northern Ireland, Roger Dixon, is familiar with Hayward's work. Although he was too young to have known him, his father, who was a musician, was friendly with him through both music and acting circles:

> There was a lot of jealousy about Hayward from the 1940s onward. People were envious of what he was doing which was inspired by his success, especially in his music and books. Academics at Queen's University were annoyed because he wrote popular history which sold well. He was populist and they did not like that. In the music world in those days the musicians had a narrow professional focus dedicated to the big bands. They looked down on folk music and the fact that someone like Hayward was making a success of it

annoyed them intensely. Although he was appreciated as a talented singer, in wider music circles he was considered something of an amateur by the professional musicians. They wanted to be part of a bigger world and had no appreciation of folk music which they thought was parochial and out-of-date. Belfast was a small place in those days where everyone knew everybody else, but a lot of people were waiting for Hayward to fall flat on his face in his ventures. Unquestionably he had the common touch, he liked journalists, and people who kept him amused and told him stories although he definitely had a high opinion of himself.[53]

Hayward ended 1959 with the satisfaction of an astonishingly productive decade. It had seen the publication of no fewer than six books, a vast amount of journalism, and the fulfilment of travelling around Europe and the US on a mix of business and pleasure. It was crowned with an honorary doctorate from an American College, a late-in-the-day recognition of his achievements. With the approach of a new decade, he was about to launch into another large-scale writing project on a part of Ireland he loved and which would happily absorb much of his life for the next four years.

FOURTEEN

Munster literary swansong
(1959–1964)

> He has a tremendous gusto that can stand an enormous amount of contradic-
> tion, a profound knowledge and admiration of Irish architecture and sculp-
> ture, and an Ulster common-sense that is both shocking and exhilarating
> – exhilarating when he agrees with you, shocking when he doesn't.
>
> Review by Frank O'Connor of *Munster and the City of Cork*, 1964

By the late 1950s the face of the music industry was changing rapidly and
Hayward's recording career suffered a dip. The technology had become obsolete
and from 1960 companies stopped making 78s. The old stock was sold off and
Hayward's work was no longer available. With the arrival on the Irish scene of
the Clancy Brothers and Tommy Makem, a new type of balladeer was emerging
in Ireland. The showband era had started to take the country by storm; the
Ronnie Drew Ballad Group took over a back room in O'Donoghue's pub in
Merrion Row and became The Dubliners; these were the new Irish rock stars.

Popular music was revolutionized as Elvis Presley burst on to the international arena while on the British pop scene the first wave of rockers included
Marty Wilde, Billy Fury, Adam Faith and Tommy Steele. The 'Trad Boom' with
Acker Bilk, Chris Barber and Kenny Ball was sweeping Britain in a craze for
traditional jazz that gave way with the arrival of four young men who made
a music club in Liverpool the most famous in the world. The Cavern Club
opened for business in 1957 and was hidden down the sloping Mathew Street
in an area steeped in history. Hayward would have known the place from his

sojourn in the city forty years beforehand when he worked at Cammell Laird. Now it was the nerve centre of an exciting pop scene, which a new generation was embracing with deafening cries. Crowds flocked downstairs to the cellar of a former warehouse to listen to skiffle, blues and the distinctive Merseybeat. This was to be the place where the Beatles made nearly 300 appearances. Out of the skiffle music emerged Cliff Richard and the Shadows who produced the film musicals *The Young Ones* (1961) and *Summer Holiday* (1963). All of this resulted in the youth of the era becoming increasingly unsympathetic to Hayward's music.

During his visit to the US to receive his honorary doctorate, he had been asked by a journalist about the changes taking place at home. Hayward said that those who see Ireland as a misty dreamland are 'utterly stupid and unthinking'. 'He remarked', reported the *Easton Express*, 'that the presence of the 'Teddy Boys' with their tight, drain-pipe trousers and long coats, is a misfortune for Ireland and the British Isles. He laughed and shook his head when asked if they were a productive group that might possibly contribute to the culture of the country'.[1]

A revolution in comedy led by Spike Milligan and the Goon Show's humour brought an end to stage shows such as those held at the Theatre Royal in Dublin. A new generation was distancing themselves from their parents' interests and values. Hayward nonetheless remained a vivid vocal presence at social events with his unique brand of humour. By the start of the sixties, even though his music was being eclipsed by pop, he had as big a fan base as ever. Within sight of his seventieth birthday, his mental faculties were sharp. He retained his twinkly amusement and his dexterous storytelling exuding his old charisma. A seasoned pro, he could still seduce his audience. Even though he may have been out of step with the times, his crowd appeal was as strong as ever. On average his records sold between 4000 and 5000 copies and given the impressive total that he produced, sales figures ran into several hundred thousand.

He was part of a regular touring line-up of musicians organized by the Committee for the Encouragement of Music and the Arts (CEMA), which included the singers Mattie Waugh and Eric Hinds as well as Cathleen Wright, a solo pianist and accompanist. Mattie, a full-time teacher, was a trained soprano and oratorio singer. One of her first appearances with Hayward was when she took part alongside him on the BBC's St Patrick's Day Special TV programme in which she sang 'The Basket of Flowers'. In subsequent years she performed with him at numerous CEMA concerts for which they were paid £8 per night. Mattie recalls that in the early 1960s they staged six shows each year to packed houses in village and church halls all over the North:

Hayward was compere and warmed up the audience with funny stories while we waited backstage. There were times when I didn't want to hear him because I laughed so much at his jokes that I could not sing. Frequently I developed a tickle in my throat from laughing. A few minutes before I went on stage, he would produce Fox's Glacier Mints from his pocket and give me one saying they are awfully good for clearing your throat and they did help. After a few anecdotes he suddenly burst into song, intertwining them with stories, and then at other times he would recite his own poems. Very soon he would have the audience eating out of his hands. People lapped it all up and they were crazy for him. I was crazy about him too. He was an absolute wonder and he could keep them laughing all evening. He had dramatic effect and a talent to keep the audience amused from the beginning and there was always thunderous applause. He sang 'The Stone outside Dan Murphy's Door' and 'The Mutton Burn Stream'. I would often sing 'The Blue Hills of Antrim' which pleased him and 'The Gartan mother's lullaby'. We used to have dinner beforehand and he would produce tiny packets of Needler's chocolates as he was great at promoting the sweets. He was very knowledgeable and had friends all over the place. But he was no slouch. He worked us up with enthusiasm for our performance and the tours were great fun. I still treasure those evenings with him as there was such a feel-good factor about being in his company.[2]

Mattie's husband, Eric, a retired BBC industrial correspondent, travelled with them to CEMA concerts, carrying their music bags:

Richard was a one-off if ever there was one, but a nice man to know nevertheless. One joke that he used to tell the CEMA audiences was about two old men discussing the arrival of a new Presbyterian minister to their church. On his first Sunday he preached for a very long time. Swapping stories outside the church about the length of the sermon, one man said, 'Thon fella fairly shortened the winter,' while the other said, 'I could feel the spit of him in the fifth row.' Although it may not have been sophisticated humour, it was finely tuned, his timing was spot on, and his public loved it.[3]

There was little danger of his jokes growing stale with the rapt audiences that he enjoyed to the end of his life. But not everything was suitable. Hayward's witty irreverence sometimes led to trouble. The retired director of the Northern Ireland Arts Council, Ken Jamison, remembers attending the opening of a gallery exhibition in Belfast run through CEMA. Afterwards he went for tea with Lady Ashby, the guest of honour:

We decided to go to Robinson & Cleaver's tea room in Donegall Place. Hayward imposed himself on us and gatecrashed our tea party, inviting himself along. When we sat down he just took over – there was no stopping him and he told a terrible joke: 'There was a mouse sitting outside on the kerbstone and a bus came along and ran over it. The mouse lost its legs but managed to struggle into the nearby Matchett's music shop and asked the man in charge if he had any mouth organs for sale.' Lady Ashby was most offended. She reacted quite fiercely, exclaiming 'Really Mr. Hayward!'[4]

As a young reporter on the *Northern Whig* in Belfast at the start of his journalistic career in the early 1960s, Billy Simpson (later a columnist with the *Belfast Telegraph*) covered talks that Hayward gave to Women's Institutes and other groups. He met him several times:

I was very impressed that he could speak off the top of his head so easily and with such wit – of course he would probably be arrested today for some of his humour. There is no doubt he had a charismatic presence, and as I listened to him I was conscious that he was a famous person. Hayward was a Renaissance man. He was multi-talented and did not confine himself to one particular thing but had expertise in a number of different fields. I would describe him as a Titan in his own time and liken some of his sayings and witticisms as being similar to those of Mark Twain.[5]

Hayward's comic stories may not have changed much over the years but the face of Belfast, the city he had lived in for more than four decades, was radically different. The horse-drawn trams of his adolescence had been replaced by a fleet of red and white trolleybuses, which swung their way around the streets operating on all the main arterial roads leading into the city centre. Modern buses also ran on the roads and cars were increasingly taking over. The countryside was being reshaped too. Car owners were getting to grips with the rules of driving on a new motorway, the first in Ireland. Six sections of the M1 opened in mid 1962, running west from Belfast following the route of the former Lagan canal. The city itself was rapidly losing its individuality. The Empire Theatre had been pulled down in 1961, reducing a century of melodrama and music to rubble. Hayward lamented the standardization of shops and the fact that in the city streets 'you wouldn't see a shawl in a day's walk nowadays'. Many of the improvements, he wrote, had brought with them 'some loss of character and of the old solidity of the people':

One by one the old Belfast family businesses have been taken over by great English cartels, or have fallen victims to the venomous estate duties, and a bare half-dozen of our sturdier traders have survived the deluge ... Belfast is fast becoming first-cousin to similar places in England and elsewhere and more and more we see the self-same shopfronts with the self-same displays of merchandise and the self-same exhortations to purchase that we see in London and Edinburgh, Manchester and Cardiff.[6]

The city's changing religious demographic and new housing developments, especially around his own part of north Belfast, motivated him to comment:

> Erstwhile Protestant preserves, such as the Antrim Road, are no longer notable for residents who 'dig with the right fut' and it is many years since Catholics lived mainly in and around the Falls region …We never had slums in Belfast, in the real meaning of that ugly word, but great strides are being made in the erection of multi-storey flats to replace low-grade out-of-date housing. These, for all their usefulness, are bringing a further deadening uniformity of shape and character into our midst.[7]

At Stormont too the old order was changing. Lord Brookeborough resigned on health grounds as prime minister of Northern Ireland at the end of March 1963 and was succeeded by Captain Terence O'Neill whose appointment ushered in a new era. Undaunted by the whirlwind of political, social and cultural upheaval taking place around him, Hayward's inexhaustible energy was continuing at the usual breakneck pace. The television producer Andrew Crockart remembers the Clancy Brothers performing at the Ulster Hall in Belfast. Hayward liked holding court and showed he could be the life and soul of any party:

> We sneaked backstage into the Ulster Hall to hear the Clancys who were all the rage at the time. They were great fun and we had never before seen people with that sort of energy. I had become involved in programmes on traditional music and wasn't entirely ignorant of the scene but the way they performed was quite something as was the way the audience loved them. They were staying in the Midland Hotel and Hayward got up on a seat in the foyer and welcomed them, which was typical of him. Nobody had asked him to do this but he would have just done it because nobody else was going to do it and at least he was an honest practitioner of what he did. He was a great self-publicist. In those days when Belfast was well known for being terribly reserved this bouncy man was selling himself. He was a salesman by profession – nothing wrong with that – but certainly my mother and father would have thought he talks a little too much.[8]

Hayward was supportive of young musicians. Members of a newly-formed Northern group, the Glenfolk Four, met him to seek guidance. Charles Hill was a singer with the group, made up of Vincent Hanna (later a BBC television political presenter and journalist) and Ivan and Yvonne McKenna. He recalls

Hayward's visits to hear them play at Hanna's home at Fortwilliam Park in Belfast, a short walk from Hayward's house:

> Hayward was very generous with his musical knowledge and willingly shared it with us. We were in our early twenties and it was remarkable that he went to so much trouble to help us. He was quite a purist and I was apprehensive that he might not approve of our modernized folk-style. We recorded a song of his, 'The Orange Maid of Sligo', which had a calypso rhythm with a change of key halfway through. We thought it was an act of desecration, but when he heard it, Hayward approved of our treatment of his carefully collected music. At that time there was a great following in Canada for folk music. Our song was played on many radio stations in Toronto and became a top twenty hit staying in the folk charts for six months. I often mention Hayward's name to young musicians but few have heard of him or appreciate his great legacy.[9]

Needler's chocolate box advertisement for Easter and Mother's Day 1964. By this stage Hayward had been working part-time for the company for forty years.

The singing and showbiz strand to his life had of course been only one element to his streams of income and he was holding a portfolio of jobs that were keeping him busy. The confectionery agencies were a continuing source of reliable income. Needler's now dealt with a range of fancy assortment packs that gloried in such names as By The Lake Box, Regal Casket, Riviera Casket and Golden Moments. By the beginning of the 1960s his writing life had entered its sixth decade. He was now starting the Munster book, which would complete his quintet of volumes on the regions of Ireland.

Behind the wheel again, he set off in 1960 on his Munster research. Accompanied as usual by Piper, he was in confident mood. It had been five years since the publication of his fourth book in the series 'This is Ireland'. This was their fifth and final collaboration and they were determined to round off the enterprise with a grand literary and artistic finale.

For both of them it must have felt like old times. They were about to undertake a marathon journey in the southwest of Ireland, a formidable task taking in some of the country's biggest counties, highest mountains and most noted antiquities. Spruce and vigorous, Hayward was well able for the challenges it presented. His mind still sparkled with intellectual curiosity. He could draw on five decades of experience as well as a wealth of first-class contacts throughout Munster. They spent three months touring Cork, Kerry, Waterford, Tipperary, Limerick and Clare but it was to be nearly four years before the book was published to a fanfare of publicity. By now Hayward was no stranger to Munster. Although it was sixteen years since he had toured for five weeks in Kerry with Theo Gracey, he had been a frequent visitor to many other parts of the province, leading field club trips to the Burren, Limerick, Kerry, Cork, and Waterford.

Their journey starts with a short section on Cork city before quickly moving on to the rest of the county to which he devotes sixty pages. They stop at the Blarney Stone, which Hayward says he has already kissed three times. 'As I write, *the Cult of the Blarney Stone* seems to have entered a new phase with the publication of a neatly designed *Certificate of Eloquence* that may be purchased for a small sum by every person who submits to the amusing and time-honoured ceremony.'[10] They are accompanied through west Cork by John T. Collins, an 'old shanachie', full of history, lore and humour. There are personal moments in the book such as Hayward's singing of 'The Iniskilling Dragoon' over the novelist Donn Byrne's grave in Rathclarin near Kilbrittain – despite the admonition of the epitaph, 'I'm in my sleeping and let you not waken me.'

He reflects on the work of Byrne – known to him as Brian – who was killed in a car accident in 1928 at Courtmacsherry Bay in Cork.[11]

As in previous books, Hayward took every aspect of his exploration of the outdoors seriously. A lined exercise book from the Belfast Education Authority is filled with handwritten details of the flora of Munster. His knowledge of botany was as sharp as ever: lists of flowers, complete with botanical nomenclature and his bracketed notes, include references to botanists such as Praeger who died in 1953, and Henry Chichester Hart.

Blossom's Gate in Kilmallock, County Limerick, the last of the five original town gates sketched for *Munster and the City of Cork* published in 1964. The town was the principal stronghold of the Fitzgeralds from the fourteenth to the sixteenth century.

Pinguicula grandiflora (one of our most beautiful Irish plants)

Limestone Pavement in Co. Limerick, nr Askeaton – interesting place with a sort of reduced Burren flora

Co. Tipperary, The Galtees: H. C. Hart, that wonderful and indefatigable hunter worked this area near the Galtees.

Lathyrus maritimus, Rossbeigh, Kerry (lost sight of for a century)

Burren: Run of interesting plants: Dryas octopetala, Potentilla fruticosa,

Saxifraga, the mossy saxifrage, Gentiana verna, Neotinea intacta,

Orchis O'Kellyi, Maidenhair Fern [12]

In Clare the two men travelled the 'marvellous new road that hugs the coast' enjoying the panorama of the cliffs of Moher, and walked the Burren's lime-stone pavement. Piper, who was developing a passion bordering on infatuation for wild orchids, produced an exquisite two-page suite of sketches of the high-lights of the Burren flora. Kerry had already been fertile ground for Hayward's 1946 book. In the intervening period more cars were on the roads and the face of the Irish countryside had changed from the war years. Frequently he wrote to people requesting information about buildings, local customs and folklore or stories from the past. For example, specific information on the history of Glen-stal Abbey in County Limerick was sent to him by the Belgian monk Dom Hubert after their visit. While at Glenstal, they enjoyed 'the hospitality of the house' hearing the monks intone a grace in plainchant.

They were slowed down by rain and cold weather during part of May but it picked up for June. In Tipperary they timed their visit to join the Kilfeacle Beagles for their annual off-season meet to the summit of Galtymore on 5 June 1960 – Whit Sunday. Participants who reached Dawson's Table by 4 pm received a buttonhole badge award known as the *Barr Buadha Na Binne*, the 'Top Victory of the Peak'. Hayward was selected that day for a special award as the most senior person on Galtymore. His notebooks from the journey record that he covered 2603 miles on his Munster odyssey. He made notes but after he had written the script, he spoke it into a Dictaphone recording machine. In April he had hired the machine for twenty-four months at a cost of £172 11s 0d. He used a Time-Master Model IR6 to dictate his whole Munster book over the following two years, handing it over to a typist with instructions on the layout and spelling of Irish place names. He requested it to be in double-line spacing to allow him to sub-edit the script. By the end of his Munster journey he had amassed sixteen Dictabelt recordings, which constituted a draft containing a staggering 180,000 words from the 1960 trip and a further one in 1961. The Dictaphone gave a voice-perfect recording quality that could not be erased or changed. Held in the public library in Belfast, they are crackly period pieces but Hayward's clipped voice comes across precise and clear.[13]

The book required a vast amount of research and fact-checking and was a protracted enterprise. Its appearance was delayed for a number of reasons. Not only was Hayward busy in many spheres, but Elma's health was deteriorating. She had suffered but fully recovered from a stroke causing paralysis and slurred speech. This was followed by an operation on her stomach and she was diagnosed with gastric cancer. In the spring Elma finally succumbed to her illness and died on 11 April 1960, having expressed regret that she would not live to attend Ricky's wedding later that year. Since there was then no crematorium in Ireland, she was cremated on 14 April at the Western Necropolis Crematorium in Glasgow. Just her husband and Ricky attended the cremation; Dion, in far-off New Zealand, could join them only in thought.

For forty-six years they had shared a richly rewarding married life enjoying many happy times together both as partners and in a professional partnership on stage that so many had loved. Elma was an accomplished actress whose work was held in high regard by the critics. Ricky fondly remembers how much her ability to imitate accents embellished anecdotes with which she entertained friends. She brought skill and enthusiasm to her stage persona. But her life was eclipsed by the fact that her husband was always the centre of the circle of their friends while in later years she mostly remained out of the limelight. Nonetheless she was his staunch supporter, standing behind him in his many business ventures and giving him strength, bringing domestic happiness in a long relationship. 'She was a retiring lady and I was very upset when she died,' said Paul Hayward who has fond memories of her. 'She had significant talent as an actress and lived a quiet and content life as his wife, providing rock-solid stability.'[14]

Although he had been prepared for it for some time, Elma's death left a void in Hayward's world. But he concealed his private sorrow and began to lead an ever more crowded life. Friends realized he would need companionship and would find it difficult looking after and running such a large house. After his mother's death, Ricky continued living at home. They managed, he recalled, to cope well and his father cooked for both of them. On 22 December 1961, Ricky married Mary Eileen Byrne, formerly a fellow chemistry student at Queen's University and then teaching at Richmond Lodge School in Belfast. He moved into her rented flat in the university area leaving his father briefly on his own. In February 1963 Ricky and Mary sailed to the US where he worked for three years in postdoctoral molecular biology research at the University of Chicago. Dion had earlier decided that he did not want to remain in Northern Ireland and accepted a job in New Zealand, moving there in 1960 to be followed by Dolly and Paul early in 1961. Having graduated from university in Auckland, Paul later went to California for postgraduate study, ultimately settling in the US.

Progress on the Munster book ground to a halt but Hayward picked himself up and was re-energized when a new love entered his life. For some years he had already known Dorothy Gamble through the Belfast artistic and cultural milieu in the mid 1950s. She was a medical secretary and as a published poet had joined PEN. They lived near each other in north Belfast. In the midst of everything that was going on in his life he embarked on a late-flowering love affair. Their friendship started with a courtship some years before Elma's death and was known initially to only a few close friends. From his trips around Ireland he had sent some piteously funny letters and postcards to her. One letter that has survived was written while Hayward was working on the Munster book in the silence of the Kilkenny countryside. He was staying as a guest at Tom Hoyne's house, which he had been using as a writing base. Less than six weeks after Elma's death, he spelled out his feelings for his new paramour, declaring how much he missed her, starting with a reference to Dorothy's niece and later using a pet name:

Dorothy, Dear heart,
    I have sent the card to dear wee Judith without delay but I'm sure she won't get it until Thursday, bless her. I'm using Tom's typewriter and its unfamiliarity accounts for a number of typographical inexactitudes already made and many more to come!

Launching into romantic rhetoric, he wrote that the look on the page of one of the typewriter's brackets reminded him of an amusing frolic.

The longer skirts are perfect bliss
To girls with legs like ( ) and) (though, thank God, not to darling Dotty Berry whose legs are all they should be, eminently strokeable and gorgeously encircling :: and perfectly 'perfect bliss' in themselves. Wish I could stroke them now: I've felt the need of them and their sweet owner very very very verrry VERRRRRRRY much these last few days. You see, I love her so much and always will to the end of my days … I'm very happy to know that he [Tom] has a very high opinion of you. I think at one time you thought otherwise. But everything he has said about you shows his warm approval of my

own sweet girl, the dear heart of my waking moments and my golden dreams. I didn't get up until 11 a.m. today. Tom insisted and brought my breakfast up to bed. Since then I have written a thousand words of Kerry and plan to finish it today and tomorrow. I have a room all to myself, a fragrant wood fire and the peace of the countryside. Tom and Nurse are kindness personified and all I miss is your own dear self, the shining comfort of my declining years, the pillar I can lean upon as I approach my century. Terrible thing it is to be old and feeble, and you know how very feeble I am, my darling horizontal companion in exercises far beyond my nonagerian [*sic*] frailty!! ... Everyone was asking for Ricky at Newtown. And for Elma. It was all rather sad and at times I was close to tears.[15]

Plainly they were deeply in love. He wrote many tender letters and post-cards to Dorothy filled with a sunny tone. Born on 27 May 1915, she was the eldest of four children and the daughter of a pharmaceutical chemist. The family lived in Chichester Park in north Belfast and later moved to Clifton Park Avenue. During the Second World War Dorothy had been a personal assistant in the Belfast Branch of the Postal Censorship Division. After the war, she moved to England, working in Leeds as a private secretary for Associated Industrial Consultants. She later became a secretary with the Manchester Medical Society, an amalgamation of all the medical societies in the city. She had excellent secretarial skills including shorthand, typewriting and bookkeeping, and returned to Northern Ireland in 1952 to work at the Royal Victoria Hospital in Belfast.

Aside from her job, Dorothy's interests lay in literary and artistic circles. She was well read and enjoyed discussing books and poetry. In 1937 her collection of twenty-six poems, *A Page Turned Back*, was published by Arthur Stockwell of London and was well received. The poems feature, amongst other places, Donegal and Connemara while some are written in dialect. She had travelled around Ireland and was familiar with many parts of the country. Apart from poetry, she painted and sketched, read widely, particularly in the arts and theology, and was an admirer of the work of the scholar and author Helen Waddell. An attractive and sociable woman, she and Hayward were ideally suited and decided to get engaged.

Dorothy was twenty-three years his junior and the worlds in which they grew up were entirely different but the age gap did not present any problems. She enjoyed his intellectual energy and they shared common interests, including a love of drama, especially Shakespeare. She was a member of the Shakespeare Society in Belfast as well as poetry and history societies. They had intended to keep the news of their courtship private but in the best traditions of the world of Belfast gossip, word slipped out to the press and it was reported in advance of the wedding. 'Dr Hayward's romance secret is out' read the headline in the *Sunday Express* on 18 February 1962. The paper reported that the 'secret engagement' had leaked out:[16]

> Yesterday the couple dined in one of Belfast's leading restaurants. Miss Gamble wore a three-diamond engagement ring. Said Dr Hayward: 'We are very happy although surprised that our engagement news has leaked. We had hoped to have kept it completely quiet.'[17]

Ten months after Elma's death, on 23 February 1962, they were married. Twelve close family members and friends attended the service in Duncairn Presbyterian Church with Raymond Piper as best man. Well-wishers congratulated the couple with cards, letters and telegrams. Amongst the greetings was one from Patrick Mahony, a friend living in Santa Barbara, California who wrote about Dorothy, 'She owns that dangerous combination of brains and looks. Watch out.'[18]

The wedding party pictured at Hayward's marriage to Dorothy Gamble. The ceremony was held at Duncairn Presbyterian Church, Belfast on 23 February 1962. Raymond Piper, standing behind the newly married couple, was best man. The marriage was solemnized in the presence of Ricky Hayward and his wife Mary, on the extreme left of the photograph.

ROMANCING IRELAND: RICHARD HAYWARD

Les Holmes, a business associate from Belfast, wrote a short letter with a nod to Hayward's confectionery job and the exclamatory 'You sly old fox!!'[19] As with so much in his life, the papers reported his second marriage. 'Poet, 70 weds the girl next door', was the headline in the *Dublin Evening Mail*.[20] Newspapers carried photographs of the beaming couple, and Ireland's social magazines reported the wedding too. The glossy monthly *Social and Personal* recorded the event:

> Another excitement has hit P.E.N. – a romantic one this time, the marriage of two of its best known members, Richard Hayward – author, singer, actor, antiquarian – and poet Dorothy Gamble. Dorothy is a sensitive writer who deserves to be better known than she is and she shares Richard's interest in Irish history, architecture and folk lore. Like him, she has travelled over most of the country and has unearthed the most extraordinary information about places and buildings, her poet's eye singles out the remarkable feature wherever she goes.[21]

As a young boy Paul Hayward was admitted to hospital in Belfast with appendicitis and remembers Dorothy visiting him in 1959:

> I recall a strange woman coming into the hospital ward to see me and ask how I was. I didn't know her but discovered it was Dorothy who was described as a friend of my grandfather. It was all a bit puzzling to me as a nine-year-old. Much later I was told that my grandfather was active extramaritally and his affair with Dorothy had been going on for several years. My parents were aware that she was his mistress although at the time I did not know this. My grandmother was dying and being cheated on but my childhood anger at the marriage was based on the quickness of it after my grandmother's death and I wondered why my parents were not as upset as I was. I suppose it was my childhood naïvety at the ways of the world that governed my feelings. Although I am not a highly moralistic person I felt the brevity between the period of her death and his marriage to Dorothy was inappropriate. I was offended that he remarried hastily although eventually I grew up and grew out of it.[22]

The newly married pair spent their honeymoon in Dublin, staying in Buswells Hotel for four nights at a cost of £31 10*s* 2*d*. The trip coincided with a Garvey banquet on 23 February while Dublin PEN held a cocktail party in the United Arts Club followed by dinner in the Royal Hibernian Hotel. His second marriage marked the start of a new life for Hayward. He had many good years ahead of him and still had much to achieve.

Entering into the spirit of the festivities at the Galway Oyster Festival in September 1961, Hayward is second on the right.

An immediate priority was to complete the Munster book and instigate new projects for the years of companionship that lay ahead. Foreign travel was high on his itinerary. He had already spent considerable time in the 1950s in Europe and had a taste for continental life as a contrast from the drab wet city streets of Belfast. Spain had become a passion and he and Dorothy were planning to visit the country later in the year. In early autumn the couple toured energetically around the country for the whole of September, returning home in early October. Hayward had become a Hispanicist, imbibing the culture and history of the country. His time in Spain though was spent dealing with letters from the publishers and queries about his Munster book, which was finally taking shape, albeit at a snail's pace.

At seventy, there was no temptation to slow down. Far from slackening, and with energy levels undiminished, he kept up his varied activities. Two months after their marriage, Dorothy accompanied her new husband on a weekend field club excursion to Limerick. She was already familiar with some people in Hayward's wide network of friends and he delighted in introducing her to others. He brought her to the Galway Oyster Festival in 1963 where they were guests of honour.

Hayward was pictured in *The Irish Times* along with Lady ffrench at the Galway Oyster Festival in 1961. At the same event, Charles Haughey, then Parliamentary Secretary to the Minster for Justice is photographed helping his wife to eat the first oysters of the season. Beneath is Lord Hemphill of Tulira Castle, owner of oyster beds in Galway Bay. The caption states that he ate nine dozen of the shellfish but was a bad second to Lady ffrench who ate a gross.

Everywhere they went they appeared to radiate an aura, brightening the lives of those around them as they shared stories and jokes. It was a loving and successful marriage – a partnership of minds locked together in harmony. Letters to Dorothy after Hayward's death shine a light on their time together, reflecting the esteem in which they were held. One writer, Ann Young, captures the mood:

> I do remember as if it were yesterday, sitting with my back to the door at the beginning of the PEN meeting, and becoming aware quite suddenly that something rare and special had happened. I had to turn round – and as you and Richard came into the room I felt that we should all get up and make an obeisance: you carried your happiness about your heads like aureoles. Every time I saw you together after that it was the same. You two brought into any room something gracious and reviving which was more than the sum total of two very distinct and mature people smiling on their friends. We all of us warmed our hands and gave thanks because the world is often so horrible and here was something so outstanding and so lovely.[23]

At the end of April 1963 Hayward was laid low with laryngitis. Barely able to speak, he cancelled all his appointments for a week and carried on whispered conversations with friends.[24] Fortunately he was concentrating on the written rather than the spoken word. His contribution to a new anthology, *Ireland and the Irish*, had just come out. The book dealt with such subjects as history, folklore, national character, the visual arts, as well as sports and horse breeding. For its second section on the Irish regions, Hayward wrote a 10,000-word feature on 'The Province of Ulster,' which incorporated 1000 words on each of the nine counties as well as Belfast. In total, fifteen writers contributed to the attractive hardback volume, including Kate O'Brien, Garret FitzGerald, Stephen Rynne, Bryan MacMahon, Micheál Mac Liammóir and John D. Sheridan.

He redoubled his efforts on the Munster book and was eagerly awaiting the proofs, the final hectic push to get it completed. Piper too was working day and night on the sketches. He told the *Belfast News Letter* in early October that he was adjusting the galley proofs before dispatching them to the publishers:

> I've been at this until five in the morning for the past few days and it is an energy-sapping job. We had some wonderful experiences. You could call this a geographical, topographical and anecdotal book as when doing our research we met all sorts of people.[25]

But despite their best efforts the book suffered further delays. It had originally been scheduled for publication in the autumn of 1963 but was now put back to the following year. Arthur Barker had sold his firm to Weidenfeld & Nicolson in 1959 and Hayward had found a new publisher in J.M. Dent. The book was to be published by Phoenix House, a subsidiary of Dent. In the snowy days of December 1963 and January 1964, the finishing touches were applied. Travel anywhere was extremely difficult that winter – the worst in living memory – but in the midst of the perishing cold he was planning trips both at home and abroad with Dorothy for later in the year. In early summer of 1963 Hayward and Dorothy, along with Tom Hoyne, visited Galtymore on 8 June for the Whit weekend climb organized by the Kilfeacle Beagle Hunt, which he had completed on his Munster tour with Piper three years earlier. The following year, 1964, he helped choose the 'Maid of the Mountain'.

Signs of a social and economic revolution were in evidence in the Republic with the election in 1959 of Seán Lemass as Taoiseach. After the moribund 1950s, a decade that saw more than 400,000 people emigrate, the country was being transformed. A new liberalism was stirring. The old Ireland of de Valera was beginning to fade and in June 1963 the visit of John F. Kennedy, seen by many commentators as a turning point in Ireland's modern history, raised the country's self-esteem.

Early in 1964 Hayward's life was tinged with sadness when he heard of the death of Maurice Walsh, the novelist, who more than anyone else in Ireland had championed his name through unstinting support of his books. Walsh died at the age of eighty-five on 18 February at his son's home in Stillorgan, County Dublin. Working tirelessly to the end, he had just completed correcting the proofs of his new short-story collection, *The Smart Fellow*, due to be published in May. Hayward wrote to his son, also called Maurice, asking 'Where shall we see his like again?'

> Dorothy and I would like you to know that your loss is also very much ours. Never again can we visit Dublin without feeling that there is a gap there that can never be filled. May I beg you to send me a photograph of your father for my 'Irish Room'? I have a row of Maurice Walsh volumes, many of them autographed but I have no picture to place near them ... and I would so much like to have one. My heart is full when I look back on the many wonderful times Maurice and I enjoyed together and both Dorothy and I remember with deep pleasure that last grand ceilidh when you sang 'Come to the Bower'. And now indeed dear Maurice has gone to the bower and left us all to mourn him.[26]

Apart from his American doctorate, Hayward was the recipient of another, more unusual overseas award. At a dinner in the Conway Hotel in Belfast, he received the Insignia of Honorary Capataz (foreman) of the San Patricio. The award was made by the Garvey sherry firm to those who had distinguished themselves in their work on behalf of sherry and promoting Hispanic culture. The company was founded in 1780 by William Garvey, an Irish aristocrat from County Waterford who made their sherry one of the principal bodegas in the province of Cadiz. Garvey wanted to build wine cellars in Jerez in southwest Spain, saying 'St Patrick will guide us' and dedicated the Garvey Bodega, a dry sherry, to the Irish patron saint using the Spanish form of the name San Patricio. Hayward, who had made several trips to Spain as guest of the House of Garvey, described it as a 'signal honour' to receive the award. He had written a number of articles in Irish newspapers promoting the drink as well as sherry brandy, sweet wines and other wines of Spain. He was so taken by the story of Garvey history, which he said read 'like a brightly-coloured romance', that he was collecting material for a book.[27]

For a long time he had been a prophet without honour in his own city, but in June 1963 he was the first Ulsterman to be elected an honoray life associate of the British Institute of Recorded Sound. Hayward received a personal letter from Sir Adrian Boult, the chairman of the Institute's executive committee and an exponent of Elgar's music. Boult, who had established the BBC Symphony Orchestra and become its chief conductor, was later appointed conductor of the London Philharmonic Orchestra. The award acknowledged Hayward's long service in folk music and its recording. In February 1964 he was re-elected to the position of president of the Ulster Folksong Society.

Recognition at home came late in the day with Establishment venera-tion. In the Queen's honours list of June 1964 he was appointed Order of the British Empire (OBE) for his services to art and literature although the award was never formally conferred on him. The *Belfast Telegraph* described him 'as a unique figure in local life and letters, jack of all trades and artist of all work'.[28] The paper's Christopher Cairns in his 'Off-stage Jottings' column also used the occasion to look ahead to the much-anticipated appearance of the Munster book now at last scheduled for publication in a few months' time:

> He was rather surprised at his publisher's temerity proposing to bring out a special edition limited to a hundred copies at ten guineas a time. He has been even more surprised to hear that this expensive de-luxe part of the general edition has already been heavily subscribed. Now Richard Hayward can start all over again with a new book on Ulster. His home province has changed so much since he started out, at least superficially. Richard Hayward has scarcely changed at all.[29]

In its coverage of the honours list, the *Belfast News Letter* described him as a man of many parts: author, actor, harpist, ballad singer, folklorist, film producer, lecturer and amateur archaeologist among them. The paper said he had written many travel books and 'uncountable newspaper and magazine articles'.[30] His longtime friend Jimmy Mageean with whom thirty-five years previously he had founded the Belfast Repertory Company wrote good-humouredly to him from his Californian home at Pacific Beach, San Diego. He had read the report of it in the 'Telly' (*Belfast Telegraph*) and at once sat down and wrote a paean in verse:

> With a Hi and a Ho and a HAYward!
> Black is white and white is black
> Catch those words and bring them back!
> There is surely something wrong …

Damn! This interrupts my song …
Give me patience, Lord, amen,
Like R. Bruce I'll start again.
White is black and black is white …
No! That simply can't be right …
White is white and black is black,
Now at last I'm on the track
All is right as right can be,
Right for Hayward right by me,
Just my blinking cupa Tea,
Let the Welkin ring with glee,
Rise and shout with all your might…
Ta Hayward! May his days be bright!
See how two wrongs become a right,
So may his day become a knight!
'Owed' to An Old Friend.
Written by Semaj Trebor Na Eegam,
Upon learning that H. Richard Hayward had received the O.B.E.

He then went on to write an Ode to Dorothy:

I lift my brimming glass of Tea
And send a wish to you from me,
May Heaven grant you strength and joy …
You'll need the strength, and how! … Oh! Boy!
With Richard and his fads galore,
He'll plague you till your heart is sore,
And then, dear Lady, just you think,
The job you'll have when he's in drink,
An eye for girls … the low down pub,
The late late nights, aye, there's the rub,
But still and all he's not the worst,
So may detractors all be cursed
Here's wishing you both health and joy,
With Richard H … Soul He's the Boy! [31]

When the news filtered through to New Zealand, Paul Hayward says his parents were delighted with the recognition: 'He was known in the family as

HRH from his original names of Harold Richard, and I remember mum and dad laughing, saying that my grandfather would have felt it more appropriate if he had received a knighthood.'[32] Shortly after the announcement of his OBE, towards the end of June 1964, with Dorothy accompanying him, they went to Scandinavia where they spent a month on a combined holiday and work trip. For a week they were delegates to the international PEN Congress in Oslo. But before going to Norway they attended a Sibelius festival in Helsinki for a week and squeezed in sightseeing. Hayward said he liked the Finns and the clean air but not the prices. 'You can wear a white shirt there for three days and it won't get dirty. However, even when I did send two shirts and a few collars to the laundry, it cost 7s 10d. An apple cost me 1s 5d.'[33]

Despite the animosity directed at him two years earlier by Patricia Kertland and the unpleasant aftertaste, Hayward retained field club links. Although by 1964 he was no longer conducting outings, he turned up for some of them including a 'Barony of Mourne' excursion to south Down led by Brendan Adams. On Saturday 22 August they visited prehistoric and medieval sites at Kilkeel and Annalong with a sunny stop for lunch at Cranfield. One of those present was David Honneyman who had been friendly with Hayward and had an interest in flora. With an idyllic background of the Cooley Mountains on one side and the Mountains of Mourne on the other, the two men decided on an afternoon swim in Carlingford Lough near Greencastle – a day that has lived long in Honneyman's memory:

> After we pulled up on the beach and explored the Anglo-Norman castle, Hayward told me he had come prepared as he had brought his bathing costume so we plunged into the lough. It was a hot day and the water was pleasantly warm. We swam for about fifteen minutes and when we came out we were regarded as heroes by the rest of the group. I was forty-six and even though Hayward was seventy-one, he was full of beans. He was sociable and good company with an outgoing personality although he was cocksure of himself. The men in the field club were very quiet; they were academics and experts on dead insects or rare flowers while others were dour Presbyterians. Some of them would say about Hayward 'Who the hell does he think he is, or what does he know about anything?'[34]

Honneyman recalls stories that Hayward used to tell him about his searches for antiquities in the countryside:

> He roamed the hills in every part of the country looking for dolmens or standing stones and was particularly interested in souterrains, the underground

tunnels. Always with a map in his hand he would wander around talking to local people picking up stories. He told me on one occasion when searching for a dolmen near Cloughmills in north Antrim that he came across an old farmer cutting turf. He questioned him about where the dolmen was to be found and the farmer asked why he wanted to know. Hayward said he had travelled all over Ireland, and the wider world, in search of such things and liked to know their exact location. The farmer replied, 'I wouldn't like you to think I'm a stay-at-home man. I've been twice to Ballymoney, never been to Belfast but I was once in Buckna.' He could talk to peasants and he could talk to intellectuals and had the gift of the gab. He could talk his way in anywhere, was verbally fluent and a master of self-control. If he walked into a room everyone would know he was the top man. When he spoke, a silence fell. He was an alpha male, the other males would slink away and the females would sit around and smile.[35]

Not only was Dorothy his wife, she was also his literary midwife. While he was finalizing work on his Munster book, she took on the task of compiling the index, which ran to twelve pages. She had a photographic memory and with her own knowledge of Ireland, was ideally placed to carry out this meticulous work. With the final editing, proofreading and indexing complete, the book was ready. In the countdown to publication, plans were being put in place for a publicity tour that would take author and artist all around Ireland again. It was the culmination of a five-volume venture that started in 1948 at the age of fifty-six and was to be an occasion worth marking. Now, sixteen years later, the Munster book, regarded as a work of *gravitas*, crowned his writing career just two months short of his seventy-second birthday. An enormous investment of time and money, *Munster and the City of Cork* was one of his proudest achievements. It was published at the end of August 1964 by Phoenix House of London. Although it was part of the series *This is Ireland* it was a larger format than the other four books published by Arthur Barker in a uniform edition but was a pleasure for readers to hold. A hefty volume, at 354 pages, it bore a dedication to Elma and their sons Dion and Richard.

Priced at three guineas, the book was finished with a green binding and gold lettering on the black panel on the spine. The mustard-yellow and green dust wrapper showed an elegant illustration of the Clock Gate at Youghal, County Cork. Piper had doubled the amount of sketches he had drawn for the other books and produced 120 high-quality halftone plates from pencil drawings, twenty-four of which were full page. Apart from the textual drawings he provided extra ones for the endpapers and preliminary pages including a title page with *Erinus alpinus* (fairy foxglove) on old walls in Cork city; others portrayed boatmen on the Lakes of Killarney and a jarvey in the Gap of Dunloe. The final sketch in the book featured Hayward with Fr Gabriel and Tom Hoyne on the bridge at Carrick-on-Suir – along with a sketch of Piper's own hands. A map of the province of Munster appeared on the preliminary pages with an inset map of Ireland, which wrongly placed County Clare in Connacht instead of Munster. Apart from this topographical flaw, the book was printed to a high standard with first-class production values. A deluxe limited edition of a hundred numbered copies, signed by both Hayward and Piper, was produced in a slipcase at ten guineas and was heavily subscribed in advance. At the end of the following year the book's worth was recognized when it was chosen for the National Book League Design Exhibition in London. Advance publicity by Phoenix House touted the book as a major publication with 'Richard Hayward, doyen of Irish topographical writers, starting from a central point in each county and leading the reader on from place to place.'

Munster hit the bookshops in early September and was released in tandem with a whirlwind round of speeches, lunches and dinners in Ireland's major cities. Signing sessions, involving both writer and artist, started on 2 September in Mullan's bookshop in Belfast and the week-long tour took them to Dublin, Cork and Limerick where a medieval banquet was held in his honour at Bunratty Castle. Although a punishing programme, the tour was a triumphant success for Hayward. The sprightly figure was well able for it and shrewd enough to realize the sales dividends.

The strain it exacted must have sometimes left him exhausted, but if this was the case he did not show it. With so many publications behind him, Hayward had immense talent for the self-promotional bonhomie required to help give the book the necessary kick-start. He was in a class of his own when it came to marketing his books and exploiting the hoopla of publicity. It was sometimes cuttingly said of him that when he was on the promotional trail, an unsigned copy of one of his travel books was worth a good deal more money than a signed one.[36] But his loyal readership regarded it as important to have a personally inscribed copy.

Michael Geare, sales manager with J.M. Dent who organized the Irish tour, had predicted a remarkable degree of press coverage. 'This is for three reasons,' he told Hayward. 'We have worked extremely hard; you are very well-known in Ireland, and it is an absolutely first-class book.'[37] Geare's prediction was well founded. A blaze of publicity in the daily and Sunday papers followed while the afterglow of the launches lingered. For the most part, the critics lavished praise with largely positive noises but in some cases it was tempered with carping criticism. Writing in the *Guardian*, Sean O'Faolain described the book as 'a blend of old time lunch-pictorial Baedeker-Murray tradition of factual-informative'. His main complaint was that the book was impractically big and heavy:

> It is not really meant to be read; it is meant to be consulted. Richard Hayward's head is full of curious information. I feel he has been toppled by the sheer poundage of information, historical, botanical, topographical etc. that he has had to supply and the foot-slogging style he has had to adopt.[38]

The *Cork Examiner* critic began his review by saying that in all parts of Ireland there are legions of enthusiastic admirers of Hayward's work. 'Perhaps no other writer has done so much to foster a love of the countryside, a knowledge of Ireland's place names and an appreciation of Irish scenic beauty.' The only disappointment, the reviewer grumbled, was the brevity of the chapter on Cork city: 'Nine pages out of 200 is surely scant treatment … Perhaps it was that Messrs. Hayward and Piper were over-eager for the open road and the green fields, or maybe John T [Collins] was so anxious to get them to his beloved West Cork that he forebore to regale them with more urban anecdotes.'[39]

In *The Irish Times*, Maurice Gorham felt that Hayward 'does not bother about being bang up to date, is not ashamed to wax sentimental on occasion and makes no effort to conform to contemporary tastes. He does not hide his dislike of the Church of Christ the King at Turner's Cross with which no doubt many Corkmen will secretly agree.' Gorham's criticism was about the absence of people. 'We get no hint of the people on whom the character of places depend. A few such glimpses might have added living humanity to a book that is rich in everything else.'[40] A similar complaint about lack of people was made in *The Irish Press* by Sean J. White who said there was 'an absence of a felt sense of life being lived. The Munsterman should marvel at the act of imaginative sympathy that makes an Ulsterman and a confessed Orangeman so knowledgeable about Munster.' He also criticized the inadequate section on Cork city that he felt Hayward had 'scanted':

> Like Belfast it has a distinctive life of its own with decidedly individual qualities. It is drisheen, and the teeming life of Blarney Street, the Opera House and competing breweries, oddly named pubs, the Butter Exchange Band and harbour excursions … There is a blinkered view about some of Mr. Hayward's pre-occupations. Chi-Ro crosses and castle and abbeys certainly

interest the traveller, but nowadays so do the buildings of the eighteenth century, the best of Victorian building, railway architecture and the like.[41]

White felt Hayward's prose had a rather embarrassing way at times. Adare Friary is 'a venerable pile', in Brandon 'the far-flung delights of Brandon Bay came into our ken,' and in Glencar he travels 'a splendid bog road that is beset by a veritable sea of mountains.'

Frank O'Connor's review of *Munster and the City of Cork* was published in the *Sunday Independent*. He said Hayward had an 'Ulster common-sense that is both shocking and exhilarating'.

In the *Sunday Independent* Frank O'Connor wrote a humorous piece in his 'Books on Sunday' column under the heading: 'Mr. Hayward is an even bigger crank than I am ...' He affects to know far more than I – or indeed, any living man – pretends to know ... I call the books remarkable because I buy them, which is the biggest compliment a professional writer can pay to another.'

He then took Hayward to task [for] 'pretending to know. He parades Irish place-names in a Gaelic dress and in that miserable Gothic lettering which is miscalled "Irish" and gets them brilliantly wrong ... But, of course, arguing with Richard Hay Ward (to give his name its proper spelling) is half the fun because you cotton on to the man in a couple of pages.' O'Connor praised Piper's sketches, which he said had 'developed beyond recognition', and called for an exhibition of them in Dublin.[42] The *Belfast Telegraph* critic, W. Brownlow White, said that Hayward's personal network of contacts had held him in good stead:

> Unlike the transient traveller, Dr. Hayward has had great advantage of having among his friendships men and women who know the feel of the country. This is reflected in the racy vein which he discusses all kinds of subjects with them and draws them into his narrative.[43]

In a review in the *Illustrated London News*, the distinguished British historian and author of Irish lineage, Sir Charles Petrie, said it was an admirable book and that Hayward's descriptive powers are 'considerable'.[44] Writing in the *New Daily*, C.R. Cammell singled out two sketches in particular: Ardfert Cathedral and Myrtle Grove in Youghal, the home of Sir Walter Raleigh: 'For such delicacy and evocative power they may be spoken of with such masterpieces as Turner's vignettes on copper illustrating the poems of Rogers and Thomas Campbell.'[45] Under the heading 'The Brave Smell of a Stone', Trevor Roycroft, in the *Irish Christian Advocate*, said that although the book was undeniably impressive he felt 'it is all over-burdened with archaeological repetitiveness which must pall upon all but the most rabid of enthusiasts.' But he added: 'One glimpses through the narrative the pleasurable journeys of happy partners in what must have been a satisfying and rewarding pilgrimage.'[46] The *Church of Ireland Gazette* reviewer, under the headline: 'Give it to your Rector', said the book was compulsory reading for clergy and laity alike and 'you could do a lot worse things with your three guineas … even if you don't want to read the text it would be worthwhile to buy the book and decorate the best bedroom with the illustrations.'[47]

Whatever the opinion of critics on his writing, there was universal praise for Piper's sketches. The five *This is Ireland* books are of their time, and his final literary milestone, *Munster and the City of Cork*, stands as Hayward's testimony. Piper's sketches (Leinster sixty-five, Ulster seventy-eight, Galway fifty-six, *MSLR* forty-two, Munster 120) collectively run to 361 for the five books, and remain a valuable record of an Ireland, in some cases, long gone. The scale of the journey was epic – not necessarily in geographical terms – but from the sheer volume of information and the number of places visited. Together they ticked off more than 500 sites of historic and archaeological importance.

Although he received many positive reviews, in some respects Hayward's stock was always higher among readers than critics, who liked to highlight his fondness of purple prose and rambling passages. The editor of the *Dictionary of Irish Literature*, Robert Hogan, while acknowledging that his travel books are informal and minutely knowledgeable, felt that they were 'finally a bit irksome to read because of obtrusive stage-Ulster jocularity.' He compares them, somewhat unfavourably, with Padraic Colum's *The Road Round Ireland*, Harold Speakman's *Here's Ireland*, and Thackeray's *Sketch Book*.[48]

Clearly certain words and phrases date the books and Hayward indulges freely in the flowery language of enthusiasm. Chapters overflow with a high density of words such as lovely, magnificent and beautiful interspersed with verily and bejewelled. In *Mayo Sligo Leitrim & Roscommon* the number of picturesque's skewed seriously out of control running to a total of twenty-seven. There is an antique flavour to some of the writing. But whatever the demerits of his prose, Hayward succeeds in answering the two essential questions that constitute engaging travel or place writing. The first is: What is a land and its people who live in it really like? And secondly: How did they come to be as they are today? Time and again, through the people he meets, he effectively links the past to the present, encapsulating the twin pillars of people and place.

He had the capacity to indulge in excursuses but also the ability to distil a vast amount of historical information into readable prose, disentangling dry facts and animating the past. Rigorous in historiography, Hayward's depth of research, sense of history and powers of observation contributed to his skill as a writer. In his 1938 Ulster book he refers to historical accuracy. He mentions the fact that the Sham Fight at Scarva in County Down is fought at a site 'that is too far north for those who are sticklers for historical accuracy.' And in a throwaway line he adds: '... and sure who cares about historical accuracy anyway?' It is fair to assume that Hayward wrote this flippantly with tongue firmly in cheek. He cared about historical accuracy, which is evident from the weight of research and fusillade of careful fact-checking. This point was highlighted by the academic Richard Kirkland in his study of the Northern Revival in Ireland from 1890 to 1960. 'Hayward,' he wrote, 'was a liberal Protestant writer of a type increasingly rare in Ireland during this period who gained some success with *In Praise of Ulster* ... a work that corrected and revised some of the enthusiastic excesses of historical detail found in the writings of more forthrightly national figures such as Bigger.'[49]

When the Munster book came out in the autumn of 1964 Hayward was again on the crest of a popularity wave. His final volume in the series, it gained wide coverage with promising early sales and his critical esteem was high. Indefatigable as ever, his life was packed with engagements. Full of schemes and projects, he was hoping to visit Europe again with Dorothy and travel with her to meet Rex, his brother in South Africa. Rex had written in early October suggesting that he should come on a lecture tour and write a book based on the impact made by the country on a stranger. 'There is so much nonsense and vituperation going around in Ireland', he wrote, 'that I would dearly love to present the facts.'[50] Rex also sent five inscribed copies of the Munster book to the prime minister at his residence in Pretoria as a token of the high regard in which he held his brother.

New ideas on Ireland were bubbling. His literary agent had mooted the possibility of a personal one-volume book on Ireland, along the lines of that originally envisaged for the American market in the 1940s. Hayward had discussed with Dorothy taking a cottage in the south or west of Ireland with a view to researching and writing a book together. No location had been chosen and the idea was at the embryonic stage. They had intended to work on it jointly, pooling their skills and experience as well as their knowledge of Ireland.

On 26 September he delighted in placing a notice in the newspaper about the birth in Chicago of his second grandson, Richard Laurence, first son of Ricky. The middle of October marked the fortieth anniversary of his life in broadcasting; it had been four decades since his first radio work with Elma and Tyrone Guthrie recording scenes from Shakespeare plays in the small BBC Studio 2BE. He had been booked to take part in Radio Balmoral, a week-long series of events, including 'Meet the Stars' organized by the Northern Ireland Radio Retailers Association at the King's Hall in south Belfast. Some of the Irish stars included Val Doonican, Brendan O'Dowda and Ronnie Carroll, part of a BBC radio anniversary programme planned for the evening of 19 October. Before an invited audience, Hayward was to record 'Irish Rhythms' with the BBC Northern Ireland Light Orchestra conducted by David Curry to be broadcast on the Northern Ireland Home Service on 22 October. He was also to give a recital on his Irish harp and would be accompanied by the singers Janette Simpson and Harold Gray. On the Saturday he was planning to visit Dublin to deliver an address to a meeting of Irish PEN on the novelist Donn Byrne. Amongst other projects on which he was working was the preparation of a 12-inch-long playing disc that would tell the history of the Orange Order in word and song from its beginnings in 1795. On the evening of Monday, 12 October he had attended a meeting at Clifton Street Orange Hall in north Belfast where details of it were discussed. His brain was fertile in many directions and such a hectic week's activities typified his life of perpetual motion. No one could have guessed the awful shock that lay in store.

FIFTEEN

Tragedy strikes

(1964)

They told me, Heraclitus, they told me you were dead,
They brought me bitter news to hear and bitter tears to shed.
I wept as I remembered how often you and I
Had tired the sun with talking and sent him down the sky.
                              William Cory, 'Heraclitus'

Most of us remember how beautifully he played the harp and how like he
seemed to one's conception of the Irish harpers of long ago.
                              Jeanne Cooper Foster

The gold dust of his zest for living seemed to brush off on everyone he met.
                              Ian Fox, Director, Fox's Glacier Mints

The next morning, Tuesday, 13 October 1964 began like any other day. As
part of his usual routine, Hayward drove his 1960 Ford Anglia into his office
in Bedford Street to deal with correspondence and finalize arrangements for
several forthcoming big events. He was due at lunchtime that day in Ballymena
to give a talk to the Rotary Club on folklore, something that he had done
with numerous organizations on countless occasions. En route he stopped for a
coffee and chat with Dorothy at Clonsilla on the Antrim Road, saying goodbye
to her just before 11.30 am. But this was the last time she saw him alive and they
were the last words he spoke to her. On his way to the Adair Arms Hotel, in the

townland of Cromkill two miles from Ballymena, his car crashed head on into another vehicle on the road and Hayward, along with two people in the other car, was killed.

The car was driven by the Rev. Stanley Dunlop, an assistant curate in Bally-willan Parish Church in Portrush. He was killed along with his mother Violet Dunlop. Another passenger (their housekeeper), Lavinia Kew received severe head injuries and was taken to the Waveney Hospital in Ballymena. The accident happened on a straight stretch of road. Newspapers reported that workmen at the side of the road were spattered with glass and had to jump clear when the cars crashed.[1] Emergency services, including fire and police, were called but by the time they arrived, the workmen had already wrenched open the doors and extricated the bodies from the cars.[2] Three ambulances were called and Hayward's body was also taken to the Waveney Hospital. No one was sure what had caused the accident. Road conditions were wet but the most likely explanation was that Hayward had suffered a heart attack. An inquest would later determine the cause of death.

It was a cruelly ironic end for a man who had spent so much of his life driving the roads of Ireland for forty years. The accident happened less than twenty miles across the mid-Antrim countryside from Larne, the place where he had spent a happy childhood. It was a profoundly shocking and sudden end to an industrious and distinguished life, a tragedy for both the Hayward and Dunlop families. Just eleven days short of his seventy-second birthday, the man who for years had entertained and enriched so many was stilled. His life, which began on an October day, ended seventy-two years later; on an October afternoon on a country road, a unique voice had fallen silent.

Dorothy was told of the accident in a phone call at 12.45 pm. In an instant her world changed irrevocably. She was devastated. They had enjoyed barely three years of companionship and shared enthusiasms but still had much to do together. Their immediate plans and everything they had been looking forward to counted for nothing. Her stepsons were a long way from Belfast. Dion worked in New Zealand while Ricky was engaged in cancer-cell research at Chicago University. Death in a car accident is never easy to cope with for grieving relatives but when the immediate family is thousands of miles away it is even more difficult.

Hayward was a man of such personal magnetism and distinctive presence that it was difficult for many to accept that his life had been snuffed out in a matter of seconds. It took time for the unexpected and heartbreaking news to sink in, for his family and close friends to come to terms with the circumstances of what had happened. Within hours, telegrams of condolence arrived. In the days that followed, letters began to pour in from stunned friends, loved ones and strangers. Dorothy was overwhelmed with a tidal wave of correspondence and sympathy cards from all corners of the world and while this offered consolation, she was in the depths of despair.

Shockwaves reverberated across Ireland. The newspaper headlines made frightful reading and all the main Irish daily papers recorded Richard Hayward's death in detail, most putting it on the front page. It was the lead news story in the daily Belfast newspapers and reported on radio and television. The *Belfast News Letter* devoted part of its front page to the accident along with a photograph of the smashed car. A report inside headlined 'Culture Loses Man of Note' reflected on the fact that he was 'an authority on so many facets of Ulster life'. The paper carried a tribute from his artist friend Raymond Piper. 'Hayward was a man of impish ways, great humour, and broad mind. Apart from the personal loss by his wife and family, Ireland has lost a man who has contributed more than anybody else to the culture of our country.'[3]

The writer and broadcaster James Boyce reflected on the fact that Hayward's abilities were recognized abroad more so than at home. 'It is sad that Richard had to wait for recognition from America, but I am sure that Ulster artists are inured to this kind of disregard.'[4] The *News Letter* reported on how he liked lunching at Belfast's Abercorn restaurant in Castle Lane. 'He was known to all members of the staff. One waitress, Vickey, since retired, had served his lunch for more than half a century.'[5] The *Irish News* spread the story over six columns on its front page under the headline: 'Three die in Ballymena Road Crash' with a subheading: 'Author Richard Hayward Killed'.[6]

Despite the fact that a British general election was about to take place that same week, the papers gave prominent coverage to his death and its aftermath with an outpouring of admiration. By the end of the week Harold Wilson had been elected the youngest prime minister in seventy years while Khrushchev had resigned as Russia's prime minister and Communist Party leader. But for Dorothy, beyond sadness, it was a week in which she and her husband's legions of friends and followers tried to make sense of what had happened.

In Dublin the news was reported with an equal sense of loss. *The Irish Press*, a paper that had frequently run extensive reviews of Hayward's plays, films and books, put the story on its front page and carried an obituary.

Newspaper front pages on the morning of 14 October 1964 tell the harrowing story of the car crash in which Hayward and two other people were killed. *The Irish News* reported the tragedy with widespread coverage.

The Irish Independent showed Hayward's car and the two workmen, John Darragh and James Douglas, who jumped clear when the crash happened.

A memoir of Hayward was written by W.A. Newman in his 'Talking Points' column. Newman eloquently summed up the views of many throughout Ireland when he wrote that: 'He was the sort of man you thought incapable of dying, so vivacious and energetic was he even in an age when most people have reconciled themselves to reminiscences and the armchair.' He had met Hayward at intervals over the years and wrote that he found him:

> Every time more zestful, every time avid of some new interest, every time more animated and more amusing company. Yes I know he infuriated some people and was somewhat of a storm petrel in the literary circles of Belfast … nevertheless he will be sorely missed and I fancy that more than a few people will follow his coffin to Carnmoney.'[7]

Newman also looked back on his literary legacy:

> And what a worker! I have lost count of his books, but six of them are on my shelves and that must be well under half of the full sum. Many of our Irish writers have grand reputations but only a small fraction of that output – and not necessarily of better quality! … How well he knew Ireland, and how many friends he has acquired in the process of acquiring his knowledge.[8]

Newspaper obituaries spoke of his genial nature and artistic legacy. *The Irish Times* gave proper weight to his achievements with a lengthy two-column 1000-word obituary:

> He took the view that the Gaelic language was the indispensable key to the understanding of Irish literature and culture, and, as such should be possessed by every Irishman … Later in his life he knew the Gaelic names of every mountain, stream, townland and village and he considered that the knowledge of these names threw a flood of light upon the past.[9]

The paper quoted a close friend: 'He was so alive in every way and he is as great a loss to Ireland as he is to his own family.'[10] The *Irish Independent* covered the story on its front page with a photograph of the wrecked car. In its obituary the *Independent* reflected on how his Munster book had been widely acclaimed and quoted Hayward's literary agent, J.N. McGarry, saying he had been mulling over writing a new book on Ireland. 'When I last saw him I suggested he should distil all his travel books into one called Hayward's Ireland. This would have completed the series. The tragedy is he died before the book could be written.'[11] In a brief news story, *The Times* said Hayward was one of Ulster's most colourful and versatile characters. His traditional ballads had a worldwide sale and the paper noted that his *Orange and Blue* record was chosen by a British panel as one of the six outstanding recordings of 1956.[12]

On Friday afternoon, 16 October, four days after the accident, a private service was held at Melville's funeral parlour in Townsend Street in Belfast followed by a short service at Roselawn Crematorium. The family had requested privacy, and a memorial service was planned. In the meantime Hayward's friends, diminished by his passing, busied themselves writing affectionate personal tributes and appreciations. Next day in the *Belfast Telegraph*, Jeanne Cooper Foster, whom he had known through the Belfast Centre of Irish PEN, of which he had three times been chairman, said he was the 'embodiment of everything an Irishman should be: witty, gay, charming and kindly':

> I often watched with fascination and no little envy how completely he could captivate an audience. He was a scholar but he carried his learning lightly, and it was typical of his generosity and lack of pomposity that he would as willingly address a dozen people in a village as a learned audience in the city. In this day and age of narrow, and frequently arid specialisation, Richard shone as a man of many talents, one who refused to have his mind cabined, cribbed or confined.[13]

In the weeks following the accident, a distraught Dorothy set about the harrowing process of dealing with hundreds of sympathy letters. She was also swamped with phone calls and condolences, mostly from Ireland and Britain but also from all over the world. One of the most poignant of all communications came the day after the accident from a Church of Ireland minister, Dr Michael Dewar. Originally from London, then rector of Magherally near Banbridge in County Down, he had known Hayward for nearly twenty years. He was one of the first to hear of the tragedy. Immediately he sent Dorothy a simple seven-word telegram from Banbridge Post Office, invoking the Greek philosopher Heraclitus:

'Ulsters Heraclitus Scholar, Entertainer, Friend, Dewar, Magherally'.[14] On a plain white postcard Dewar wrote a moving 'In Memorian', quoting William Cory's 'Heraclitus':

> They told me, Heraclitus, they told me you were dead,
> They brought me bitter news to hear and bitter tears to shed.
> I wept as I remembered how often you and I
> Had tired the sun with talking and sent him down the sky.

But now that thou art lying, my dear old Carian guest,
A handful of grey ashes, long, long ago at rest,
Still are thy pleasant voices, thy nightingales, awake;
For Death, he taketh all away, but them he cannot take.[15]

It was a fitting epitaph. Dewar had collected Hayward's books and ballads and often discussed literature, history and other aspects of Irish culture with him far into the night. Hayward had promised to pay a visit to Magherally church in the new year to give a talk to parishioners. One week after his death, Dewar wrote a tribute in the *Belfast News Letter:*

> As the years found me more deeply rooted in Ulster I discovered that this vivacious scholar, poet and humorist was not only an Ulsterman but also in the fullest sense of the word, an Irishman. Now he has become part of the living history of that Ireland he loved and lived in. As long as his songs are sung, the harp strings touched, and the tales are told, Richard of the Welcomes will never be dead.[16]

Hayward's remarkable personality touched many people. Numerous adjectives summed up his life: benign, merry, jolly, cheerful, kind, convivial, and sparkling were some of the words used by sympathizers in the 350 letters Dorothy received. From arts-related groups, institutions, commercial organizations, social clubs and individuals, they are the tangible proof of his popularity. Some were from strangers. Reading through them, the esteem in which he was held by all who knew him, however fleetingly, is apparent. Aside from disbelief about the accident, many speak of his zest for life and highlight his contribution to Ireland. Others mention his gift for friendship and his many qualities; a common theme is the fact that his name will be cherished for a long time to come. He gave endless enjoyment to countless people and epitomized the spirit of Ulster. A sense of desolation about his loss is palpable. Some of the most moving correspondence is between Dorothy and her stepsons. Two days after the accident, Dion wrote from New Zealand:

> Inadequate as the written word may be, it is unfortunately our only means of expressing to you our profound grief at the awful news this week has brought us. I find it hard to marshal my thoughts at a time when I have much to say. One of the hardest things is the feeling of utter helplessness to assist you to bear the burden of your sorrow.[17]

At the end of the month, his brother Rex, whom he had planned to visit, wrote from South Africa:

The news had a terrible effect upon me and I had a haemorrhage and was ordered to stay in bed. Richard and I were so close with our common love of Ireland. I don't know what more to say. I am heartbroken and know you must feel the same. If we cannot meet in person do let us write regularly. Our love for Richard deserves it. The tears are coming again so I must close now with all our love.[18]

Several weeks later Rex again wrote to Dorothy, saying he would like to get to know her better.

Richard was a changed man when he married you. Before then, rightly or wrongly, I thought him a selfish man in some ways ... and so I must agree that Richard had 'deepened to a new maturity' to use your words. Mind you in this modern world it is the selfish ones who get on. So you can take full credit for bringing about a closer coming together of Richard and me.[19]

In a letter six weeks later, Dorothy replied, 'I don't think I will ever get over Richard's tragic death. Nothing has ever affected me so much.'[20] Dorothy had in mind to write a book on Richard and she had asked Rex for ancestral information. He replied, providing some illuminating details of his brother's life:

Richard's first interest was the boy scout movement and from that developed his interest in the theatre and the Ulster Players. Our father was one of the greatest riders to hounds in Ireland hunting with the Wexford harriers. Richard's family life had nothing to do with his parents' interests. He was a lone wolf, starting from scratch, and attaining a stature of which we are all very proud. We were a family of children influenced by our Ulster environment with many diametrically opposed views on politics and religion. In spite of opposing views we always remained loving to each other as brothers and sisters to the end.[21]

Touching letters and many tributes are reflected in the archive and range alphabetically from the Amstel Brewery in Amsterdam to the Young Ulster Society. Scores of letters arrived from organizations for whom he worked such as Fox's and Needler's, publishing firms, newspapers, the BBC and UTV, and a large number of clubs and social groups to whom he had delivered talks. Amongst these were the Belfast Shakespeare Society, Belfast Naturalists' Field Club, Ulster Unionist Party, Orange Order, Donaghadee and District Horticultural Society, Dublin Gramophone Society and the Public Record Office of Northern Ireland. The headmaster of Larne Grammar School wrote to say that he had been a good friend of theirs and had given encouragement to pupils to find out for themselves the richness of the life of the countryside and in this he 'rendered a valuable service to education'. John-Lewis Crosby, the secretary of the National Trust in Northern Ireland, wrote, 'A light has gone out over Ulster and indeed Ireland'.[22] Capt O.W.J. Henderson, the owner of the *Belfast News Letter* said, 'How tragically sad it was to hear of the news this afternoon about Richard. Only last night he was at L.O.L. 7, and as usual, was the life and soul of our meeting.'[23] The director of Fox's Glacier Mints, Ian Fox and his wife Marjorie, sent sympathy: 'He enjoyed life to the full and some of the gold dust of his zest for living seemed to brush off on everyone he met.'[24] Ivan Grainger from the Irish Astronomical Society wrote that 'he spread an aura of friendship and happiness around him wherever he went, a warmth that one could not resist, with his twinkling eyes and good natured humour.'[25]

Some of the most effusive praise came from longtime friends in acting, writing and broadcasting. The actor John D. Stewart wrote:

It consoles his friends, although not you, that he got so much of himself on permanent record in one medium or another. New generations can go meeting him in his books and appreciate his times, his places and the man himself. He needs no other monument. I am so glad that he got the Munster book finished and published, that he lived long enough to receive his honours from university and state and to greet his grandson. His lifetime of work and achievement had reached its peak and crown and that is all I can say. Thousands of people in many places, all classes and creeds, will miss him and speak of him with great affection.[26]

Harold Goldblatt, who thirty years earlier had made his stage debut in Hayward's production of Carnduff's *Castlereagh*, wrote:

His roots were implanted in the soil of the country he loved, and he dreamed and worked for a great cultural renaissance. I never knew him to lose his temper. He had a great sense of humour. It is hard to believe that that noble countenance and jaunty gait is no more but he has left behind him an affectionate memory and a wealth of folklore and culture which will remain for all time. Truly he lived a noble and useful life.[27]

Ray Rosenfield, a journalist and drama critic, wrote from Oxford: 'I can't think that I shan't ever again enjoy his quips and be dazzled by his memory for detail and his sheer zest for life, which, of course, was his most exciting characteristic.'[28] The distinguished historian, J.C. Beckett, Professor of Irish history at Queen's University, who two years later wrote *The Making of Modern Ireland*, felt a sense of personal loss:

He was such good company, so much alive, so full of eager interest in what was going on, that he brought with him a kind of infectious friendliness wherever he went. It is not easy to offer any comfort in so great a loss; but you have at least the consolation of knowing that for half a century or more he has given interest and pleasure to vast numbers of people not only those who met him personally, but also through his books, broadcasts and recordings to thousands of people all over the world.[29]

In an exchange of letters between Dorothy and Michael Geare, who worked for J.M. Dent and masterminded the promotional tour of Ireland, Geare wrote of his deep shock. 'Few people have packed more information, and wasted less time in their lives. And I am certain he enjoyed every moment of it.' He said an American firm had made an enquiry about handling the Munster book.[30] Dorothy replied to say that Richard had always hoped that one day the American market might be open to him and she wondered if the books in the *This is Ireland* series could be published in a paperback edition:

> One gets so tired of 'off the cuff' type of travel books, on some superficial level with the countries concerned as the 'Darling, do drop in for a drink.' Richard's quality of writing had always derived from a combination of knowledge, long loving and the humility of truth. I and my stepsons would be delighted if his books were to be welcomed in new markets. But here's the contrariness and the rub!! God save Ireland from the Tourist Hordes. Amen.[31]

A London-based friend of Hayward's, Philip Duncan, offered words of condolence:

> Later you will be proud of the affection he inspired. He was a darlin' man and I have good reason to remember much kindness and help from him. It was my ambition to travel amongst Ireland that Richard wrote so wonderfully about. I realized quite a bit of that ambition wherever I went I met people and mentioned that I knew Richard and faces would light up and one could feel a bond had been established between us ... Wherever I go in Ireland, be it North or South, I will always feel his presence near me and shall be thankful for his help and guidance.[32]

Another London business associate, L. Duncan-Doring, who knew him through the confectionery trade, wrote about their friendship: 'What a marvellous chap he was. He virtually rivalled Abou Ben Adhem with his love for his fellow men. The last occasion I met him was when we went up to Leicester for a farewell party. We sat yarning late into the night with a lot of other people and at breakfast we were still celebrating. Instead of the proverbial hotel coffee, we drank champagne.'[33] Betsy and Patric Stevenson from Hillsborough in County Down said their pen was inadequate to express their sorrow:

An unfailing vein of gaiety has been rudely wrecked out of the life of Ireland and the source of many a good-humored chuckle – whether in the Drawing Room of Government House or in a cottage or a pub in Connemara or Cork or on 'The Road to Athy', and has been taken from us. We are all immeasurably the poorer by his death: Ireland will not be the same island without him but wherever they go in future years all Irish travellers will be companioned by him, for his writings will live and prove the best and most dependable of guides to so much of enduring interest in the national heritage.[34]

Jerome Coffey from Kate Kearney's Cottage near Killarney said he was 'deeply grieved as he was one of my best friends.'[35] The City Manager and Town Clerk of Cork Corporation sent a letter on behalf of the Lord Mayor regretting 'the tragic death of your distinguished husband.'[36] The writer Stephen Rynne sent sympathy from Prosperous, Naas in County Kildare: 'The tragic news has cast a shadow over our house. He was so kindly, debonair, witty and a splendid Irishman. One consolation is that he lived to see the success of the Munster book. I am glad of that triumph.'[37] Sympathy letters came from the County Louth Archaeological Society of which Hayward had been a member since 1950. Rev. Diarmuid Maclomhair wrote that the society all had pleasant memories of him.[38] From Lord Moyne (the poet Bryan Guinness) of Castleknock in County Dublin to people who knew him only through his books, songs or films, they poured out their sorrow.

Some of the saddest correspondence came from people who had never met him but knew him by reputation. Mrs K. Thompson wrote from Liverpool to say that she had served in the sweet and tobacconists shop in Queen's Arcade, Belfast and had got to know him there and later read his books.[39] Many referred to his essential goodness, warm personality and sense of humour. One man, Giff Pitney, wrote to say that his 'regard for Richard was almost idolatrous.'[40] Elsie Patton, a member of PEN and friend of Dorothy's from Bangor, County Down, wrote: 'He really put into practice the second great tenet of Christianity, the brotherhood of man. Richard liked all kinds of human beings and in his mind there were no barriers between the races or social classes.'[41] Meta Reid, from Crawfordsburn, County Down, felt personal loss:

I am heartsick for you at the terrible waste of Richard – cut off before the ink on his new reviews was barely dry. I grieve personally too. He was part of my early literary life in Ulster. He was one of the last (I think) of the Irish wits and raconteurs, the blessed charming people who stayed young and made a party go, who kindled good talk. And so much more of course.[42]

Hazel Staples, the granddaughter of the artist Ponsonby Staples who formerly lived at Lissan House near Cookstown in County Tyrone, wrote from London:

I know how much his friendship meant to Pop who had so few real friends and I know how much Mummy looked forward to his visits to 'Lissan.' I shall remember him always playing upstairs in our old bathroom with its shabby paint and faded paper while Jimmy and Pippa sat up in bed in their pyjamas listening to his harp: they too will remember though the sound of the music is hushed, because for children today there are too few Richards who can spare the time to soften the edges of reality. I wish I could see you and do something for you but I send my love and my friendship.[43]

Many letters came from across the Atlantic. Gene Tunney wrote from New York:

Polly and I were very fond of your husband. We had the good fortune to be guided by Richard on a week's tour of Ireland some twelve or thirteen years ago, and saw him whenever he visited this country. Richard was an extraordinarily unusual man with many facets – intellectual, humorous and musical. All who knew him on this side of the ocean loved him.[44]

An envelope in the Folk Museum Hayward archive contains more than thirty telegrams, sent on either 13 or 14 October. They include one from Frank O'Connor, offering deepest sympathy from himself and the members of the Dublin branch of PEN.[45] From the National Museum of Ireland, Neil Prendergast referred to 'the sunshine of his happiness', adding that he achieved more for 'the good relations and happiness of Irish people from Belfast to Cork than anyone in our time.'[46] Another Dublin friend with whom he had enjoyed so many happy times, Mollie Quinn, expressed deep sorrow to Dorothy:

I was so upset and worried about you since our telephone conversation on Wednesday that I made up my mind at once to do something about it. The enclosed card may not be very clear to you but briefly it means that you will be prayed for every day by the Capuchins for the rest of your life. It may help you in your present very sad and lonely time.[47]

On behalf of Sligo Field Club, Michael Cahalane recalled the pleasure Hayward's visits had brought:

His work for Ireland in archaeology and folklore will serve as a lasting monument to his memory but, above all, he shall be remembered by all who had the pleasure of knowing him, for his charming company, ready wit and deep understanding of his fellow men everywhere.[48]

One place where his death was most heartfelt was Kilkenny. For twenty years Hayward had been a member of the Kilkenny Archaeological Society. Always interested in its activities, he was one of the original guarantors of the Rothe House scheme. Maureen Hegarty of the KAS wrote: 'Here in Kilkenny where he was well known and admired, the news was heard with widespread grief.'[49] Daisy Phelan, also from Kilkenny, asked: 'Where will we meet his like again? So original, sincere, humorous and spontaneous – god rest him and comfort you – all here who knew him are distressed for you – and sorry for themselves to have lost so loyal a friend to Kilkenny. His Way, his own 'Hayward' way was but much appreciated by us all.'[50] Ten days after his death a tribute was published in the *Kilkenny People*:

His abrupt passing has caused great regret and distress for his wife, and nowhere is this regret and distress more sincere than in Kilkenny. He had a great liking for us down here, and we for him – not for the scholar merely, or the raconteur, but for the man himself, so approachable, friendly, lively and young. I think we all got a shock when we saw his age was 72. His ways were not those of a septuagenarian. In 1961 the annual outing was to Belfast. He had been inviting us for years and he was a wonderful host and guide. None could resist his enthusiasm. The rain that fell on some occasions was just ignored. Before the light of his bright knowledge and scholarship all little disturbances just faded away ... May the clay lie lightly on him.[51]

SIXTEEN

Final parting

Are we to believe that the fine mind of Richard Hayward is to be extinguished? We can only hope that his spirit of friendship will live for ever.

Rev. D. Frazer-Hurst

Three weeks after the dark shadow of the fateful crash, close friends, acquaintances and admirers of Hayward's work gathered in Belfast to honour the passing of a man of many parts. More than 300 people filled St Anne's Cathedral on 4 November, swapping stories and remembering the wealth of different roles he had played in a packed life. They came, many still incredulous, to pay unstinting tribute, not only to 'a great Irishman'[1] but also a charismatic, mercurial character who had done so much to delineate the cultural history of the land he loved.

The sheer range of his preoccupations was reflected in the many-sidedness of the mourners and the affection in which he was held. Richard Hayward was never short of friends. Political, literary, artistic and business Ireland came out in force to replay his life. Churchmen, politicians, writers, journalists, broadcasters, historians, librarians, actors, singers and artists filled the seats of St Anne's. Prominent figures in the Commercial Travellers' Association and the confectionery trade included representatives of Needler's and Fox's Glacier Mints, the two firms for whom he had worked for a lifetime. Many in attendance were from organizations and societies with which he was associated. The Lord Mayor of

Belfast, Councillor William Jenkins, was present. RUC officers, including the Inspector General, and staff from Queen's University sat alongside friends from the Young Ulster Society and a contingent from Belfast Naturalists' Field Club. Members of the Sligo Field Club as well as the Kilkenny and County Louth Archaeological Societies travelled to Belfast. The bond that Hayward had established with his public was evident.

Distance prevented Ricky being at the service although Dion did make the journey from New Zealand. Ricky had come over from the US three weeks earlier to attend his father's funeral. Some who attended had never met Hayward and knew him only through his films, songs or books. Brendan Adams, his nephew and close associate, was in the congregation. His friend from the field club trips of the 1950s, Prof Richard Clarke, recalls the mood of disbelief at the service:

> There was a lot of shock and grief and we were all horrified at what happened. It was a huge crowd and was one of the biggest events ever held in the cathedral as he was such a great local figure. His charisma and personality created the image that led to his popularity and once the man and the personality had gone then people could not identify with him and sadly they later forgot about him.[2]

The tall thin figure of Raymond Piper quietly contemplated the fulfilling years they had spent together driving around the back roads, the people they met and friendships enjoyed.[3] Amongst the writers who turned up were Mary Lavin and Frank O'Connor who just weeks earlier had written a whimsical review of the Munster book for the *Sunday Independent*. Tyrone Guthrie, now Sir, the man who gave Hayward his singing break forty years earlier and who had been appointed Chancellor of Queen's University in 1963, was also present.

The order of service booklet listed a varied career, comprising some of his roles but was by no means exhaustive: 'Author, Actor, Poet, Humorist, Lecturer, Naturalist and Singer, he loved the company of his fellowmen.' They came to remember a man who had lived through the Boer War, two devastating World Wars and a Cold War, the Easter Rising, the Irish war of independence and civil war. In a life stretching from the Victorian to the early years of the Elizabethan era, he witnessed the reign of six monarchs. He lived through the decline of the British Empire and the changing cultural face of twentieth-century Ireland, which he recorded so graphically.

Five clergymen, including the Bishop of Connor, the Rt Rev. R.C.H.G. Elliott, and the Dean of Belfast, the Very Rev. C.I. Peacocke, took part. Although a solemn service, warm tributes were paid and Hayward's humour was reflected. In his address, the Presbyterian minister, Rev. Dr Frazer-Hurst, who had officiated at the marriage to Dorothy in 1962, referred to 'the abrupt and harsh finality' to his life:

> I had known him for many years and was familiar with his numerous accomplishments but I came within the orbit of his friendship when I had the privilege of marrying them and thought they were ideally suited to one another with their kindred interests. Their marriage was so harmonious and so happy and you felt their warm radiance. I appreciated Richard Hayward's many sided personality in fuller measure. He had reached out into many fields of knowledge of which I knew little and acquired a great respect for his breadth of mind and the sanity of his judgements. He knew everything related to his own business and knew not a little but a very great deal about a quite extraordinary number of things. He had that prerequisite of all knowledge – a desire to learn … his Protestant faith did not prevent him from having a full understanding of the religious feeling in Catholic poetry such as in Padraic Colum's 'Cradle Song' and the line 'O men from the fields' with its touching simplicity. He was very sensitive to the spirit of a place and in his visits to churches and monastic ruins he would remark on the peace that still seemed to dwell in places where prayer was wont to be made. In his love of nature there was a strain of awe and wonder at the mystery that lies behind all the beauty of this visible universe. His wife tells me that if he found some little plant clinging precariously to life in the crevice of a rock or stone wall he would almost invariably quote with deep feeling the beautiful lines of Tennyson's poem 'Flower in a crannied wall.'[4]

Rev. Frazer-Hurst said that with such insight and depth of sympathy it is not surprising that Hayward responded to many appeals for help and good causes or to assist friends through his gifts as singer, musician or lecturer. 'I am sure there is not a person present in this cathedral this afternoon who is not beholden to Richard Hayward for some personal kindness.' He continued:

> His humour sprang up like a fountain sparkling in the sunshine. His wit was iridescent and wherever he was there was laughter and friendship and one was sure to find happiness … One would have thought at his age he would have been contented to rest on his laurels, but Dr Hayward had made it clear that he intended to visit Europe and to take part in the forthcoming BBC anniversary programme.[5]

Rev. Frazer-Hurst told the congregation that Hayward's books would be a permanent reminder of 'this great man' as would his many recordings:

Through his work he can still speak to his friends and to later generations. We can put on some of his many records and listen to him singing the songs and ballads for which he was famous or open one of his books in his company and travel the highways of Ireland wandering with him amongst monastic ruins or the green loanings that he loved. Are we to believe that the fine mind of Richard Hayward is to be extinguished? We can only hope that his spirit of friendship will live for ever.[6]

The eyes of the world that bleak November day were focused on the announcement of President Lyndon B. Johnson sweeping back to the White House in the biggest election win in America's history. But in Belfast those who attended the poignant service in St Anne's were caught up with their own personal thoughts of the past rather than the present.

Hot on the heels of the service, the inquest was held the next day into the deaths of all three killed in the accident. Dorothy did not attend the hearing in Ballymena courthouse but instructed a solicitor, Henry Catchpole, who had known Hayward for many years, to read a statement on her behalf. A graphic description was read of Hayward's last few minutes and of how workmen on the side of the road had to jump clear when the cars crashed. Two labourers, John Darragh from Kilrea and James Douglas from Rasharkin, were working at the scene. They described how Hayward's car veered suddenly to the wrong side of the road for no apparent reason. The other car had no time to take evasive action. Both vehicles collided head on. No evidence was offered as to why Hayward's car had swerved to the wrong side although questions were raised about his tiredness and general workload.[7]

Dorothy's statement said that her husband had been in his usual good health and spirits when he left her on the morning of 13 October. He had had a medical examination on 8 October and felt well, except for a little tiredness that he attributed to recent pressure of work. The inquest was told that the insurance company proposed to take the line that he was unconscious and perhaps died as a result of a heart attack or seizure before the impact. The state pathologist, Dr D.J. Carson, concluded that all three individuals died from injuries received in the crash. Post-mortem examinations of both drivers showed no disease to cause or accelerate death or collapse. Open verdicts were returned on each of them.[8] The inquest marked the close of a series of sad events that kept Hayward's name in the public domain – but as Dorothy continued to mourn her loss, his name refused to disappear from the public imagination.

Less than two weeks after the service, the question of a memorial was raised in press correspondence columns. The *Belfast News Letter* carried a letter from Miss V.I.D. Stewart of Donaghadee, County Down, who wrote that she was 'voicing the opinions of a great many people regretting his untimely and tragic death':

> I know that for 10 years with a team of co-workers he compiled and edited a dictionary of dialect words and this was hard work – Dr Hayward himself said. The dictionary, illustrated by maps, is now in the Folk Museum at Cultra. Dr Hayward's books on the Irish provinces are now available but pensioners like myself can not afford all these. As a graduate of Queen's University I should now like to see recognition of worth and not let a great man go unwept, unhonoured and unsung. He will not be unwept.[9]

In a detailed response a week later, Brendan Adams rose to his late uncle's defence. 'Miss Stewart,' he wrote 'is sadly misinformed' about Hayward's contribution to dialect studies in Ulster:

> It does ill service to the memory of Dr Hayward, and to the painstaking field-work and consultation which he was wont to undertake before publishing his numerous books, to obscure the genuine contribution which he made to promote the study of Ulster dialects by attribution to him work which he did not, and in some respects, could not have done, especially when your correspondent could so easily have checked the substance of her statements before rushing into print … A fitting memorial would be to bring together all the Ulster speech which abounds throughout his public works.[10]

Two weeks later it was mooted that one of four new blocks of multi-storey flats in the Rathcoole estate in Newtownabbey, north of Belfast, should be named after Hayward. The Urban Council recommended to the Northern Ireland Housing Trust that instead of one of the suggested names – Barna House, Belmore House, Iona House and Innis House – one of the blocks be named Hayward House. The council felt that because the family had lived nearby at Silverstream in Greenisland it would be a fitting memorial.[11] Nothing came of this proposal but the question of a memorial periodically raised its head in the years that followed.

Two events honoured his name in the spring of 1965. On 12 March, the youth guild from the parish of Magherally near Banbridge presented 'A Richard Hayward Evening', a social night of stories, songs and scenic slides. Held in Magherally Presbyterian Hall, it was introduced by Michael Dewar, a man determined to retain his memory. The following week, at a St Patrick's Tide morning service in St John the Evangelist Church at Magherally, Dewar dedicated a memorial oak book rest for the Holy Table in Hayward's honour. Presented as a gift from Dorothy – who attended the service – and her stepsons, it reads:

In Loving memory of
Richard Hayward, Ulsterman 1892–1964
Presented by his wife, Dorothy and his sons Dion and Richard
St. Patrick's Tide, 1965

In his sermon, Dewar paid tribute to 'the friend who, more than any man, brought me to Ulster, and helped make me what I am proud to be – an Ulsterman by adoption … for this I have to thank my friend, Richard of the Welcomes, Richard of the Songs and Laughter.' Originally from London, Dewar had first come across *In Praise of Ulster* in the summer of 1943 in a book-shop in Charing Cross Road. A staunch supporter of Orangeism, he wrote five booklets on its history and relevance. He referred to the fact that Hayward had agreed to come to Magherally early in 1965 to give a talk to parishioners and friends of the church:

But he could not come. Fate decreed otherwise. I saw him once weaving his way like a sprightly twenty-year-old among the traffic of Royal Avenue. I held my breath, and did not distract him – and two weeks later it was my sad, proud lot to help comfort the widow whom I had never met …. How perfectly the old writer of Ecclesiasticus describes the art of Richard Hayward in those lines – 'such as found out musical tunes, and recited verses in writing.' More than fifty years ago this perennially 'young man' gave to Ulstermen and women, in song and story, the age-old lyrics and ballads of their race … he saved the traditions of the truest folk life of a mighty folk – the Ulstermen … And as he sang, so he wrote. A dozen stout volumes show that all Ireland had his heart, but none will 'speak home' to one louder, or more heartsomely, than *In Praise of Ulster* – greatest and most famous of his books. There he writes in rich, poetic prose of gem-like, pictorial quality. He lived long enough to know that at least one reader in distant England was infected. So you see, perhaps, why his widow has come on behalf of her step-sons and herself to worship with us, 'near Banbridge town' where once shone the 'Star of the County Down' where grew 'The Flower of Magherally-O.' She comes also to perpetuate her loved one's memory in our little church with a lasting gift – a beautiful oak book rest for use at the Celebration of the Lord's Supper at His Holy Table. She comes also to lay a tribute of white heather beside the new-made grave of Dr Helen Waddell, who also shall speak to us down the corridors of memory, as she, too, pays tribute to the land she loved – our kindly County Down, its little round hills, likened by Dr Hayward to a basket of eggs.[12]

The musical theme alluded to in Dewar's tribute continued that year with the posthumous release of two LPs. One record, in early summer, was a back-catalogue compilation 'Irish Night Out'. As well as singles by Richard and Elma Hayward, it included songs and sketches by names familiar to his followers over the years: Jimmy O'Dea, Harry O'Donovan, and Jimmy Mageean, plus the Loyal Brethren. The cover artwork featured sketch portraits of all the musicians but by this stage, with the Beatles dominating the charts, the music – for the critics at least – was past its listen-to date. *English Dance and Song* magazine said 'the songs are fine, but the Irish country humour (which once provided the ingredients for best selling 78s) sounds incredibly dated.'[13]

That summer Fontana also produced '12th of July Souvenir, The Songs and Sounds', which as well as being a 'best of' collection of his Orange ballads was also a tribute to Hayward. Leslie Mann, the Irish representative of the Philips group, had approached him in spring 1964 about bringing together a sound picture of the annual Orange celebrations and including his most popular songs. Hayward suggested that during the Twelfth parades that year tape recorders should be used in Sandy Row in the loyalist heart of Belfast, and in other areas, to record the scenes at the bonfires on the evening of 11 July. As well as the dedication of flags, the Lambeg drummers and pipers, the cheering children and thud of marching feet, the general musical atmosphere of the day was recorded on tape. In the event, he did not live long enough to see it produced, and a replacement, Roy Dickson, a young folk singer from Bally-money in north Antrim, was found to record the songs. They include ones that Hayward frequently performed: 'The Sash My Father Wore', 'The Ride on the Goat', 'Derry's Walls' and 'No Surrender' as well as Hayward's own trademark song 'The Wee Shop'. Dickson also added 'The Ballad of Richard Hayward', a tribute to the man who started it all.

On the sleeve cover, Mann described Hayward as 'the original Orange balladeer.' The extent of his posthumous popularity can be measured in the praise bestowed in an article in *Gramophone* in which W. A. Chislett wrote about '12th of July Souvenir':

> I confess that my eyes misted over when I heard this memorial to an old friend, as they did also when I heard 'The Sash My Father Wore', one of Richard's most famous songs and here sung by a man young enough to be his grandson with the same relish and fervour.[14]

Farther afield his memory was also being preserved too. On Whit Monday, June 1965, on the summit of Galtymore Mountain – the highest point in

Tipperary – a plaque was erected in memory of Hayward and of James Blake, a local man who drowned in a boating accident in Tangier. Hayward had known Blake through the Kilfeacle Beagles. The memorial bears the words 'The top victory of the peak', the motto on the buttonhole badge, which the Beagles issue to those who climb to the top.[15]

All this, during 1965, was a testing time for Dorothy. The fact that she was left with a large house as well as his estate, private matters and financial affairs to sort out, caused her stress. She was also told that she was ineligible for the widow's pension since she was not his first wife, a decision Ricky described as 'unnecessarily harsh'.[16] Alone with her thoughts, Dorothy lived a cloistered life in the house on the Antrim Road. Some words of Hayward's friend, John Hewitt, are apposite, 'sealed off from sight, rooms hugged bright memories'.[17] Left with the unenviable task of sorting out the estate she began to try to make some sense of a lifetime's mountain of private papers, letters, photographs and treasured books. There were also films, records and an *omnium gatherum* of artefacts including clothes such as Sam Mulhern's shirt worn by her husband in the 1930s' feature films and boxes of magic tricks. In a neatly typed letter some months after his death she wrote to Dion and Ricky about the income from the books:

> The royalties of the books for the three years 1962/3/4 and the estimate for the three years ahead make a total of £5,000 while money, stocks and shares come to £3,500. Royalties have been falling steadily due to the fact that all books, save the new one, are now out of print though odd copies of Border Foray can be bought.[18]

A Personal Accident Insurance Policy, she said, was to be met in full of £5000. The company was satisfied that his death was caused by the accident. 'But it is so terrible. It is literally blood money. I shall never know why it all had to happen as it did, when in the ordinary way I would have been with him and, if I had been, the accident would not have happened, at least I feel so.'[19] Hayward's estate totalled £13,460 and included Richard Hayward Film Productions Ltd., building society savings, life insurance policies and premium saving bonds. In his will he left £50 to the Ulster Unionist Party. Dorothy kept in touch with some of his friends, receiving annual letters and Christmas cards. But she refused to accept that he had died. Filled with self-pity, she indulged in magical thinking, an 'inner voice' that believed he would come back. Peter Cavan, who had known Hayward through the field club, was invited to the house for tea three years after his death:

The blinds were always kept down, and the blood-spattered raincoat that he'd been wearing hung in the cloakroom while his shoes were laid out; it was quite a gloomy atmosphere. Dorothy would break into tears from time to time and it was very emotional but the house was like a mausoleum and was kept that way for some time. His harp was also there in a downstairs room. I can still see it now sitting at an angle in the corner of the drawing room. Dorothy said that at the time of the crash on the day he was killed, a string broke on the harp. She attached great significance to that as a sign of something or perhaps a harbinger of doom.[20]

Her next-door neighbour, Jack McIlvenna, who moved to live in the area in 1975, described her as a 'genteel lady who minded her own business':

I was in her house a few times and there was never any heat. She had a small grate with a few sticks or twigs in it but it was rarely ever lit. She was very friendly but seemed to me to be a recluse and didn't go out much. She was house-proud and was often washing and brushing the path outside her front door although I don't think she ever changed the curtains or anything inside the house. Some of the furnishings, including the cooker, were very old and she didn't seem interested in modernizing any of it. It was just left the way it was when her husband died.[21]

Dorothy did not live a completely reclusive life. She gave occasional talks such as one to the John O' London Literary Circle in Belfast on the life and work of the critic F.C. Moore. Some years after Hayward's death George Thompson, the director of the Folk Museum, suggested to her that his films should be lodged with them. Most were in cans in the house and their condition was deteriorating:

Some were nitrate and others were acetate and since they were dangerously flammable they eventually would self-destruct. Initially Dorothy refused but then reconsidered and agreed that the films should be given to the museum on the condition that we erect a permanent statue of Hayward wearing his doctorate robes. This was obviously a condition we could not agree to as it would have opened the floodgates and led to other requests. Many people had doctorates and Hayward's was an American one. Dorothy eventually relented and the films were received by the museum in 1991.[22]

Throughout the 1970s and eighties Hayward's travel books were in demand. Fred Collins, who in those days worked in Greene's secondhand bookshop in Clare Street in Dublin, says there were a number of reasons for the continuing popularity of his books:

Hayward's books sold like hot cakes and we couldn't get enough of them. As soon as we got them in, they had a high resale turnover and sold within a few days. They were generally in very good condition as the owners looked after them carefully. He was opinionated and outspoken about some places and it wasn't tourist board sponsored writing but personal writing – unlike the *Shell Guide to Ireland*, which was a completely different style. There is a wonderful element of discovery in Hayward. As some of the books were never reprinted, demand petered in the late 1980s, although the book-collector interest is always there. I have copies of all his books and cherish them. I remember certain vignettes from them; for example, in the Shannon book in 1939, there's a lovely piece of writing after he had gone for a swim on a summer's morning and he describes the birdsong when the announcement comes through about the declaration of war.[23]

During this period stories continued to be written about him in the press. Occasionally a fleeting mention cropped up in the newspapers or on radio or television but as his peers in the journalistic world had either retired or died, he disappeared from the limelight. The opening sequence in John Betjeman's BBC Northern Ireland TV documentary on Belfast in 1976 referred to him. Betjeman played a recording of one of his best-known songs and in his intro-duction said, 'In my mind the ghostly melodious voice of Richard Hayward singing a traditional song, 'The Mutton Burn Stream' …'

But as the years passed, the name of Richard Hayward barely impinged on the public mind, his reputation fell into abeyance and a curious silence descended. Through it all Dorothy's commitment to guarding his reputation never wavered. She protected his name, correcting misunderstandings and dealing with requests from anyone asking permission to quote from or use his material. Her niece Judith Wilson said, 'She adored Richard and never really got over his death. At times she could become quite emotional when she recalled memories of him.'[24] Ricky also felt that Dorothy dwelt on his father's death:

Even though they barely had three years together, they were inseparable companions and led an energetic cultural life together. She had great energy while in his company and was full of energy even after his death. Clearly she missed him dreadfully and guarded his work like a lioness.[25]

Increasingly, as the years wore on, Dorothy was worried about money, calling her situation a 'financial nightmare'.[26] By 1982 Dion had retired and moved to Waiheke Island, Auckland, where he said he was 'living quietly with Dolly with a very small emergency fund'. Dion's letter said that he imagined the main cause of her concern was the stewardship of their father's books and music recordings:

> Dad always lived life to the full and I'm sure my childhood was the richer because of this, but he was never a saver. I can recall even now a number of financial crises which were only solved by assistance from the Nelson side. And so I was conditioned to, and satisfied with the early realization that my inheritance and Ricky's, in a different sense, would be the memories of a rich and varied childhood full of music and theatre, and musical and artistic and theatrical people, who were my parents' friends and collaborators. In many ways a more precious legacy than mere money.[27]

Dion went on to say that Dorothy should make the best use of what had been left to her and to dispose of his father's affairs as best she can:

> He could never have visualized the changes which have taken place in Ulster life. I honestly believe you must reassess your options and think more about yourself, the living woman. By marrying you Dad became responsible for you like any other man. Your present position and difficulties arise from your marriage which did not, as I see it, obligate you to sacrifice your whole future health and happiness in order to preserve an image. You should feel no shame or guilt if you are now obliged to capitalize on your inheritance. I can honestly speak this way, who loved and admired and was proud of my Father, but who, despite or because of this, can see that he had responsibilities to you who only seem to perceive responsibilities to him. Yours need not be a 3rd rate existence. Every time you face a decision, just ask yourself what would Richard do? He can live with you to the end on the spiritual place.[28]

Twenty-six years after his death, the Folk Museum wrote to Dorothy in connection with acquiring items for their collection. She pointed out that she still held responsibility for his estate:

> Even after a lapse of so many years since his death, I still find it an emotional experience to see and handle memorabilia of Richard's busy, cheerful and high-hearted life. Might I ask that, should you consider it necessary, mention be made of the fact that in accordance with the terms of Richard's will, I alone have the privileged responsibility of decision making as to his effects.[29]

Dorothy continued living in the house right through the Troubles for a further thirty-four years until 1998, which marked the signing in Belfast of the Good Friday Agreement. That March she suffered a serious stroke. She was severely incapacitated and moved into a private nursing home near Belfast. Although unable to write or speak, apart from a few words, she was mentally alert. By that stage, with her house something of a time capsule, she had already made an agreement through her solicitor with the trustees of the museum that her husband's estate should be handed over to them. Shortly after moving into the care home, four museum staff cleared the house. The police had expressed concerns about it being left vacant and worries over the security of the contents. Staff spent two days packing boxes, crates and bags into a van. Clifford Harkness, the head of collections management at the Folk Museum, was one of those involved in removing the personal effects:

> The house was quite dark with high-quality antique furniture and Dorothy seemed to spend her time in the library on the first floor. It was a bright room at the front of the house and quite homely. She did not seem to cook very much but once invited me for lunch in the dining room which had a big table with a Lazy Susan in the centre. The lunch turned out to be a Chinese takeaway meal that was delivered but presented by her. The kitchen had 1950s appliances and had not been modernized. The house was never heated and was always cold with an electric bar fire used to heat the library but it was clean and everything was pristine. Quite a bit of stuff was stored upstairs in boxes. The house was a bit run down although there was no sense of decay – it was more like a well-preserved museum with Dorothy as curator. The drawing room had a good music centre with an elaborate radiogram and classical music collection. It was a fabulous snapshot of a wealthy or refined Belfast family that had gone into limbo land. I remember the harp and an easel with a painting at the top of the stairs. She was there, and it was as if *he* was there ... almost as a ghost.[30]

The museum Librarian, Roger Dixon, also helped in the house clearance. Hayward had amassed an impressive library covering a diverse range of subjects, which included the book collection of R.A.S. Macalister. He recalls that the library was stocked with more than 1500 books shelved in antique bookcases:

> The house was like a miniature stately home and was frozen in time. But Dorothy was no Miss Havisham, there were no cobwebs or mice running about; she had her support mechanisms although it was an odd life she was living.[31]

When Dorothy was told that the museum had now acquired the bequest material, which was sealed from public access, she was upset but in full agreement.[32] But her health was declining and at the age of ninety she died on 26 November 2005. After forty-one years of widowhood, her death marked the end of a long life spent acting as the still centre of her husband's posterity.

Left: Raymond Piper photographed at his home in Belfast in 1985 working on an orchid drawing. After Hayward's death he described him as 'a man of impish ways, great humour and broad mind'. Right: *Cruiscín lán* stoneware jug designed from a mould by Piper encapsulating Hayward's visage. Piper entitled it: 'Richard Hayward as the Joker'.

Across the city in leafy south Belfast Raymond Piper reminisces about his times spent motoring around Ireland with his friend. In 2001, for a magazine profile of Hayward, I interviewed him at length. On more than a dozen visits to his flat, between 2001 and 2007, the year of his death, and on occasions over lunch at the Wellington Park Hotel, he talked about Hayward and their time together. One item stood out on all my visits. On his mantelpiece, in between postcards, dinner invitations and cigar packets, sat a twelve-inch-tall *cruiscín lán* stoneware jug of Hayward smiling down at him like a happy Buddha with a beatific expression. The jug, in the form of a small statuette that at one time contained whiskey, served as a reminder of their time on the road. Piper had designed it from a mould and said that sometimes he would talk to 'this wee man' recalling jokey stories of their travels around Ireland. The image, he felt, represented him well as he looked a picture of contentment. He called it: 'Richard Hayward as the Joker', perfectly encapsulating his visage. As he looked back on the places they had visited and the people they had met, a wistful look spread over his face:

> My memories of him are all happy ones. He was a gregarious man and had a great sense of humour as well as a broad mind. He liked a drink, particularly whiskey and ginger. People gravitated towards him because of his charisma and attractive character. He sparked off an interest in me in archaeology and helped start my artistic career. Working with him was a great age of discovery for me as he instilled enormous enthusiasm for all Ireland's attributes. He was like a man with an electric current running through him – always on the go and always with a twinkle in his eye. He has been terribly neglected, which in my view is grossly unfair considering his achievements. But to me he was ageless and if anything, he got younger as he got older.[33]

Paul Hayward feels his grandfather has been neglected because Dorothy kept such a tight rein on all his property:

> He was relegated to the dustbin and this is related to his second marriage. Dorothy took over sole possession of everything and I felt that was bizarre. It was a twist of fate for someone so gregarious that his memory should be so jealously guarded. This was the number one reason his reputation has fallen into abeyance. She had to have him for herself and would not share him, to the detriment of the rest of us. After my grandfather's death, my father would like to have taken some of the pictures by William Conor that were earmarked for him. This was not so much for the monetary value as he was never mercenary, but for personal reasons. But he never got the opportunity. I believe that Dorothy is the main reason that his voice for sanity was extinguished. It was the last thing Richard would have wanted. She had a disorder – it was abnormal and she would not accept he was dead. She should have been living in the reflected glory of the life of my grandfather and promoting his name but she could not let it out of the house. She was the keeper of Richard Hayward but she killed his legacy. In my opinion she is the primary culprit as to why his name disappeared.[34]

Richard Hayward received awards and an honorary doctorate, but among the tributes after his death, one that perhaps he might just have valued most was from the secretary of the Fermanagh Field Club who wrote:

He lit the fields of Ireland with a brilliant light.[35]

Portrait of Richard Hayward painted by Raymond Piper in 1961.

Postscript: Richard Hayward Assayed

> You will tell me that you have executed
> A monument more lasting than bronze;
> But even bronze is perishable.
> Your best poem, you know the one I mean,
> The very language in which the poem
> Was written, and the idea of language,
> All these things will pass away in time.
>
> Derek Mahon, 'Heraclitus on Rivers', *New Collected Poems*

On a crisp spring day in April 2007 four people gathered on the shore of Belfast Lough to perform a simple ceremony. Ricky Hayward came over from Edinburgh to scatter his father's and Dorothy's ashes on the lough shore with the giant canary-yellow shipyard cranes Samson and Goliath looming in the distance. The ashes were spread in a short ceremony on 18 April attended by Ricky's partner, Karin, Judith Wilson and a local minister. His stepmother died two years earlier and the urn with his father's ashes had now passed to him. More than four decades had elapsed since he had felt the personal grief of his father's loss. Three months later, on 13 July, another historical link was severed with the death of Raymond Piper. Tributes were paid to his skill as an orchid painter and the obituaries in national British and Irish newspapers made mention of his book illustrations.[1]

Like the work of many mid-twentieth-century writers, Hayward's books have been moribund for a considerable time, but by the start of the second decade of the twenty-first century the early stages of a resurgence of interest in him is palpable. Although there are few people alive who recall him, those who do remember him acknowledge his centrality – frequently with a hint of his playfulness – in the Irish cultural mainstream. Interest in his writing and music is being rekindled. Irish tourist organizations, including Tourism Ireland, Fáilte Ireland and Shannon Development, used quotations from his work in a raft of glossy brochures.[2] BBC Radio Ulster began to play some of his music on Saturday morning light-entertainment shows such as *Your Place and Mine*, which coincided with a BBC Writers exhibition on Hayward, reflecting the diversity of his work with the corporation.[3] RTÉ's long-running Saturday evening radio music and song programme *Fáilte Isteach* liked to play Hayward's 'The Three Roses'. A new interest is being created through the internet. Many of his feature films have been digitized and can be viewed in libraries and museums with some clips online. In its 2014 edition, *Fodor's Ireland*, the internationally renowned guidebook, listed a walking tour of Richard Hayward's Belfast.[4]

His presidential role in the Belfast Naturalists' Field Club was celebrated in a 150th anniversary exhibition at the Ulster Museum in spring 2013, bringing him to the attention of a younger generation of naturalists. Appropriately, alongside him, a separate panel featured Piper, who had served twice as president – in 1971 and 1983.[5] The exhibition created considerable media interest with Hayward's club tours receiving a mention en passant in *The Irish Times*.[6]

But still he continued to suffer municipal neglect; despite Dorothy's best efforts no monument or statue was ever likely to be erected. Walk across the black granite stones in Writers' Square in the heart of Belfast's Cathedral Quarter and you will find the names of more than twenty authors embedded into the ground. The square was set up to honour famous local writers with their words inscribed into the paving stones. Potter around and you will stumble across Louis MacNeice with a verse of his poem 'See Belfast'. Nearby is a quotation from C.S. Lewis, and a few paces away is the poet John Hewitt whose name lives on in the eponymous pub in Donegall Street. The roll-call of names underfoot includes the novelist Michael McLaverty, playwright Sam Thompson and author Denis Ireland. Hayward's friends such as St John Ervine and Robert Lloyd Praeger merit a mention as does the shipyard poet Thomas Carnduff. But the only Hayward handiwork etched into the ground is in some of Belfast's manhole covers.

You will search Writers' Square in vain for the name Richard Hayward. Yet unlike many of those mentioned, some of whom deserted their native city and moved to live and work in England or Dublin, Hayward spent his adult life in Belfast. The powers-that-be do not deem him worthy of mention or of a single quotation from any of his books of poetry, plays, fiction and travel, never mind his output of songs and comedy revues. The man who wrote lovingly of the city where he lived and worked, entertained and socialized, is forgotten, consigned to a footnote in history.

In the streets around central Dublin, the Hayward name is particularly prevalent. Walk along College Green, turn into Church Lane and along St Andrew Street, Trinity Street and Suffolk Street, look carefully at the ground and you will discover numerous Hayward Brothers pavement lights. In South Anne Street, off Grafton Street, the name is also found in similar well-worn pavement lights with glazed glass.

Hayward's posthumous reputation was affected by changing fashions, both in the reading habits of the public and in the nature of the publishing business. After the death of many writers there is often a falling off in interest and their books become unfashionable, remaining stubbornly out of print. Hayward's work matters for the lasting pleasure it affords, for the breadth of his achievements, and the glimpse it offers of an Ireland that has long since disappeared.

On a sunny May morning in 2013, more than fifty people turned up to honour the memory of Richard Hayward at the unveiling of a blue plaque on Belfast's Antrim Road. The Ulster History Circle decided to acknowledge his work, raising his profile and name with a plaque on the front of Clonsilla, the house where he lived for more than twenty years. Blue plaques commemorate men and women who have made a significant contribution to the history of Ulster and its development. The plaque lists three of his roles: Writer, Actor, Singer.

Nearly half a century after his death, speakers talk effusively about his warmth, his twinkling humour and how on his conducted tours around Ireland he illuminated places largely unknown to all but the locals. The crowd stands inside railings on gravel stones in the shade of two bright pink-blossoming cherry trees. The house from which he launched himself into so many enterprises in the prime of his life is occupied now by two businesses: a firm of solicitors and a burglar alarm company. The chairman of the Ulster History Circle, Chris Spurr, referred to the many sides to Hayward. 'His life was entertaining and edifying and he made a distinctive and endearing impression across the many areas of his work. He brought pleasure to thousands and gave them an appreciation of their heritage and traditions.'

'The tale goes round' – Piper's sketch of Dunne's Bar, Carrick-on-Shannon, County Leitrim in 1952, which appeared in *Mayo Sligo Leitrim & Roscommon*. Seated in the centre, Hayward is third from left. Also in the drawing are, from left, Paddy Dillon, the chemist, Jack Cassidy, dentist, Patrick Dunne, editor of the *Leitrim Observer*, Paddy Hyland, the paper's manager, John Dunne, jeweller and former owner of Dunne's bar, and Tommy Flynn, the former owner of P. Flynn and Company. The bar has been renovated but the sketch now hangs on a wall.

Ricky travelled from Kent and along with his nephew Paul from the San Juan Islands, Washington State, carried out the unveiling by pulling the string of a navy curtain. He spoke of his father's talents and boundless energy, saying he had passed on much information and enthusiasm in many different fields. He saluted the memory of his father and his mother Elma, 'his faithful wife and no mean actress'. He also mentioned Dorothy who had shared this house for just a few years and was 'a good companion'. Melding into the crowd, holding on to his rollator but listening attentively, was a fresh-faced eighty-eight-year-old man. Seventy-five years earlier, at the age of thirteen, Liam Mulvenna was in the St Gall's Boys' Choir that sang in Hayward's film *In the Footsteps of St Patrick*. He spoke of his memories:

I have never forgotten my time in the choir when Richard Hayward organized us to sing. It has been embedded in my mind and I am overjoyed to see that at long last he is being recognized and they are doing something about him. I was in this house just a few years ago and it was an overwhelming experience. I went up to the attic to pray for him. I would have come to the unveiling of this plaque even if I had to crawl here. I'll never forget him until the day I die. He is looking down on us all now and smiling – God have mercy on him.[7]

One hundred and twenty miles west, in Dunne's bar in Carrick-on-Shannon hangs a line drawing by Raymond Piper entitled 'The tale goes round'. It features six well-dressed Carrick businessmen in a cosy group, some on high stools with glasses in hand, shooting the breeze. Seated in the centre, a relaxed and puckish Hayward – his face radiating pleasure – wears an open-neck shirt with a sports jacket. As ever, holding court, he plays the role expected of him with his finely-honed oratorical skills.

Hayward and Piper were on their 1952 research tour for *Mayo Sligo Leitrim & Roscommon* and the sketch appeared in the book three years later.[8] It was presented by Gregory Dunne to Paul and Anne-Marie Maye, the owner of Dunne's renovated bar on their first anniversary, 12 March 2002. It serves as a reminder of the esteem in which Hayward was held in a place that had a strong emotional pull for him and which he frequently revisited. He had a burning affection for Carrick and never forgot the camaraderie he found in 'the little town of my heart'. For him it exemplified the commonplace soul of Ireland. Gregory Dunne, a nephew of Patrick Dunne, recounted how Hayward would sing in the bar accompanied on the piano by Anna Neagle:

> Dunne's was a small squared-shaped bar that held no more than fifteen people. It was well known for its after-hours drinking and if the Guards knocked on the door the customers went out the back door and into the kitchen of the jewellery shop waiting until they were gone.[9]

Although the honour had no official status, Hayward was made a 'freeman' of Carrick in 1945 for his services to the Inland Waterways Association of Ireland. This was in recognition of his work promoting the Shannon region in his writing and filmmaking. Pubs were a tremendous source of knowledge for Hayward. He often described them as 'a natural clearing-house for information,' and in his Shannon book, after 'two wild nights' he renamed Carrick-on-Shannon 'Cirrhosis-of-the-Liver.'[10]

One of Carrick's enduring landmarks, the town clock erected to Owen McCann in 1905 and sketched by Piper, still presides at the junction of Bridge and Main streets. In Hayward's time it stood on the road but in the 1970s was moved back on to the pavement. He says in the book it has not worked since 1921. With seats around it, the clock is still a meeting place, now keeping the correct time. Although the rhythm of the streetscape has not changed he would not recognize much of the bling of modern day *Cora Droma Rúisc* ('the stony ford of the ridge in the marsh').

In 2013, during my visit to Dunne's, I asked a fellow drinker on a stool at the bar if he knew the name Richard Hayward. He said, 'I *think* I've heard of him', and he asked the barman, 'Was he in here the other night?'

And the barman said, 'He's here every night.'

The Ballad of Richard Hayward (1965)

by Roy Dickson

Fare thee well, fare thee well
Richard Hayward has left us
No more will we hear him
As in days gone by.

Cruel fate tore him from us
In Antrim, in autumn
And Ireland's the loser
You'll hear people sigh.

For he loved Erin's Isle
From the North to Cork city
This author and actor and folksinger too
On the Twelfth of July we will always remember
Our friend Richard Hayward, an Orangeman true.

At dinner his folk stories charmed us
His books about Ireland are famous it's true.
And his songs will live on
For a hundred or more years,
The Sash, Dolly's Brae and the Orange and Blue.

Bibliography

BOOKS BY RICHARD HAYWARD

Poems, Morland, Amersham, Buckinghamshire, 1917

Poems, Morland, Amersham, Buckinghamshire, 1920

The Jew's Fiddle, with Abram Rish, Talbot, Dublin, Unwin, London, 1921

Love in Ulster and Other Poems, Talbot, Dublin, Unwin, London, 1922

Sugarhouse Entry, Arthur Barker, London, 1936

In Praise of Ulster (illustrations by J.H. Craig), Arthur Barker, 1938

Where the River Shannon flows (photographs by Louis Morrison), Dundalgan & G. Harrap, 1940

The Corrib Country (illustrations by J.H. Craig), Dundalgan, 1943

In the Kingdom of Kerry (illustrations by T.J. Gracey), Dundalgan, 1946

This is Ireland: Leinster and the City of Dublin (illustrations by Raymond Piper), Arthur Barker, 1949

Ulster and the City of Belfast (illustrations by Raymond Piper), Arthur Barker, 1950

Connacht and the City of Galway (illustrations by Raymond Piper), Arthur Barker, 1952

Belfast through the Ages (illustrations by Raymond Piper), Dundalgan, 1952

The Story of the Irish Harp, Guinness, Dublin, 1954

Mayo Sligo Leitrim & Roscommon (illustrations by Raymond Piper), Arthur Barker, 1955

Border Foray, Arthur Barker, 1957

Munster and the City of Cork (illustrations by Raymond Piper), Phoenix, Dent, 1964

Books edited by Richard Hayward

Ulster songs and ballads of the town and the country, Duckworth, London, 1925

Excursion guide, Belfast, British Association for the Advancement of Science, 1952

Richard Hayward contributions to anthologies

The Autumn Anthology, A Compilation of Representative Verse from the World's Living Poets, (various eds.), Mitre Press, London, 1930

H.P. Swan (ed.), *'Twixt Foyle and Swilly,* 'A Donegal Ceilidhe', Hodges, Figgis, Dublin, 1949

The P.E.N. in Ulster, 'An Ireland that Never was,' Belfast P.E.N. Writers Centre, 1943

Brave Crack! An Anthology of Ulster Wit and Humour, 'Brave Crack,' Carter, Belfast, 1951

Concord of Harps, An Irish P.E.N. Anthology of Poetry, Talbot Press, Dublin, 1952

Two Islands – One Common Market?, McConnell Group, 1962

M. Gorman (ed.), *Ireland by the Irish,* 'The Province of Ulster,' Galley Press Ltd., London, 1963

FOREWORDS WRITTEN BY RICHARD HAYWARD

Lucas, L.W., *Mevagh Down the Years, A History of Carrigart, Downings, Glen and the Surrounding District,* Mevagh, 1962

Swan, H. P., *'Twixt Foyle and Swilly,* Hodges, Figgis, Dublin, 1949

———— *Flashes of Wit & Wisdom,* Quota Press, 1952

———— *Gems of Wit and Wisdom,* Carter, 1956

A Programme of Ulster Records, Arranged by Hayward, Decca, circa 1933

MUSIC BOOKS AND SHEET MUSIC BY RICHARD HAYWARD

Ireland calling, copyright arrangement of words and music by Richard Hayward, Mozart Allan, Glasgow, 1935

'The Star of Ulster', written and composed by Richard Hayward, Ulster Publications, Belfast, 1937

'The Three Flowers', music arranged by Richard Hayward and Anna Meakin, words by Norman Reddin, Walton, Dublin, 1940

'The Humour is on Me Now', Richard Hayward and Anna Meakin, Walton, Dublin, 1942

Orange Standard, 18 Selected Songs, by Richard Hayward, Mozart Allan, Glasgow, 1958

ABOUT RICHARD HAYWARD:
SELECTED ARTICLES AND PROFILES

Adams, G.B., 'Richard Hayward, A bibliography of his published works', *Irish Booklore,* vol. 3, no.1, W. McCann (ed.), Blackstaff Press, 1976, pp. 50–55

Ballymena Observer, 'Co. Antrim personalities: Richard Hayward', 2 February 1976

Clarke, R., 'Hayward, (Harold) Richard (1892–1964)', *Oxford Dictionary of National Biography,* vol. 26, H.C.G. Matthew & B. Harrison (eds), OUP, 2004, pp. 91–2

Clements, P., 'Richard Hayward: Irish Travel Writer and Broadcaster', *Book and Magazine Collector,* no. 222, September 2002, (London) pp. 56–66

———— 'Great Walkers of the Past: Mountain Man in a Morris Minor', *Walking World Ireland* 2006 annual, pp. 52–3

———— 'Irishman's Diary', *Irish Times*, 4 August 2007

———— *Ireland's Own*, 'Raymond Piper: A love affair with Ireland', 23 November 2007, pp. 5–6

Easton Express, 'Ireland of Shillelaghs and Shamrocks is Myth, Visiting Poet Declares,' 5 June 1959

Eason Bulletin, 'Irish Authors, Richard Hayward: 30', 1947

Foster, J.C., 'Richard Hayward: An appreciation' *Belfast Telegraph*, 17 October 1964

'Gramophone Personalities, 6: Richard Hayward', Discus, Bristol Gramophone Society, vol. 2, no. 7, summer 1948

Irish Radio Journal, 'H. Richard Hayward: Ulster Poet and Dramatist', 15 July 1925, pp. 948–9, p. 952

Lagan, P., *Irish Press*, 'Here's a man who knew about the Six Counties', 2 March 1962

———— *Irish Press*, 'The liveliest of Irish writers', 8 May 1964

Limerick Leader, 'Outstanding Acting: Adjudicator's Awards and Comments', 27 March 1950

Lunney, L., 'Hayward, (Harold) Richard', *Dictionary of Irish Biography*, vol. 4, G-J, J. McGuire and J. Quinn (eds), Royal Irish Academy & Cambridge University Press, 2009, pp. 551–2

Orr, C., 'This early morning lark', *Sunday Review*, 28 October 1962

Orr, M., 'Richard Hayward: His 21st anniversary as a recording artist', Decca, 1948

Patton, J., 'Richard Hayward: An appreciation', *Ulster Tatler*, August 1969

The Nationalist, 'The Glory that is Galteemore', 8 June 1963

ARCHIVAL MATERIAL CONSULTED IN THE FOLLOWING HOLDINGS

Abbey Theatre Archive, Dublin
BBC Northern Ireland Community Archive, UFTM
BBC Written Archives, Caversham, Reading
Belfast Naturalists' Field Club Archive
Bodleian Library
British Library
Central Newspaper Library, Belfast
Forces War Records
Glucksman Library, University of Limerick
Grand Orange Lodge of Ireland Archive, Belfast
Irish Film Institute Archive, Dublin
Irish Traditional Music Archive, Dublin
Larne Grammar School Library
Larne Heritage Centre

Linen Hall Library Theatre Archive, Belfast
Manuscript & Archives Research Library, Trinity College Dublin
National Archives Ireland
National Library Ireland
Newtown School Archives, Waterford
Public Record Office, Northern Ireland
Richard Hayward Archive, Belfast Central Library
Richard Hayward Archive, UFTM
Royal Irish Academy, Dublin
Royal Mersey Yacht Club Archive, Birkenhead, Liverpool
Royal Society of Antiquaries of Ireland, Dublin
RTÉ Radio and Television Archive, Dublin
Special Collections, Queen's University Belfast
Tyrone Guthrie Centre Library, Annaghmakerrig, Newbliss, County Monaghan
UCD Archive, University College Dublin
Ulster Television Film Library Archive

SECONDARY BIBLIOGRAPHY

Agee., C. (ed.) *Irish Pages, Unfinished Ireland, Essays on Hubert Butler*, Linen Hall Library, Belfast, 2003
Bardon, J., *Beyond The Studio: A History of* BBC *Northern Ireland*, Blackstaff Press, 2000
Barry, M., & P. Tilling (eds) *The English Dialects of Ulster, An anthology of articles on Ulster speech by G. B. Adams,* Ulster Folk and Transport Museum, 1986
Barton, B., *The Blitz, Belfast in the War Years*, Blackstaff Press, 1989
Bell, S. H., *The Theatre in Ulster*, Gill and Macmillan, 1972
Blakeston, O., *Thank You Now, An Exploration of Ulster*, Anthony Blond, 1960
Boyd, J., *The Middle of My Journey*, Blackstaff Press, 1990
Breathnach, C., *The Congested Districts Board of Ireland, 1891–1923*, Four Courts Press, 2005
Butler, H., *Escape from the Anthill*, Lilliput Press, 1985
——— *In the Land of Nod*, Lilliput Press, 1996
Byrne, O., (ed.) *State of Play, The Theatre and Cultural Identity in 20th Century Ulster*, Linen Hall Library, 2001
——— *The Stage in Ulster from the Eighteenth Century*, Linen Hall Library, 1997
Cathcart, R., *The Most Contrary Region, The* BBC *in Northern Ireland, 1924–1984*, Blackstaff Press, 1984
Clements, P., *The Height of Nonsense*, Collins Press, 2005
——— *Burren Country*, Collins Press, 2011
Connell, G. A., *James Humbert Craig, The Natural Talents of J. H. Craig, The Peoples' Artist*, Arches Art Galley, Belfast, 1988
Connolly, R., *The Evolution of the Lyric Players Theatre, Belfast: Fighting the Waves*, Edwin Mellen, 2000

Corcoran, D., *A Tour of East Antrim*, Friar's Bush Press, 1990

Craig, P., (ed.) *The Ulster Anthology*, Blackstaff Press, 2006

Delaney, R., *The Shannon Navigation*, Lilliput Press, 2008

Durrell, P., & Kelly C., (eds) *The Grand Tour of Kerry*, Cailleach Books, 2001

Fitz-Simon, C., *Eleven Houses: A Memoir of Childhood*, Penguin, 2007

Gallagher, L., *The Grand Opera House, Belfast*, Blackstaff Press, 1995

Gray, J., (ed.) *Thomas Carnduff, Life and Writings*, Lagan Press, 1994

Grene, N., (ed.) *J. M. Synge, Travelling Ireland, Essays 1898–1908*, Lilliput Press, 2009

Grevatt, W., BBC *Children's Hour, A Celebration of Those Magical Years,* The Book Guild, Sussex, 1988

Gribbon, H. D., *The History of Water Power in Ulster*, David & Charles, Newton Abbot, 1969

Hailes, A., *Standby Studio*, Shanway Press, 2009

Hartnoll, P., (ed.) *The Oxford Companion to the Theatre*, OUP, 1951

Hewitt, J., *Art in Ulster 1, 1557–1957*, Blackstaff Press, 1977

Hill, J., *Cinema and Northern Ireland, Film, Culture and Politics*, British Film Institute, 2006

Hogan, R., (ed.) *Dictionary of Irish Literature*, Aldwych Press, London, 1996

Houlihan, M., *Puck Fair, History and Tradition*, 2013

Hutton, C., (ed.) *The Oxford History of the Irish Book, Vol V: The Irish Book in English, 1891–2000*, OUP, 2011

Kennedy, S.B., *With an angler's eye, The Art of James Humbert Craig,* W&G Baird and Ulster Museum, 2001

Killen, J., *A History of the Linen Hall Library, 1788–1988*, Linen Hall Library, Belfast, 1990

King, S. H., and McMahon, S., (ed.) *Hope and History, Eyewitness accounts of life in twentieth-century Ulster*, Friar's Bush Press, Belfast, 1996

Kirkland, R., *Cathal O'Byrne and the Northern Revival in Ireland, 1890–1960*, Liverpool University Press, 2006

Livingstone, P., *The Fermanagh Story, Cumann Seanchais Chlochair*, St. Michael's College, Enniskillen, 1969

Loughlin, J., *Ulster Unionism and British National Identity since 1885*, Pinter, 1995

Loughran, G., & M. McCavana (eds), *The Radio Catalogue*, Ulster Folk and Transport Museum, 1993

Macafee, C.I., (ed.) *A Concise Ulster Dictionary*, OUP, 1996

Mac Liammóir, M., *An Oscar of No Importance*, Heinemann, 1968

MacQuitty, W., *A Life to Remember*, Quartet Books, 1991

————*Titanic Memories: The Making of a Night to Remember*, National Maritime Museum, London, 2000

Matheson, S., *Maurice Walsh, Storyteller*, Brandon, 1985

Matthew, H.C.G., & B. Harrison (eds), *Oxford Dictionary of National Biography*, vol. 26, OUP, 2004

McCann, W., (ed.) *Irish Booklore*, vol. 4, no.1, Blackstaff Press, 1978, 'Thomas Carnduff, 1886–1956: chapters from an unpublished autobiography', John Gray

McCrea, C.T., *Tempest of Dundalgan, Portrait of a Perfectionist*, Dundalgan Press, 1988

McHenry, M., *The Ulster Theatre in Ireland*, Philadelphia, 1931

McIlroy, B., *Irish Cinema: An Illustrated History*, Anna Livia Press, 1988

McLoone, M., (ed.) *Broadcasting in a Divided Community, Seventy years of the* BBC *in Northern Ireland*, Institute of Irish Studies, 1996

McMahon, S., (ed.) *The Derry Anthology*, Blackstaff Press, 2002

McVeagh, J., *Irish Travel Writing, A Bibliography*, Wolfhound, n.d.

Morton, H.V., *In Search of Ireland*, Methuen, 1930

Muirhead, L. R., (ed.) *Muirhead's Ireland*, Ernest Benn, 1949

Needler, R., *Needlers of Hull*, Hutton Press, 1993

Nelson, C., *The Burren: A companion to the wildflowers of an Irish limestone wilderness*, Boethius Press, 1991

Newman, K., (ed.) *Dictionary of Ulster Biography*, Institute of Irish Studies, Belfast, n.d.

O'Farrell, P., *Shannon Through Her Literature*, Mercier Press, 1983

O'Hara, A., *I'll live till I die: The story of Delia Murphy*, Drumlin Publications, 1997

Patton, M., *Central Belfast: An Historical Gazetteer*, Ulster Architectural Heritage Society, 1993

Robinson, T., *Stones of Aran, Pilgrimage*, Viking, 1986

———*Connemara, Listening to the Wind*, Penguin Ireland, 2006

Rockett, K., *Irish Film Censorship: A Cultural Journey from Silent Cinema to Internet Pornography*, Four Courts Press, 2004

Rose, J., & P.J. Anderson (eds), *Dictionary of Literary Biography*, vol. 112, 'British Literary Publishing Houses, 1881–1965', Gale Research Inc. 1991

Ryan, R., *A History of the West Lancashire Yacht Club 1894–1994*, Carnegie, 1993

Sandford, E., *Discover Northern Ireland*, Northern Ireland Tourist Board, 1977

Slide, A., *The Cinema and Ireland*, McFarland and Company, 1988

Smyth, A., M. Montgomery & P. Robinson (eds), *The Academic Study of Ulster-Scots: Essays for and by Robert J. Gregg*, Ulster Folk and Transport Museum, 2006

Smyth, D., *Poet of the People, Thomas Carnduff, 1886–1956*, North Belfast History Workshop, 1991

Snoddy, T., *Dictionary of Irish Artists 20th Century*, Wolfhound Press, 1996

Tobin, R., *The Minority Voice, Hubert Butler and Southern Ireland Protestantism, 1900–1991*, OUP, 2012

Tohill, J.J., *Pubs of the North*, Portaferry, 1990

Ulster Dialects: An Introductory Symposium, Ulster Folk Museum, 1964

Wilson, J. C., *Conor, 1881–1968, The life and work of an Ulster artist*, Blackstaff Press, 1981

Years of Reflection, 1783–1953: The Story of Haywards of the Borough, Harley Publishing, London, 1953

Unpublished dissertation

Ludlow, J., *Aspects of economic and social change in the town of Larne during the period 1850–1900*, presented to the School of Social Sciences of Queen's University, Belfast, September 1991

RICHARD HAYWARD FILMOGRAPHY

Richard Hayward acted in, narrated, directed, produced or contributed music to the following feature films, travelogues and documentaries

The Voice of Ireland, 1932
Irish Travelogue, 1935
Flame in the Heather, 1935
The Luck of the Irish, 1935
Shipmates O' Mine, 1936
Star of Ulster, 1936
The Early Bird, 1936
Irish and Proud of It, 1936
Devil's Rock, 1937
Anna Liffey goes to Dublin, 1938
In the Footsteps of Saint Patrick, 1939
Where the Shannon Flows down to the Sea, 1940
Simple Silage, 1942
Tomorrow's Bread, 1943
Loch Corrib, 1944
Kingdom of Kerry, 1944
Back Home in Ireland, 1946
The Quiet Man, 1952
A Night to Remember, 1958

Undated films

Holiday, personal, and business documentaries, including films Hayward made on behalf of companies for advertising, are in the following list. The films were made between the 1930s and 1960:

Armagh, Cashel, Cardinal MacRory's Funeral, Concert scenes in Tonic Cinema, Bangor, County Down, Conferring of honorary doctorate, Lafayette, USA, Flowing Waters, Harp Trade Mark, Holiday Ramble England, In Ireland's Garden, Sligo Advertising film, The Dawn of Beauty Ball, Gresham Hotel, Dublin, Thomas Heiton & Co., Coal merchants

RICHARD HAYWARD PLAYOGRAPHY

Playwrighting credits

Richard Hayward as author or co-author

The Jew's Fiddle with Abram Rish, 1920
Huge Love, 1924

Acting credits

Between 1920 and 1937 Richard Hayward appeared as actor with the Ulster Players and the Belfast Repertory Theatre Company in the following plays (with playwright's name)

The Jew's Fiddle, Richard Hayward, 1920
Loaves and Fishes, Charles K. Ayre, 1921
The Drone, Rutherford Mayne, 1922
The Mist that Does be on the Bog, Gerald Macnamara, 1922
Turncoats, Lynn Doyle, 1922
Love and Land, Lynn Doyle, 1922
The Throwbacks, Gerald Macnamara, 1922
Phantoms, Rutherford Mayne, 1923
The Turn of the Road, Rutherford Mayne, 1923
The Skipper's Submarine, Charles K. Ayre, 1923
The Land of the Stranger, Dorothea Donn Byrne, 1924
The Ship, St John Ervine, 1924
The Lilac Ribbon, Lynn Doyle, 1924
Missing Links, Charles K. Ayre, 1925
Thompson in Tir-na-nog, Gerald Macnamara, 1926
Passed Unanimously, N.F. Webb, 1928
No Surrender, Gerald Macnamara, 1929
Who Fears to Speak, Gerald Macnamara, 1929
French Leave, Reginald Berkeley, 1929
Cartney and Kevney, George Shiels, 1930
Workers, Thomas Carnduff, 1932
Machinery, Thomas Carnduff, 1933
Mrs McConaghey's Money, Hugh Quinn, 1933
Traitors, Thomas Carnduff, 1934
Castlereagh, Thomas Carnduff, 1935
The Early Bird, James Douglas, 1936
A Quiet Twelfth, Hugh Quinn, 1937
Collecting the Rent, Hugh Quinn, 1937

Broadcasts

'A table in the window', BBC N.I. Home Service, 9 November 1961, BBC Radio Archive, UFTM
'Mr Doyle of Ballygullion', BBC N.I. Home Service, 19 June 1962, BBC Radio Archive, UFTM, Cultra
'Betjeman's Belfast', BBC Northern Ireland TV, 1976, BBC Archive, UFTM, Cultra
'The Story of Richard Hayward', Downtown Radio, Presented by Bobbie Hanvey, 'The Ramblin' Man', 1981, Larne Heritage Centre

Notes

1. 'SOAKED IN IRISH SONGS AND STORIES'

1. Rex Hayward to DH, 30 October 1964, RHA, UFTM.
2. *Yachting World*, 'Yachting Celebrities', 20 January 1899, p. 174.
3. *Belfast News Letter*, 24 August 1910; *Southport Guardian*, 24 August 1910.
4. *In Praise of Ulster*, 5th edn, (Belfast 1945), p. 81.
5. *Larne Times*, 14 April 1900.
6. *IPU, op. cit.* p. 81.
7. Quoted in H.D. Gribbon, *The History of Water Power in Ulster*, (Newton Abbot 1969), p. 140.
8. *IPU, op. cit.* pp. 81–2.
9. *Larne Weekly Reporter*, July 1891, quoted in McKillop, *History of Larne and East Antrim*, (Glenarm 2005), p. 95.
10. *IPU, op. cit.* p. 82.
11. *Ibid.* p. 78.
12. *Ibid.* p. 317.
13. *Ibid.* p. 81.
14. *Ibid.* p. 216.
15. *Ibid.* pp. 94–5.
16. *Ibid.* p. 81.
17. *Ibid.* p. 81.
18. R.H. McIlrath, *Larne Grammar School: The First 100 Years*, (Larne, 1985), p. 130.
19. Roger Ryan, *A History of the West Lancashire Yacht Club 1894–1994*, (Preston 1993), p. 65.
20. *British Yachts and Yachtsmen*, (London 1907), p. 438.
21. 'The Gramophone Record', Mid-June, 1951.

22. *Ibid.*
23. Ricky H in conversation with PC, 15 June 2013.
24. *IPU, op. cit.* p. 289.
25. *Belfast Telegraph*, 23 January 1960.
26. *Oxford Dictionary of National Biography*, vol. 26, 'Walter Scott Hayward' by Roger Ryan, H.C.G. Matthew & B. Harrison (eds), (Oxford, 2004), p. 96.
27. *Belfast and Ulster Street Directory, 1910*, (Belfast 1910), p. 920.
28. *Southport Guardian*, 24 August 1910.
29. *J.M. Synge, Travelling Ireland, Essays 1898–1908*, N. Grene, (ed.) (Dublin 2009), p. xxvi.
30. Quoted in Tim Robinson, *Stones of Aran: Pilgrimage*, (London 1986), p. 216.
31. Michael Scott-Hayward, family history documents.
32. *Ibid.*
33. Ryan, *op. cit.* p. 66.
34. *Yachting World*, 25 August 1910, p. 152.
35. *Yachting World*, 9 March 1911, p. 132.
36. *Belfast News Letter, op. cit.*
37. Ryan, *op. cit.* p. 66.
38. Ricky H (quoting his mother, Elma Hayward) in conversation with PC, 10 February 2013.

2. SWEET POETIC ASPIRATIONS

1. *Belfast Telegraph*, 22 March 1958.
2. *Ibid.*
3. *Ulster Illustrated*, vol. 6, no. 2, April 1958.
4. William MacQuitty, *A Life to Remember*, (London 1991), p. 6.
5. Ricky H in conversation with PC, 13 January 2012.
6. *Belfast through the Ages*, (Dundalk 1952), p. 27.
7. *Evening Press*, 26 November 1962.
8. Note from Sir Francis Evans, RHA, UFTM, n.d.
9. *Irish Press*, 28 December 1962.
10. *Ibid.*
11. *Ibid.*
12. *Ibid.*
13. Census of Ireland, Larne, County Antrim, 2 April 1911, NAI.
14. Ricky H in conversation with PC, 14 May 2013, letter 18 July 2013, quoting Michael Scott-Hayward, Cape Town.
15. David McNeill, Larne historian, in conversation with PC, 8 March 2013.
16. Gladys Jenks' personal papers, Judith Wilson collection.
17. *The Buildings of England: Lancashire, Liverpool and the South-West*, R. Pollard & N. Pevsner, (London, 2006).
18. Raymond Needler, *Needlers of Hull*, (Beverley 1993), p.47, p. 58.

19. Confectionery customer ledger, RHA, UFTM.
20. Ricky H letters to PC, 11 June 2013, 18 July 2013.
21. *Poems*, (Amersham 1920), p. 58.
22. *Irish Press*, W.A. Newman, 14 October 1964.
23. *Love in Ulster and Other Poems*, (Dublin, London 1922), p. 6.
24. Tom Clyde, *Irish Literary Magazines*, (Dublin 2003), p. 171.
25. Campbell photo album, 1922–24, BNFC archive.
26. Proceedings of BNFC, summer season, 31 May 1924, BNFC archive.
27. Jack Johnston, *In the Days of the Clogher Valley and its railway 1887–1942*, (Belfast 1987), p. 15.
28. *Irish Naturalists' Journal*, October 1950.
29. *Irish Naturalists' Journal*, vol. one, November 1925.
30. Campbell, *op. cit.*
31. Estyn Evans, *UJA*, 3rd ser. 14, 1951.
32. *In the Kingdom of Kerry*, (Dundalk 1946), p. 138.
33. *Corrib Country*, (Dundalk 1943), p. 103.
34. *Ulster Review*, October 1924.
35. *Ibid.*
36. *Ibid.*
37. *Northern Whig*, 16 August 1924.
38. *Ibid.*

3. 'THEY LIE WHO SAY I DO NOT LOVE THIS COUNTRY!'

1. *Evening Press*, 26 November 1962.
2. www.ulsteractors.com.
3. *Liverpool Echo*, 5 September 1922.
4. Quoted in 'Mr Doyle of Ballygullion', BBC N.I. Home Service, transmitted 19 June 1962, BBC Radio Archive, UFTM, Cultra.
5. Quoted in Margaret McHenry, *The Ulster Theatre in Ireland*, (Pennsylvania 1931), p. 54.
6. V.S. Pritchett, *Dublin: A Portrait*, (London 1967), p. 15.
7. Ricky H letter to PC, 13 January 2013.
8. McHenry, *op. cit.* p. 68.
9. *Irish Times*, 1 December 1931.
10. RH, 'A few random notes about the foundation of a Belfast Repertory Theatre', RHA, UFTM, n.d. note circa 1930.
11. 'The Autobiography of Thomas Carnduff', quoted in *Thomas Carnduff: Life and Writings*, John Gray (ed.), (Belfast 1994), p. 109.
12. *Irish Independent*, 12 October 1932.
13. *Ibid.*
14. *Irish Independent*, 11 October 1932.

15. *Irish Times*, 11 October 1932.
16. 'Thomas Carnduff: Unpublished autobiography', Carnduff archive QUB Special Collections, MS21/2.
17. *Irish Press*, 14 October 1932.
18. *Irish Independent*, 14 October 1932.
19. *Irish Press*, 14 October 1932.
20. *Irish Independent*, 14 October 1932.
21. *Northern Whig*, 14 October 1932.
22. *Belfast News Letter*, 22 November 1932.
23. *Irish News*, 22 November 1932.
24. *Northern Whig*, 22 November 1932.
25. John Gray, *Irish Book Lore*, vol. 4, no.1, Wesley McCann (ed.), 'Thomas Carnduff, 1886–1956: chapters from an unpublished autobiography', (Belfast 1978).
26. 'Thomas Carnduff', *op. cit.*
27. Gray, *op. cit.*
28. *Sunday Dispatch*, 21 March 1933.
29. *Irish Times*, 7 March 1933.
30. *Dublin Evening Herald*, 7 March 1933.
31. *Belfast News Letter*, 22 January 1935.
32. Sam Hanna Bell, *The Theatre in Ulster*, (Dublin 1972), p. 55.
33. *Irish Independent*, 19 February 1935.
34. *Irish Times*, 19 February 1935.
35. *Irish Press*, 19 February 1935.
36. *Dublin Evening Herald*, 19 February 1935.
37. *Sunday Independent*, 22 February 1935.
38. Ricky H in conversation with PC, 14 October 2012.
39. *Ibid.*
40. *Daily Express*, 11 October 1933.
41. Bell, *op. cit.* p.53.
42. www.ulsteractors.com
43. *Belfast Telegraph*, 16 April 1956.
44. *IPU*, pp. 32–3.
45. *Northern Whig*, 18 May, 1937.
46. *Irish Independent*, 11 October 1932.

4. CRUSADERS OF THE ETHER

1. Quoted in Rex Cathcart, *The Most Contrary Region: The BBC in Northern Ireland 1924–1984*, (Belfast 1984), p. 25.
2. *IRJ*, July 1925.
3. John Cowley letter to Tyrone Guthrie, 13 August 1925, Tyrone Guthrie Letters (1920–29), PRONI D3585/F/5/1/1.

4. *Radio Times*, 1927.
5. Cathcart, *op. cit.* p. 55.
6. *Sunday Independent*, 19 January 1930.
7. *The* BBC *in Northern Ireland, Silver Jubilee 1924–1949*, '2BE Calling, 1924', Guthrie, BBC publications, 1949.
8. *Ibid.*
9. *Belfast News Letter*, 16 October 1929.
10. Cathcart, *op. cit.* pp. 41–2.
11. *Belfast News Letter*, 21 October 1929.
12. *Ibid.*
13. *Northern Whig*, 3 April 1931.
14. RH letter to Ursula Eason, n.d. BBC files, RHA, UFTM.
15. Eason letter to RH, 6 May 1941, RHA, UFTM.
16. Franklin Engelmann letter to RH, 10 December 1941, RHA, UFTM.
17. Eason letter to RH, 29 April 1941, RHA, UFTM.
18. *Border Foray*, (London 1957), p. 63.
19. *Leinster and the City of Dublin*, (London 1949), p. 242.
20. *The Story of the Irish harp*, (Dublin 1954).
21. *Manchester Guardian*, 6 December 1954.
22. Nicholas Carolan recorded interview with PC, 13 May 2010.
23. D.L. Ross letter to RH, 2 February 1959, BBC files, RHA, UFTM.
24. Walter Love interview with PC, 30 October 2012.
25. Michael Baguley email to PC, 11 January 2013.
26. Andrew Crockart recorded interview with PC, 23 November 2012.
27. Gerry Hobbs in conversation with PC, 18 April 2013.
28. *Ibid.*
29. James Greene phone conversation with PC, 12 January 2013.

5. MASTER OF HIS ART

1. Quoted in Moore Orr interview with RH, twenty-first anniversary brochure as recording artist, Decca, London, 1948.
2. *Irish Saturday Night* record sleeve notes, Decca, 1954.
3. *Ulster Songs and Ballads*, (London 1925), pp. 5–6.
4. *Ibid.* pp. 7–11.
5. *Irish News*, 21 November 1925.
6. *Ibid.*
7. *Ibid.*
8. *Studies*, vol. XV, no. 57, March 1926.
9. *Irish Statesman*, 12 December 1925.
10. Monk Gibbon quoted in W.R. Rodgers, *Irish Literary Portraits*, (London 1972), p. 198.

11. *IPU*, p. 182.
12. *Gramophone*, July 1931.
13. *From the Irish Roads*, Decca, 1948.
14. *Ibid.*
15. *Ibid.*
16. *Daily Express*, 23 February 1934.
17. *Northern Whig*, 19 June 1936.
18. Orr, *op. cit.*
19. Nicholas Carolan recorded interview with PC, 13 May 2010.
20. Gerry Hobbs in conversation with PC, 18 April 2013.
21. Quoted in Brian Barton, *The Blitz: Belfast in the War Years*, (Belfast 1989), p. 122.
22. *Irish News*, 17 April 1942.
23. Ricky H in conversation with PC, 14 May 2013.
24. *Ibid.*
25. *Evening Herald*, 6 August 1940.
26. Personal papers, RHA, UFTM.
27. *Ibid.*
28. Orr, *op. cit.*
29. 'Disc: The Pocket Miscellany for the Music Lover and the Gramophone Enthusiast', by "Discus", Donald J. Thornton, (ed.) vol. 2, no. 7, Bristol Gramophone Society, Summer 1948.
30. *Ibid.*
31. *Ibid.*

6. NAME IN LIGHTS

1. Brian McIlroy, *Irish Cinema: An Illustrated History*, (Dublin 1988), pp. 26–7.
2. *Belfast News Letter*, 11 November 1932.
3. *Irish News*, 11 November 1932.
4. *Kinematograph Weekly*, 2 April 1936.
5. *Ulster Illustrated*, vol. 6, no. 5, July 1958.
6. *Irish News*, 11 September 1935.
7. *Ulster Tatler*, August 1969.
8. John Clifford diary, February 1970, Larne Heritage Centre.
9. *Belfast News Letter*, 4 February 1936.
10. *Belfast Telegraph*, 4 February 1936.
11. *Irish News*, 14 December 1935.
12. *Irish Press*, 18 February 1936.
13. *Dublin Evening Herald*, 15 February 1936.
14. *Limerick Leader*, 3 February 1936.
15. *Daily Express*, 3 September 1935.
16. *Irish News*, 14 December 1935.

17. *Ulster Illustrated, op. cit.*
18. *Daily Mail*, 26 January 1937.
19. *Variety*, 20 January 1936.
20. *Irish News*, 29 May 1936.
21. *Ibid.*
22. Quoted in John Hill, *Cinema and Northern Ireland*, (London 2006), p.8.
23. *Ibid*, footnote, p. 11.
24. *Irish News*, 13 March 1935.
25. *Irish News*, 14 December 1936.
26. *Belfast Telegraph*, 17 November 1936.
27. *Irish News*, 8 August 1936.
28. *Ibid.*
29. *Irish Press*, 9 February 1937.
30. Hill, *op. cit.* p. 33.
31. Censor's Decision Reserve Books, Film Censors Office, NAI, 98/28/13, p.3730 no. 11061.
32. Quoted in Kevin Rockett, *Irish Film Censorship, A Cultural Journey from Silent Cinema to Internet Pornography*, (Dublin 2004), p. 63.
33. McIlroy, *op. cit.* p. 27.
34. *Belfast News Letter*, 5 November 1936.
35. *Irish News*, 5 November 1936.
36. *The Times*, 26 November 2012.
37. *Guardian*, 26 November 2012.
38. *Ulster Illustrated*, vol. 6, no. 4, June 1958.
39. *New York Times*, 3 November 1938.
40. *Irish Echo*, 12 November 1938.
41. *Irish News*, 26 November 1938, quoted in *The Gaelic American*, 5 November and 12 November.
42. *Ibid.*
43. *Ibid.*
44. *Irish News*, 30 November 1937.
45. *Ibid.*
46. *Belfast Telegraph*, 30 November 1937.
47. *Daily Express*, 4 December 1937.
48. *Monthly Film Bulletin*, 1938.
49. F.J. Caraher letter to RH, 13 January 1945, RHA, UFTM.
50. Hill, *op cit.* p. 163.

7. 'AS WONDERFUL AS FATHER O'FLYNN'

1. *Sugarhouse Entry*, (London 1936), p. 1.
2. *Ibid*, pp. 28–9.

3. *Spectator*, 9 October 1936.

4. *Irish Independent*, 24 November 1936.

5. *Belfast Telegraph*, 10 October 1936.

6. *Sunday Times*, 4 October 1936.

7. *Daily Telegraph*, 6 October 1936.

8. *Derry Journal*, 23 October 1936.

9. *Ibid.*

10. Máirín Allen, *Father Mathew Record*, 'Contemporary Irish Artists, XII: 'James Humbert Craig, R.H.A.', June 1942.

11. *Ibid.*

12. *IPU*, pp. 3–4.

13. *Ibid.* p. 8.

14. *Ibid.* p.8.

15. *Ibid.* p. 106.

16. *Ibid.* p. 243.

17. *Ibid.* p. 278.

18. *Ibid.* p. 177.

19. *Ibid.* p. 336.

20. *Book Society*, July 1936.

21. *Observer*, 9 August 1938.

22. *The Times*, 5 July 1938.

23. *Manchester Guardian*, 22 July 1938.

24. *Sunday Times*, 14 August 1938.

25. *Belfast Telegraph*, 27 August 1938.

26. *Irish Times*, 10 September 1938.

27. *Irish Independent*, 26 July 1938.

28. *Sunday Independent*, 7 August 1938.

29. *IPU*, p. 252.

30. *Dublin Magazine*, Jan–Mar. 1939.

31. John Hewitt, *Art in Ulster, 1557–1957*, (Belfast 1977), p. 141.

32. *IPU*, p. 1.

33. Govt. information service, November 1945, PRONI CAB 9/F/123/34.

34. *Ibid.*

35. *DLB*, vol. 112, 'British Literary Publishing Houses, 1881–1965', Jonathan Rose & Patricia Anderson (eds), essay on Arthur Barker by John Hewish, (Gale Research Inc. 1991), p. 35.

36. RH letter to Mullan & Son, 9 November 1949, RHA, UFTM.

37. *Ibid.*

38. Private papers, RHA, UFTM

39. *Ibid.*

40. *Ibid.*

41. Caravan hire receipts, RHA, UFTM.

42. *Where the River Shannon flows*, (Dundalk, London), 1940, p. 180.

43. *Ibid.* p. 181.
44. *Ibid.* pp. 307–8.
45. *Ibid.* p. 326.
46. *Irish Times*, 13 July 1940.
47. *Ibid.*
48. *Belfast News Letter*, 24 April 1939.
49. *Sunday Independent*, 7 July 1940.
50. *Tablet*, 6 July 1940.
51. *Sunday Times*, 7 July 1940.
52. *Studies*, vol. XXX, June 1941.
53. *Ibid, DLB*, essay on George G. Harrap by Kirk Beetz.
54. Nick Kaszuk in conversation with PC, 18 May 2011.
55. Ricky H letter to PC, 13 January 2013.
56. RH to MW, 13 March 1943, MWP, Glucksman UL, P7, 138.
57. Dion Hayward, war journal, 1944.
58. Paul Hayward in conversation with PC, 13 May 2013.
59. *IPU*, p. 143.
60. *Ibid*, p. 254.
61. Ricky H letter to PC, 13 January 2013.
62. *Munster and the City of Cork*, (London 1964), p. 169.
63. Leslie Matson phone conversation with PC, 11 September 2013.
64. Ricky H letter to PC, 12 June 2013.
65. *Who's Who in Northern Ireland, 1938*, (Belfast 1938).

8. 'A STUBBORN DIVIL'

1. Seamus Brennan, (Noel Huggard's son-in-law), in conversation with PC, 2 November 2012.
2. *Corrib Country*, p. 2.
3. *Ibid.* p. 19
4. *Ibid.* p. 1.
5. *Ibid.* p. 5.
6. *Ibid.* p. 105.
7. *Ibid.* pp. 72–4.
8. *Ibid.* p. 95.
9. *Ibid.* pp. 101–03.
10. *Ibid.* p. 104.
11. *Tempest of Dundalgan: Portrait of a Perfectionist,* Charles Tempest McCrea, Dundalgan, 1968, p. 68.
12. *Belfast News Letter*, 4 June 1943.
13. *Belfast Telegraph*, 21 May 1943.
14. *Irish Independent*, 31 May 1943.

15. *Irish Press*, 12 May 1943.
16. *TLS*, 24 July 1943.
17. *Dublin Magazine*, October 1943.
18. *Studies*, June 1944, vol. XXXIII, pp. 286–7.
19. *Ibid.*
20. *The Bell*, vol. 11, no. 6, September 1943, pp. 534–5.
21. *CC*, foreword.
22. *Irish Times*, 15 May 1943.
23. Donovan Pedelty letter to RH, 11 June 1943, RHA, UFTM.
24. Tempest letter to RH, 24 June 1963, RHA, UFTM.
25. Ricky H in conversation with PC, 14 May 2013.
26. *Ibid.*
27. Avril Cotton-Taylor phone conversation with PC, 10 June 2013.
28. Ricky H in conversation with PC, 15 November 2012.
29. Ricky H in conversation with PC, 14 May 2013.
30. *In the Kingdom of Kerry* pp. 228–9.
31. *Ibid.* p. 231.
32. *Ibid.* pp. 231–2
33. *Ibid.* p. 232.
34. *Ibid.* pp. 234–5.
35. *Ibid.* p. 236. (A wassail is a toast or salutation.)
36. *Ibid.* p. 190.
37. *Ibid.* pp. 244–5.
38. *Ibid.* p. 246.
39. *Ibid.* p. 260.
40. Ricky H in conversation with PC, 14 May 2013.
41. Richard Hilliard letter to PC, 9 July 2013 and phone conversation, 29 July 2013.
42. McCrea, *op. cit.* p. 71.
43. *Ibid.* pp. 71–2.
44. Tempest letter to RH, 21 March 1945, RHA, UFTM.
45. *Ibid.*
46. *Ibid.*
47. *Ibid.*
48. RH letter to Tempest, 22 March 1945, RHA, UFTM.
49. *Ibid.*
50. *Ibid.*
51. *Ibid.*
52. *Ibid.*
53. *Ibid.*
54. *Ibid.*
55. Tempest letter to RH, 3 April 1945, RHA, UFTM.
56. RH letter to Tempest, 6 April 1945.
57. RH letter to Tempest, 12 April 1945.

58. *Ibid.*

59. RH letter to Tempest, 24 April 1945.

60. McCrea, *op. cit.* p.72.

61. *Ibid.*

62. *Ibid.*

63. *Irish Independent*, 19 August 1946.

64. *The Bell*, vol. XIII, no. 1, October 1946, p. 82.

65. *Irish Bookman*, vol. 1, no. 2, September 1946.

66. Theo Snoddy, *Dictionary of Irish Artists: 20th Century*, Wolfhound, 1996, p. 151.

67. *Illustrated London News*, 20 July 1946, p. 82.

68. *Manchester Guardian*, n.d.

69. *JRSAI*, Miscellanea, vol. LXXX, part 1, 1950.

70. Daniel O'Sullivan letter to RH, 12 December 1947, RHA, UFTM.

71. Michael Glazier letter to RH, 1 August 1953, RHA, UFTM.

72. Eason Bulletin, Irish Authors, Richard Hayward: 30, 1947.

73. MacMahon, *op. cit.*

9. ULSTER VERSUS IRELAND: A 'SUGAR-COATING' BATTLE

1. *Belfast News Letter*, 17 May 1939.

2. *Irish Press*, 14 March 1939.

3. Gerard Turley letter to PC, 7 February 2012.

4. *Irish Press*, 13 March 1944.

5. RH letter to Hungerford, 26 February 1940, PRONI, CAB9F/123/3A.

6. *Ibid.*

7. L.G.P. Freer letter to Hungerford, 1 March 1940, PRONI CAB9F/123/3A.

8. MacQuitty, *A Life to Remember*, p. 270.

9. *Ibid.*

10. *Northern Whig*, 5 February 1942.

11. Hill, *Cinema and Northern Ireland*, p. 88.

12. *Belfast News Letter*, 5 February 1942.

13. *Belfast Telegraph*, 5 February 1942.

14. MacQuitty, *op. cit.* pp. 271–2.

15. *Ibid.* p. 272.

16. *Irish Press*, 16 November 1943.

17. *Irish Press*, 13 December 1943.

18. *Dublin Herald*, 15 November 1943.

19. *Irish Times*, 16 November 1943.

20. *Kinematograph*, 21 March 1946.

21. *To-day's Cinema*, 15 March 1946.

22. Quoted in Hill, p. 111.

23. *Ibid.* pp. 111–12.

24. Adams letter to Northwood, 19 November 1945, PRONI CAB9F/123/81.
25. Northwood letter to Adams, 24 November 1945, PRONI CAB9F/123/81.
26. RH letter Robert Gransden, 9 April 1946, PRONI CAB9F/123/81.
27. Gransden letter to RH, 16 April 1946, PRONI CAB9F/123/81.
28. RH letter to Gransden, 12 April 1946, PRONI CAB9F/123/81.
29. RH letter to Gransden with film unit proposal, 9 April 1946, PRONI CAB9F/123/81.
30. *Ibid.*
31. Gransden letter, 9 May 1946, PRONI CAB9F/123/81.
32. Minutes of Stormont Cabinet Publicity Committee, 6 May 1946, PRONI CAB9F/123/37.
33. Cabinet Publicity Committee, note by F. M. Adams, 11 April 1946, PRONI CAB9F/123/37.
34. *Ibid.*
35. RH letter to Gransden, 19 April 1946, PRONI CAB9F/123/81.
36. *Ibid.*

10. 'WE USED TO ROW LIKE HELL AT TIMES – AS GOOD FRIENDS DO'

1. Devin Garrity letter to RH, 17 February 1947, RHA, UFTM.
2. RH letter to Garrity, 12 August 1947, RHA, UFTM.
3. Garrity letter to RH, 10 October 1947, RHA, UFTM
4. *Ibid.*
5. RH letter to Garrity, 23 October 1947, RHA, UFTM.
6. *Ibid.*
7. *Ibid.*
8. Garrity letter with reader's report to RH, 28 November 1947, RHA, UFTM.
9. *Ibid.*
10. Garrity letter to RH, 28 November 1947, RHA, UFTM.
11. RH letter to Garrity, 9 December 1947, RHA, UFTM.
12. Garrity letter to RH, 20 January 1948, RHA, UFTM.
13. RH letter to Garrity, 2 February 1948, RHA, UFTM.
14. *Ibid.*
15. Garrity letter to RH, 29 April 1948, RHA, UFTM.
16. RH letter to Garrity, 5 May 1948, RHA, UFTM.
17. Personal papers, RHA, UFTM.
18. *Leinster and the City of Dublin,* (London 1949), p. 33.
19. *Ibid.* p. 37.
20. *Ibid.* p. 47.
21. *Ibid.* p. 50.

22. *Ibid.* p. 54.
23. *Ibid.* p. 52.
24. *Ibid.* p. 62.
25. Private papers, RHA, UFTM
26. *LCD, op. cit.* p. 126.
27. *Ibid.* p. 147.
28. Alan Pim phone conversation with PC, 28 January 2013.
29. *LCD, op. cit.* p. 179.
30. *Ibid.* p. 230.
31. *Ibid.* p. 202.
32. *Oxford Companion to Irish Literature,* (Oxford 1996), pp. 149–50.
33. *LCD, op. cit.* pp. 5–6.
34. *Ibid.* p. 249.
35. Harold Leask letter to RH, 7 January 1949, RHA, UFTM.
36. *LCD, op. cit.* p. 9.
37. *Ibid.* pp. 6–7.
38. Leask letter to RH, 10 August 1949, RHA, UFTM.
39. *Irish Times,* 13 August 1949.
40. *Irish Independent,* 20 August 1940.
41. *Irish Press,* 28 July 1949.
42. *Irish Geography,* vol. 2, no. 2, 1950.
43. *Dublin Magazine,* Oct.–Dec. 1949, p. 57.
44. *TLS,* 19 August 1949.
45. *The Bookman,* n.d.
46. *Truth,* n.d.
47. *LCD, op. cit.* p. 256.
48. Arthur Barker letter to RH, 20 April 1949, RHA, UFTM.
49. Raymond Piper in conversation with PC, 21 May 2001.

11. 'TALKATIVE TRAVELLER'

1. *Ulster and the City of Belfast,* (London 1950), p. 18.
2. RH letter to Mathew O'Mahony, 17 May 1949, O'Mahony papers, NLI MS 24,900 (iii) acc 3844.
3. *Belfast Telegraph,* 27 May 1950.
4. *Northern Whig,* 1 July 1950.
5. *Dublin Magazine,* vol. XXV, no. 5, Jan–Mar. 1950.
6. *Studies,* March 1951.
7. *TLS,* 23 June 1950.
8. RH travel notebooks, RHA, UFTM.
9. *MSLR,* (London 1955), p. 162.
10. RH travel notebooks, *op cit.*

11. Tom Maher in conversation with PC, 21 August 2009.
12. RH travel notebooks, *op. cit.*
13. *MSLR*, p. 65.
14. *Ibid.* p. 33.
15. RH travel notebooks, *op. cit.*
16. *MSLR*, p. 92.
17. *Ibid*, p. 144.
18. *Ibid.* pp. 148–9.
19. *Ibid*, p. 214.
20. RH letter to Leask, 21 October 1949, RHA, UFTM.
21. Leask letter to RH, 23 October 1949, RHA, UFTM.
22. Leask letter to RH, 15 August 1949, RHA, UFTM.
23. RH letter to Mathew O'Mahony, 10 November 1949, *op. cit.*
24. *DLB*, vol. 112, 'British Literary Publishing Houses, 1881–1965', Jonathan Rose & Patricia Anderson, (eds), Arthur Barker essay by John Hewish, 1991, p. 35.
25. Van Thal letter to RH, 24 October 1951, RHA, UFTM.
26. Van Thal letter to RH, 2 November 1951, RHA, UFTM.
27. Van Thal letter to RH, 17 March 1952, RHA, UFTM.
28. *New Statesman and Nation*, 17 May 1952.
29. *TLS*, 2 May 1952.
30. *Northern Whig*, 30 August 1952.
31. *Irish Book Lover*, June 1952.
32. Van Thal letter to RH, 17 March 1952, RHA, UFTM.
33. Des Kenny phone conversation with PC, 28 February 2013.
34. Henry Comerford letters to PC, 7 July and 25 July 2013, phone conversation 22 July 2013.
35. Van Thal letter to RH, 24 October 1951, RHA, UFTM.
36. RH letter to Liam Gógan, 26 June 1958, Liam S. Gógan papers, UCD LA27/711.
37. George Thompson in conversation with PC, 9 March 2013.
38. *Ibid.*
39. RH October 1951 diary, RHA, UFTM.
40. Thomas Carnduff Archive, QUB Special Collections, PEN file, Box 5, MS/21/17.
41. Geoffrey Taylor letter to John Hewitt, July 1953, PRONI D3838/7/16/61–80.
42. *Kavanagh's Weekly*, vol. 1, no. 4, 3 May 1952.
43. J. J. Tohill in conversation with PC, 28 February 2013.
44. Wilson Graham phone conversation with PC, 1 July 2013.
45. Jay R. Tunney, *The Prizefighter and the Playwright: Gene Tunney and Bernard Shaw*, (Buffalo 2010), p. 271.
46. Denis O'Hara, *I nearly met Gene Tunney*, (Cushendun 2011), p. 2; Randal McDonnell phone conversation with PC, 9 August 2013.
47. O'Hara, *op cit.* p. 6.
48. *Northern Whig*, 28 August 1952.

49. Austin Carty letter to PC, 25 July 2013 and phone conversation 9 August 2013.
50. *TLS*, 22 July 1955.
51. *Western Mail*, 21 September 1955.

12. FRIENDLY INVASION FROM THE NORTH

1. Alun Evans email to PC, 9 May 2013.
2. HB, 'Down the Parade', *In the Land of Nod*, (Dublin 1996), p. 3.
3. HB, 'Beside the Nore', *Escape from the Anthill*, (Dublin 1985), pp. 93–4.
4. RH to HB, 30 October 1951, TCD MS 10304/571/2.
5. Walter Smithwick letter to HB, 29 December 1945, TCD MS 10304/571/5.
6. RH letter to HB, 4 January 1952, TCD MS 10304/571/6.
7. RH letter to HB, 29 February 1952, TCD MS 10304/571/12.
8. HB telegram to RH, 3 March 1952, TCD MS 10304/571/13.
9. RH letter to HB, 4 March 1952, TCD MS 10304/571/14.
10. RH letter to HB, 12 March 1952, TCD MS 10304/571/15.
11. *Irish Times*, 10 April 1952.
12. *Kilkenny People*, 19 April 1952.
13. *Kilkenny Journal*, 19 April 1952.
14. 'North and South', 'Weekly Bulletin of the Department of External Affairs', NLI, 28 April 1952, no. 133, p. 6.
15. Quoted in Robert Tobin, *The Minority Voice: Hubert Butler and Southern Irish Protestantism, 1900–1991*, (Oxford 2012), p. 165.
16. Christopher Fitz-Simon, *Eleven Houses: A Memoir of Childhood*, (Dublin 2007), pp. 172–7.
17. HB, untitled note, 1952, TCD MS 10304/188b1.
18. HB, 'The Sub-Prefect Should Have Held His Tongue', *Escape from the Anthill, op. cit.* p. 279.
19. *Old Kilkenny Review*, (Kilkenny 1953), p. 54.
20. RH letter to HB, 17 November 1952, TCD MS 10304/597/752/4.
21. *Northern Whig*, 24 April 1954.
22. Proinsias Ó Drisceoil, 'The Kilkenny Debates', in C. Agee (ed.), *Unfinished Ireland: Essays on Hubert Butler* (Belfast 2003), p. 112. See this for an account of the background to the debate.
23. *Belfast Telegraph*, 24 April 1954; the song was not identified but was 'County Kildare Fragment.'
24. *Ibid.*
25. HB, 'The Sub-Prefect Should Have Held His Tongue' (1956), *Escape from the Anthill, op. cit.* p. 274. For more on the controversy see the book's appendix containing HB letter.
26. *Wexford People*, 11 April 1953.
27. Prof Richard Clarke recorded interview with PC, 10 December 2012.

28. *Ibid.*
29. Peter Cavan recorded interviews with PC, 9 November 2012 and 22 November 2012.
30. RH letter to Gógan, 12 May 1958, Liam S. Gógan papers, UCD LA27/407.
31. Cavan, *op. cit.*
32. *Ibid.*
33. *Ibid.*
34. *Irish Naturalists' Journal*, vol. X, October 1950.
35. *Ulster and the City of Belfast*, (1950), p. 7.
36. BNFC AGM minute book, 1951–2, p. 123, BNFC archive.
37. *Ibid.*
38. *Ibid.*
39. Cavan, *op. cit.*
40. *PRIA*, vol. 52. Section C: Archaeology, Linguistics and Literature, July 1948 (Paper presented 9 December 1947) (Dublin 1948).
41. *The English Dialects of Ulster*, Barry and Tilling (eds), (Cultra 1986).
42. RH general notebooks, RHA, UFTM.
43. *Northern Whig*, 28 July 1951.
44. *Border Foray*, p. 185.
45. Anne Smyth recorded interview with PC, 15 February 2013.
46. RH general notebooks, RHA, UFTM.
47. BNFC Report, 1959–60, BNFC archive.
48. Adams, BNFC minute book, 21 April 1959, BNFC archive.
49. *Ulster Dialects: An Introductory Symposium*, (Cultra 1964).
50. Quoted in 'The Dictionary Project', *Concise Ulster Dictionary*, C. I. Macafee, (ed.), (Oxford 1996), p. ix.
51. Smyth, *op cit.*
52. *Ibid.*
53. *Belfast News Letter*, 16 November 1964.
54. *Ibid.*
55. Quoted in *Newry Telegraph*, 11 April 1953.
56. RH private papers, RHA, UFTM.

13. MANY-WAYED MAN WITH AN 'EYE FOR THE MAIN CHANCE'

1. *Border Foray*, (1957), pp. 10–11.
2. *Ibid.* p. 30.
3. *Ibid.* p. 64.
4. *Ibid.* p. 11.
5. *Ibid.* p. 133.
6. *Ibid.* p. 59.
7. *Ibid.* p. 60.

8. *Ibid.* pp. 64–5.
9. *Ibid.* p. 68.
10. *Ibid.* p. 119.
11. *Ibid.* p. 89
12. *Ibid.* p. 146.
13. *Ibid.* pp. 150–1.
14. *Ibid.* p. 173.
15. *Ibid.* p. 148.
16. *TLS*, 24 January 1958.
17. John Hewitt, *Art in Ulster, 1557–1957*, (Belfast 1977), p. 143.
18. *Book and Magazine Collector*, no. 222, September 2002.
19. James Loughlin, *Ulster Unionism and British National Identity Since 1885*, (London 1995), p. 170.
20. *Ibid.* p. 171.
21. Eldon Orange lodge, general correspondence file, 1945–1958, Orange Order HQ, Belfast.
22. *Ibid.* general correspondence file, 1964–65.
23. Angus McConnell phone conversation with PC, 26 June 2013.
24. Paul Hayward in conversation with PC, 14 May 2013.
25. Compton Mackenzie, n.d.
26. Quoted on *The Orange Sash*, LP sleeve notes, Fontana, 1959.
27. Anne Smyth interview with PC, 15 February 2103.
28. *Ibid.*
29. *Gramophone*, January 1960.
30. *Belfast Telegraph*, 2 December 1959.
31. 'The Sash My Father Wore', BBC Radio Ulster, presented by Tommy Sands, produced by Cameron Mitchell, transmitted 7 July 2013.
32. *The Orange Sash*, LP, *op. cit.*
33. *Ibid.*
34. *Belfast through the Ages*, 'Books, Ships and some Town-Planning', (Dundalk 1952), pp. 12–13.
35. *Belfast Telegraph*, 8 March 1958.
36. *Ulster Illustrated*, vol. 7, no. 9, September 1959.
37. *Ibid.*
38. *Ibid.*
39. *Easton Express*, 5 June 1959.
40. Brookeborough letter to RH, 6 May 1959, RHA, UFTM.
41. Alfie Byrne letter to RH, 16 April 1955, RHA, UFTM.
42. Ricky H in conversation with PC, 14 May 2013.
43. *Belfast Telegraph*, 19 April 1958.
44. Seán McCann letter to RH, 23 August 1962, RHA, UFTM.
45. *Irish Astronomical Journal*, 'Astronomy Sixty Years ago, The Ulster Astronomical Society, 1890–1894', RH and John H. McElderry, vol. 1, no. 3, September 1950.

46. RH letter to editor, *UJA* 'Archaeology and the ordinary farmer', 3rd ser. vol. 10, 1947.
47. George Thompson phone conversation with PC, 9 March 2013.
48. Thompson Steele phone conversation with PC, 15 April 2013.
49. John Killen in conversation with PC, 15 April 2013.
50. 'A table in the window', BBC N.I. Home Service, presented by Sam Hanna Bell and Jack Loudan, produced by Maurice Leitch, transmitted 9 November 1961, BBC Radio Archive, UFTM, Cultra, ref. no. 26984(1), cat. no. 904028.
51. Roma Tomelty phone conversation with PC, 12 January 2013.
52. James Campbell phone conversation with PC, 10 December 2012.
53. Roger Dixon in conversation with PC, 5 August 2013.

14. MUNSTER LITERARY SWANSONG

1. *Easton Express*, 5 June 1959.
2. Mattie Waugh phone conversation with PC, 10 April 2013.
3. Eric Waugh phone conversation with PC, 10 April 2013.
4. Ken Jamison phone conversation with PC, 29 January 2013.
5. Billy Simpson phone conversation with PC, 9 May 2013.
6. *Evening Press*, 26 November 1962, 'Nostalgia in a changing city, My Home Town.'
7. *Ibid.*
8. Andrew Crockart recorded interview with PC, 23 November 2012.
9. Charles Hill letter to PC, 4 July 2013; phone conversation, 31 July 2013.
10. *MCC*, p. 44.
11. *Ibid.* pp. 51–2.
12. RH notes, RHA, UFTM.
13. RHA, BCL.
14. Paul Hayward in conversation with PC, 9 November 2012.
15. RH letter to Dorothy Gamble, 23 May 1961, RHA, UFTM.
16. *Sunday Express*, 18 February 1962.
17. *Ibid.*
18. Patrick Mahony letter to RH, RHA, UFTM.
19. Len Holmes letter to RH, RHA, UFTM.
20. *Dublin Evening Mail*, 23 February 1962.
21. *Social and Personal*, vol. 17, no. 10, March 1962.
22. Paul Hayward in conversation with PC, 14 May 2013.
23. Ann Young letter to Dorothy Hayward, 18 October 1964, RHA, UFTM.
24. *Belfast Telegraph*, 24 April 1963.
25. *Belfast News Letter*, 8 October 1963.
26. RH letter to Maurice Walsh, 23 February 1964, MS P7/147/47, MWP, Glucksman, UL.
27. Garvey papers, RHA, UFTM.

28. *Belfast Telegraph*, 13 June 1964.
29. *Ibid.*
30. *Belfast News Letter*, 13 June 1964.
31. Mageean letter and poem to RH, 20 August 1964, RHA, UFTM.
32. Paul Hayward in conversation with PC, 14 May 2013.
33. *Belfast Telegraph*, 6 July 1964.
34. David Honneyman in conversation with PC, 15 March 2013.
35. *Ibid.*
36. Harry Irvine in conversation with PC, 10 March 2002.
37. Michael Geare letter to RH, 16 July 1964, RHA, UFTM.
38. *Guardian*, 4 September 1964.
39. *Cork Examiner*, 3 September 1964.
40. *Irish Times*, 5 September 1964.
41. *Irish Press*, 19 September 1964.
42. *Sunday Independent*, 20 September 1964.
43. *Belfast Telegraph*, 3 September 1964.
44. *Illustrated London News*, 19 September 1964.
45. *New Daily*, 2 September 1964.
46. *Irish Christian Advocate*, 3 September 1964.
47. *Church of Ireland Gazette*, September 1964.
48. Robert Hogan, (ed.) *Dictionary of Irish Literature*, (London 1996), p. 532.
49. Richard Kirkland, *Cathal O'Byrne and the Northern Revival in Ireland, 1890–1960*, (Liverpool 2006), p. 199.
50. Rex Hayward letter to RH, 4 October 1964, RHA, UFTM.

15. TRAGEDY STRIKES

1. *Irish Independent*, 14 October, 1964.
2. *Ballymena Observer*, 15 October 1964.
3. *Belfast News Letter*, 14 October 1964.
4. *Ibid.*
5. *Ibid.*
6. *Irish News*, 14 October 1964.
7. *Irish Press*, 14 October 1964.
8. *Ibid.*
9. *Irish Times*, 14 October 1964.
10. *Ibid.*
11. *Irish Independent, op. cit.*
12. *The Times*, 15 October 1964.
13. *Belfast Telegraph*, 17 October 1964.
14. Michael Dewar telegram to DH, 14 October 1964, RHA, UFTM.
15. Dewar to DH, 15 October 1964, RHA, UFTM.

16. *Belfast News Letter*, 21 October 1964.
17. Dion Hayward letter to DH, 15 October 1964, RHA, UFTM
18. Rex Hayward letter to DH, 29 October 1964 RHA, UFTM.
19. Rex Hayward letter to DH, 18 November 1964, RHA, UFTM.
20. DH letter to Rex Hayward, 12 December 1964, RHA, UFTM.
21. Rex Hayward letter to DH, n.d. RHA, UFTM.
The following correspondence is all dated October 1964, RHA, UFTM
22. John-Lewis Crosby to DH.
23. O.W.J. Henderson to DH.
24. Ian Fox to DH.
25. Ivan Grainger to DH.
26. John D. Stewart to DH.
27. Harold Goldblatt to DH.
28. Ray Rosenfield to DH.
29. J.C. Beckett to DH.
30. Michael Geare to DH.
31. DH to Geare.
32. Philip Duncan to DH.
33. L. Duncan-Doring to DH.
34. Betsy and Patric Stevenson to DH.
35. Jerome Coffey to DH.
36. Cork town clerk to DH.
37. Stephen Rynne to DH.
38. Diarmuid Maclomhair to DH.
39. K. Thompson to DH.
40. Giff Pitney to DH.
41. Elsie Patton to DH.
42. Meta Reid to DH.
43. Hazel Staples to DH.
44. Gene Tunney to DH.
45. Frank O'Connor to DH.
46. Neil Prendergast to DH.
47. Mollie Quinn to DH.
48. Michael Cahalane to DH.
49. Maureen Hegarty to DH.
50. Daisy Phelan to DH.
51. *Kilkenny People*, 23 October 1964.

16. FINAL PARTING

1. *Belfast News Letter*, 5 November 1964.
2. Richard Clarke recorded interview with PC, 10 December 2012.

3. Raymond Piper in conversation with PC, 14 May 2005.
4. Douglas Frazer-Hurst, RH memorial service recording, 4 November 1964, (kindly supplied by Paul Hayward to PC, 17 May 2013.)
5. *Ibid.*
6. *Ibid.*
7. Inquest papers, RHA, UFTM.
8. *Ibid.*
9. *Belfast News Letter*, 9 November 1964.
10. *Belfast News Letter*, 16 November 1964.
11. *Belfast Telegraph*, 1 December 1964.
12. *Banbridge Chronicle*, 2 April 1965.
13. *English Dance and Song*, August 1965.
14. *Gramophone*, September 1965.
15. *Belfast News Letter*, 10 June 1965.
16. Ricky H letter to DH, January 1965, UFTM, RHA.
17. 'A House Demolished', *The Collected Poems of John Hewitt,* Frank Ormsby, (ed.) (Belfast 1992), p.p 323–4.
18. DH letter to Ricky H and Dion, n.d., RHA, UFTM.
19. *Ibid.*
20. Peter Cavan in conversation with PC, 9 November 2012.
21. Jack McIlvenna in conversation with PC, 17 May 2013.
22. George Thompson phone conversation with PC, 9 March 2013.
23. Fred Collins phone conversation with PC, 27 June 2013.
24. Judith Wilson in conversation with PC, 16 April 2013.
25. Ricky H in conversation with PC, 14 May 2013.
26. Dion Hayward letter to DH, 21 November 1982, RHA, UFTM.
27. *Ibid.*
28. *Ibid.*
29. DH letter to UFTM, 16 May 1990, RHA, UFTM.
30. Clifford Harkness in conversation with PC, 13 March 2013.
31. Roger Dixon in conversation with PC, 13 March 2013.
32. Judith Wilson in conversation with PC, 16 April 2013.
33. Raymond Piper in conversation with PC, 25 November 2001.
34. Paul Hayward in conversation with PC, 9 November 2012, 14 May 2013.
35. Walter Brady letter to DH, 18 October 1964, RHA, UFTM.

POSTSCRIPT: RICHARD HAYWARD ASSAYED

1. *Irish Times*, 21 July 2007; *Guardian*, 27 September 2007.
2. *A Walk through Carrick-on-Shannon,* Failte Ireland, 2009; *Offaly at your leisure,* Shannon Development, 2010; *Lough Derg, Ireland's Pleasure Lake*, Shannon Development, 2011; *Irish Cities Market Book,* Tourism Ireland, 2013; *Donegal*

Holiday Guide, Donegal County Council, 2014.

3. BBC N.I. exhibition, 2014.
4. *Fodor's Ireland 2014*, Random House, 2014, pp. 583–4.
5. 'Citizen Science: 150 years of the Belfast Naturalists' Field Club', BNFC, 2013, pp. 14–15.
6. *Irish Times*, 'Irishman's Diary', 15 March 2013.
7. Liam Mulvenna in conversation with PC, 17 May 2013.
8. *MSLR*, p. 185.
9. Gregory Dunne in conversation with PC, 22 August 2008.
10. *Where the River Shannon flows*, 1940, p. 91.

Acknowledgments

The art of biography is more difficult than is generally supposed.
Thornton Wilder, *The Bridge of San Luis Rey*, 1927

This biography would scarcely have been possible without the generous support of Richard Hayward's son, also called Richard, and known as Ricky. Patiently and cordially he answered innumerable queries, whether face-to-face, by letter, email or phone call, sharing his knowledge as well as memories and anecdotes of his father. During the course of my seven years of enquiries he has given unstintingly of his time, making available letters, family trees, photographs and other personal material. I have been privileged to hear stories from his family's past; his kindness, which included reading a section of the manuscript for accuracy, enriched the experience.

Richard Hayward's grandson, Paul Hayward (son of Dion Hayward), supplied information and agreed to be interviewed at length about his grandfather. He kindly supplied the loan of a recording of the memorial service and provided specific wartime facts from his father's Second World War journal. Judith Wilson, niece of Dorothy Hayward, responded with goodwill to my phone calls and emails bringing newly uncovered paperwork, photographs, and nuggets of information to our meetings.

There is a vast paper trail in connection with Hayward's life and work. I have truffled about in dusty archives, heritage centres and museums, and like Coleridge's 'library-cormorant' have flown from library to library as part of my research. Hayward's personal archive is held at the Ulster Folk and Transport Museum at Cultra in County Down. I was kindly given access to it by the Librarian Roger Dixon – a good counsel on many matters – and was constantly refreshed and excited by its contents. Other museum employees who helped include Clifford Harkness who advised on aspects of the Hayward film archive and images, and Sally Skilling. Peter Carson tracked down song and sketch recordings. Anne Smyth, Curator of the Ulster Dialect Archive, agreed to be interviewed while Dr Vivienne Pollock, Curator of History, opened photographic archives. The retired museum director, George Thompson, was full of insightful knowledge and stories, and considerably illuminated Hayward.

I wish to thank the staff at the Central Library in Belfast, where a range of archival material is kept containing Hayward manuscripts, typescripts, photographs and Dictabelt voice recordings. I am grateful to Patricia Walker, specialist manager at the library for help in locating these. As part of RASCAL: Research and Special Collections Available Locally, the Lynn Doyle Archive, Francis Joseph Bigger Archive and Ulster Writers' Archive are held in the library and all fed into the wider picture. I would like specifically to thank Jolene Weller, Yvonne Lynn and Dawn Ramsey. Thanks also to Jenny Browne for her help with the library's archive on the Empire and Abbey theatres. On numerous occasions, I consulted the priceless collection of papers in the Central Newspaper Library in Belfast where many productive hours were happily spent poring over relevant articles and sometimes irrelevant news stories. The staff was similarly solicitous and delivered a stream of bound volumes from the early and mid twentieth century.

Few cities can boast of such a venerable institution as the Linen Hall Library in Belfast and I benefited from its remarkable collections. The Librarian John Killen, Deputy Librarian, Monica Cash, as well as Deborah Douglas, Mary Delargy, Kelsey Ockert, and other members of staff, pointed me in the direction of the theatrical ephemera in the Mageean Collection and Empire Theatre Archives, an outstanding resource that was digitized in 2013. I would also like to acknowledge the helpfulness of the staff at the McClay Library at Queen's University Belfast. Deirdre Wildy, head of special collections and archives, and Susan Kirkpatrick allowed me to consult the private letters, papers, notebooks, theatrical ephemera and cuttings books in the Thomas Carnduff Archive. Ursula Mitchell at Queen's answered specific queries while Donna McCleary, senior library assistant in Arts Humanities and Social Sciences, and Diarmuid Kennedy made useful suggestions pointing me in fresh archival directions.

An important debt is to the staff at the BBC Northern Ireland Community Archive at the UFTM. Niamh Macnamara was resourceful in locating sound recordings and BBC-related material while her successor, Evelyn Ellison, carried on the task and suggested several Hayward-related books that I was not aware of. The head of corporate and public affairs at the BBC, Mark Adair, took an early interest in Hayward and was a keen supporter of the project while Sarah Rutherford helped organize travel practicalities. Michael Baguley, Andrew Crockart and Walter Love shared their memories of Hayward in the BBC in Belfast in the 1950s and I am grateful for their stories. Elsewhere in the BBC, I would like to thank Cameron Mitchell, Owen McFadden, John Toal and Jennifer Dupree. At the BBC Written Archives Centre at Caversham, Trish Hayes, Louise North and Marian Fallon facilitated my visit helping locate letters, magazines, books and BBC contracts.

A former BBC colleague, Trevor Ferris worked wonders with old photographs and preparation of images, as well as the recording of interviews and transfer of recording material and compilation of DVDs and slideshows. He took photographs for the book and was full of inventive suggestions, original ideas, and gave willingly of his time.

At the Ulster Television film library and archive, Pauline Russell and archive assistant Charlene McLean helped locate early TV broadcasts. With her bulging book of journalistic and broadcasting contacts, Anne Hailes was an indefatigable source, providing leads to many informants. Likewise, Yvonne Friers made suggestions of people to speak to, and cast her net wide, paving the way for telephone calls. I am grateful to both of them. At PRONI in Belfast's Titanic Quarter, Ian Montgomery helped source important information. The Office holds the Tyrone Guthrie and John Hewitt archives as well as government information files and cabinet papers with Hayward correspondence. The private records archivist, Dr Bethany Sinclair, reconnoitred the Guthrie archive and came up with useful information.

I am grateful to Angela Campbell, secretary of Larne Grammar School and to Jimmy Christie on the teaching staff for their advice on school archives and for allowing access to the library. Jenny Caldwell and Marian Kelso at Larne Heritage Centre produced diaries, recordings and other useful information on Hayward. Charlie and Jean Ludlow supplied historical detail on Larne; Jean kindly allowed me to quote from her invaluable dissertation on social changes in the town between 1850 and 1900 and supplied postcard images of Larne in Victorian times.

For many years I drew on the memory of Raymond Piper who died in July 2007. As well as personal reminiscences, Piper also generously provided hospitality in the form of a frequent glass of red wine on my visits to his home. I offer posthumous thanks to a warm and friendly man who knew Hayward better then most and I treasure the memories I have of him. Several other people who helped me with information: Harry Irvine in Belfast and Tom Maher in Carrick-on-Shannon, are no longer with us.

It was a pleasure to meet and come to know members of the Belfast Naturalists' Field Club. I am indebted to Dr Peter Crowther for opening the club's extensive archive, assisting my research and making suggestions about whom I should contact. He was particularly cooperative, producing minute books, records of club proceedings, scrapbooks and albums from which sepia photographs leapt to life. Through the crossing of their paths with Hayward, Prof Richard Clarke, David Honneyman and a former club secretary, Peter Cavan, recalled him in the flesh showing what he was *like* as a person. They spoke eloquently of their memories of field club trips and activities in the 1950s and early sixties bringing a fresh perspective. Liam McCaughey, club secretary, was also helpful as was Margaret Marshall.

Over many cups of coffee and spirited conversations, J.J. Tohill kindly supplied information, as well as rare Hayward film and music recordings, and I thank him for his generous support. Similar thanks are due to Gerard Turley, Gerry Hobbs and Liam Mulvenna each of whom recalled their involvement with Hayward through the St Gall's boys' school choir. Other memories, anecdotes and photographs came from Dr Austin Carty, Henry Comerford, James Davidson, Jimmy Greene, Charles Hill, Richard Hilliard, Ken Jamison, Angus McConnell, Billy Simpson and Roma Tomelty – collective thanks are due to all of them. An extra dimension to my research was added by Alan Cobb who opened his personal collection of Hayward books and records allowing me to draw on previously unseen and unheard material. Dr David Hume, Director of Services of the Grand Orange Lodge of Ireland and David Cargo provided access to archives at the Order's headquarters at Schomberg House in Belfast.

For information on Walter Scott Hayward, Maeve Bell kindly put me in touch with Northern Irish sailing clubs and I wish to thank Gordon Finlay, archivist of the Royal Ulster Yacht Club and Michael McKee, as well as Robert Hume of the Royal North of Ireland and Noel Johnston of Donaghadee Yacht Club. At the Royal Mersey Yacht Club in Birkenhead, Brian and Mary Smyth opened up the club archive and extensive yachting library, a fruitful source of material.

A former Librarian of the Linen Hall Library, John Gray, kindly read and commented on a draft of the theatre chapter offering useful suggestions. Nicholas Carolan, Director of the Irish Traditional Music Archive in Dublin, read the music chapter draft and made helpful comments. Treasa Harkin and Maeve Gebruers, also from ITMA pinned down music details. At their near neighbours based in Society House at 63 Merrion Square, the staff at the Royal Society of Antiquaries of Ireland, including Director Niamh McCabe, and Librarian Donal Fenlon, opened their journals and archives for perusal.

The staff of the National Library of Ireland in Dublin tracked down journals, magazines, newspapers and manuscripts and I am particularly indebted to Bernie Metcalfe, Lorraine Teavoy, Anita Joyce and Evie Monaghan. The library holds the Mathew O'Mahony Papers and the James Holloway Collection. Ellen O'Flaherty and Aisling Lockhart of the Manuscript & Archives Research Library at Trinity College Dublin helped guide me through the papers of Hubert Butler and the diaries and scrapbooks of Richard Marmaduke Hilliard, while Gillian Whelan and Sharon Sutton supplied digital images. At the UCD Archive, Orna Somerville facilitated my visit to consult the Liam S. Gógan papers. Christopher Sweeney at the Royal Irish Academy showed me the Praeger archive while Bernadette Cunningham helped source information in the Academy library. Simon O'Connor at the Little Museum of Dublin sourced letters from the former Lord Mayor Alfie Byrne. At the Abbey Theatre Archive, Mairéad Delaney kindly searched scrapbooks and other records from the theatre's history. In RTÉ I would like to thank John Glendon at the radio archive and Michael Talty at the Written Documents Archive information office for their help.

At the Irish Film Institute Archive I am grateful to Fiona Rigney at the Tiernan MacBride Library and to Raelene Casey who located several hard to find cinema books and other archive film material relating to 1930s' Ireland. Francis Jones, archive education officer with the Northern Ireland Screen Digital Film Archive, advised on permissions in relation to accessing footage of Hayward's films and I am grateful to him and to Tony Dykes of the British Film Institute for their assistance. I am indebted to the fruits of Bill Dean-Myatt's research in compiling a discography of Hayward's music recordings and in providing valuable information.

In Carrick-on-Shannon, Joe Dolan of the Bush Hotel, as well as John Bredin and Dermot MacNabb from Carrick-on-Shannon & District Historical Society aided me immeasurably on several visits to one of Hayward's favourite haunts. Martin A. Timoney and Pat O'Brien from the Sligo Field Club helped shed light on his Sligo connection. Vinnie Browne from Charlie Byrne's bookshop in Galway was a passionate provocateur and sounding board for ideas. Des Kenny of Kenny's Bookshop dug into his well of memory to recall stories from his mother about Hayward's visits to the family bookshop; Peadar O'Dowd, of Galway Archaeological Society brought light to bear on Hayward's Galway and Corrib writings. At the University of Limerick, Ken Bergin and Jean Turner of Special Collections in the Glucksman Library allowed me access to the Maurice Walsh Papers. Mary Kenehan from the Thomond Archaeological and Historical Society in Limerick suggested some names to speak to, including Mary Geary, a former president who was helpful. Alan Pim in Waterford conjured up memories of his childhood at Anngrove in County Laois when his parents were entertained by Hayward and Piper in 1948. Leslie Matson, a former teacher at Newtown School, recalled Richard and Elma Hayward's visits with Ricky.

I spent a considerable amount of time in bookshops in Ireland. I owe a large debt to the following bookshop owners: John Donohue in Athlone Bookshop, Caroline O'Brien of the Celtic Bookshop in Limerick, Nick Kaszuk, owner of Trinity Rare Books, Carrick-on-Shannon, Art Byrne and Ken Thatcher, Foyle Books, Derry, and Fred Collins formerly of Greene's bookshop, Dublin.

No book is completed alone. Many individuals responded to specific enquiries in newspapers while others offered encouragement as well as inspiration, frequently going out of their way to assist. I am indebted to the following for help in many forms: Celia and Angeline Adams, Maureen Baguley, Fergus Hanna Bell, Nigel Black, Sir Kenneth Bloomfield, Aeneas Bonner, Iain Bradley, Seamus Brennan, Ronan Browne, Olive Byers, Emma Caffrey, Denis Carson, Jan Carson, Derek Clements, Nick Condon, Patricia Craig, Robert Cumbers, Lucy Dallas, James Davidson, Sé Merry Doyle, Gregory Dunne, James Ellis, Prof Alun Evans, Michael Fewer, John Fitzgerald, Barry Fitzsimmons, Marie Forrester, Ann-Marie Foster, Francis Gilbride, Paul Gilmore, Diana Gleadhill, Brian Gógan, Len Graham, Jayne Greer, Kieran Guinness, Alan Hailes, Maud Hamill, Bobbie Hanvey, John Harcourt, Maureen Hegarty, Vicky Herbert, Alannah Hopkin, Angela Huggard, Peter Huggard, Vicky Jaglarz, Tim Jenkins, Anne Jensen, Roger and Joan Johnson, Jack Johnston, Sam Kane, Bobby Kelly, Donna and Ronan Kelly, Vivienne Kirk, James Lamont, Robert Lamrock, Brian Little, Wilson Logan, Anne Marshall, Eamon Matthews, Colin McAlpin, Hector McDonnell, Randal McDonnell, Rev. Peter McDowell, Sean McGeown, John McGuinness, Jack McIlvenna, Eddie McIlwaine, Cathal McKeown, Jimmy McLaughlin, Tony McMinn, Mary Molloy, Dr John Moulden, John Mullaney, Martin Nelson, Jim O Halloran, Denis O'Hara, Tim O'Sullivan, Mervyn Rainey, Tim Robinson, Sam Ruscica, Paddy Scully, Lisa Smyth, Tim Smyth, Thompson Steele, Mark Steen, Annie Stephens, Noel Spence, Chris Spurr, Angeline Starr, Lila and Phil Stuart, Thomas Teehan, Deirdre Vickers, Charlie Warmington, Norman Weatherall, Roger Weatherup, Helen White, Leo Wilson and George Woodman. Any errors of fact or interpretation are mine, not theirs.

I would like to thank the staff of the Tyrone Guthrie Centre, at Annaghmakerrig, County Monaghan, particularly Robbie McDonald, Mary Clerkin and Ingrid Adams. They permitted unrestricted access to the Guthrie library and facilitated a week-long stay in 2013 where I benefited from the collegiality of meeting new people which triggered ideas. Not for the first time, my agent Jonathan Williams offered encouragement during the various stages of the project. He provided incisive criticism and made valuable suggestions.

Research and interview work for this book was carried out with the aid of a grant in 2011 from the Arts Council of Northern Ireland under the Support for the Individual Artist Programme (SIAP) through the General Art Award Scheme which helped buy valuable time and I am grateful for this. In 2013, a second SIAP grant from the Arts Council of Northern Ireland allowed me to buy writing and editing time to prepare the manuscript and photographs for publication. I would like to acknowledge the support and interest of Damian Smyth, Head of Literature and Drama at the Arts Council.

Without the assistance of a number of other funding agencies this would have been a much less well produced book. Financial help towards publication costs is gratefully acknowledged from the following: MAGUS: The Ministerial Advisory Group Ulster-Scots Academy, Arts Council of Northern Ireland, Belfast Naturalists' Field Club, Esme Mitchell Trust, and the Ulster Local History Trust. Specific thanks to Edel McMahon and Richard Sproule from the MAG Ulster-Scots Academy for their help, and to Vicky Herbert from the ULHT.

I would like to thank Kitty Lyddon at The Lilliput Press for her sterling work through the production lifecycle of this book. Djinn von Noorden, a sympathetic and skilful editor, suggested comments and cuts, saved me from mistakes, and shepherded the manuscript to publication.

I owe thanks beyond measure to my wife Felicity and son Daniel for their interest in what turned out to be a lengthy project – but they have been down this boreen with me before. In Belfast, Dublin, Oxford and London they proved adept as spotters of Hayward Brothers manhole covers and pavement lights, and helped with scanning images, fact-checking, proof reading and compilation of the index.

Henry James once wrote: 'Never say you know the last word about any human heart.' You can never know the last word about anyone but my last, although by no means least words of thanks are to Richard Hayward himself for giving us the music, the books, the films, the plays, the talks, the jokes and much more; and for leading such a fun-filled, zestful and until now, largely uncelebrated life.

Permissions and photo credits

Every effort has been made to trace the copyright of images reproduced. Any inadvertent omission of acknowledgment or permission can be rectified in future printings. I would like to thank the Trustees, National Museums Northern Ireland for permission to quote material from the Hayward Bequest at the Ulster Folk & Transport Museum, Cultra, and those who administer this remarkable archive. Acknowledgments are due to the Deputy Keeper of the Records at PRONI for permission to reproduce material from Stormont cabinet papers as well as from the John Hewitt Papers. Excerpts from letters between Hayward and Maurice Walsh are reproduced from the Maurice Walsh Papers at the Glucksman Library, University of Limerick. Other excerpts are quoted from letters in the Liam S. Gógan Papers held in the UCD Archive, the Hubert Butler Archive held at Trinity College Dublin, and the Mathew O'Mahony Papers held at the National Library of Ireland. The excerpt quoted from *Kavanagh's Weekly* is reprinted by kind permission of the Trustees of the Estate of the late Katherine B. Kavanagh, through the Jonathan Williams Literary Agency.

In addition, I am most grateful to the following individuals and institutions for allowing reproduction of material: Eric Nathan, copyright image page xxii. Photographs on pages 44 and 45 are courtesy of the archive of the Belfast Naturalists' Field Club. The photograph on page 51 and images on pages 56 and 75 are courtesy of the Linen Hall Library, Belfast. The photograph on page 155 is courtesy of Newtown School Archives, Waterford. The sketch on page 240 is copyright Dr Austin Carty.

Index

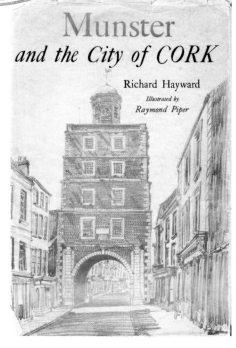